From Stonehenge to the Baltic

Living with cultural diversity
in the third millennium BC

Edited by

Mats Larsson
Mike Parker Pearson

BAR International Series 1692
2007

This title published by

Archaeopress
Publishers of British Archaeological Reports
Gordon House
276 Banbury Road
Oxford OX2 7ED
England
bar@archaeopress.com
www.archaeopress.com

Archaeopress
10 years

BAR S1692

From Stonehenge to the Baltic: Living with cultural diversity in the third millennium BC

ISBN 978 1 4073 0130 3

Front cover illsutration: Adam Stanford of Aerial-Cam
Back cover illustrations: Adam Stanford of Aerial-Cam (excavations at Durrington Walls and Woodhenge), Stonehenge Riverside Project (Stonehenge trilithons and reconstruction of Southern Circle), National Museums of Wales (Naaboth's Vineyard Beaker pot)

Printed in England by CMP (UK) Ltd

All BAR titles are available from:

Hadrian Books Ltd
122 Banbury Road
Oxford
OX2 7BP
England
bar@hadrianbooks.co.uk

The current BAR catalogue with details of all titles in print, prices and means of payment is available free from Hadrian Books or may be downloaded from www.archaeopress.com

Contents

Part 3 – Stonehenge and the Stonehenge Riverside Project

Part 4 – Research on other Neolithic World Heritage Sites in Britain and Ireland

List of Contributors

Kenneth Alexandersson   Institute of Humanities and Social Sciences, University of Kalmar, 391 82 Kalmar, Sweden

Wayne Bennett   Somerset County Council, Dillington House, Ilminster, Somerset, UK

Conor Brady   Dundalk Institute of Technology, Dundalk, Ireland

Nick Card   Archaeology Centre, Orkney College, University of the Highlands & Islands, Kirkwall, Orkney, KW15 1LX, UK

Andrew Chamberlain   Department of Archaeology, University of Sheffield, Sheffield, S10 2TN, UK

Jonathan Cluett   School of Biological and Environmental Sciences, University of Stirling, FK9 4LA, UK

Rachel Cooper   Department of Archaeological Sciences, University of Bradford, Bradford, West Yorkshire BD7 1DP, UK

Jane Downes   Archaeology Department, Orkney College, University of the Highlands & Islands, Kirkwall, Orkney, KW15 1LX, UK

Gunilla Eriksson   Archaeological Research Laboratory, Stockholm University, SE-106 91 Stockholm, Sweden.

Jane Evans   NERC Isotope Geosciences Laboratory, British Geological Survey, Keyworth, Nottinghamshire, NG12 5GG, UK

David Field   English Heritage, Kemble Drive, Swindon, Wiltshire, SN2 2GZ, UK

John Gater   GSB Prospection Ltd., Cowburn Farm, Market Street, Thornton, Bradford, BD13 3HW, UK

Alex Gibson   Department of Archaeological Sciences, University of Bradford, Bradford, West Yorkshire BD7 1DP, UK

Ole Grøn   Langelands Museum, Langeland, Denmark

Mandy Jay   Department of Archaeology, University of Durham, Durham, UK

Maria Magdalena Kosko   Institute of Archaeology, University of London, 31-34 Gordon Square, London, UK

Lars Larsson   Department of Archaeology and Ancient History, University of Lund, Box 117, SE-221 00 Lund, Sweden

Mats Larsson   Institute of Humanities and Social Sciences, University of Kalmar, 391 82 Kalmar, Sweden

Kerstin Lidén   Archaeological Research Laboratory, Stockholm University, SE-106 91 Stockholm, Sweden

Patrick Mahoney   Department of Archaeology, University of Sheffield, Sheffield, S10 2TN, UK

Janet Montgomery   Department of Archaeological Sciences, University of Bradford, Bradford, West Yorkshire BD7 1DP, UK

Stuart Needham   Old Pitts Farm, Langrish, Hampshire, GU32 1RQ, UK

Susan Ovenden — Archaeology Centre, Orkney College, University of the Highlands & Islands, Kirkwall, Orkney, KW15 1LX, UK

Ludvig Papmehl-Dufay — Archaeological Research Laboratory, Stockholm University, SE-106 91 Stockholm, Sweden

Mike Parker Pearson — Department of Archaeology, University of Sheffield, Sheffield, S10 2TN, UK

Joshua Pollard — Department of Archaeology and Anthropology, University of Bristol, Woodlands Road, Bristol, UK

Colin Richards — School of Arts, Histories and Cultures, University of Manchester, Manchester

Michael Richards — Department of Human Evolution, Max Planck Institute for Evolutionary Anthropology, Deutscher Platz 6, 04103 Leipzig and Department of Archaeology, University of Durham, Durham, UK

David Robinson — Department of Archaeology and Anthropology, University of Bristol, Woodlands Road, Bristol, UK

Alison Sheridan — National Museums Scotland, Chambers Street, Edinburgh, EH1 1JF, UK

Anne Teather — Department of Archaeology, University of Sheffield, Sheffield, S10 2TN, UK

Julian Thomas — School of Arts, Histories and Cultures, University of Manchester, Manchester

Christopher Tilley — Department of Anthropology, University College London, Gower Street, London, UK

List of Figures and Tables

(NB These are in abbreviated form here)

Tables

Preface

Mike Parker Pearson and Mats Larsson

In 1980 the two editors of this volume met at a crayfish party in Malmö, in Scania. ML was then working at the Institute of Archaeology in Lund and MPP was visiting Sweden whilst working on his PhD thesis on the Iron Age in southern Scandinavia. Crayfish parties can be wild events, involving the drinking of large quantities of schnapps and beer, singing of songs and reciting of poems until no one remains sitting at the table. Almost quarter of a century later, ML contacted MPP in 2002 with a view to developing collaborative research between the Swedish universities of Kalmar and Stockholm and the University of Sheffield in the UK. MPP's colleagues John Barrett and Marek Zvelebil were also involved as was Kerstin Lidén at the University of Stockholm, and colleagues in the Stonehenge Riverside Project – Colin Richards, Julian Thomas and Chris Tilley; over the next five years collaborative exchanges involved the training of research students and undergraduates, the holding of two conferences – one in Kalmar and one in Sheffield – and a host of staff exchanges across the North Sea.

The research theme of the conference was the investigation of cultural diversity in the 3rd millennium BC in the British Isles and Scandinavia, not so much to divine any prehistoric cultural links between the two in that period but to compare and contrast empirical evidence and theoretical approaches. The collaboration was also an important means of fostering new research projects in both Sweden and Britain. The academic exchange programme was principally funded by the Swedish Foundation for International Cooperation in Research and Higher Education (STINT) with further financial support from the universities involved. The proceedings of the conference held in Kalmar in 2004 were published in the *Journal of Nordic Archaeological Science* in 2005. This present volume contains papers presented at the conference held in Sheffield in May 2006. Some of these are synthetic overviews whilst others are interim reports on on-going field and laboratory-based projects.

In Scandinavia the archaeological evidence from the 3rd millennium BC has been characterized as a series of cultures: the Pitted Ware Culture, the later part of the Funnel-necked Beaker Culture (Trichterbecher Kultur or TRB), the Battle Axe Culture, the Single Grave Culture, and the Corded Ware Culture. The aim of the project was to investigate this cultural diversity to gain some understanding of what these archaeological assemblages might have represented in human terms, whether they really constituted discrete groupings of material culture, and whether these long-lived cultural historical labels had any relevance for understanding the complex relationship between material culture and social identities.

Similar diversity in material assemblages can be identified in Britain, particularly in terms of ceramic styles: Peterborough Ware and other impressed styles (*c.* 3200-2500 cal BC) broadly pre-dated Grooved Ware (*c.* 3000-2200 cal BC) which was followed by Bell Beakers (*c.* 2400-1700 cal BC). The substantial overlaps between styles within the radiocarbon chronology can be partly explained by plateaux in the calibration curve but new approaches were required to explain why and how certain material culture styles were replaced by others. Although the culture historical notion of pots as indicative of ethnic groups has been largely discredited in British prehistory, the concept of a Beaker 'folk' immigrating across continental Europe into Britain has proved remarkably resilient since the initial attacks on culture history as a theoretical tool in the 1970s. Two new research projects were set to explore these issues in Britain. The Beaker People Project (or Beaker Isotope Project), directed by MPP, Andrew Chamberlain and Mike Richards, set out to investigate diet, mobility and migration patterns. The Stonehenge Riverside Project (directed by MPP, Josh Pollard, Colin Richards, Julian Thomas, Chris Tilley and Kate Welham) has been investigating, amongst other things, the relationship between the Beaker-associated monument of Stonehenge and the nearby Grooved Ware-associated henge of Durrington Walls.

The Middle Neolithic in Sweden

The Middle Neolithic in Scandinavia (c. 3300-2300 BC) is a period in which the later part of the Funnel-necked Beaker Culture (Trichterbecher Kultur or TRB) ended around 2800 BC (at the transition between the early and late Middle Neolithic) with a series of material culture changes in ceramic styles and other portable artefacts, together with a new fashion for individual inhumation burial. In Jutland and western Denmark, these are known as the Battle Axe Culture or the Single Grave Culture (Ebbesen 2006; Hübner 2006). Further south in Germany and Poland, as well as in southern Sweden, these are termed the Corded Ware Culture. These Middle Neolithic styles were succeeded by the Late Neolithic around 2300 BC, a time when bronze was adopted elsewhere in northern Europe including Britain but was only rarely deposited in Scandinavian archaeological contexts.

An important ceramic style within the eastern Baltic in this period, overlapping with both late TRB and the Battle Axe/Corded Ware/Single Grave Cultures, is Pitted Ware (Larsson 2006). This pottery, with its rows of impressed pits and pointed bases, is found on settlements located in primarily coastal locations. Debate has fluctuated between viewing these sites as inhabited by hunter-fisher-gatherers whose identities were entirely separate from the TRB/BAC/CWC/SGC agriculturalists or interpreting them as seasonal variations or devolved versions of these agricultural societies.

Two small excavations were carried out within the broad remit of the project on Middle Neolithic sites on the island of Öland; on the Pitted Ware settlement of Ottenby Royal Manor by Ludvig Papmehl-Dufay, and on the megalithic chamber tomb at Resmö.

The papers in the first part of this book address the question of what these 'cultures' represented, in terms of material culture (Lars Larsson), ceramics (Papmehl-Dufay), dietary practices (Lidén and Eriksson), lithics (Alexandersson) and ritual practices (Mats Larsson).

The Beaker People Project

The identity of the Beaker folk has been a perennial question in the study of British prehistory. Were they European immigrants? Or were they indigenous communities who adopted a pan-European material culture 'package' that included drinking cups, martial display and single burial? The Beaker People Project is run by a consortium of university teams (from Sheffield, Durham, Leipzig and the British Geological Survey), with the help of local and national museums, to get some answers to these questions (Parker Pearson 2006). The project is also aimed at finding out just how mobile these people were, what their diets consisted of, and whether their nutrition and health were affected by gender and status. The long-recognised anatomical distinction between a long-headed Neolithic population of the 4th millennium BC and broad-headed Beaker people of the late 3rd millennium BC certainly still seems to hold but, given the long time period between them, the differences are as likely to be due to genetic drift as to immigration. Unfortunately, ancient DNA seems not to survive well in prehistoric skeletons kept in museums so other methods have to be employed.

Isotopic analyses are being carried out on 250 Beaker-period burials: carbon (δ^{13}C) and nitrogen (δ^{15}N) to find out about diet, strontium (^{87}Sr/^{86}Sr) and oxygen (δ^{18}O) to investigate mobility and migration, and sulphur (δ^{34}S) to identify those who lived in coastal areas. Preliminary results of carbon (δ^{13}C) and nitrogen (δ^{15}N) isotope analyses have shed light on dietary patterns (Jay and Richards). The project is also providing new radiocarbon dates as well as thorough osteological and dental analyses of aspects such as age and sex, health and trauma, and dietary patterns from dental microwear analysis (Mahoney). The project began with a sample of Scottish burials, followed by a large group from the Yorkshire Wolds. The final regional groups to be sampled are from Wessex, southern England and the Peak District, as well as the few Beaker burials from Wales.

The discovery that the Amesbury Archer grew up in central Europe, probably in the Alpine foothills (Evans *et al.* 2006), has been something of a bombshell for prehistorians. Three of the Boscombe Down Bowmen, also found near Stonehenge by Andrew Fitzpatrick of Wessex Archaeology, were also not local to the Wessex chalk. Their strontium and oxygen values are consistent with an origin in Wales although northwest France is another possibility. Yet not all the Stonehenge Beaker people had migrated. The Stonehenge Archer (found with arrow wounds in the Stonehenge ditch) and an individual buried nearby at Wilsford had both grown up on the chalkland. It is too early for the Beaker People Project to have any results from strontium and oxygen isotopic analysis but the pilot study by Montgomery *et al.* gives a taste of what is to come.

Currently, the earliest Beaker burials in England and Scotland do not appear to date to before 2400 BC (see papers by Needham, Sheridan and Gibson in this volume). But was Beaker pottery in use in Britain before the appearance of the inhumation rite? Two Beaker sherds were found in 1954 in one of the bluestone pits at Stonehenge. This first arrangement of bluestones pre-dates the sarsen circle, which was probably erected before 2480 BC. These Beaker sherds may therefore be much older than Beaker pots in burials. Nonetheless, it may be that the idea of a single movement of people bringing Beakers, metallurgy, horses, wheeled vehicles and fancy goods has outlived its credibility. Over the next few years, the project might just change what we thought we knew about the Beaker folk.

The Stonehenge Riverside Project

In 1998 a new interpretation was proposed for Stonehenge, explaining the construction of its stone circle as a monument to the ancestors (Parker Pearson and Ramilisonina 1998) and suggesting a direct relationship between Stonehenge and the timber circle complex at Durrington during the third millennium BC, articulated primarily along the River Avon. Most of the inhabitants of Late Neolithic Wessex were not buried in barrows and it has long been suspected that the bodies of many of the dead were disposed of in rivers (Bradley and Gordon 1988). The relationship between Durrington Walls and Stonehenge is proposed as a process by which the dead were transformed into ancestors. The theory proposed that the rites of passage by which the dead left the physical world entailed entering the river at Durrington Walls, a domain of the living and the beginning of a physical and incorporeal journey down the river to the domain of the ancestors at Stonehenge.

The project, running between 2003 and 2010, addresses many of the research issues and objectives listed in the archaeological research framework (Darvill 2005: 107-36; Parker Pearson *et al.* 2004). Its aims are:

1. To better understand social change in third millennium BC Britain, including the rise and decline of the great henges, the adoption of metal and transformations in funerary practice.
2. To explore alternative explanations for Stonehenge and its surrounding monuments, including investigation of theories concerning materiality and permanence.
3. To reassess and redate Stonehenge's landscape history from the fourth to the second millennium BC.
4. To contribute to public enjoyment of, and improved management of the wider Stonehenge landscape through close co-operation with English Heritage, the National Trust and other stakeholders.
5. To train students and volunteers within a scheme that integrates university researchers with professional archaeological contractors.

In 2003 and 2004 a programme of topographic and geophysical survey, combined with coring, mapped most of the area of Durrington Walls and its immediate vicinity, enabling reconstruction of pre-colluvial topography and recognition of sub-surface features.

Excavations were carried out from 2004 onwards at Durrington Walls' east entrance as well as within its interior (Parker Pearson *et al.* 2006). In 2005 the team excavated the stonehole of a large sarsen which had originally been set up as a standing stone 2005 at Bulford, east of Durrington. It lay within a ring ditch and there was a well-provisioned double Food Vessel burial whose 32 grave goods included a rock crystal artefact. Excavations on top of Larkhill in 2005, along the line of the midsummer sunrise axis from Stonehenge, failed to locate any substantial prehistoric activity on this summit, although the plan of the early 20th century barracks was mapped, together with other post-medieval features. In 2006 excavations were extended to Woodhenge to confirm that the decayed timber posts of the wooden monument had been replaced by a standing stone monument.

Within the wider landscape, there have been successful results from palaeochannel and topographic investigations. Palaeochannel sequences have been identified and sampled on the Avon floodplain both north and south of Durrington Walls. Relict channels likely to date to the third millennium have also been identified at the point where the Stonehenge Avenue meets the river.

This volume presents interim results of the excavations to date at Durrington Walls and Woodhenge (Parker Pearson, Thomas, Pollard and Robinson), as well as studies of Stonehenge in its landscape (Tilley *et al.*), units of megalithic measurement (Chamberlain), a study of phalli from Durrington Walls and other sites in southern Britain (Teather), and an ethnographic comparison with Sami cosmology (Grøn). It concludes with papers on two other Neolithic World Heritage Sites: Brú na Bóinne (Bend of the Boyne) in Ireland (Brady) and Orkney in Scotland (Card *et al.*).

References

Bradley, R. and Gordon, K. 1988 Human skulls from the River Thames, their dating and significance. *Antiquity* 62: 503-9.

Darvill, T.C. 2005 *Stonehenge World Heritage Site: an archaeological research framework*. London and Bournemouth: English Heritage and Bournemouth University.

Evans, J., Chenery, C. and Fitzpatrick, A.P. 2006. Bronze Age childhood migration of individuals near Stonehenge, revealed by strontium and oxygen isotope tooth enamel analysis. *Archaeometry* 48: 309-21.

Ebbesen, K. 2006. *The Battle Axe Period*. København: University of Copenhagen.

Hübner, E. 2006. *Jungneolithische Gräber auf der Jütischen Halbinsel. Typologische und chronologische Studien zur Einzelgrabkultur*. København: Nordiske Fortidsminder (Serie B, Band 24:1–3).

Larsson, M. 2006. *A Tale of a Strange People: the Pitted Ware Culture in southern Sweden*. Kalmar Studies in Archaeology 2. Kalmar: Institutionen för humaniora och samhällsvetenskap, Högskolan i Kalmar.

Parker Pearson, M. 2006 The Beaker people project: mobility and diet in the British Early Bronze Age. *The Archaeologist* 61: 14-15.

Parker Pearson, M. and Ramilisonina. 1998 Stonehenge for the ancestors: the stones pass on the message. *Antiquity* 72: 308-26.

Parker Pearson, M., Richards, C., Allen, M., Payne, A. and Welham, K. 2004. The Stonehenge Riverside project: research design and initial results. *Journal of Nordic Archaeological Science* 14: 45-60.

Parker Pearson, M., Pollard, J., Richards, C., Thomas, J., Tilley, C., Welham, K. and Albarella, U. 2006. Materializing Stonehenge: the Stonehenge Riverside Project and new discoveries. *Journal of Material Culture* 11: 227-261.

Chapter 1

Walking on the wild side: on cultural diversity and the Pitted Ware Culture along the Swedish east coast during the Middle Neolithic

Kerstin Lidén and Gunilla Eriksson

Archaeological Research Laboratory, Stockholm University, SE-106 91 Stockholm, Sweden

Abstract

There was a rich diversity in material culture during the Middle Neolithic in Scandinavia and the Baltic region, and the archaeological remains have therefore generally been labelled as one out of several parallel archaeological cultures. What these "cultures" represent, and whether or not they correspond to actual groups of people has long been debated. Particularly the Pitted Ware Culture has given rise to various hypotheses. By applying stable carbon and nitrogen isotope analyses on human and faunal skeletal remains from Pitted Ware contexts, and to compare these data with stable isotope data derived from sites of other cultural attribution, we were able to demonstrate that the Pitted Ware Culture in fact represents a separate group of people, not only distinguished by their characteristic pottery, but also by their food culture, which was mainly based on the utilization of seal. On the basis of stable isotope, radiocarbon and archaeological data, various other hypotheses regarding the Pitted Ware Culture and its stance vis-à-vis the Funnel Beaker and Battle Axe (Corded Ware) Cultures could thus be refuted.

Introduction

The Middle Neolithic period in Scandinavia (roughly 3300–2300 BC) has traditionally been described as a period with three separate archaeological cultures, based on ceramic typology (for a recent review, see Papmehl-Dufay 2006). Whereas the Funnel Beaker Culture (TRB), which appeared already in the Early Neolithic, is superseded by the Battle Axe/Corded Ware Culture (BAC) halfway into the Middle Neolithic, the Pitted Ware Culture (PWC) overlaps chronologically with both the TRB and the BAC.

This is one of the reasons why the existence, definition and extent of the Pitted Ware Culture in Scandinavia has been the subject of archaeological controversy (Becker 1950; 1980; Janzon 1974; Österholm 1989; Wyszomirska 1984; Browall 1991; Damm 1991; Edenmo et al. 1997; Papmehl-Dufay 2006).

Whereas both the Funnel Beaker and Battle Axe Cultures have been associated with agriculture, based on finds of animal bones or cereals, the coastal Pitted Ware Culture has been suggested to represent a number of different life styles. Thus, there are almost as many hypotheses regarding the Pitted Ware Culture as there are scholars. Here we focus not so much on its origin, but rather on what the PWC represents, especially in terms of its relationship to the TRB and BAC. Within that particular framework, the existing hypotheses can be narrowed down to four principal scenarios:

1. The TRB developed into the PWC, i.e. TRB societies changed their material culture due to social/cultural/ideological change within the group (Browall 1991; Carlsson 1998; Larsson 2006). The shift is sometimes seen as a response to neolithicization – a protest against the Neolithic way of life, either by regressing to a hunter–gatherer ideal, or by simply glorifying hunting and gathering while retaining agriculture. This hypothesis, which regards the TRB as the predecessors of the PWC, would seem to suggest only a small chronological overlap between the two. It has therefore been suggested that the transformation took place rather rapidly on the local scale, in less than 50 years, although not synchronically over the whole region (Browall 1991).

2. The PWC represents the hunting and fishing sites, or merely ritual sites for pot destruction, of the TRB and the BAC. In other words, they were actually the same people performing certain activities at the coast, leaving traces of Pitted Ware material culture, and other activities inland, resulting in material culture of the TRB or BAC (Persson 1986; Carlsson 1987; 1998; Andersson 1998). This hypothesis accordingly acknowledges the great chronological overlap between the PWC on the one hand, and the TRB and BAC on the other.

3. People of the Pitted Ware Culture were part-time farmers, practising pig herding and/or other types of animal husbandry alongside seal hunting and fishing (Wincentz Rasmussen 1993; Zvelebil 1996). This hypothesis is mainly based on the frequent presence of wild boar tusks or pig mandibles in PWC graves (cf. Figure 1.1), as well as the occurrence of pig remains in occupation layers. It generally makes no proposition about the relationship to the TRB or BAC, and is compatible with the first as well as and the second hypotheses, although not both at the same time.

4. The Pitted Ware Culture represents a distinct group of people with their own cultural identity, hard-core seal hunters who existed parallel to FBC and BAC groups of people respectively (Wyszomirska 1984; Werbart 1998; Eriksson 2004; Papmehl-Dufay 2006). Some even see the group as a continuation of the Mesolithic life style.

Since the above interpretations are partially or entirely incompatible with each other, they obviously cannot all be correct. In order to test some of these hypotheses we

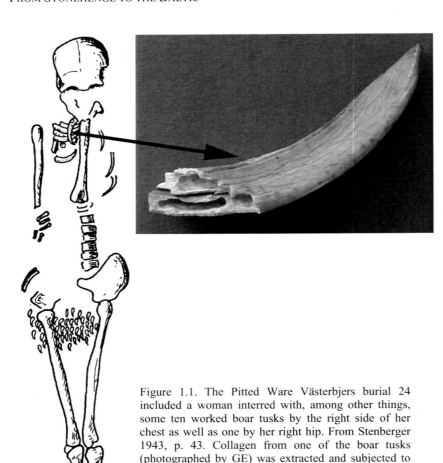

Figure 1.1. The Pitted Ware Västerbjers burial 24 included a woman interred with, among other things, some ten worked boar tusks by the right side of her chest as well as one by her right hip. From Stenberger 1943, p. 43. Collagen from one of the boar tusks (photographed by GE) was extracted and subjected to stable isotope analysis and radiocarbon dating.

analysed: Jettböle on the Åland Islands (*Finnish* Ahvenmaa, an autonomous region of Finland), Korsnäs on the Swedish mainland, Ire, Visby and Västerbjers on Gotland, and finally Köpingsvik on Öland (Figure 2.2). All human and faunal skeletal remains derive from museum stores, since the majority of sites were excavated (sometimes in many episodes during several decades) in the early or mid-twentieth century. Human bone and dentine collagen representing more than 100 distinct individuals were subjected to stable carbon and nitrogen isotope analysis. The analyses were supported by extensive faunal stable isotope data for Korsnäs and Västerbjers, as well as radiocarbon dates of both human and faunal remains from most of the sites.

The large Jettböle site in Jomala parish on Åland was first discovered, and some 700 m^2 subsequently excavated, in the early 20th century (see Götherström *et al.* 2002 and references cited therein). In addition to vast amounts of Pitted Ware pottery and well-preserved human and faunal remains, the most striking features about this site are the large number of anthropomorphic clay figurines recovered, and the cut-marks found on some human bones, leading to the discussion of possible cannibalism (Núnez and Lidén 1997). Only one certain burial was recovered, but disarticulated skeletal remains from at least another thirteen individuals have been identified. Limited excavations at the site have also been performed during the past ten years (see Storå 2001 and Stenbäck 2003 for reviews). Radiocarbon dates suggest that the site was mainly in use during the first half of the Middle Neolithic (MN A).

Korsnäs in the province of Södermanland comprises extensive cultural layers containing pottery, bone and stone implements typical of the Pitted Ware Culture, as well as considerable amounts of faunal remains along with a number of dispersed human bones. Six burials – both certain and possible ones – were also recovered. The exceptional preservation conditions are unique for the eastern Swedish mainland, although Korsnäs during the Middle Neolithic was actually situated in what was then an inner archipelago. Like many other PWC sites, it has undergone several excavations with varying levels of documentation. Discovered and subsequently partly excavated in the 1930s, it was not until the mid-1960s that something of the extent and size of the site was realized. In preparation for a planned gravel quarry,

have therefore chosen to use stable isotope analysis to reconstruct the diet of the people buried at the sites attributed to the PWC, because diet is such a strong cultural marker (e.g. Parker Pearson 2003 and references cited therein). Food habits are closely tied to cultural and social identity and might as such be an even stronger indicator of group identity than any artefacts customarily used for attribution to an archaeological culture (Eriksson 2003). While faunal and botanical remains in occupation layers, or palaeo-ecological surveys, may provide information on the range of available food resources, and burial depositions of food related items such as animal bones or food containers could give important insights into the ritual and symbolic world of those handling the funeral, it does not really provide evidence of the daily practice of food culture. By contrast, the use of stable isotope analyses to investigate what people ate, offers information on actual food consumption and thus the everyday expression of food culture.

Material and methods

Human and faunal remains from six Pitted Ware Culture sites in the Baltic Sea along the Swedish east coast were stripping of some 2000sq m then exposed extensive cultural layers, and subsequent surface collection of finds, sieving of dump heaps and minor excavations by various agencies, produced the bulk of those human and faunal remains now present in the museum stores (see Fornander 2006 and references cited therein). Recent radiocarbon dating of human and faunal remains from the site places it in the first part of the Middle Neolithic (MN A).

Ire, located on the north-western coast of Gotland, is one of the better documented PWC sites, mainly excavated in the 1950s, revealing nine burials and extensive cultural deposits (Janzon 1974). Radiocarbon dating of human bone was performed during the 1970s, but recent analyses have revealed problems with the chemical pre-treatment of the bones at the radiocarbon laboratory at that time, so they are not considered reliable (see Eriksson 2004 for a detailed discussion).

During the Middle Neolithic, Västerbjers was situated on the shore of a long narrow inlet of the Baltic on eastern Gotland. The majority of the more than 50 burials was excavated during the 1930s, in connection with gravel quarrying (see Eriksson 2004 and references cited therein). In addition to graves, the site included extensive cultural layers with several hearths, and a few post-holes and pits, although radiocarbon dating of bovid and ovicaprid bones from these layers revealed the presence of Bronze Age intrusions. Direct radiocarbon dates of the interred indicate continuous use during several hundred years half-way into the Middle Neolithic (MN A–MN B transition).

Both Visby on Gotland (Nihlén 1927; Janzon 1974) and Köpingsvik on Öland (Papmehl-Dufay 2006 and references cited therein) are present-day towns with rich medieval cultural deposits and cemeteries superimposed on the Neolithic layers, which has generated fairly complicated research histories including a high number of rescue excavations performed throughout the 20th century. In Visby at least 42 PWC graves have been discovered, and in Köpingsvik the corresponding figure would be 19, although we have identified and analysed at least another 15 individuals represented by disarticulated human bones. No reliable radiocarbon dates for Visby are presently available. Radiocarbon dates for Köpingsvik reveal that the cemetery was in use already during the Mesolithic, although they suggest an emphasis during the first half of the Middle Neolithic.

Basically the carbon and nitrogen isotopes used in this study provide information about the source of the ingested protein. The stable carbon isotope value, $\delta^{13}C$, tells us if the protein derives from marine or terrestrial sources, whereas the stable nitrogen isotope value, $\delta^{15}N$, tells us from what level in the food web the protein derives. Both $\delta^{13}C$ and $\delta^{15}N$ are expressed in *per mil* (parts per thousand, ‰) relative to a standard (for further information, see Lidén 1995a; Eriksson 2003).

The stable isotope analyses were performed on collagen extracted from bone or tooth dentine. Whereas bone collagen provides an average dietary signal for the individual's last 10–15 years, depending on biological age, the dentine collagen provides a dietary signal for the time of tooth formation, i.e. childhood (see Lidén and Angerbjörn 1999; Eriksson 2003). Where available, the first, second and third molar teeth, as well as bone, were sampled for each individual in order to trace intra-individual variation. In effect, this expanded the material to include children who survived childhood – a group otherwise severely underrepresented in archaeological data.

In addition to the human skeletal remains analysed, animal bones from a wide range of species found at two of the sites, Korsnäs and Köpingsvik, have also been analysed (not included in the plots here; for detailed data see Fornander 2006 and Eriksson 2004). The faunal analyses serve two purposes: one is to establish the isotope ecology for the area and period by determining isotopic end-point values, and the other is to provide reference data for potential foodstuffs consumed at the sites. In both cases they serve to provide an isotopic framework and considerably increases the precision in the interpretation of human stable isotope data. It must be emphasized that stable isotope signatures of the same species could vary substantially between different regions, ecological systems and time periods, so it is important to analyse fauna with the same geographical and chronological origin as those human remains analysed.

We have in all cases extracted the collagen according to Brown *et al.* (1988) where ultrafiltration is an important last step to remove residues smaller than 30kDa. The stable isotope analyses were performed combusting the samples with a Carlo Erba NC2500 elemental analyser connected via a split interface to reduce the gas volume to a Finnigan MAT Delta+ isotope ratio mass spectrometer (IRMS), where the precision was ±0.15‰ or better for both $\delta^{13}C$ and $\delta^{15}N$.

For comparison, we have also included stable isotope data for a number of human subjects from TRB and BAC sites in Sweden and Latvia (Figures 1.2–1.3, Table 1.1). Both Hjelmars rör (Axelsson and Persson 1999) and Rössberga (Cullberg 1963) are passage graves in the "megalithic centre" of mainland Sweden, within the province of Västergötland, and are represented by five and eleven data points respectively. Although the Rolfsåker burial in Halland (Nordqvist 1998), a man buried with an axe in a natural shell midden on the Swedish west coast, cannot safely be associated with the Funnel Beaker Culture, the skeleton has been radiocarbon dated (twice!) to the first part of the Middle Neolithic. The only excavated megatlithic tomb on Öland, situated in Resmo parish (Arne 1909), is here represented by eleven data points. Radiocarbon dates of human bone

Figure 1.2. Map of the Baltic region with sites mentioned in the text indicated.

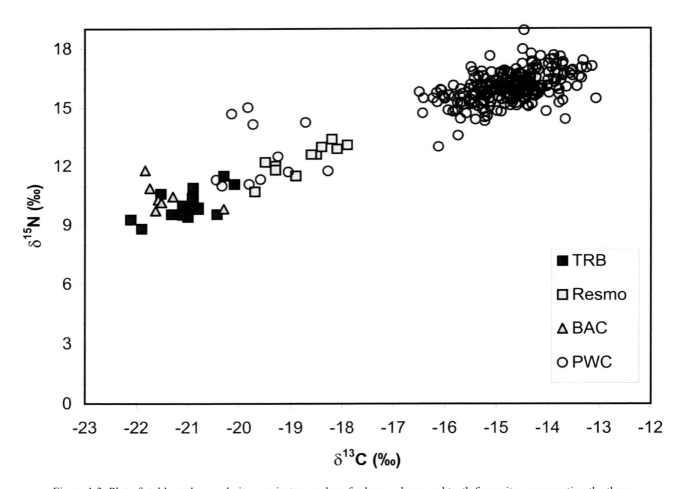

Figure 1.3. Plot of stable carbon and nitrogen isotope values for human bone and teeth from sites representing the three archaeological cultures of the Middle Neolithic (cf. Table 1 and Figure 2).

Site	Archaeological culture	Stable isotope data from
Hjelmars rör	TRB	Eriksson unpublished
Rolfsåker	TRB	Lidén et al. 2004
Rössberga	TRB	Lidén 1995b, Eriksson unpublished
Resmo	TRB	Lidén 1995b
Kastanjegården	BAC	Lidén et al. 2004
Zvejnieki crouched burials	BAC	Eriksson et al. 2003
Sarkani	BAC	Eriksson et al. 2003
Selgas	BAC	Eriksson et al. 2003
Jettböle	PWC	Eriksson unpublished
Korsnäs	PWC	Fornander 2006
Ire	PWC	Eriksson unpublished
Visby	PWC	Eriksson unpublished
Västerbjers	PWC	Eriksson 2004
Köpingsvik	PWC	Eriksson unpublished

Table 1.1. List of sites assigned to the various archaeological cultures for which stable isotope data has been produced, as plotted in Figure 3.

from Resmo span both the Early and Middle Neolithic periods.

One burial from the Kastanjegården BAC cemetery in the province of Skåne (Scania) (Winge 1976) is represented by one data point. Corded Ware burials from two sites in the interior of Latvia, Sarkani and Selgas (Grasis 1996), produced four data points. Also included here are two crouched burials from the Zvejnieki Stone Age complex in northern Latvia. Even though this cemetery spans several millennia and includes mostly hunter–gatherer burials, these two burials differ distinctly in both manner of deposition and grave goods from the other burials at the cemetery, and both have produced direct radiocarbon dates completely corresponding to the Selgas and Sarkani ones.

Results

Stable carbon and nitrogen isotope analyses of 106 individual human subjects (247 data points) from Pitted Ware contexts are presented in Figure 1.3, along with stable isotope data for 28 human subjects from TRB contexts and six individuals (seven data points) from BAC contexts. The stable isotope data illustrate the great diversity in food culture during the Middle Neolithic. This diversity is not, however, completely arbitrary. With the exception of Resmo (n=11), all of the TRB and BAC data points are more negative than –20‰ for δ^{13}C, and below 12‰ for δ^{15}N. These stable isotope signatures are consistent with a diet derived mainly from terrestrial plants and animals, possibly with the addition of some freshwater fish. The overwhelming majority of PWC data points, on the other hand, are more positive than –16‰ for δ^{13}C and higher than 14‰ for δ^{15}N, which indicates food resources extracted mainly from the sea. In between those two extremes, are the TRB Resmo data points, exhibiting δ^{13}C values roughly ranging from –20‰ to –18‰, and most δ^{15}N values centring around 12‰–13‰. Accordingly, these values suggest a diet composed of foodstuffs originating from both terrestrial and marine sources.

Discussion

The plot of the Pitted Ware stable isotope data shows a solid cluster with stable carbon isotope values ranging between –16.5‰ and –13‰, and the corresponding stable nitrogen isotope value range 14‰–18‰. Analysed seals from Pitted Ware contexts include grey seal (*Halichoerus grypus*), harp seal (*Phoca groenlandica*) and ringed seal (*Pusa hispida*), deriving from Västerbjers (n=11), Ire (n=4) and Korsnäs (n=3). For these seals, δ^{13}C values range between –17.7‰ and –14.5‰ (–16.1‰±0.7‰ [average ± standard deviation]), whereas δ^{15}N values are within the 11.1‰–16.1‰ range (13.5±1.3‰). Taking into account a trophic level offset of 1‰ for δ^{13}C, and 3‰ for δ^{15}N (Minagawa and Wada 1984; Schoeninger and DeNiro 1984), a hypothetical average isotope signature for individuals feeding exclusively off seal would thus be δ^{13}C –15.1‰ and δ^{15}N 16.5‰. This is very close to the actual case, δ^{13}C –15.0±1.2‰ and δ^{15}N 15.9±1.1‰, indicating a massive intake of marine protein of seal and other marine resources from a high trophic level, within this group of people.

There are a few outliers, however, which deviate significantly from this general pattern, particularly in terms of their carbon isotope values, which range between –20.4 and –18.3‰ (Figure 1.4). The specimens with deviating stable isotope signatures derive from Visby and Köpingsvik – both sites where the Stone Age deposits are superimposed by Viking Age or medieval cultural layers. Four of the data points derive from bone and teeth from a single mandible, which on the one hand is marked 'Visby sk[eleton] 2, 1909' but, on the other hand, does not match the description for this context, 'a 40–50 year old male' (Janzon 1974). It is hence likely that this jaw has been mixed up in the museum stores with medieval skeletal remains from the many excavations in Visby.

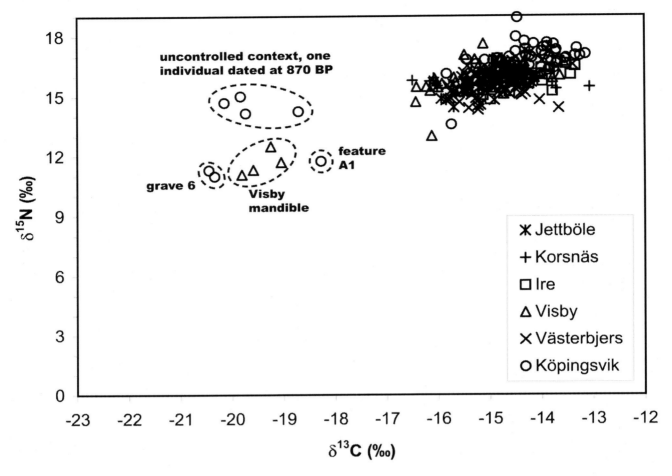

Figure 1.4. Stable isotopic data for bone and teeth from Pitted Ware contexts. For detailed arguments regarding the outlying values, see main text.

The remaining seven outlying values all derive from skeletal remains excavated in Köpingsvik. Out of the ten radiocarbon dates on human bone/dentine collagen produced from the site thus far, only one is later than the Middle Neolithic: 870±35 BP (Ua-32182; Papmehl-Dufay 2006: 112), that is, clearly medieval. It is therefore not surprising that four of the outlying data points (representing three individuals) stem from the same uncontrolled context as the medieval one, and they should consequently be discarded as possible intrusions.

It is intriguing that another of the outlying Köpingsvik values originates from one of the most interesting contexts at Köpingsvik, feature A1 (Papmehl-Dufay 2006: 99ff). This unique feature contained, apart from scattered human skeletal remains and regular PWC finds, two sherds of BAC ceramics and one battle axe – to our knowledge, the only finds of BAC attribution recovered at the whole site of Köpingsvik. The two final deviating carbon isotope values derive from a child burial, grave 6, at Köpingsvik. The child was buried in a crouched position, lacking chronologically diagnostic finds clearly associated with it. Radiocarbon dating of all specimens exhibiting deviating stable isotopic signatures is underway, and will be helpful in ruling out later intrusions.

To sum up, there are six individuals with deviating stable isotope values, four of which are likely to be later intrusions, one possibly associated with BAC artefacts, and one from a burial of uncertain date. This leaves us with 236 remaining data points, originating from 100 individuals, which all have a strong marine signal in their diet. Indeed, this makes a strong case for arguing that the Pitted Ware Culture actually represents a distinct group of people. Especially in the light of stable isotope analyses performed on skeletal remains from TRB or BAC contexts, the PWC stable isotope signatures stand out. With the exception of the Resmo megalith on Öland, there are no traces of any considerable marine protein intake among any of the TRB or BAC individuals (n=24) from various Swedish sites (Figure 1.3, Table 1.1). And although the analysed individuals from the Resmo passage grave (n=11) do display stable isotope signatures indicating some marine protein intake, none of the data points are within even three standard deviations of the average for the PWC cluster based on 236 individuals (−14.7±0.7‰ for $\delta^{13}C$ and 16.0±0.8‰ for $\delta^{15}N$).

So, returning to the four hypotheses on the PWC, how should we interpret our results? There is nothing in the data to suggest any gradual change of diet, as stated in the first hypothesis, unless the Resmo TRB population is regarded as forming a transitional stage. However, radiocarbon dates for Resmo suggests that the megalith was in use for at least 500 years, a period which overlaps extensively with radiocarbon dates for Köpingsvik PWC (Papmehl-Dufay 2006). The location of both Resmo and Köpingsvik on the small island of Öland would seem to correspond to the condition of studying change on a local scale, and the chronological overlap is therefore not coherent with the hypothesis.

The interpretation that the PWC sites were places where ritual pot destruction took place cannot really be tested by means of stable isotope analysis – we can only conclude that the ceramic tradition was important, although not in what way. We can, however, rule out the second hypothesis on other grounds. In contrast to people buried in TRB or BAC contexts, individuals in Pitted Ware burials exhibit a distinctly marine diet. Even assuming that these belong to a particular group within the TRB or BAC cultures, with special tasks associated with coastal activities, this would not explain why all kinds of people, regardless of age or sex, are buried, nor why their overall diet is so homogeneous, and demonstrates such a massive intake of marine resources, or why this diet at the individual level is so consistent throughout their life courses – from childhood to old age.

The third hypothesis postulates that the PWC combined hunting and fishing with animal husbandry, particularly pig herding. If the pigs were domestic, one would expect the people to, at least occasionally, feed them with left-overs of seal, fish or other marine resources. However, stable isotope analyses of pigs from Korsnäs, Västerbjers and Ire revealed no marine protein input to the pig diet – accordingly suggesting that they were actually wild boar (see Rowley-Conwy and Storå 1997 for a review of previous arguments regarding PWC pigs). Moreover, although sporadic finds of cattle or sheep/goat are recovered in PWC contexts, there is a lack of positive evidence of securely associated finds of any considerable number. In fact, radiocarbon dating of a number of allegedly PWC cattle and sheep/goat from Åland and Gotland have demonstrated them to be later intrusions, i.e. of Late Neolithic, Bronze Age or Iron Age date (Storå 2000; Eriksson 2004). Futhermore, it would be reasonable to expect that the alleged farming also implied inclusion of some domestic meat or dairy products in the cuisine. However, there is nothing in the stable isotope data to support any such substantial consumption.

Only the fourth hypothesis remains, then, viewing the Pitted Ware Culture as representing a distinct group of people, with their specific cultural identity, distinguished by their material culture, their burial practice, their diet and their subsistence pattern. This scenario has extensive support in the archaeological record as well as in the stable isotope data. In addition, a recent study of PWC ceramics from Öland (Papmehl-Dufay 2006) refutes previous ideas about PWC ceramic being merely "simple and inferior TRB pottery". The ceramic craft of the Pitted

Ware Culture was technologically advanced and an important part of society, with deeply rooted norms about proper pottery production and design – in fact very similar to ideas and norms concerning diet and what was considered edible.

Conclusion

Based on the analysis of stable carbon and nitrogen isotopes, we conclude that people buried in what has traditionally been described as Pitted Ware contexts, were very homogeneous in terms of actual diet. This shared dietary culture was mainly based on the utilization of seals and other marine protein sources. It is furthermore distinctly different from the diets of people from TRB or BAC contexts. Based on stable isotope, radiocarbon and archaeological data, we therefore reject the hypotheses that the PWC represents the ideological transformation of TRB groups, or that it represents coastal activities of TRB/BAC groups, or part-time farmers. So, in conclusion, the people of the Pitted Ware Culture were distinguished not only by their pottery, but also by their diet.

Acknowledgements

Thanks go to Heike Siegmund for running the mass-spectrometer, the Swedish Research Council and STINT for funding, the Swedish Museum of National Antiquities, the Swedish National Heritage Board and the Åland Museum for providing bone material, and Mike Parker Pearson and Mats Larsson for arranging a stimulating meeting.

References

Andersson, C. 1998. Kontinuitet i de mellanneolitiska samhällsstrukturerna. In C. Fredengren and I. Tarsala (eds) *Aktuell Arkeologi VI*. Stockholm Archaeological Reports. New Series vol. 35. Stockholm: Dept. of Archaeology, Stockholm University. 65–75.

Arne, T. J. 1909. Stenåldersundersökningar. *Fornvännen* 4: 86–108.

Axelsson, T. and Persson, P. 1999. *Arkeologisk undersökning 1998: Gånggriften Hjelmars rör, Raä nr 3, Falköping stad, Västergötland*. GOTARC Serie D. Arkeologiska rapporter 45. Göteborg: Institutionen för arkeologi, Göteborgs universitet.

Becker, C. J. 1950. Den grubekeramiske kultur i Danmark. *Aarbøger for nordisk oldkyndighed og historie* 1950: 153–274.

Becker, C. J. 1980. Om grubekeramisk kultur i Danmark: Korte bidrag til en lang diskussion (1950–1980). (In Danish with an English summary: On the Pitted Ware Culture in Denmark: Brief contributions to a lengthy discussion (1950–1980)). *Aarbøger for nordisk oldkyndighed og historie* 1980: 13–33.

Browall, H. 1991. Om förhållandet mellan trattbägarkultur och gropkeramisk kultur. In H. Browall, P. Persson and K.-G. Sjögren (eds)

Västsvenska stenåldersstudier. GOTARC serie C. Arkeologiska skrifter No 8. Göteborg: Institutionen för arkeologi, Göteborgs Universitet. 111–142.

Brown, T. A.. Nelson, D. E., Vogel, J. S. and Southon, J. R. 1988. Improved collagen extraction by modified Longin method. *Radiocarbon* 30: 171–177.

Carlsson, A. 1987. The prehistory of Gotland in Swedish archaeological research. In A. Carlsson, D. Damell, P. Hellström, Å. Hyenstrand and A. Åkerlund (eds) *Swedish Archaeology 1981–1985.* Stockholm: Svenska Arkeologiska Samfundet. 91–100.

Carlsson, A. 1998. *Tolkande arkeologi och svensk forntidshistoria: Stenåldern.* Stockholm Studies in Archaeology 17. Stockholm: Department of Archaeology.

Cullberg, C. 1963. *Meglitgraven i Rössberga.* Stockholm: Riksantikvarieämbetet.

Damm, C. 1991. The Danish single grave culture – ethnic migration or social construction? *Journal of Danish Archaeology* 10: 199–204.

Edenmo, R., Larsson, M. Nordqvist, B. and Olsson, E. 1997. Gropkeramikerna – fanns de? Materiell kultur och ideologisk förändring. In M. Larsson and E. Olsson (eds) *Regionalt och interregionalt: Stenåldersundersökningar i Syd- och Mellansverige.* Riksantikvarieämbetet Arkeologiska Undersökningar, Skrifter vol. 23. Stockholm: Riksantikvarieämbetet. 135–213.

Eriksson, G. 2003. *Norm and Difference. Stone Age Dietary Practice in the Baltic Region.* Theses and papers in scientific archaeology 5. Stockholm: Archaeological Research Laboratory.

Eriksson, G. 2004. Part-time farmers or hard-core sealers? Västerbjers studied by means of stable isotope analysis. *Journal of Anthropological Archaeology* 23(2): 135–162.

Eriksson, G., Lõugas, L. and Zagorska, I. 2003. Stone Age hunter-fisher-gatherers at Zvejnieki, northern Latvia: Radiocarbon, stable isotope and archaeozoology data. *Before Farming* (www.waspjournals.com) 2003/1(2): 1–26.

Fornander, E. 2006. The Wild Side of the Neolithic: A study of Pitted Ware diet and ideology through analysis of stable carbon and nitrogen isotopes in skeletal material from Korsnäs, Grödinge parish, Södermanland. MA theis, Archaeological Research Laboratory, Stockholm University. Available in full text at http://urn.kb.se/resolve?urn=urn:nbn:se:su:diva-1144

Götherström, A., Stenbäck, N. and Storå, J. 2002. Jettböle Middle Neolithic site of the Åland Islands – human remains, ancient DNA and pottery. *European Journal of Archaeology* 5: 42–69.

Grasis, N. 1996. Auklas kermaikas kulturas apbedijumi Sarkanos un Selgas (in Latvian). *Zinatniskas atskaites sisijas materiali par arheologu 1994. un 1995. gada petijumu rezultatiem.* Riga: Latvijas vestures instituta apgads. 60–65.

Janzon, G. O. 1974. *Gotlands mellanneolitiska gravar.* Stockholm: Almqvist & Wiksell.

Larsson, M. 2006. *A Tale of a Strange People: the Pitted Ware Culture in southern Sweden.* Kalmar Studies in Archaeology 2. Kalmar: Institutionen för humaniora och samhällskunskap, Högskolan i Kalmar.

Lidén, K. 1995a. *Prehistoric Diet Transitions.* Theses and Papers in Scientific Archaeology 1. Stockholm: Archaeological Research Laboratory.

Lidén, K. 1995b. Megaliths, agriculture, and social complexity: A diet study of two Swedish megalith populations. *Journal of Anthropological Archaeology* 14: 404–417.

Lidén, K. and Angerbjörn, A. 1999. Dietary change and stable isotopes: Problems with growth, Physiology and collagen turnover time. *Proceedings of the Royal Society London Series B* 266: 1779–1783.

Lidén, K., Eriksson, G., Nordqvist, B., Götherström, A., and Bendixen, E. 2004. "The wet and the wild followed by the dry and the tame" – or did they occur at the same time? *Antiquity* 78: 23–33.

Minagawa, M. and Wada, E. 1984. Stepwise enrichment of ^{15}N along food chains: Further evidence and the relation between $\delta^{15}N$ and animal age. *Geochimica et Cosmochimica Acta* 48: 1135–1140.

Nihlén, J. 1927. *Gotlands stenåldersboplatser.* Stockholm: Kungl. Vitterhets Historie och Antikvitets Akademiens handlingar.

Nordqvist, B. 1998. Fyndplatsen för Rolfsåkersmannen. In B. Nordqvist, C. Bramstång, R. Hernek, and J. Streiffert (eds) *Vin och vatten: Arkeologiska undersökningar i Bohuslän och Halland.* UV Väst rapport vol. 1998:14. Kungsbacka: Riksantikvarieämbetet, Byrån för arkeologiska undersökningar. 117–122.

Núñez, M. & Lidén, K. 1997. Taking the 5000 year old "Jettböle skeletons" out of the closet: A palaeo-medical examination of human remanins from the Åland (Ahvenanmaa) Islands. *International Journal of Circumpolar Health* 56: 30–39.

Österholm, I. 1989. *Bosättningsmönstret på Gotland under stenåldern: En analys av fysisk miljö, ekonomi och social struktur.* Theses and Papers in Archaeology 3. Stockholm: Dept. of Archaeology.

Papmehl-Dufay, L. 2006. *Shaping an Identity. Pitted Ware Potters in Southeast Sweden.* Theses and Papers in Scientific Archaeology 7. Stockholm: Archaeological Research Laboratory.

Parker Pearson, M. 2003. Food, identity and culture: an introduction and overview. In M. Parker Pearson (ed.) *Food, Culture and Identity in the Neolithic and Early Bronze Age.* Oxford: BAR International Series S1117. 1–30.

Persson, P. 1986. Några kommentarer till en lista över STY boplatsfynd från den svenska västkusten. In C. Adamsen and K. Ebbesen (eds) *Stridsøksetid i Sydskandinavien: Beretning fra et symposium 28.–30.X1985 i Vejle.* København: Forhistorisk Arkæologisk Insititut, Københavns Universitet. 266–275.

Rowley-Conwy, P. and Storå, J. 1997. Pitted Ware seals and pigs from Ajvide, Gotland: Methods of study and first results. In G. Burenhult (ed.) *Remote Sensing, vol. I.* Theses and Papers in North-European Archaeology, vol. 13:a. Stockholm: Dept. of Archaeology, Stockholm University. 113–127.

Schoeninger, M. J. and DeNiro, M. J. 1984. Nitrogen and carbon isotopic composition of bone collagen from marine and terrestrial animals. *Geochimica et Cosmochimica Acta* 48: 625–639.

Stenbäck, N. 2003. *Människorna vid havet: Platser och keramik på ålandsöarna perioden 3500–2000 f.Kr.* Stockholm Studies in Archaeology 28. Stockholm: Dept. of Archaeology, Stockholm University.

Storå, J. 2000. Sealing and animal husbandry in the Ålandic Middle and Late Neolithic. *Fennoscandia archaeological* 17: 57–81.

Werbart, B. 1998. Subneolithic: What is it? – "subneolithic" societies and the conservative economies of the Circum-Baltic Region. In eds M. Zvelebil, L. Domanska, and R. Dennell (eds) *Harvesting the Sea, Farming the Forest: The Emergence of Neolithic Societies in the Baltic Region.* Sheffield archaeological monographs, vol. 10. Sheffield: Sheffield Academic Press. 37–44.

Wincentz Rasmussen, L. 1993. Pitted Ware settlements. In S. Hvass and B. Storgaard (eds) *Digging into the Past: 25 years of Archaeology in Denmark.* København: The Royal Society of Northern Antiquaries. 114–115.

Winge, G. 1976. *Gravfältet vid Kastanjegården.* Malmöfynd 3. Malmö: Malmö Museum.

Wyszomirska, B. 1984. *Figurplastik och gravskick hos Nord- och Nordösteuropas neolitiska fångstkulturer.* Acta Archaeologica Lundensia, Series in 4° 18. Lund: Institute of Archaeology, University of Lund.

Zvelebil, M. 1996. The agricultural frontier and the transition to farming in the circum-Baltic region. In D. R. Harris (ed.) *The Origins and Spread of Agriculture and Pastoralism in Eurasia.* London: UCL Press. 323–345.

Chapter 2

Regional development or external influences? The Battle Axe period in south-western Scandinavia

Lars Larsson

Department of Archaeology and Ancient History, University of Lund (Lars.Larsson@ark.lu.se)

Introduction

What is the reason that scholars working with the Battle Axe Culture usually produce gigantic publications? It started on a more normal scale with P. V. Glob's study of the Single Grave Culture in 1944. Despite its rather restricted size it contains an important solid basis for our understanding and for future studies with a terminological and chronological presentation. But the next major work, *Jungneolithische Studien,* about the Battle Axe Culture of the Scandinavian peninsula by Mats P. Malmer in 1962 turned out to be one of the largest dissertations in archaeology so far, with some 959 pages. Despite its size, it is an eminent opus and easy to read.

The Battle Axe period in eastern Denmark

Other studies have been published since then, but early in 2006 two large publications about the Single Grave Culture appeared. The first one is Klaus Ebbesen's book *The Battle Axe Period*, altogether 858 pages, most of which consists of different find lists and presentations of important grave finds. It should be stated that Ebbesen's dissertation was finished back in 1992 and the main aspects, with the exception of the settlement sites, have not changed considerably since then. Ebbesen's study takes as its point of departure the situation in the east Danish islands. The number of finds and especially graves of typical Battle Axe origin is small. Some scholars have even maintained that the Single Grave Culture never really existed in eastern Denmark.

As long as the Funnel Beaker Culture and the Single Grave Culture were regarded as parallel cultural entities, there was not too much of a problem. The Funnel Beaker Culture had a longer existence in eastern than in western Denmark. But when more and more evidence appeared which contradicted this model, the problem of the cultural representation of eastern Denmark, in what Ebbesen names the Battle Axe period, became very significant. This is the situation that Ebbesen set out to solve. But, in order to do so, his intention was to obtain firm information about what constituted the primal materiality of the Single Grave Culture. With the exception of pottery, he worked with a typology based primarily on Glob's terminology, with the addition of sub-divisions of flint axe classifications based on previous studies of his own.

Despite intense studies of archives and collections, the number of graves typical of the Single Grave Culture remains low in eastern Denmark – about ten, mostly concentrated in the westernmost part, but they do appear in the east as well (Figure 2.1). They are all of a late date according to the typologically based chronology. Battle axes, which are so numerous in western Denmark where they appear to be an important personal belonging in graves, do exist in eastern Denmark, even the earliest types, but the majority are single finds; a considerable number have been found in wetland environments. This shows that the function of the battle axes was slightly different within eastern Denmark.

The large flint tools of different shapes, such as axes, gouges and chisels, are the largest group that can be referred to as the main representatives of the period. The main types are similar to what were produced in the late Funnel Beaker Culture. However, the examples of this period are not made with the same excellent knapping and polish as the previous ones and have a less marked trapezoidal shape. They are also generally smaller. The hollow-edged shaping of the gouges also became a common feature.

A considerable number of these large flint tools, as well as other artefact groups dated to the Battle Axe period, are found in the megalithic tombs of eastern Denmark. This is a phenomenon with parallels in western Denmark, but the frequency in the east is much higher (Figure 2.2). The position of most finds indicates that they were used as grave goods. However, there is no totally convincing example of a typical grave situation with a skeleton combined with these personal belongings. Yet this absence is also evident within the late Funnel Beaker Culture as well.

In some cases where axes show traces of fire or intentionally destroyed edges, the situation is similar, with special forms of ritual deposition. Thus we have no solid grounds for determining how many deposits of these artefact types should be regarded as funerary or burial contexts and how many reflect other forms of ritual activity. An interesting aspect is that the number of battle axes in megalithic tombs is rather small. This is a criticism of Ebbesen, who judges almost all finds as coming from former burial sites.

The study presents a period of certain influences between what is today western and eastern Denmark during the period. The already old megalithic tombs continued to be used as monuments for ritual activities while the new burial practice of single graves covered by a small barrow

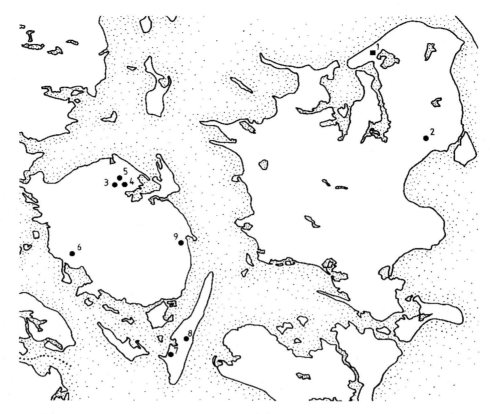

Figure 2.1. The distribution of graves typical for the Single Grave Culture, with a central grave and a small mound (dots) and flat graves (rectangle), within eastern Denmark (Ebbesen 2006: figure 96).

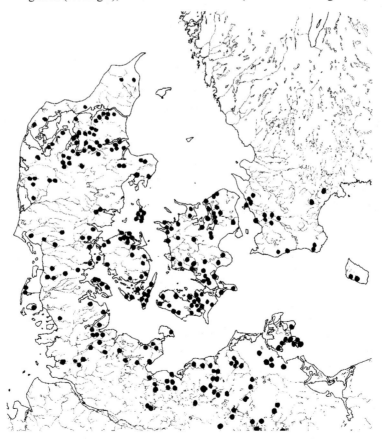

Figure 2.2. Megalithic tombs in Southern Scandinavia with finds dated to the Younger Neolithic (Ebbesen 2006: figure 93).

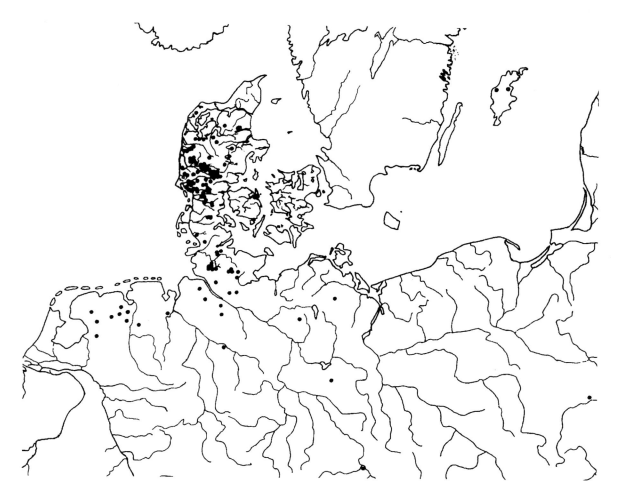

Figure 2.3. The distribution of the earliest types of battle axes (Ebbesen 2006: figure 120).

was rarely applied. The links to traditional behaviour, for instance ritual deposition in wetlands, was more marked in the east than in the west.

The origin of the Single Grave Culture

A question of importance for Ebbesen is the origin of the Single Grave Culture. At the transition from the early to late Middle Neolithic at about 2800 cal BC, there is evidence for marked deforestation of the southern and central parts of the Jutland peninsula. Large areas of heather heath replaced the forest. These had to be cultivated in order to create pastures of major importance. In order to pinpoint their cultural origin, Ebbesen uses the distribution of the earliest battle axes, which turn out to have a marked concentration in the southern part of central Jutland (Figure 2.3). This area is thereby regarded as the focal area.

After a systematic study of the so-called Corded Ware cultural complex, this term is totally disregarded by Ebbesen. There are common features within central and northern continental Europe. However, the Corded Ware folk are viewed as fictional. The concept of the Corded Ware Culture must be given up since there is no uniform

archaeological complex in Europe during this period. On the contrary, regional differences are very clear. The subsistence strategy has to be described as local adaptations to the ecological resources of each part of northern and central Europe. But Ebbesen does not indicate that this is not new. These were the same subsistence practices as in the Funnel Beaker Culture across a vast area with many differences but quite acceptable to Ebbesen. That the battle axe was a personal male belonging in quite a different way from previous periods is accepted, as well as inter-regional features of ceramic decoration and form. In most areas small concentrations of graves provide a picture of a marked tribal organisation. The contacts between these tribal centres were low, so that surplus was not exchanged. Ebbesen states that no single area can be identified in which the new international elements that characterise the period were created. For Ebbesen this development is a natural step in the process of European development. However the reasons and explanations for such changes, or natural steps, however unnatural, are totally neglected. He more or less explicitly states that the origin of these developments is to be found in southern Jutland. In traditional Danish style, the publication is filled with tables and diagram, most of them rather meaningless and

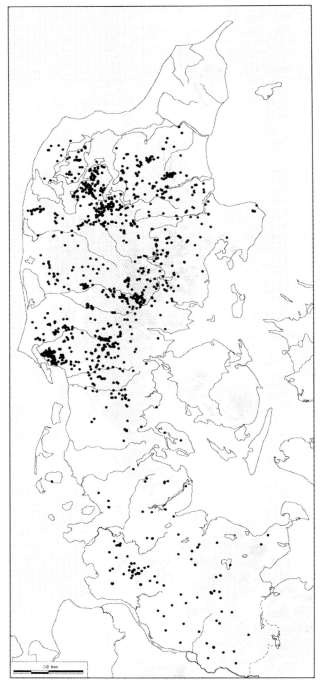

Figure 2.4. The distribution of excavated graves from the Single Grave Culture (Hübner 2006: abb. 8).

impossible to use when comparing one factor with another.

The essence of the Single Grave Culture

The second publication issued in 2006 is Eva Hübner's *Jungneolithische Gräber auf der Jütischen Halbinsel* in three volumes - 1,500 pages altogether. Luckily, and typically for a German dissertation, most of the pages include grave finds and illustrations. While Ebbesen views the cultural changes from the north, Hübner regards the development as originating from the south, in other words northern continental Europe. Her intentions are to make a thorough study of the Single Grave Culture. In contrast to Glob's study of almost 600 graves, Hübner is able to include almost 2400. This is a huge increase, but without a comparable rise in the number of excavated new graves after the Second World War. Most graves were found at the turn of the last century, caused by the intensity of enlarging farmland at the expense of heathland. It also includes the graves of Schleswig and Holstein, but these account for only 8% of all burials. As in Ebbesen's book, the chosen problems are very straightforward without much novelty in relation to the problems tackled by other scholars.

It has been stated that people connected to the Single Grave Culture lived on sandy soil. But a thorough study of the distribution of small mounds shows that about a quarter of them are located on clay and just slightly fewer (20%) on poor heath sand. Two counties include about half the number of mounds from the Single Grave Culture (Figure 2.4). Based on the present-day number, the total number of mounds is calculated to be about 30,000. Over a duration of 600 years (in relation to Ebbesen's 450 years; 2850–2400 BC) about fifty mounds would have been constructed in each year on average.

A considerable number, varying from 54% to 18% depending on the region, have been investigated professionally as regards documentation and information on which to base interpretation.

The chronology of the Single Grave Culture

The chronological sequences of the culture have been based on the relation of graves within the same mound, from underground graves to the overground graves but, as Hübner states, the number of mounds with two or more graves is very small. This provides too small a basis for a firm chronological analysis. Instead Hübner uses correspondence analysis on about four hundred graves. The result is a division into seven groups that has some divergences from the chronology presented by Glob and Ebbesen (Figure 2.5). The most remarkable difference is the early typological sequence of the battle axes. The earliest type (Glob's A1) is actually later than subtypes B1–B3, previously regarded as later than A1. This might seem exaggeratedly pedantic but actually it presents quite a new picture of the spread of the earliest Single Grave Culture in contrast to Ebbesen's view. Instead of a marked concentration of early graves in southern Jutland, the new version presents a more uniform spread of early graves along the axis of the peninsula (Figure 2.6). This has similarities to a process of change that was already in its earliest stage affecting most of the area of the Single Grave Culture.

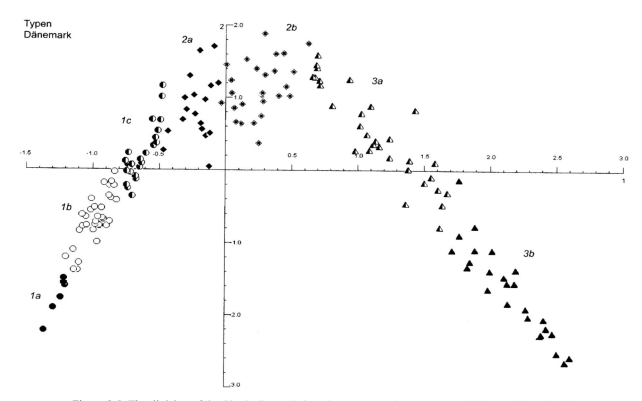

Figure 2.5. The division of the Single Grave Culture by correspondence analysis (Hübner 2006: abb. 24).

	YN 1	YN 1–2	YN 2	YN 2–3	YN 3	undated	Total
Males	635 89,2%	118 74,2%	231 77,8%	20 22,2%	202 34,1%	118 24,3%	1324 56,7%
Females	22 3,1%	22 13,8%	25 8,4%	50 55,6%	50 8,5%	144 29,7%	313 13,4%
Children	5 0,7%	7 4,4%	11 3,7%	3 3,3%	21 3,5%	15 3,1%	62 2,7%
Indeter- mined	50 7,0%	12 7,6%	30 10,1%	17 18,9%	318 18,9%	208 42,9%	635 27,2%
Total	712	159	297	90	591	485	2334

Table 2.1. The number of males, females and children in the graves dated to the Younger Neolithic (after Hübner 2006: abb. 454).

Hübner's book includes as many tables and diagrams as Ebbesen's but they are much easier to compare and do provide valuable information about the division of certain artefact group such as the axe and gouge sub-types.

The Single Grave Culture in social perspective

Hübner's book includes a detailed presentation of the different types of grave within the cultural framework of the Single Grave Culture. Apart from ordinary grave-pits covered by a small mound, some more exquisite structures are present such as mortuary houses. But they are small in size as well as number and the quality or quantity of grave goods does not differ significantly from other graves.

There is a well known division in the placing of men and women in the grave pit; males have their heads to the west (lying on their right sides) and women to the east (lying on their left sides), while both sexes face towards the south. In most cases, all that survives of the skeletons are stains in the acidic soils so gender has been estimated by grave good provision. Based on the postulate that battle axes were personal belonging for males and that certain amber ornaments belonged to females, Hübner calculates the proportions of men and women (Table 2.1). In the early part of the Single Grave Culture the percentage of male graves is as high as 90%, a figure that is reduced in the late part of the culture to about 30%. At the same time the number of sex-neutral graves increases. The social structure is interpreted as markedly patriarchal. Graves for children are almost lacking, and the distribution of grave goods in some graves indicates that they were buried together with adults.

According to Hübner, the Single Grave Culture covers the period 2850 until 2250 BC. In her discussion of the chronology she is well aware of the wiggle effect of the radiocarbon calibration curve. Despite that, she suggests a certain chronological overlap with the Funnel Beaker Culture at the beginning as well as with the Late Neolithic at the end. The basis used for these statements is fragile to say the least. It is very much a question of terminology – *i.e.* what one means by Late Neolithic.

According to Hübner, the Single Grave Culture did not appear in eastern Denmark until a later phase. Instead a society based on traditions from the Funnel Beaker and the Pitted Ware Cultures existed for at least two hundred years. At the end of the Battle Axe period eastern Denmark was well incorporated in the same cultural sphere as western Denmark.

Due to this new chronological setting, the introduction of the Single Grave Culture is marked by a number of graves spreading from the Elbe to Limfjorden (Figure 2.6). The contrasts with the Funnel Beaker Culture in the east and the Pitted Ware Culture in the north are clear. Hübner views the change as a rapid process within the existing population. Increasing sheep farming created a more individualistic society, in contrast to the communal herding of cows. The reason for the differences between the well-made flint axes of the Funnel Beaker Culture and those of the Single Grave Culture is interpreted as the more manifest symbolic importance of the artefact in the former than in the latter.

In her investigation of contemporaneous societies in continental Europe, Hübner, just like Ebbesen, does not identify any intensive connections. Like Ebbesen, she does not accept the idea of copper as a trading commodity of importance. Since more than 80% of graves with early battle axes are located in Jutland, both favour this regional development as the origin for the Single Grave Culture but neither presents a firmly based model for why and how this cultural change was initiated and extended.

References

Ebbesen, K. 2006. *The Battle Axe Period.* København: University of Copenhagen.

Glob, P. V. 1944. Studier over den jyske Enkeltgravkultur. *Aarbøger for Oldkyndighed og Historie* 1944: 1–283.

Hübner, E. 2006. *Jungneolithische Gräber auf der Jütischen Halbinsel. Typologische und chronologische Studien zur Einzelgrabkultur.* København: Nordiske Fortidsminder (Serie B, Band 24:1–3).

Malmer. M. P. 1962. *Jungneolithiische Studien.* Lund: Acta Archaeologica Lundensia (Series in 8°, No. 2).

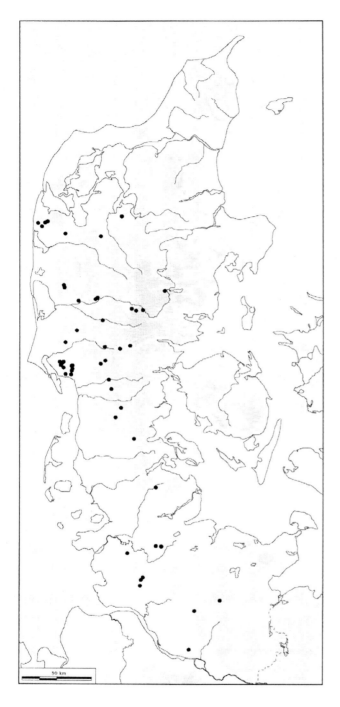

Figure 2.6. The distribution of the earliest graves from the Single Grave Culture (Hübner 2006: abb. 470).

No differences in style of grave good types are evident during the early part of the culture. However, in the later part a south-eastern and a north-eastern group are distinctive, especially in the stylistic differences within the pottery.

Chapter 3

The Guardians and Protectors of Mind:[1] ritual structures in the Middle Neolithic of Southern Sweden

Mats Larsson

Institute of Humanities and Social Sciences, University of Kalmar, Kalmar, Sweden

Introduction

This article concerns itself with what has been interpreted as ritual deposits and structures in the later part of the Middle Neolithic in both Southern Sweden and Denmark. During the time span 2900-2600 cal BC, we see the erection, and sometimes destruction, of huge palisade enclosures, causewayed enclosures as well as more insubstantial structures. The radiocarbon dates clearly indicate that they all belong to the transition between Middle Neolithic A (MN A) and Middle Neolithic B (MN B). The erection of these enclosures, for example the one at Dösjebro, happened at the same time as the large Funnel Beaker Culture (FBC) settlements were abandoned, and instead we find many small-scale settlements in the landscape.

It is, in other words, clear that something happened to the fundamental structure of society at this period and those public meanings and interpretations were negotiated and contested. In times of rapid change people used, re-invented, and re-used different forms of material culture.

Ritual sites in the late Middle Neolithic: a case study

Something that has often been overlooked in the debate concerning the late Middle Neolithic is the evidence for ritual. The following sites of Åby, Siretorp, Bollbacken, Dösjebro, Hyllie, Stävie and Hunneberget (Figure 3.1) will be briefly discussed in this vein.

Åby

Burned and unburned human bones were found in trench 2 as well as in trench 3 (excavated in 1997) but no evidence of any grave features or red ochre were noted. The bones seem to come from at least two, but probably more, adults (Sigvallius 1999). In the same trench a fragment of a burned thin bladed flint axe, two hollow-edged chisels, a thick-butted stone axe as well as two tanged arrowheads were found. Most of the worked flints from the site also derive from this area (Larsson 2006).

The human bones were found in several squares in trench 2, together with the above-mentioned artefacts and some highly decorated pottery, but no actual concentration is visible. Parts of pointed shaped vessel bottoms were also found in trench 2. They were actually still standing in

small pits. In the same context we also found animal bones; fish, pig, seal and beaver. The site has been briefly discussed recently by Richard Bradley (2005:134) where he also notes that it is possible that the human bones found on several Pitted Ware Culture (PWC) sites derive not from graves but from culture layer contexts of the kind discussed above. The dating of the deposits is not that easy. The youngest date (2400-2040 cal BC) is from organic residue on a sherd with a characteristic pattern that we call 'hanging triangles' (Larsson 2004). This sherd was found in trench 2 and therefore in association with the deposit. As has been discussed elsewhere, this date is too young and a radiocarbon value of 2880-2490 cal BC is more in accordance with the material. This sherd also has a 'hanging triangle' motif (Larsson 2006). Åby is not the only PWC site with traces of rituals. For example, at the nearby site of Fagervik, Axel Bagge excavated a pit (feature 3) with about 20 skull fragments together with other smaller human bones (1938).

Siretorp

The site of Siretorp, situated in Blekinge in south-eastern Sweden, is one of the most famous of all PWC sites. In the context of this article, an excavation in 1990 at Siretorp 4:19 is highly interesting for many reasons. No proper site report has been written so the following is based on the author's own impressions of the material (Larsson 2006). In total, about 150sq m was excavated and the trench was situated less than 20 m from Bagge and Kjellmark's (1939) main trench (A) from 1931. Two pits (A18 and A 26), found beneath Björkquist's layer L3: II, are of special interest and might be interpreted as ritual features.

The two pits were situated close together in the northwestern part of the excavation. Pit A 18 was about 1.2m x 0.8m across and 0.32 m deep. The filling in the pit consisted of grey-black, slightly sooty sand, and contained some interesting and unusual finds. For example, the amount of fire-damaged flint debris was quite large. The total weight of the worked flint (both Kristianstad flint and Baltic flint) was not especially great (only about 200g) but 40% of it was damaged by fire. The most unusual finds, however, were a fragment of a thin-bladed flint axe and a fragment of a thick-butted chisel, both made of Baltic flint (Figure 3.2). On both items, both the narrow and broad sides are polished. Interestingly enough, the axe and the chisel were heavily damaged by fire and were found lying close together at the bottom of the pit.

---

[1] Bob Dylan 'Chimes of freedom' 1964

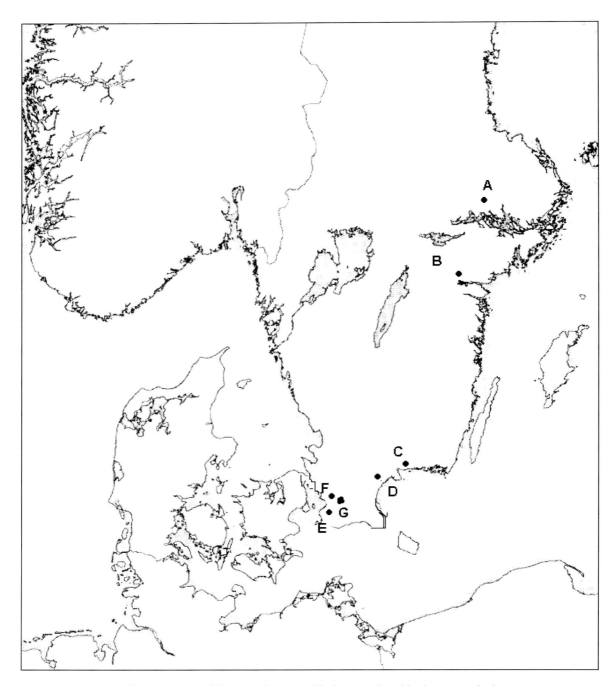

Figure 3.1 Map of Southern Sweden with sites mentioned in the text marked
(A Bollbacken; B Åby; C Siretorp; D Hunneberget; E Hyllie; F Dösjebro; G Stävie)

The pottery from the pit has some interesting features. The total weight of pottery from pit A18 is 1214g, of which 200g (16%) is decorated. It is highly fragmented, making it difficult to say anything about vessel shape, but there are some interesting decorative motifs. One sherd has a spruce twig-shaped decoration in incised lines, and a couple more sherds show similar decoration. These are small, however, and only show vertical incised lines but they are similar to the above in technique.

Pit A18 and the culture layer are dated by three radiocarbon dates on charcoal. Charcoal from the pit A18 is dated to 3300-2700 cal BC (LuA-4503; 4340±110 BP) and from the culture layer to 2700-2490 cal BC (LuA-4505 4090±120 BP). A second determination from the pit (LuA-4504) dates to the Late Bronze Age and is not discussed further here.

The other pit (A26) was situated very close to A18 and the two of them might be seen as parts of the same structure. The pit was 1.2m x 0.2m wide and had a depth of 0.1m-0.2m. The filling in the pit consisted of blackish sand. As was the case in A18, only a very small amount of pottery (c. 100g) was found in A26, and only a couple

Figure 3.2 Fire-damaged chisel and thin-bladed flint axe from Siretorp

of sherds were decorated with horizontal lines. Otherwise the material in A26 was similar to that in A18: fire-damaged flint of both Kristianstad and Baltic types. The total weight of the flint waste (100g) is not significant, but about 90% of it was fire-damaged. It included 16 burned fragments of polished axes made from Baltic flint. They are small but it is possible to identify one as deriving from of a thin-bladed axe and one from a thick-butted axe.

Bollbacken
At the Bollbacken site in middle Sweden several house plans were excavated, of which house 3 is the most interesting (Artursson 1996). A post wall was probably embedded into a trapezoidal ditch about 0.2m-0.4m deep. There were cremated human bones and animal bones in the construction fill, as well as in other features associated with it. The excavator interprets the construction as a ritual building with an associated area around it that was used for ritual activities such as funerary rites (*ibid.*: 76). Several radiocarbon dates place the Bollbacken site in the period *c.* 2600-2300 cal BC (*ibid.*: 97, 204).

Hunneberget
During a rescue excavation outside Kristianstad in northeast Scania in 2002 three small timber circles, as well as two post-built structures of another type, were found (Figure 3.3; Edring 2005). The diameter of these circles varies between 2m and 5m; they are, in other words, quite small. The circles were restricted to a small area on the Hunneberget hill. Two rows of smaller posts run towards the largest of the circles. This has been interpreted as a passageway running into this particular circle. Materials interpreted as ritual depositions were found both in the actual post-holes as well as in pits outside the circles.

Hyllie
The enclosure of Hyllie was discovered during a rescue excavation in the southern outskirts of Malmö in 1989 (Figure 3.4; Svensson 2002). This was the first enclosure of its kind to be found in southern Scandinavia. Only parts of the palisade were excavated at that time and further excavations were carried out in 2001-2002, providing a full plan of the entire enclosure and some areas outside the palisades. This made it the most extensively excavated palisade enclosure in Scandinavia. The enclosure was oval in shape and measured about 250m x 160m. It consists of 3229 postholes in which posts with a diameter of 0.1m-0.4m were erected. The height of the palisade has been estimated at between 1.5m and 2m. The radiocarbon results and finds in post-holes and a few other related features place the enclosure within the Battle Axe Culture (BAC) and the transition between MN A and MN B. Flakes from the production of

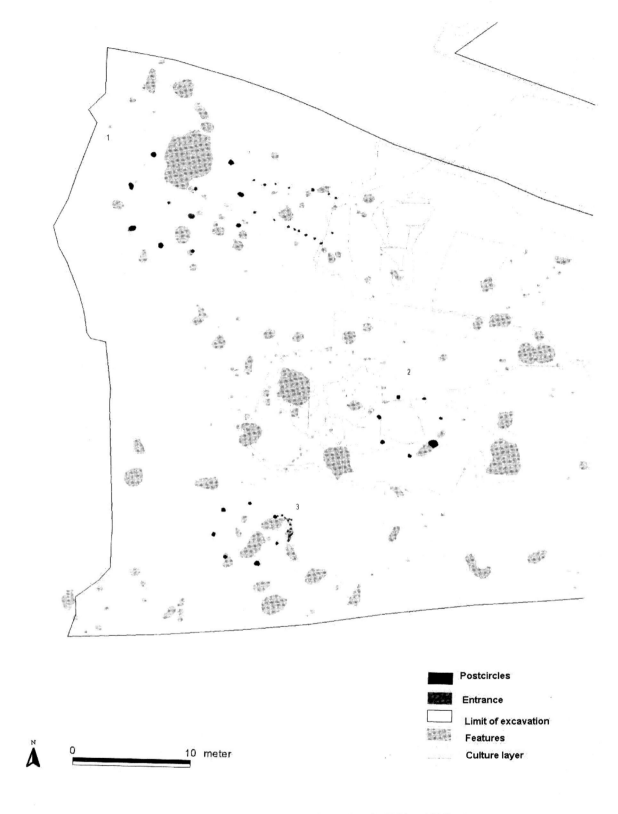

Figure 3.3 Hunneberget in NE Scania (Edring 2005)

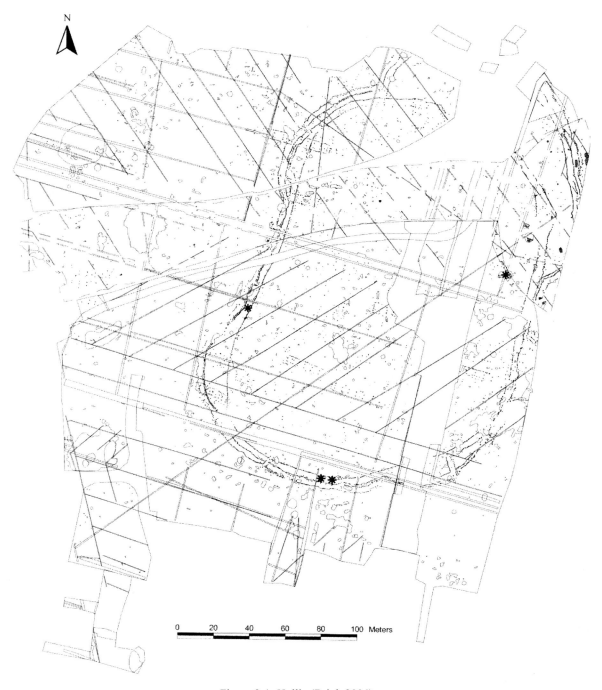

Figure 3.4 Hyllie (Brink 2004)

square-sectioned axes or chisels were found in post-holes and pits, together with flake scrapers, bones of both domestic and wild animals and pottery. Small fragments of burned clay in several postholes could indicate that the palisade was burned down (Brink 2004).

Dösjebro
Between 1995 and 1998 extensive archaeological excavations were carried out at Dösjebro in western Scania (Svensson 2002; 2003), not far from the causewayed enclosure at Stävie, 6km to the south. The area enclosed by the palisade at Dösjebro is about 3ha

(Figure 3.5). Several components belonging to the palisade have been identified: a main palisade, supporting posts and entrances. About 500 posts have been recorded, each set about 1m apart. In the postholes, pottery both from the late FBC as well as the BAC were found. Several axe-manufacturing sites were found outside, but close to the palisade. The flint assemblage is completely made up of waste material. In one posthole 1640 flakes were found packed tightly together. As was the case with Hyllie, this palisade was also burned down: at the top of every posthole there was a pipe of charcoal.

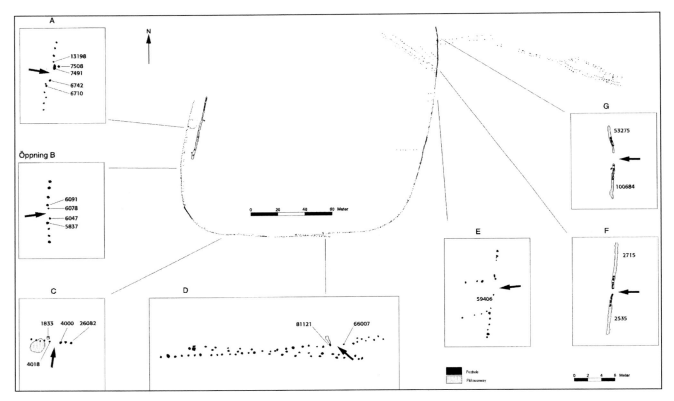

Figure 3.5 Dösjebro (Svensson 2002)

Stävie

Between 1973 and 1978, extensive excavations at Stävie in western Scania located an extensive system of pits in the eastern part of the excavated area. The sizes of the pits varied between 0.4m and 3m, and more than 100kg of pottery was found in them. The pottery has been dated to the late MN A and represents the type site for the late FBC ceramic group called Stävie. Interestingly enough, there is heavy influence from the PWC in the flint industry with many characteristic PWC items such as tanged arrowheads (Larsson 1982).

The protectors of the mind and society: ritual specialists and changes in society

People were active agents in the way in which the material was deposited, in the kind of material selected, in the structuration of the material, and in the telling of stories and myths. At sites like the ones discussed above, there is evidence for what might be interpreted as ritual activities. In this way it all made sense and reaffirmed domestic duties. This is how the *habitus* worked; confirming practices and re-working them in new ways. Rituals also imply the legitimacy of age and tradition; they are a matter of deep structure that does not change (Bell 1997: 210). They were, in other words, an important part of the structuration of society and they helped people not only to connect and re-connect with the ancestors, but also to realize the future.

What happened, then, in a society when monuments were closed, like the passage graves, or the palisade enclosures which were deliberately destroyed by fire? As Bell (1997: 251) has stated, ritual is a medium for appropriating changes while maintaining a sense of cultural continuity.

This is, to my mind, an important statement for the interpretation of societal change in the late Middle Neolithic. If we apply this to the period in question we can see how the destruction and closing of monuments like, for example, Dösjebro and Hyllie must have been of huge importance and the consequences must have been radical. An important dimension of social practices is the relationship with the past, and the extent to which (routine) practices repeat earlier practices as a form of memory of them. This is why I think that Bell's interpretation is of importance.

In a social structure there are traditions and established ways of doing things and, if we accept the common notion that rituals formed a central role in society and that ritual leaders were high-ranking members of society, we can imagine the importance of ritual in the reproduction of human social lives. In this way, we can see those officiating at rituals as human agents. John Barrett (1994: 81) writes that ritual practices enabled those who participated to rework their collective experiences against a 'text', whose origin and authority derived from other, sacred worlds but it also means that these can be changed when people start to ignore them, replace them or reproduce them differently.

In the same period of time, we also see the destruction of flint axes by fire as well as the cremation of human bone.

22

This is known from several places normally dated to the late FBC. We can here only briefly mention sites like Kverrestad and SvartskylIe in Scania where large amounts of flint axes were consciously destroyed by fire (L. Larsson 2000; 2004).

All of these manifestations of ritual behaviour, together with the evidence for a change in the settlement system, in the period 2900-2600 cal BC can, I believe, be traced back to a change in ritual. The ritual specialists were active agents in changing society and I believe that the outcome of this period of upheaval is the Battle Axe Culture with its completely new set of rules and affiliations.

References

Artursson, M. 1995. *Bollbacken: En sen gropkeramisk boplats och ett gravfält från äldre järnålder* RAÄ 258, Tortuna socken, Västmanland. Rapporter från Arkeologikonsult . Slutundersökningsrapport, MBM402. ATA Dnr: 421-4805-1996.

Bagge, A. 1938. Stenåldersboplatsen vid Fagervik I Krokeks sn, Östergötland. Ett preliminärt meddelande. *Meddelanden från Östergötlands Fornminnesförening* 1937-1938.

Bagge, A. and Kjellmark, K. 1939. *Stenåldersboplatserna vid Siretorp i Blekinge.* Stockholm: KVHAA.

Barrett, J. 1994 *Fragments from Antiquity: an archaeology of social life in Britain, 2900-1200 BC.* Oxford: Blackwell.

Bell. 1997. *Ritual: perspectives and dimensions.* Oxford: Oxford University Press.

Bradley, R. 2005. *Ritual and Domestic Life in Prehistoric Europe.* London: Routledge.

Brink, K. 2004. The palisade enclosure at Hyllie, SW Scania. *Journal of Nordic Archaeological Science* 14: 61-71.

Larsson, L. 1982. A causewayed enclosure and a site with Valby Pottery at Stävie, western Scania. *Meddelanden från Lunds Universitets Historiska Museum 1981-1982.*

Larsson, L. 2000.Axes and fire-contacts with the gods. In D. Olausson and H.Vandkilde (eds) *Form, Function and Context. Material culture studies in Scandinavian archaeology.* Lund: 93-105.

Larsson M. 2004. Living in cultural diversity. The Pitted Ware Culture and its relatives. *Journal of Nordic Archaeological Science* 14: 61-71.

Larsson, M. 2006. *The Tale of a Strange People: the Pitted Ware Culture in southern Sweden.* Kalmar/Lund: Kalmar Studies in Archaeology vol. 2, University of Lund.

Sigvallius, B.1999. *Åby. Raä 36, Kvillinge sn., Östergötland. Osteologisk undersökning.* UV-mitt. Stockholm.

Svensson, M. 2002. Palisade enclosures – the second generation of enclosed sites in the Neolithic of Northern Europe. In A.Gibson (ed.) *Behind Wooden Walls: Neolithic enclosures in Europe.* Oxford: BAR International Series 1013. 28-59.

Svensson, M. 2003. I det neolitiska rummet. *Skånska spår-arkeologi längs Västkustbanan.* Lund: Riksantikvarieämbetet.

Chapter 4

Shaping an identity: pottery and potters of the Pitted Ware Culture

Ludvig Papmehl-Dufay

Archaeological Research Laboratory, University of Stockholm, Stockholm, Sweden

Abstract

This paper deals with pottery and cultural identity during the Middle Neolithic (*c.* 3300–2300 cal BC) in southeast Sweden. The problem area treated is very large, and what is said below reflects several of my previously published cases on the subject (Papmehl-Dufay 2003; 2004; in press) as well as my recently published PhD thesis (2006). Here I approached ceramic materials from a specific time period in a specific area and, with the aid of different analytical methods, tried to illuminate various technological and practical issues that I assume to have been socially embedded. The general aim of the study was to investigate the role of pottery within the so-called Pitted Ware culture in southeast Sweden. Two large pottery assemblages from two sites on the island of Öland were approached with similar questions and similar methods, intending to reveal similarities and differences in the production and use of ceramic products on the island during the period. Methods used include recording and statistical treatment of large ceramic assemblages, lipid residue analysis by means of Gas Chromatography combined with Mass Spectrometry (GC/MS), and technological analysis of clays and wares by binocular microscope and thin section. In the following a brief review of the problems and the results will be given, and the issue of pottery and cultural identity will be touched upon.

Cultural diversity and pottery

In archaeology, the design of pots is often expected to reflect different groups of people and contact between areas, and large-scale geographical similarities in pottery form and decoration are believed to reflect the expression of some form of common cultural identity. However, as has been emphasised by numerous authors in recent years this is not an altogether straightforward point, and the way identity is expressed through pottery design certainly needs to be discussed further (Jones 2002: 105ff; Boast 2002). In recent studies on Swedish Neolithic pottery, it has been argued that expressions of identity not only should be sought in general aspects of design such as vessel shape or decorative styles, but that small details may have been manipulated as part of the expression of a local identity (e.g. Gruber 1995; Hallgren 2000: 184ff; Larsson 2006: 87ff). This further indicates something which I think is important to consider: that pottery design should not be seen as one single element that either does or does not reflect cultural identity, but rather specific elements of the design, or the manner of execution of specific stages of the production process, may signify identity on different levels and in different contexts (see Gosselain 2000; Boast 2002: 104). This is why, in any study attempting to address issues of pottery design and identity, as many aspects of the pottery as possible should be covered by the investigation. It is also important to bear in mind that, besides the expression of various forms of identity, pottery design depends on a range of other factors that are relevant to consider in relation to studies of pottery variation. Intended practical vessel use, raw material availability and use, technological tradition, design tradition, metaphorical representations in vessel shape and decoration, and not least the personal influence of individual potters – all these and other factors combine to make up what we see as pottery design.

A Pitted Ware cultural identity

In common archaeological parlance, the Pitted Ware culture represents a Middle Neolithic hunting-fishing-gathering culture, conceptually closely associated with the coastal environment and heavily dependent on seal hunting and fishing (e.g. Storå 2001; Stenbäck 2003). Large cemeteries have been found on the islands of Gotland and Öland in the Baltic Sea, and along the Swedish east coast a very large number of sites have been found from northeast Scania in the south to Hälsingland in the north (Figure 4.1; Edenmo *et al.* 1997; Papmehl-Dufay 2006: 32ff). The sites are characterised by the overwhelmingly large assemblages of pottery (Figure 4.2), as well as by their coastal locations and the occurrence of fish and seal bones. In earlier studies the Pitted Ware culture was often regarded as primitive in relation to the agricultural TRB culture, and it can easily be demonstrated that this conception, to a large extent, has influenced the kind of interpretations drawn regarding various aspects of the Neolithic (Papmehl-Dufay 2006: 32ff). In recent years, the use of the concept of culture in Neolithic studies has been intensely debated, however, and the very existence of a cultural entity corresponding to what we refer to as the Pitted Ware culture has been questioned. In fact, it is still a matter of heated discussion whether or not we should talk about different 'cultures' in the Neolithic (e.g. Edenmo *et al.* 1997).

In my view, from among other things, evidence on diet (Eriksson 2004; Fornander 2006), subsistence and hunting patterns (Storå 2001) and burial practice (Janzon 1974; Sjögren 2004), the Pitted Ware culture in eastern Sweden stands out as one quite clear example of what indeed most probably should be seen as a large cultural entity with specific ways of living, specific myths of origin, specific perceptions on life and death and, not least, a specific socially embedded ceramic craft tradition. The latter includes not only the production and design of

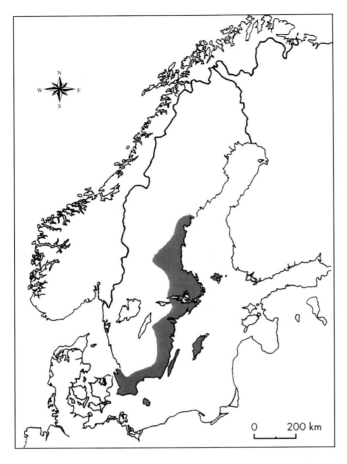

Figure 4.1. Map of Scandinavia with the distribution area of the eastern Swedish Pitted Ware culture indicated.

Figure 4.2. Pitted Ware pot from Siretorp, Blekinge, SE Sweden (after Bagge and Kjellmark 1939: 317). The rim diameter of the original vessel is *c*. 38cm.

ceramic vessels and the social activities surrounding these, but also the use of the pots in specific contexts as seen in the enormous assemblages typically deposited in near-the-shore settings. It is important to emphasise that, within this entity, numerous local identity groups were most likely included and, regarding the pottery aesthetically as well as technologically and possibly also contextually, there are some significant regional differences to be seen within the overall Pitted Ware tradition. Apart from the general Pitted Ware cultural identity governing certain aspects of pottery design, on a higher level of detail smaller identity groups such as lineages or extended family units may have been important for the rules surrounding production of pottery in a particular community (see Hallgren 2000; Larsson 2006).

The Pitted Ware life style outlined above agrees poorly, one might argue, with the existence of a lively and socially important ceramic craft tradition. Factors like small population size and residential mobility are generally believed to put serious constraints on the possibility of (and use for) pottery production (Arnold 1985; Núñez 1990: 35ff; Eerkens *et al.* 2002), and often the production and use of pottery is believed to be closely connected to an agricultural economy (e.g. Gebauer 1995). A number of recent studies clearly show, however,

that this association of pottery production with sedentary agricultural societies cannot be maintained (Bougard 2003; Zvelebil and Jordan in press). In northern Europe the ceramic craft was generally adopted within hunter-gatherer societies and, in most cases, was not connected in any clear way to the introduction of agriculture (Hallgren 2004: 131ff). The ceramic craft of the Pitted Ware culture is interesting in this context; dating to the middle Neolithic and thus post-dating the introduction of agriculture in the area with some 1000 years, it occurs in a distinctly non-agricultural setting and in very large amounts. In his study of Neolithic pottery from the Åland islands, Niklas Stenbäck showed that the amount of pottery recovered from Pitted Ware sites by far exceeds that on both earlier and later sites in the region (Stenbäck 2003: 98ff). This pattern seems to be true for Pitted Ware sites all over eastern Sweden (Segerberg 1999: 61; Malmer 2002: 112ff). It seems clear that the ceramic craft held a prominent position within the Pitted Ware Culture, and that this position had nothing to do with agriculture. An interesting observation in this context is that the earliest Pitted Ware pottery seems to occur in eastern central Sweden, outside or on the northeastern periphery of the Ertebölle and early TRB cultures further south. In Finland to the east, however, Comb Ware pottery appeared in the Late Mesolithic (Hallgren 2004), and it has often been argued that similarities in design can be

Figure 4.3. a) Detail of grave 42 at Västerbjers, b) Base fragments and small conical vessel from burials at Västerbjers. The height of the vessel from grave 42 (lower right in Figure 3b) is *c.* 7cm (after Stenberger *et al.* 1943).

seen between Finnish Comb Ware and Swedish Pitted Ware. Given the disturbing time gap, the 'Mesolithic' design of Pitted Ware pottery has been explained as a re-activation of 'historical' symbols; *i.e.* the pit decoration and the pointed base refer to an old hunter-gatherer ideology in contrast to the 'agricultural' pottery of the TRB culture (Stenbäck 2003; Knutsson 2004). In this view the ceramic craft played a central role in the expression of identity, and the design of the pots had a deep symbolic significance connected to perceptions of 'us and them' (insiders and outsiders).

The archaeology of Pitted Ware ceramics

For almost precisely a century, Pitted Ware pottery has been a hot topic of discussion for Swedish Stone Age researchers. Since the 1970s pottery technology has been investigated on a small scale (e.g. Hulthén 1977; 1998), and in recent years chemical analyses of organic residues found in association with pottery have contributed to the discussion (M. Isaksson 2000; S. Isaksson in press; Papmehl-Dufay 2006). Pottery design on the other hand has always been the central aspect of Pitted Ware culture studies, and most often patterns of decoration have been considered to reflect chronological or cultural differences or both. The classic work on the subject is Axel Bagge's study of the Fagervik assemblage (Bagge 1951), in which a sequence of five stages (Fagevik I-V), based mainly on decorative patterns and ware quality, was presented. The sequence has been heavily criticised, but it is still frequently used as a tool for relative dating. In my view it suffers from a generalised view of pottery design, where change over time is the main answer to the problem of pottery variation. Instead, as has been argued above, pottery design should be approached from a ceramic craft perspective where the individual potters and their culturally embedded craft traditions are seen to govern the way in which the pots are designed. In this view, variation is not a result of chronological or ethnic differences alone, but rather depends on a large number of factors. Despite this variation, the great homogeneity

in design seen in Pitted Ware pottery in eastern Sweden is highly interesting in this respect, addressing questions concerning the organisation of pottery production in the Pitted Ware culture as well as the connection between pottery design and expressions of identity.

Pitted Ware pottery assemblages generally derive from what has been classified archaeologically as settlement sites. Most often pottery is recovered from the cultural layers as well as from pits and various other sunken features and, in most studies, the pottery is held to reflect mainly functional hunting- and eating-related activities (Segerberg 1999: 62). Not all potsherds found on a site should be regarded as waste, however. The most straightforward example of this is the occurrence of pottery in Pitted Ware burials. Complete ceramic vessels in Pitted Ware burials are more or less restricted to miniature vessels; the vast majority of the ceramics recorded from graves are fragments of vessels. Single potsherds frequently occur, and in many cases there can be no doubt that they have been deposited as sherds and not as complete vessels. A most interesting phenomenon in this context is the occurrence of conical base fragments in burials and other specific contexts of deposition (Papmehl-Dufay 2006: 54). The deliberate deposition of fragmented pottery could possibly be connected to the metaphor of the pottery vessel as a human body, which is widely documented ethnographically (*e.g.* Gosselain 1999). The fragmentation of pots in connection with death may be understood as the killing of the vessel through fragmentation, with its subsequent placement in the burial with the dead, or its deposition in some other way in connection with death-related rituals (see Barley 1994: 92). At the cemetery of Västerbjers on Gotland, pottery was recorded as being part of the burial goods in 12 of the 54 graves excavated (Stenberger *et al.* 1943). Six of the burials contained pottery in the form of a conical base fragment, usually deposited together with other objects by the head or the feet of the buried individual. Only one burial contained a complete vessel. This is a small conical pot very similar in size and shape to the conical base fragments, and the possibility should perhaps be considered that this pot actually represents an imitation of a base fragment (Figure 4.3; Papmehl-Dufay 2006: 54ff).

The Middle Neolithic of Öland

The island of Öland is situated between the island of Gotland and the Swedish mainland. With its 140 km in length and 20 km in width, it is the fourth largest island in the Baltic Sea. Ancient remains are numerous, particularly from later prehistory. Stone Age remains are also abundant, but so far little research has been carried out in the area (see Papmehl-Dufay 2006: 65ff). Only two Pitted Ware sites have been excavated: Köpingsvik and Ottenby Royal Manor (Schulze 2004; Papmehl-Dufay 2005). Pottery from these two sites was used in my study of the ceramic craft within the Pitted Ware Culture, the results of which are briefly outlined below.

Working with material from an insular geographic setting is advantageous in several respects. First of all, the island represents a clearly delimited area that can be assumed to have been of relevance as an identifiable region in the period under study as well. Secondly, island societies often develop contact networks more extensive than those seen in mainland contexts, resulting in a more varied and complex archaeological situation (see Broodbank 2000; Papmehl-Dufay 2006: 20ff). On Öland this is expressed during the Neolithic in a particularly wide range of archaeological evidence representing the different 'cultures'; for instance the occurrence of four TRB megalithic tombs in the parish of Resmo, alongside several Boat Axe Culture settlements and burials and a number of large Pitted Ware settlements and at least one cemetery. The megalithic tombs and the Pitted Ware burials have been shown to overlap chronologically, and finds at the Pitted Ware sites of Boat Axe Culture-related artefacts indicate that this might be the case concerning the Pitted Ware and Boat Axe Cultures as well (Papmehl-Dufay 2006: 132ff). Also, one of the megalithic tombs has been re-used within the Boat Axe Culture (Arne 1909). It seems that society on Öland during the Middle Neolithic saw a complex cultural development apparently lacking on the neighbouring mainland where, for instance, no megalithic burials are to be found.

The two Pitted Ware sites concerned in the present study are Köpingsvik on central Öland and Ottenby Royal Manor on the southernmost part of the island (Figure 4.4). The site of Köpingsvik has been excavated on more than 20 occasions, and the finds assemblage is very extensive (see Schulze 2004; Papmehl-Dufay 2006: 84ff). Apart from cultural layers with various sunken features, more than 20 burials have been recorded, most probably all dating to the Neolithic. The pottery so far collected amounts to c. 220kg and, apart from this, some 30kg of animal bones were found, mainly of marine species, as well as a large number of bone artefacts, lithic waste and artefacts including axes and arrowheads. Of the pottery,

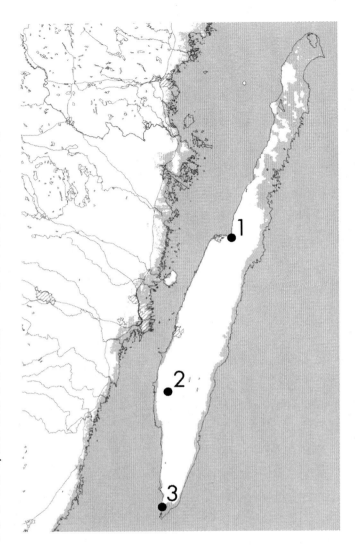

Figure 4.4. Öland with sites mentioned in the text indicated; 1) Köpingsvik, 2) Resmo, 3) Ottenby Royal Manor. The black line represents the shoreline of today, and the white area illustrates an estimation of land at c. 3100 BC, i.e. the early Middle Neolithic (map adapted from Claesson and Mikaelsson 2001).

some 18kg was recorded in detail in connection with my PhD project. In addition to this, 54 sherds from Köpingsvik were selected for thin section analysis and 18 sherds subjected to lipid residue analysis. The Pitted Ware site of Ottenby Royal Manor was found in the late 1980s and, until recently, had not been properly investigated. The analysis presented in detail in my PhD thesis was based on the material of c. 23kg pottery from a limited excavation performed by myself at the site in 2004 (Papmehl-Dufay 2005; 2006). Apart from pottery, the excavation produced finds of 3.5kg animal bones, some lithic waste and a small number of stone artefacts. No bone artefacts were found. Sunken features included small post holes and a circular ditch. No burials were found but, considering the small scale of the excavation, the possibility of a cemetery also at Ottenby Royal Manor should not be excluded. The pottery assemblage was recorded in detail and, in addition, 24 sherds were selected for thin section analysis and 15 sherds were subjected to lipid residue analysis.

These two Pitted Ware sites are broadly contemporary (*c.* 3100-2900 cal BC), and they are similar in their geographic setting in immediate proximity to the sea shore. Possible differences between the sites include the occurrence of burials, as well as the occurrence of bone artefacts. No such items were found at Ottenby Royal Manor, despite the favourable conditions for preservation of bone. The faunal assemblage at Ottenby contains a larger portion of terrestrial animals than is the case at Köpingsvik. However, six radiocarbon dates clearly suggest that a lot, if not all, of the bones from pig, sheep/goat and cow at Ottenby date to later periods. Concerning the pottery, at first glance the two assemblages are very similar, with decorative and formal elements characteristic for Pitted Ware pottery in southeast Sweden (*e.g.* Bagge 1936; Bagge and Kjellmark 1939). The detailed analysis of the pottery assemblages presented in my PhD thesis targeted aspects of design, technology and raw material utilisation as well as aspects of pottery use. Apart from the above-mentioned analyses, a clay survey was carried out within the surroundings of the sites. The raw clay samples were analysed in thin section and compared with the pottery samples. As will be briefly outlined in the following, the analysis of the Öland Pitted Ware pottery clearly showed that some small but distinctly articulated differences exist between the two sites.

Results of the pottery analysis

The formal and decorative analysis showed that on a general level of pottery design, the same kind of pots were produced at both sites. The frequency of some specific vessel shape details and the placing of decoration on the vessel body are practically identical. Vessel sizes range from just a few centimetres across up to 30cm–40cm in rim diameter and, at both sites, at least four standard size groups can be identified within this range. In both assemblages pits have been applied in one or several horizontal rows on practically every single vessel regardless of size. Concerning the rest of the decoration, despite some clear differences, obvious similarities can also be noted in the choice of patterns and not least the placing of the decoration on the vessel wall. This significant accordance between the two sites in certain aspects of vessel design is an important result and supports the idea that the archaeological category "Pitted Ware" in fact corresponds to a category identifiable during the Middle Neolithic as well. That is, the potters at these two sites had clearly defined and similar ideas about what the pots should look like and how they should be shaped, where the decoration should be placed and what decorative patterns should be used. This degree of homogeneity of Pitted Ware translates to a larger geographical scale, to a large extent; certain elements of pottery design, such as the horizontal rows of cylindrical pits and the carinated shoulder, are indeed remarkable in

their frequency and geographic distribution within the Pitted Ware culture in eastern Sweden, suggesting a widespread tradition of pottery design in this area. This is not to say, however, that all Pitted Ware assemblages are similar, as will be explained below.

Apart from the above mentioned similarities in pottery design, some differences were also demonstrated. While the placement of the decoration on the neck and around the shoulder was practically identical, the decorative elements 'comb stamp' and 'line stamp' were shown to differ regarding the way they have been applied to the vessel wall, and this difference was shown to be statistically significant. Another difference in design between the two sites concerns the shape of the rim and the frequency of decoration on the rim edge. These observations suggest that, within the overall ceramic tradition governing production at both sites, individual potters or groups of potters were able to develop some unique traits in ways of designing their pots. It is possible that some elements of design were more readily allowed to be modified by individual potters than others, and thus that some of the differences mentioned above represent intentional expressions of some sort intended to communicate to the receiver. It is also possible, however, and perhaps even probable, that some of the small differences in pottery design were not identified by the potters themselves, but rather reflect individual patterns of habitual learning by different groups of potters. This, in turn, would mean that the potters at the different sites had developed specific ways of their own in producing the pots, and that these small differences were transmitted through generations of potters at the respective sites.

Whoever made the pots recovered from the Pitted Ware sites, it is clear from, among other things, the dominance of relatively thin-walled vessels and the above-discussed homogeneity in design over large areas that these potters were skilful and deeply immersed in their own craft tradition. The variability noted in vessel wall thickness and general quality of execution should be seen against the social context of production, where potters of different ages and skill were engaged to a varying extent and at different stages of the production sequence. It should also be recalled that, even though potting during the Neolithic was not a full-time profession, most likely the practice was ascribed to certain categories of individuals, meaning that not everyone in a community was a skilful potter. From ethnographic studies of pottery production in traditional societies, it is clear that gender categories most often define the actors at different stages of the production process (Gosselain 1999). This does not necessarily mean that either women or men produced pottery, but rather that different gender categories were associated with different activities surrounding the process of producing pottery, and also that, for certain stages in the production process, specific gender groups may have been prohibited from participating. Potters may have been afforded a certain status in their community due to their profession and skill, not only for their economic importance but also for the metaphorical and magical aspects provided by pottery production (Gibson 2002: 50). From a modern perspective, the way pottery brings together the four elements in the production of a cultural object makes it rather special; clay is extracted from the ground (*earth*), moisture allows it to be shaped into almost any form (*water*), the object is then dried (*air*) and finally fired (*fire*) in order to reach the desired result – pottery – which is, in essence, artificial rock. Although the concept of the four elements is of course a historical construct and probably not relevant in a Middle Neolithic context, it is not difficult to imagine the possible range of magical associations that this process of transformation provided.

The technological analysis of clays and wares showed that clays suitable for pottery production are generally scarce on the island, and they seem to be especially difficult to find on the southernmost part of the island. At Köpingsvik a greater variation of clays was found in the pottery, which probably reflects the fact that a slightly greater number of clay sources are possible to utilise in the area. At Ottenby the variability in clay was smaller, and thus any suitable clay sources found within a reasonable distance from the site would have been kept and utilised as long as possible. The dominating tempering tradition at Köpingsvik was addition to the clay of c. 5–15% crushed sandstone, and this has been used on all different clays noted. Those wares displaying a different temper material generally have temper qualities (relative amount and grain size) similar to the ones in the dominant sandstone wares, suggesting that, for example, the granite-tempered wares at Köpingsvik were produced within the same tradition as the sandstone-tempered wares. It should also be mentioned that this tempering tradition deviates quite markedly from what is commonly observed on the mainland, where crushed granite generally makes up c. 15%–25% of the ware. At Ottenby Royal Manor the dominant practice was either to rely completely on the naturally occurring inclusions or to add unsorted sand, thus deviating strongly both from the tempering traditions at Köpingsvik and from Neolithic pottery-making in Sweden at large. Nonetheless, it is important to emphasise that, despite these obvious difficulties and obstacles, large amounts of pottery were produced at the site. Clearly the production of pottery of this specific design, in these large quantities and in this specific geographical and cultural setting during this particular period was regarded as important to perform, and not to be hampered simply by the difficulties of finding suitable raw materials in a particular area.

The technological study of clays and ceramics from Öland support the argument above that potters of different local traditions are represented in the two Pitted Ware assemblages. The sites were shown to differ in clay sources used as well as in tempering traditions followed, meaning that the individual potters, or rather groups of closely culturally related potters, despite adhering to the same overall ceramic tradition had their own ways of preparing the clay and producing the pots.

In connection with the discussion of the results from the lipid residue analysis, it should be emphasised that signals for pottery use do not equate directly with signals for diet; there are lots of ways to prepare food besides the use of pottery, and lots of things besides food can be processed in a ceramic vessel (*e.g.* Isaksson in press). Furthermore, organic residues encountered in ceramic ware may, in some cases, be the result of activities other than the use of the vessel as a container; various organic mixtures can be used on fired vessels for coating or other forms of surface treatment on the ceramic product (Gosselain and Livingstone Smith 1995: 156ff), such as the use of beeswax and other substances for sealing and waterproofing the pot (Charters *et al.* 1995). So far, the use of organic matter for surface-treatment has not been detected on prehistoric pottery in Sweden, and thus the extent of such practices is difficult to estimate.

At Köpingsvik the fortunate circumstances of having well preserved skeletons from inhumation burials contemporary with the large Pitted Ware assemblage present an opportunity for comparing data on diet from stable isotope analysis of the buried individuals with data on pottery use from the lipid residue analysis on potsherds. The dietary studies (Lidén and Eriksson this volume) and the values of $\delta^{13}C$ from available radiocarbon determinations (Papmehl-Dufay 2006: 110ff) both suggest a completely marine-oriented diet for the Neolithic individuals at Köpingsvik. Regarding pottery use, the lipid residue analysis suggests a strong preference for cooking marine animals and/or fish and vegetables. Only a small number of samples at Köpingsvik displayed a different signature, and the fish/marine animal signature was absent only in one sample. At Ottenby Royal Manor, there are so far no human bones dated or analysed for stable isotopes and thus direct evidence for diet is still lacking. The Neolithic faunal assemblage at Ottenby is dominated by marine species, and this, together with its geographical location, clearly suggests that marine sources were of considerable importance. Pottery use as seen in the lipid residue analyses, however, presents a quite different image. The signature of cooking of marine animals and vegetables dominating at Köpingsvik is altogether lacking at Ottenby where, instead, vegetables dominate whilst terrestrial animals and marine animals and/or fish occupy equally small portions of the sample analysed. Also, three of the analysed sherds contained no traceable lipid residues at all. One sample at Ottenby was strongly deviating in several respects and deserves a special comment. The sherd (Figure 4.5) was made from a non-local clay and contained very large amounts of lipid residues involving terrestrial animals, green plants and beeswax (possibly representing honey). Thus, from the presently analysed material pottery use seems to have differed between the two sites, with Köpingsvik displaying the 'expected' pattern of cooking of marine

Figure 4.5. The deviating sample OT 9 from Ottenby Royal Manor.

catch mixed with vegetables and Ottenby Royal Manor lacking this signature and, instead, displaying traces of terrestrial products not as clearly visible in the faunal remains at the site. This means that, at Köpingsvik, pottery use was fully incorporated in the marine-oriented ideology at large, completely separated from the contemporaneously expressed megalithic ideology at Mysinge and, in many ways, similar to the Pitted Ware Culture on Gotland and further north on the Swedish mainland. At Ottenby Royal Manor, on the other hand, it seems from the location and the faunal assemblage that seal and fish were indeed of great importance for the subsistence economy, yet the pottery seems to have been used mainly for processing of terrestrial products. Thus at this site some specific elements of the 'Pitted Ware ideology' were adopted and clearly expressed, whereas other aspects were neglected or manipulated. The number of samples analysed from both sites is small and hence source-critical factors should be considered; however, the possibility emerges that the role and use of pottery in fact differed between the two sites.

Concluding remarks

Pitted Ware pottery is one of the most discussed and debated aspects of the Middle Neolithic period in eastern Sweden. The large amounts of ceramics on Pitted Ware sites, however, have resulted in a homogenisation of the category, where variation and the unusual have been seen as something undesirable (Isaksson 2000). Most studies have concentrated on typo-chronological aspects of the pottery, reflected mainly in the separation of various decorative designs into vaguely defined groups of perceived chronological difference. Looking into the history of research on Pitted Ware ceramics (*e.g.* Papmehl-Dufay 2006: 32ff), it is clear that this practice of identifying chronologically different styles of pottery, and effectively different levels of cultural development, began right after the first large sites were discovered and excavated in the early 20th century. The practice developed to become the standard approach to Neolithic settlement pottery assemblages, and the proposed sequences from Säter and Fagervik, established during the following decades, soon achieved a normative role held to be valid across large parts of eastern Sweden. The fact that the Fagervik sequence still holds a dominant position in Pitted Ware studies in effect means that the

principal ideas of cultural development and pottery design, held as sound in the first decade of the 20th century, still endure to some extent – something I find quite disturbing. The potentially dynamic aspects of pottery design are effectively diminished; differences within an assemblage are explained through the typo-chronological sequences, and Pitted Ware pottery is represented as a homogeneous, simple and rough category of past material culture. In the present study, I have tried to show that this image is over-generalised and erroneous; the variations observed in the Öland assemblages cover the whole range from coarse thick-walled vessels to smooth and thin wares and, at both Köpingsvik and Ottenby, the great majority of the vessels have been decorated. Although not necessarily meaning that the pottery had a non-domestic function (see Tilley 1996: 257ff), this clearly points towards an elaborate and socially embedded ceramic craft tradition. Regarding pottery use, this has previously been discussed mainly from preconceptions governed by views of the Pitted Ware Culture as primitive and simple, and the homogeneity in design has been suggested to reflect homogeneity of use as well. The analyses presented briefly above indicate that uniform pottery design should be seen as reflecting a widespread ceramic craft tradition, and pottery use is shown to be more variable than previously suggested. The archaeological potsherds represent a long-lasting and socially important craft tradition, and thus variations are not explained by one single factor. Context of production, context of use, the individual potter, as well as chronology and cultural identity all are relevant to the discussion.

References

Arne, T. J. 1909. Stenåldersundersökningar. *Fornvännen* 4: 86-108.

Arnold, D. E. 1985. *Ceramic theory and cultural process.* Cambridge: Cambridge University Press.

Bagge, A. 1936. Stenåldersboplatsen vid Humlekärrshult, Oskarshamn. *Kalmar läns fornminnesförening, meddelanden* 24: 55-101.

Bagge, A. 1951. Fagervik. Ein Rückgrat für die Periodeneinteilung der ostschwedischen Wohnplatz- und Bootaxtkulturen aus dem Mittelneolithikum. Eine vorläufige Mitteilung. *Acta Archaeologica* 22: 57-118.

Bagge, A. and Kjellmark, K. 1939. *Stenåldersboplatserna vid Siretorp i Blekinge.* Stockholm: KVHAA.

Barley, N. 1994. *Smashing pots: feats of clay from Africa.* London: British Museum Press.

Boast, R. 2002. Pots as categories: British Beakers. In A.Woodward and J.D. Hill (eds) *Prehistoric Britain: the ceramic basis.* Oxford: Oxbow. 96-105.

Bougard, E. 2003. Ceramic in the Upper Palaeolithic. In A. Gibson,(ed) *Prehistoric pottery: people, pattern and purpose.* Oxford: BAR International Series 1156. 29-34.

Broodbank, C. 2000. *An Island Archaeology of the Early Cyclades.* Cambridge: Cambridge University Press.

Charters, S., Evershed, R. P., Blinkhorn, P. W. and Denham, V. 1995. Evidence for the mixing of fats and waxes in archaeological ceramics. *Archaeometry* 37(1): 113-127.

Claesson, T. & Mikaelsson, J. 2001. Berg och jord. In M. Forslund (ed) *Natur och kultur på Öland.* Kalmar: Länsstyrelsen i Kalmar län. 15-41.

Edenmo, R., Larsson, M., Nordqvist, B. and Olsson, E. 1997. Gropkeramikerna –fanns de? Materiell kultur och ideologisk förändring. In M. Larsson and E. Olsson (eds) *Regionalt och interregionalt. Stenåldersundersökningar i Syd- och Mellansverige.* Stockholm: Riksantikvarieämbetet Arkeologiska undersökningar, Skrifter nr 23. 135-213.

Eerkens, J. W., Neff, H. and Glascock, M. D. 2002. Ceramic production among small-scale and mobile hunters and gatherers: a case study from the southwestern Great Basin. *Journal of Anthropological Archaeology* 21: 200-229.

Eriksson, G. 2004. Part time farmers or hard-core sealers? Västerbjers studied by means of stable isotope analysis. *Journal of Anthropological Archaeology* 23: 135-162.

Fornander, E. 2006. The wild side of the Neolithic. A study of Pitted Ware diet and ideology through analysis of stable carbon and nitrogen isotopes in skeletal material from Korsnäs, Grödinge parish, Södermanland. Unpublished seminar paper, Archaeological research laboratory, Stockholm University.

Gebauer, A. B. 1995. Pottery production and the introduction of agriculture in southern Scandinavia. In W.K. Barnett and J.W. Hoopes (eds) *The emergence of pottery: technology and innovation in ancient societies.* Washington DC: Smithsonian Institution Press. 99-112.

Gibson, A. 2002. *Prehistoric pottery in Britain & Ireland.* Stroud: Tempus.

Gosselain, O. P. 1999. In pots we trust. The processing of clay and symbols in Sub-Saharan Africa. *Journal of Material Culture* 4(2): 205-230.

Gosselain, O. P. 2000. Materializing identities: an African perspective. *Journal of Archaeological Method and Theory* 7(3): 187-217.

Gosselain, O. P. and Livingstone Smith, A. 1995. The ceramics and society project: an ethnographic and experimental approach to technological choices. In A. Lindahl and O. Stilborg (eds) *The aim of laboratory analyses of ceramics in archaeology.* Stockholm: KVHAA (Konferenser 34). 147-160.

Gruber, G. 1995. Åby elva undersökningar senare... En gropkeramisk boplats för flera mindre hushåll? Unpublished seminar paper, Stockholm University.

Hallgren, F. 2000. Lineage identity and pottery design. In D. Olausson and H. Vandkilde (eds) *Form, function and context: material culture studies in Scandinavian archaeology.* Lund: Acta Archaeologica Lundensia, series in 8° No 31. 173-191.

Hallgren, F. 2004. The introduction of ceramic technology around the Baltic Sea in the 6th millennium. In H. Knutsson (ed) *Coast to Coast – arrival. Results and reflections.* Uppsala: Coast to Coast-book 10. 123-142.

Hulthén, B. 1977. *On ceramic technology during the Scanian Neolithic and Bronze Age.* Theses and Papers in North-European Archaeology 6. Stockholm.

Hulthén, B. 1998. *The Alvastra Pile Dwelling Pottery. An attempt to trace the society behind the sherds.* Stockholm: Museum of National Antiquities Monograph 5.

Isaksson, M. 2000. Forskning i Platons skuggvärld? Om kulturteori och variation i neolitiskt källmaterial utifrån analys av tidigare forskning och organiska beläggningar på gropkeramik från Jonstorp, Jonstorp sn, Skåne. *CD-uppsatser i laborativ arkeologi 99/00 Del 1.* Stockholm: Archaeological Research Laboratory, Stockholm University.

Isaksson, S. in press. Vessels of change. A long-term perspective on prehistoric pottery-use in southern and eastern middle Sweden based on lipid residue analyses. *Ny forskning om gammal keramik.* Lund: Laboratory for Ceramic Research, Lund University.

Janzon, G. O. 1974. *Gotlands mellanneolitiska gravar.* Stockholm: Acta Universitatis Stockholmiensis.

Jones, A. 2002. *Archaeological theory and scientific practice.* Cambridge: Cambridge University Press.

Knutsson, K. 2004. The historical construction of 'Norrland'. In H. Knutsson (ed) *Coast to Coast – arrival. Results and reflections.* Uppsala: Coast to Coast-book 10. 45-71.

Larsson, M. 2006. *A Tale of a Strange People: the Pitted Ware Culture in southern Sweden.* Kalmar: Kalmar Studies in Archaeology vol. 2.

Malmer, M. P. 2002. *The Neolithic of south Sweden. TRB, GRK and STR.* Stockholm: KVHAA.

Núñez, M . 1990. On Subneolithic pottery and its adoption in late Mesolithic Finland. *Fennoscandia Archaeologica* 7: 27-52.

Papmehl-Dufay, L. 2003. Stone Age Island Archaeology. Aspects of insularity, cultural identity and cosmology during the Neolithic on the island of Öland in the Baltic. In C. Samuelsson and N. Ytterberg. (eds) *Uniting Sea. Stone Age societies in the Baltic Sea region.* Uppsala: OPIA 33. 180-203.

Papmehl-Dufay, L. 2004. Kulturell identitet på Öland under mellanneolitikum. Om keramikens betydelse inom den gropkeramiska kulturen. In T. Werner and K. von Hackwitz (eds) *Aktuell Arkeologi* 8: 31-46.

Papmehl-Dufay, L. 2005. *Mellanneolitikum vid Ottenby Kungsgård. Arkeologisk undersökning av raä 40, Ås socken, Ölands sydspets, Augusti – September 2004.* Stockholm: Rapporter från Arkeologiska forskningslaboratoriet 2, Stockholm University.

Papmehl-Dufay, L. 2006. *Shaping an identity. Pitted Ware pottery and potters in Southeast Sweden.* Stockholm: Theses and papers in scientific archaeology 7.

Papmehl-Dufay in press. Pitted Ware culture ceramics. Aspects on pottery production and use at Ottenby Royal Manor, Öland, Sweden. In M. Zvelebil and P. Jordan (eds) *Origins of Ceramics and Hunter Gatherers of northern Eurasia.* London: UCL Press.

Schulze, H. 2004. *Köpingsvik på Öland. 30 undersökningar 1970-1994.* Kalmar: Rapport Kalmar läns museum.

Segerberg, A. 1999. *Bälinge mossar. Kustbor i Uppland under yngre stenåldern.* Uppsala: Aun 26.

Sjögren, K.-G. 2004. Megalithic tombs, ideology and society in Sweden. In H. Knutsson (ed) *Coast to coast – arrival. Results and reflections.* Uppsala: Coast to coast-book 10. 157-182.

Stenberger, M., Dahr, E. & Munthe, H. 1943. *Das grabfeld von Västerbjers auf Gotland.* Stockholm: KVHAA.

Stenbäck, N. 2003. *Människorna vid havet. Platser och keramik på ålandsöarna perioden 3500 – 2000 f.Kr.* Stockholm: Stockholm Studies in Archaeology 28.

Storå, J. 2001. *Reading Bones: Stone Age hunters and seals in the Baltic.* Stockholm: Stockholm Studies in Archaeology 21.

Tilley, C. 1996. *An ethnography of the Neolithic. Early prehistoric societies in southern Scandinavia.* Cambridge: Cambridge University Press.

Zvelebil, M. and Jordan, P. (eds) In press. *Origins of ceramics and hunter gatherers of northern Eurasia.* London: UCL Press.

Chapter 5

Why use different raw materials?
Raw material use during the Late Mesolithic to Middle Neolithic along the coast of Kalmarsund

Kenneth Alexandersson

Institute of Humanities and Social Sciences, University of Kalmar, 391 82 Kalmar, Sweden

Introduction

In this article I will give a short introduction to the use of different lithic raw materials for tool production in the area of Kalmarsund. I will also discuss the regional settlement pattern and show how some of the lithic raw materials could be distributed across regional and inter-regional networks.

Changes in tool production and raw material use are dynamic processes which have no absolute boundaries within time or geographical extent. In the Kalmarsund area it is possible to see how different raw materials tend to vary within lithic assemblages over time. Many aspects of change and stability are easier to analyze over the long term. For this reason, I have chosen to look at the use of lithic raw materials during the period from the Late Mesolithic to the Middle Neolithic (Figure 5.1).

Knowledge about the Stone Age in the Kalmarsund area comes from both field walking projects and archaeological excavations. A considerably large number of prehistoric sites in the region contain lithic material. There are also many stray finds from the area (Åberg 1913; Westergren 1988; 1995). Many of the stray finds consist of round-butted ground stone axes, mainly dated to the Late Mesolithic. Some of the axes are found on low contours which would have been submerged beneath the sea during the Mesolithic period and are thus likely to date to the Early or Middle Neolithic (Alexandersson 2001: 119).

Along the coast of Kalmarsund there is lithic material from sites ranging in time from the Early Mesolithic to the Late Neolithic. About 40 of these have been excavated and their finds assemblages often consist of large quantities of lithic material. One problem with these excavated sites is the absence of features deriving from specific activities. Archaeological excavations on some of these have indeed uncovered postholes and hearths but so far it has not been possible to establish whether any of them belong to houses or other post-built constructions; the oldest excavated house in the region dates to the Late Neolithic (Alexandersson et al. 2001). It is not always possible to characterize the sites according to specific activity categories. The presence of large amounts of lithic materials and flakes from many different cores and nodules make it clear that these sites were the results of more than occasional and brief visits to these spots.

A history of lithic survey

During the 19th century and the beginning of the 20th century, flint was often regarded as the primary choice of raw material for lithic tool production. Use of other local raw materials was considered only as a response to a lack of flint (Nilsson 1866). This interpretation was deep-rooted and was supported by the fact that Stone Age research during this period has its origin in Denmark and Scania, where lithic assemblages were dominated by flint. This idea remained unchallenged for a long time within Nordic Stone Age research. Flint was considered as having made human life possible and decent for these prehistoric societies, and was often regarded as being synonymous with culture itself. In the early 20th century Knut Stjerna from Uppsala University set up a nationwide inventory to find out when different parts of Sweden were colonized during the Stone Age (Baudou 2004: 214ff). In connection with this research new knowledge about the use of different raw materials slowly emerged, so that today new approaches in Scandinavia have been put forward to shed light on uses of different raw materials and their social meanings. These attempts to turn away from the old perspective have looked at the raw material in ways other than rationality and functionality, examining the variation in raw material use within a regional perspective, considering the various lithic raw materials as potential reflections of social identity, and studying how different raw materials were adopted in different social and ritual contexts (Bergsvik 2004; Lindgren 2004).

By adopting a large-scale perspective on material culture from the Early Neolithic, it is possible to identify common cultural attributes over large areas of southern Scandinavia. During the Middle Neolithic the picture is different. The material from the south Scandinavian Middle Neolithic have been divided into three different cultures; Funnel Beaker Culture, Pitted Ware Culture and Battle Axe Culture. A separation into these three cultures is based mainly on differences in pottery decoration, pottery form and economy. There are also clear differences among some of the lithic artefacts, notably axes, chisels and arrow heads. At first glance, it might

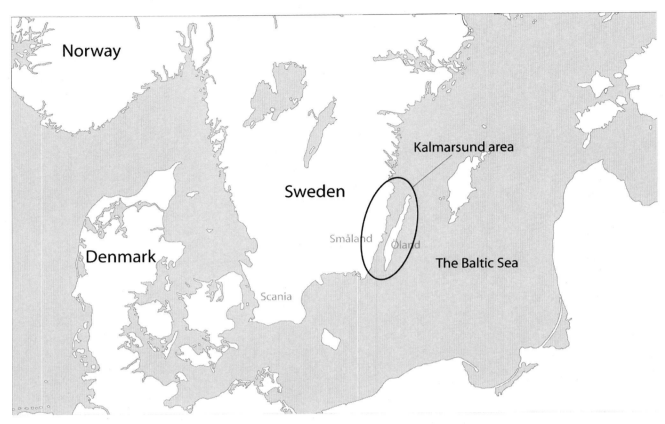

Figure 5.1. The location of the investigation area.

appear that these three cultures replaced each other in strict chronological order, but today we know that there were long periods of overlap (Edenmo *et al.* 1997: 138ff). Even so, it is still almost impossible to analyse the period without using the old 'culture history' concept.

At the same time it is also possible to see significant regional variations in local material culture during the Middle Neolithic in south Scandinavia, especially if one looks at the use of different lithic raw materials and day-to-day tool production. The often large quantities of lithic waste and the minor tools have often been neglected despite the fact that they are usually abundant on sites. I have chosen to incorporate this material in a discussion about the use of different raw materials in the Kalmarsund area. The intention has been to take the focus away from technological aspects and, instead, focus on the raw material and the social meanings that it reflected.

The presence of local versus non-local raw materials

Generally, lithic tool production in areas south of the Kalmarsund, Skåne and Blekinge regions are dominated by flint. On the other hand, in areas north of Kalmarsund lithic materials are often dominated by quartz. A closer look at the Kalmarsund region reveals considerable variation in the use of lithic raw materials. Some of them can be obtained locally, as nodules in the moraine or from the bedrock, but so far there is no physical evidence in

the region of raw material quarries; this contrasts with eastern middle Sweden where sometimes large quantities of quartz were quarried (Gutafsson 2006). On the other hand, some of the raw materials do not occur naturally within the region and have their sources in more remote areas. In certain parts of southern Scandinavia, ice- and water-transported flint can be found in moraine deposits. In most cases different local rocks are fairly easy to distinguish due to specific textural traits. In certain cases it can be more problematic to distinguish, for example, quartz from quartzite. This is not a problem if the intention of the research is to establish whether the raw materials are of local extraction; both quartz and quartzite are available locally. It is more problematic if the intention is to understand why different raw materials were used in different situations, whether for aesthetic, social or technical reasons.

It is possible to separate lithic raw materials from the Kalmarsund area into three different categories:

- *Non-regional access.* Raw materials whoch do not occur naturally in the region and have to have been brought by humans.
- *Regional access.* Raw materials occurring naturally in the region and common both in the bedrock and as nodules in the moraine. These raw materials are often abundant and easy to attain.
-

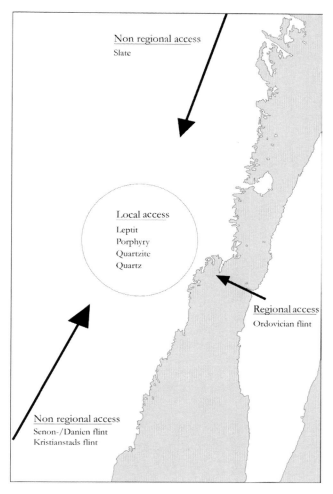

Figure 5.2. Origins of different raw materials used on the mainland in the southern part of the Kalmarsund area.

- *Local access*. Raw materials that have a very localized distribution within the region.

The most common raw materials used in the region are quartz, quartzite, porphyry, leptite and various types of flint (Figure 5. 2).

In the bedrock of southern Scandinavia there are natural occurrences of flint from different geological periods. On settlement sites in the Kalmarsund region one finds flint from several of these different sources. On the east coast of Öland it is possible to find flint washed ashore from Upper Ordovician strata (Königsson *et al.* 1993). So far there is no evidence suggesting that Ordovician flint occurred naturally on the coast of Småland. The Ordovician flint exhibits a wide range of different colours - from light grey to red and green - and it also has a wide range of different textures (Tralau 1973).

Networks, settlement patterns and the spread of raw materials

To determine what different types of raw materials are represented on settlement sites in the region is one thing.

Another is to understand where, when and how non-local raw materials reached the area. Studying the appearance of inter-regional networks could be one way to understand how separate regions were connected to each other. It is also important to analyse long-term changes in settlement patterns to see if these changes are reflected in the use of different raw materials.

Lithic debris on settlement sites along the coast of Kalmarsund shows activities from Early Mesolithic times onward. Small dispersed sites, mainly along waterways and coastlines during the Middle Mesolithic, suggest a settlement pattern of small, mobile hunting units moving over large areas. There is a large range of different raw materials represented on these Middle Mesolithic sites.

Between the Late Mesolithic and the Early Neolithic, there were clear changes in settlement pattern. Large sites appeared as a result of increased focus on river mouths and lagoons along the coast of the Kalmarsund mainland (Alexandersson 2001). Activities in areas around river mouths and lagoons tended to leave large amounts of lithic waste, and archaeological excavations on some of these sites suggest that they consisted of many small activity areas that gradually fused into single large spreads. An analysis of the lithic waste from these sites shows that an increasing proportion of non-local raw materials dominated tool production during the Late Mesolithic-Early Neolithic. Extension of activity into certain areas of the landscape is a phenomenon known from other parts of southern Scandinavia at this time and reflects the emergence of a more permanent settlement pattern (Tilley 1996: 52). At the same time, distribution networks in the region around Kalmarsund appear to have become more consolidated (Alexandersson 2001).

One of these large sites at Hagbytorp is situated close to Hagbyåns rivermouth. The main activity at Hagbytorp dates to from the Late Mesolithic to the early Middle Neolithic (Alexandersson 2001; Källström 1993). Due to the regression of water levels during the Neolithic, it is possible to identify a systematic relocation of activity within this area; Hagbytorp is followed chronologically by Igelösa Åsar which dates from the early Middle Neolithic to the late Middle Neolithic (Gurstad-Nilsson 2001) and the evidence for activity tends to move closer to the rivermouth in line with falling water levels in the Baltic Sea.

The lithic material from Hagbytorp is dominated by Kristianstads flint from northeast Scania while Igelösa Åsar is dominated by Senon and Danien flint from Denmark and southwest Scania. On these two sites it is possible to see both domestic and ritual treatment of the lithic material (Alexandersson 2001; Gurstad-Nilsson 2001). The vast amount of lithics from Hagbytorp derives from day-to-day knapping activities. The presence of flint nodules and large pieces of flint amongst the lithic debris supports the interpretation of these sites as important links in an inter-regional network; on smaller sites the flint debris often consists of minor pieces. The presence of large amounts of non-local raw materials also suggests frequent contacts with areas south of Kalmarsund. These sites also seem to be important for activities such as exchange, social interaction and different forms of ritual. In the vicinity of Igelösa Åsar there is a deposit of burnt offerings and axes whilst at the site of Igelösa Åsar itself there is waste from the final stages of manufacturing square-sectioned flint axes. Hagbytorp and Igelösa Åsar are, in some aspects, similar to Early Neolithic gathering sites in eastern middle Sweden. At Fågelbacken it has been possible to identify a site that was important for social interactions during the Early Neolithic period (Sundström 2003: 121).

The patterning in the use of raw materials at Hagbytorp and Igelösa Åsar is not typical for the whole of the Kalmarsund region. In the northern part of the study area it is possible to see that local raw materials dominated in lithic tool production during the Early and Middle Neolithic (Dahlin 2004; 2005). A distribution map of all sites with Ordovician flint shows good correspondence with the areas where it occurs naturally; however, dispersed finds of Ordovician flint in the northern part of the study area indicate some contacts across the region (Figure 5.3).

Naturally, it is to be expected that more than just lithic raw materials spread along these distribution networks; knowledge and ideas about what was happening in the world arrived with them. Some of these ideas were incorporated by local groups while others were rejected.

Why different raw materials?

There are various reasons why different raw materials were used within certain situations. Common norms and mythologies within society can, for example, affect the circumstances in which different lithic raw materials are used, and affect choices of which lithic raw materials might be used to produce specific tools.

Raw material use can be analysed within a chain of actions, from nodule to final discard:

- What raw materials are used?
- How are the raw materials received, whether pre-prepared or as nodules?
- What tools were produced and where?
- Under what circumstances were different tools or raw materials discarded?

The aim of this modified form of *chain opératoire* is to distinguish changes in how different raw materials were dealt with in certain social contexts, and to see if this treatment of various lithic raw materials altered over time.

It is also important to take into consideration the meaning of the different qualities of the various raw materials, not

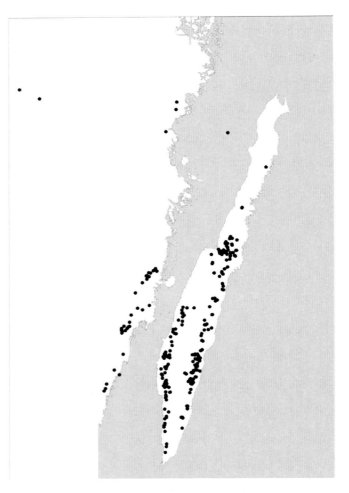

Figure 5.3. All sites in the Kalmarsund area with presence of Ordovician flint.

only in their technological aspects, but also their different colour, smoothness, feeling *etc*. The meanings of these qualities are hard to evaluate, but must have been given considerable importance during prehistoric times. In many cases the choice of raw material for certain purpose may have been so natural as to have been unnoticed or unremarked.

Finally, the use of different raw materials also has a historical dimension. Every new generation did not have to rediscover different properties in the different raw materials. Technological skills and knowledge about restrictions and taboos connected to different raw materials were probably learned from childhood and transferred from one generation to another. This was of course no static transference. Every new individual had their own ability to tailor traditional knowledge after their own personal preferences.

References

Åberg, N. 1913. Kalmar läns stenålder. *Meddelande från Kalmar läns fornminnesförening* 7. 5-56.
Alexandersson, K. 2001. Möre i centrum: mesolitikum i sydöstra Kalmar län. In G. Magnusson (ed.) *Möre*

historien om ett småland. Kalmar: E22-projektet Kalmar läns museum. 111-128.

Alexandersson, K., Hennius, A., Lloyd-Smith, L., Persson, M., Petersson, M. and Svensson, I. 2001. *Söderåkra. Ett boplatsområde från sten- och järnålder.* Kalmar: E22-projektet. Kalmar läns museums arkeologiska rapporter 2001:8.

Baudou, E. 2004. *Den nordiska arkeologin - historia och tolkningar.* Stockholm: Kungl. Vitterhets historie och antikvitets akademien.

Bergsvik, K.A. 2003. *Ethnic boundaries in Neolithic Norway.* Bergen: Department of Archaeology, University of Bergen.

Dahlin, M. 2004. *Fåror i forntidens spår: en studie av sten- och bronsålderns bosättningsmönster med utgångspunkt från specialinventeringen av Misterhults och Döderhults socknar i Oskarshamn.* Forntid i Oskarshamn kommun FOK-rapport 2004:1.

Dahlin, M. 2005. *Mellan åsar och vattendrag: en studie av sten- och bronsålderns bosättningsmönster med utgångspunkt från specialinventeringen av Kristdala församling i Oskarshamns kommun.* Forntid i Oskarshamns kommun. FOK-rapport 2005:1.

Edenmo, R., Larsson M., Nordqvist B. and Olsson E. 1997. Gopkeramikerna fanns de? In M. Larsson and E. Åkerlund (eds) *Regionalt och interregionalt, stenåldersundersökningar i Syd- och Mellansverige.* Kalmar: Riksantikvarieämbetet arkeologiska undersökningar skrifter nr 23. 135-213.

Gurstad-Nilsson, H. 2001. En neolitisering – två förlopp: tankar kring jordbrukskulturens etablering i Kalmarsundsområdet. In G. Magnusson (ed.) *Möre, historien om ett småland.* Kalmar: Kalmar läns museum E22-projektet. 129-164.

Gustafsson, P. 2006. Kvartsbrott och aktivitetsytor, Senneolitikum-Bronsålder. Toresund 281:1, Sandåsa 2:1, Toresunds socken, Strängnäs kommun, Södermanslands län, Sörmlands museum. Arkeologiska meddelanden 2006:01.

Källström, M. 1993a. *Hagbytorp, en basboplats från jägarstenålder.* Kalmar: Kalmar län 1993. Årsbok för kulturhistoria och hembygdsvård.

Königsson, L.-K., Königsson, E.-S., Bendixen, E. and Possnert, G. 1993. Topography and chronology of the Alby Stone Age settlement on southeastern Öland, Sweden. In *Sources and Resources: studies in honour of Birgit Arrhenius.* PACT 38. Belgium. 13-39.

Lindgren, C. 2004. *Människor och kvarts: sociala och teknologiska strategier under mesolitikum i östra Mellansverige.* Stockholm: Stockholm Studies in Archaeology 29, Riksantikvarieämbetets Arkeologiska undersökningar, skrifter no. 54. Coast to Coast books no.11.

Nilsson, S. 1866. *Skandinaviska nordens Ur-invånare, ett försök i komparativa etnografien. Ett bidrag till menniskoslägtets utvecklings historia. andra upplagan.* Stockholm: Norstedt.

Sundström, L. 2003. *Det hotade kollektivet: neolitiseringsprocessen ur ett östmellansvenskt*

perspektiv. Uppsala: Uppsala Universitet. Department of Archaeology and Ancient History.

Tilley, C. 1996. *An Ethnography of the Neolithic: early prehistoric societies in southern Scandinavia.* Cambridge: Cambridge University Press.

Tralau, H. 1973. Ålders- och proveniensbestämning av flintor. En paleobotanisk problemställning. *Svensk naturvetenskap Årsbok* 26: 119-122.

Westergren, E. 1988. Kalmarbygden fick en "ny" stenålder. *Populär arkeologi* 6 (1). 20-23.

Westergren, E. 1995. The Mesolithic settlement of the Kalmar area. In A. Fisher (ed.) *Man and Sea in the Mesolithic: coastal settlement above and below present sea level.* Oxford: Oxbow Monograph 53. 209-220.

Chapter 6

Isotopic aliens: Beaker movement and cultural transmissions

Stuart Needham

Honorary Research Fellow, Department of Archaeology, University of Reading

Introduction

In recent years the interpretive pendulum has swung back a little. During the 1970s and 1980s, Beaker cultural phenomena came to be seen to be effectively indigenous processes in the respective regions in which the culture became established. Burgess and Shennan (1976) were among the first to react against invasionist models, of which a late expression is seen for Britain in David Clarke's Beaker opus magnum (Clarke 1970). They, instead, saw the primary Beaker artefact package as having transcended cultural frontiers, its desirability to the multifarious indigenous cultures being due above all to the allure of the typical contents of the Beakers themselves – either alcoholic beverage or hallucinogenic substance (Burgess and Shennan 1976: 312). More recently, however, researchers have returned to the part played by moving people within the broader patterns of cultural change. This is not a return to sweeping pan-European uniform migration processes, but a series of more nuanced approaches which take account of local cultural contexts.

Neil Brodie was among the first to be explicit about potential mechanisms at the people level (Brodie 1997; 2001). Like Burgess and Shennan, he saw the pots as playing a key role in the carriage of the cultural package, but now seen in the context of cross-cultural marriage. Female marriage partners were hypothesised by Brodie to be in the vanguard of early Beaker dissemination, carrying with them special craft skills: potting in the Beaker tradition and spinning and weaving cloth (also Clarke 1976: 471). In this way he was able to explain the steady and extensive spread of the distinctive pottery style without invoking any significant exchange of the ceramics themselves, and certainly not long-distance exchange which has consistently been denied when fabrics have been analysed. This was a really important conceptual step forward, but I will argue that another dominant mode of inter-marriage better explains the material record of the Beaker pioneering phase in many regions (see also Needham 2005: 207-8).

When we look at the so-called 'Beaker phenomenon' cross-regionally and over its full duration we are faced with an immediate problem. The initial uptake of Beaker culture was extremely varied, there was furthermore variation in the cultural elements absorbed in the medium term, and there were also tremendous regional differences in the longer-term historical legacy (for a recent summary see Vander Linden 2006). Increasingly better characterisation of the contextual specificity of 'Beaker culture' on the regional scale had in the 1970s and 1980s eroded the case for any large-scale progressive movement of a 'people'. However, we have to be careful not confuse this conclusion with the possibility that in an early horizon – let's call it the *pioneering phase* – certain elements of the 'culture' were carried to new lands by individuals and communities who thought of themselves as being of a certain social group that was distinct from those inhabiting the terrains into which they had moved.

Without prejudging the quantitative aspect of the populations involved, I would suggest that there are three key issues arising at a theoretical level:

1) how many people might be moving
2) the degree to which those movements were one-way
3) the nature of interaction between those mobile elements of Beaker groups and the pre-existing populations they encountered.

Such questions may be pertinent at any stage of the Beaker culture trajectory although they tend to assume more importance, or at least are more capable of archaeological visibility at the pioneering stage when the cultural contrasts were generally most stark. To my mind these are irreducible questions – they pertain regardless of the particular interpretation and they have a significant bearing on any particular historical outcome. In asking such questions about the Beaker-using people, we should not forget that there were probably also mobile individuals among the reciprocating societies which would inevitably complicate the map of social interaction.

It follows from what I have postulated so far that it is imperative to consider the process of dissemination at any regional level as a series of stages, *viz.*: first awareness and contact, pioneering interaction sometimes involving settlement, consolidation of relations and/or settlement, changes in the character of the initial co-existent cultures and in the balance of their respective populations. Since it is no longer considered plausible that large numbers of Beaker people had overwhelmed the newly occupied areas and since any development must follow from the preconditions present in the previous stage (as in any historical trajectory), it should come as no surprise that there is no generally applicable common sequence cross-regionally.

Pioneering movements and reinforcing circles

Taking it as read that, in the pioneering phase, two cultural groups who seemed quite alien to one another would have come face to face, it is natural to seek evidence for either conflict or mechanisms for inter-societal accommodation. This is where Brodie's model for intermarriage becomes so important, for there is little direct evidence for widespread (as opposed to isolated) contesting of cultural supremacy through violence. The forging of cross-cultural marriage alliances among the elite would be an obvious way of cementing ties that allowed the respective groups to obtain something that the other had, or could offer. This was the first time since the beginning of the Neolithic that two ways of life based on radically different ethoses had come into direct contact across large parts of western to central Europe.

And this leads us on to another key question: what might have been the underlying cause of this expansion on a scale hitherto not seen? The familiar and extensive spatial co-existence of Beaker and indigenous final Neolithic groups was the *product* of whatever caused Beaker and Beaker-acculturated people to expand their geographical range. This may seem a self-evident statement, but all too often we are guilty of looking in our retrospective way at the expansion phenomenon as if it were solely driven by the particular cultural and psychological constitution or material objectives of the first Beaker groups – a kind of *wanderlust*. One example of internal motivation on the part of Beaker people that has often been voiced is the quest for new metal sources. The pattern of Beaker settlement, across many non-metal bearing as well as metalliferous terrains, and the notable lack of success in opening up more than a few metal sources in the early period suggest, however, that prospecting for these resources could hardly have been a driving force (see also Burgess and Shennan 1976: 312).

One way of conceptualising the expansion of Beaker culture is as the result of a *reinforcing circle*. During the pioneering phase, which seems to have been fairly contained in terms of archaeological timescales – let us suppose perhaps ten to twelve generations for much of the distribution – each stage of expansion brought further inter-group contacts into the sphere of potential social/exchange relations. They involved not only communities in the newly occupied areas, but also those just beyond. This would lead to a new and contextually specific indigenous response, and whenever that response was positive, in the sense of the indigenes seeing some benefit in interacting with the incomers, then it had the strong potential to draw onward some of the Beaker community (Figure 6.1). This further extends the spatial range and continues the cycle. The continuance of such a cycle for long enough to allow the culture to spread across half a continent would seem to be a matter of fact; it helps explain why this cultural entity had the capacity to spread on a pan-European scale at a time when few others were more than regional in their extent. But it is

also part of the explanation for the patchiness of the distribution of consolidated Beaker culture. Quadrant 3 in the reinforcing circle is the key here, for this determined whether a seed of Beaker culture was implanted in a region.

In applying this kind of model, we have to be clear from the outset that it directly explains only the 'bow-wave' of Beaker expansion. The bow-wave would be measured in one locality within a generation or two, so in archaeological terms it would only be a fraction of an archaeologically identifiable phase. After the bow-wave, there would doubtless be a period of consolidation and mutual adjustment between the Beaker incomers and the respective indigenous groups and we need to consider, hypothetically at least, whether interactions between them would continue in the same vein or would change in certain respects. For example, if a certain kind of exchange was crucial for a Beaker group to first establish their right (in the eyes of the indigenes) to be accepted in a new territory on peaceable terms, would it necessarily need to be perpetuated through later generations? Once in occupation, it would be difficult to evict the Beaker incomers without use of force, and this may not anyway have been desirable if they continued to provide an important service to the local culture. Beaker people might quickly have developed a sense of a rightful place in the territory especially as they began to mark their ancestral presence there.

To give substance to this so-far hypothetical argument, it is worth considering reactions to spreading Beaker culture in different parts of northwest Europe. We have dismissed the 'quest for metal sources', but there is the other side of the metal equation, the fact that Beaker people and the growing network by which they were interlinked carried this material. It has often been pointed out (*e.g.* Vander Linden 2006) that many of the regions in which Beaker culture became established - the Midi, the Rhone valley, the upper Danube - had known metal for centuries before and therefore Beaker groups would not seem special on account of possessing the material. However, it is the writer's view that this *was* one of the most influential factors in Beaker spread to those regions that only first encountered the material in the hands of Beaker incomers. Metal objects cannot have failed to have made a big impression on societies that had never seen them before, that could not have comprehended this novel and versatile stuff from description alone. This helps explain the advance to Atlantic France and the British Isles, parts of northern France and perhaps the Low Countries. It may also have been a factor for much of northern Iberia which was not within the early metal-using zones of the south.

One area that has always stood out as lacking significant Beaker material is the Paris basin and this seems unlikely to be entirely due to poor recovery. However, while not necessarily a determining factor, it may be significant that metal objects had been circulating in the region in small

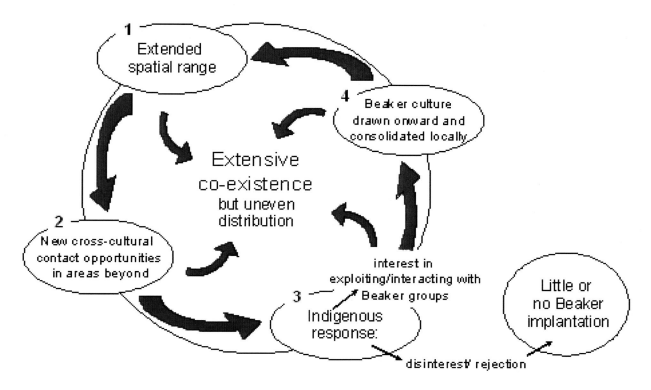

Figure 6.1 The reinforcing circle at the bow-wave of Beaker expansion

numbers for some time before contact with Beaker groups (Mille and Bouquet 2004). This, combined with a strong pre-existing cultural tradition, may have been sufficient to nullify the magic of Beaker people and their metal, hence no interest in entering into formal relations and no sequence of Beaker-influenced cultural change set in motion.

It is possible that there was an essential difference between Beaker metallurgy and that of the earlier metallurgical centres in the *way* the material was exploited within the power structures of society. Beaker people may have been more willing to pass on some of the *products* of their special knowledge to socially/ethnically quite distinct groups in order to secure other advantages and goods. If this was the case, we can nevertheless presume that metallurgical knowledge itself would be carefully guarded – this was the real source of Beaker power in relation to others. These are just tentative ideas in so far as central and northern Iberia are concerned, but the particular way of life that was highly adapted to and tolerant of periodic small-scale expansion must presumably originate early in the overall history of (maritime) Beaker culture. This became a core element within Beaker ethos – even a part of their psyche.

Consolidation and cultural marriage in Britain

If we do not envisage any large-scale migration of the kind that was once held to be responsible for Beaker culture spread, then it is necessary to explain how, in some regions such as Britain, Beaker cultural values came to prevail over pre-existing ones. This can happen over a passage of time simply through different reproductive rates within different cultural groups who operate different economies and/or different social practices (for example, infanticide) (Shennan 2002). On present evidence it is hard to evaluate these as potential contributory factors; higher infant mortality, never easy to identify, is nigh impossible to perceive in the Grooved Ware populations of Britain because of the virtual absence of a burial record, while what little is known of Grooved Ware and Beaker economies does not present obvious distinctions in reproductive potential.

There are, however, two processes that seem plausible if not likely to have upheld a demographic swing towards Beaker culture. Brodie's model would have Beaker people being married out into Grooved Ware communities, at least early on during the pioneer phase, but it is hard to see how such isolated individuals could have a dramatic effect on their adopted cultural group, who would still have greatly out-numbered them. If instead the reverse direction of marriage exchange was the dominant one (Grooved Ware females married into Beaker groups), then it would more directly lead to the numerical bolstering of the Beaker cultured population and inversely to a reduction in Grooved Ware-user numbers, albeit at first in very small numbers. I have suggested elsewhere that marriage partners were offered to small Beaker groups in return for access to metal, and perhaps other things (Needham 2005: 208). Success breeds success and, whatever the initial reason for the desirability of contact with Beaker people, any perception of preferential success in terms of faster swelling ranks could well persuade some within the Grooved Ware camp – especially perhaps young men – to 'defect'.

Once Beaker people first crossed the Channel they seem to have spread far and wide quickly, if in very small numbers. Although previously Britain had been relatively insular in its cultural outlook, there was clearly a high degree of flux across the archipelago (including Ireland). Given such a dense reticulated pre-existing network and much cultural uniformity, it is perhaps unsurprising that a similar response to the incomers was reiterated in rapid succession across many parts of the country. It is clear that for the subsequent consolidation phase we have to think in terms of a reproductive advantage – taking the term here to represent the combination of actual physical reproduction and cultural 'conversion'. There must have been a continual process of groups budding-off previously established groups, rather than simply moving on as 'vagrants'. Once the initial 'colonisation' had taken place, there would have been a progressive strengthening of Beaker groups and values at the expense of indigenous ones in those areas where they got established.

The second process is simply that of emulation of what may increasingly have seemed to be a preferable way of life because of the advantages it brought. I have already introduced this idea in the context of 'defections', but there may eventually have been a more general conversion process at a community level. In the writer's view this is what led to the collapse of Grooved Ware culture around the 22nd century BC and the simultaneous flowering of Beaker culture (Figure 6.2; *Beaker as Instituted Culture*; Needham 2005). It may also have led to the formulation of a new set of ideals and cultural goods (among them Food Vessels) by the rump of indigenous society which may have felt itself to have been marginalised or relegated in social terms.

The character of Beaker identity and its maintenance

At first sight, it is easy to be overawed by the geographical range of Beaker cultural connections, but we must always remember that this was not just a product of some haphazard vagrancy. All the time there would have been consolidation going on behind the bow-wave, albeit with variable degrees of long-term historical success. Because of the relative speed of expansion, there was limited time for the pioneer groups to culturally mutate and since, anyway, they would always initially be in the small minority relative to indigenous populations, this was doubtless good reason to strive to remain true to their cultural identity. This would certainly have been desirable if vital aspects of their economy depended on long-range contacts; the further the network spread, the more potentially attenuated it became and the more vital it was to maintain one's place in the 'Beaker network'. Hence the expansive early Beaker network became endemically central to the maintenance of both identity and specific exchange economy – in other words, it

became a part of the fabric of the Beaker way of life (Clarke 1976: 473-4). It can be suggested that later, as the individual character of regional host countries impacted on incoming Beaker ones with diverse results, the urge and necessity for conformity over a vast area diminished. This diachronic element is crucial to recognise.

Whatever the detailed motivations for the initial expansion, there can be little doubt that by the time Beaker populations had reached the Channel shores, the principle of budding-off into new terrain and the readiness to do so had become engrained in Beaker psyche. It can be postulated that by this time it seemed a natural thing for aspiring Beaker individuals or households to venture further beyond the limits of their existing network. Their internal oral tradition including origin myths would instil in them that this was part of the natural order, the way to live life. To explain the expansionist mode in this way, because of a remembered and defining cultural history, is not to dismiss it vaguely as 'wanderlust'.

Aspects of Beaker group psyche in the 'pioneering' phases have been raised by Case in his explanation of the classic and well-known pan-European grave package for men of status (Case 2004). The 'package' is constituted of Beaker pot, copper dagger/knife, stone wristguard, and flint arrowheads, which occur in graves in varying combinations over much of the full Beaker range. Case interprets these elements in terms of a 'symbolical hunting equipment … for the hunting of big game… mankind and perhaps monsters in the spirit world' (*ibid.*: 29). The burials featuring this package, or a part of it, represent individuals entitled to exceptional burial because of their exceptional role as communicators with the Otherworld. While this kind of embedded mythological structure could readily explain the relative durability of the specific funerary rite, it does not seem likely that such a hunting ethos would in itself explain the persistent expansion of the Beaker culture in its early phases.

Regional contrasts and implications

It is helpful in coming to terms with the British situation to stand back and compare it with some neighbouring lands. It has been appreciated for some time now that the Beaker cultures of the various regions of their broad western European distribution represent a range of very different responses to initial encounters between indigenous groups and the expanding Beaker phenomenon. Regional contrasts are not only apparent, but stark in north-west Europe.

While in Britain, Beaker culture - or certain critical and highly visible attributes of it - became at some stage virulent, this was not the case in either Ireland or northern France, at least not in the same way. In Ireland, not a single 'classic' Beaker burial has been recorded; in Britain we may be looking at two thousand. And yet the

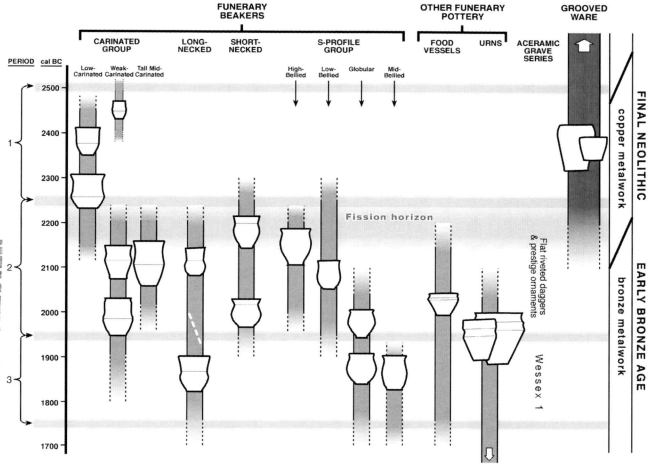

Figure 6.2 Transforming Beakers: the ceramic chronology

earliest metallurgy in Ireland is apparently associated with Beaker material (O'Brien 2004) while other Beaker style artefacts were also adopted in Ireland enthusiastically (Harbison 1976). Moreover, certain Beaker practices had subsequent impact. By the turn of the last quarter of the third millennium BC, early Food Vessel burials had emerged (O'Ríordáin and Waddell 1993). In most respects these are the direct equivalent of Beaker burial in Britain and mainland Europe, but they only emerged at a secondary stage, this perhaps explaining the incorporation of pottery bearing a distinct cultural ancestry rather than Beakers.

The evidence from northern France and Belgium (excluding Brittany) tells a different story and I have already mentioned the dearth of Beaker material from the Paris basin. Elsewhere in this region the practice of distinctive Beaker burial marks, as in Britain, the inception of the phenomenon sometime around the middle of third millennium. But while Beaker culture appears to express an important affiliation for a while, it does not leave the same centuries-long legacy that we are so familiar with from the British evidence. Good dating evidence is still thin on the ground, but I suspect that the burial record is mostly contemporary with phase 1 for Britain (*Beaker as circumscribed exclusive culture*; Needham 2005: 209). The reasons for this speedier

demise of Beaker culture on the southern shores of the Channel are doubtless complex and cannot be explored here, but there are some salient points to extract from these brief inter-comparisons:

i) successful implantation of Beaker culture in a region was not automatically accompanied by a so-called 'single-grave' burial rite

ii) similarly, successful implantation did not necessarily lead to long-term continuation of a recognisable Beaker cultural complex

iii) although there was undeniable contact across the Irish Sea and the Channel, not least to service the growing exchange in metals (Needham 2002), this in itself was not sufficient to cause culture to develop along closely parallel lines in the connected regions.

There are some other general and perhaps well established points that may be made. Whatever the gross history of population movements accounting for the spread of Beaker culture, all scholars seem to accept the creation of a far-flung network which facilitated the long distance movement of goods and ideas (Clark 1976). Now the isotopic data for the Amesbury Archer and the Boscombe Bowmen also tell us that on occasion individuals too could travel long distances during their life-times (Fitzpatrick 2002; Evans *et al.* 2006). We

45

should not jump to an instant correlation between these two independently valid observations and see the majority of Beaker culture-carrying people as wide-range roamers. The importance of the network was that it provided a ready mechanism for exchange, much of it conducted down-the-line. And it is instructive to look at the Amesbury Archer's wide array of goods, some at least of which can be seen to come ultimately from different sectors of the network, ranging potentially from central Europe to northern Spain and, of course, more locally. Perhaps the key significance of the assembled grave goods with him is that they reflect *par excellence* the world-view and life-way which he and his culture stood for in the early phase of Beaker expansion.

The 'Amesbury Archer' and the 'Boscombe Bowmen' graves both constitute exceptional contexts in their own ways and this may be the key to them containing well travelled individuals. We are certainly not yet in a position to generalise on the strength of these exceptional contexts, however exciting they may individually be. Indeed two children in the latter grave and two adults from single graves elsewhere in the Stonehenge area have already given results consistent with a more local upbringing for the individuals concerned (Evans *et al* 2006). The Beaker Isotopes Project should in time give us the more balanced view.

References

Brodie, N. 1997. New perspectives on the Bell Beaker culture. *Oxford Journal of Archaeology* 16: 297-314.

Brodie, N. 2001. Technological frontiers and the emergence of the Beaker Culture. In F. Nicolis (ed), *Bell Beakers Today: Pottery, People, Culture, Symbols in Prehistoric Europe.* Trento: Officio Beni Archeologici (2 vols). 487-96.

Burgess, C. and Shennan, S. 1976. The Beaker phenomenon: some suggestions. In C. Burgess and R. Miket (eds) *Settlement and Economy in the Third and Second Millennia B.C.* Oxford: BAR (British Series) 33. 309-31.

Case, H. 2004. Beakers and the Beaker culture. In J. Czebreszuk (ed.) *Similar but Different: Bell Beakers in Europe.* Poznan: Adam Mickiewicz University. 11-34.

Clarke, D.L. 1970. *Beaker Pottery of Britain and Ireland.* 2 vols. Cambridge: Cambridge University Press.

Clarke, D.L. 1976. The Beaker network – social and economic models. In J.N. Lanting and J.D. van der Waals (eds) *Glockenbecher Symposium, Oberried 1974.* Bussum/Haarlem: Fibula-van Dishoeck. 459-76.

Evans, J., Chenery, C.A. and Fitzpatrick, A.P. 2006. Bronze Age childhood migration of individuals near Stonehenge, revealed by strontium and oxygen isotope tooth enamel analysis. *Archaeometry* 48: 309-21.

Fitzpatrick, A. 2002. 'The Amesbury Archer': a well-furnished Early Bronze Age burial in southern England. *Antiquity* 76: 629-30.

Harbison, P. 1976. *Bracers and V-perforated Buttons in the Beaker and Food Vessel Cultures of Ireland.* Bad Bramstedt: Archaeologia Atlantica, Research Report 1.

Mille, B. and Bouquet, L. 2004. Le metal au 3e millénaire avant notre ère dans le Centre-Nord de la France. *Anthropologica et Praehistorica* 115: 197-215.

Needham, S. 2002. Analytical implications for Beaker metallurgy in North-west Europe. In M. Bartelheim, E Pernicka and R. Krause (eds) *Die Anfänge der Metallurgie in der Alten Welt.* Freiberg, Forschungen zur Archäometrie und Altertumswissenschaf 1. 99-133.

Needham, S. 2005. Transforming Beaker culture in north-west Europe; processes of fusion and fission. *Proceedings of the Prehistoric Society* 71: 171-217.

O'Brien, W. 2004. *Ross Island: Mining, Metal and Society in Early Ireland.* Galway: National University of Ireland, Bronze Age Studies 6.

O'Ríordáin, B. and Waddell, J. 1993. *The Funerary Bowls and Vases of the Irish Bronze Age.* Galway: Galway University Press.

Shennan, S. 2002. *Genes, Memes and Human History: Darwinian Archaeology and Cultural Evolution.* London: Thames & Hudson.

Vander Linden, M. 2006. *Le Phénomène Campaniforme dans l'Europe du 3ème millénaire avant notre ère.* Oxford: BAR (International Series) 1470.

Chapter 7

A Beaker veneer? Some evidence from the burial record

Alex Gibson

School of Archaeological Sciences, University of Bradford, Bradford, UK

Introduction

Almost throughout the entire 20th century the perceived wisdom regarding the Beaker Folk was that there had been a wave or waves (Clarke 1970) of 'invasions' of Britain by round-headed warriors who dominated and subjugated the local populations. Fundamental to this theory was the appearance in the archaeological record of distinctive artefact types and single, crouched inhumations beneath round barrows (Figure 7.1). These Beaker burials were often accompanied by the characteristic eponymous pots themselves as well as various 'toolkits' of both a martial (arrowheads, wristguards, daggers and battle-axes) and a more mundane nature (copper awls, flint strike-a-lights and leatherworking tools). In addition, there were burials that were perceived to be prestigious or 'rich', associated with rare grave goods such as goldwork and jet and amber items and these further illustrated the almost aristocratic (plutocratic?) importance of these new people: a social ranking gained by their martial and technological superiority, and their exploitation of local metal ores. Previous 'native' or insular burial traditions had involved the deposition of multiple inhumations or cremations beneath long barrows or within chambered tombs. This was taken to represent the importance of group ancestors in processes such as claims to land and territories and also the concept of social equality in egalitarian agrarian societies. Therefore, not only did the Beaker round barrow stand in marked contrast to what had gone before, but also the Beaker celebration of the individual must surely be taken to reflect fundamental changes in belief systems and/or the manifestation of new social identities.

That the Beaker Folk introduced this burial tradition remained an unchallenged belief in the archaeological literature despite the circularity of argument that it involved. For example, 'Beaker people' introduced single crouched inhumations beneath round barrows therefore any crouched inhumation beneath a round barrow must, by necessity, be Beaker or post-Beaker in date. This, of course, was to an extent supported by the association of early Bronze Age (post-Beaker) vessels such as Food Vessels with a similar burial rite. In addition some unaccompanied burials were found within round barrows, often secondary to a primary Beaker burial. Cremations within early Bronze Age urns were also seen as a celebration of the individual, possibly of high status given the perceived expense of the burial rite. There was also a large number of unaccompanied inhumations, without datable grave goods or without stratigraphic

relationships to other burials and/or monument types (*e.g.* flat graves), and these too were generally considered to be Early Bronze Age in date for the burial rite that they involved was held to be a Beaker introduction.

The lasting appeal of this thesis (in essence considered a fact) was largely due to its simplicity, particularly in an environment where radiocarbon dates were few, often unreliable (based on the use of unidentified charcoal in early dates, for example) and when the technique itself was comparatively expensive. In those (fairly recent) days, the tendency was to date burials that were associated with other types of grave good so that not only did the burial get dated, but also a variety of artefact types which, by inference, could be used to extend an absolute chronological framework to refined relative sequences. This strategy undoubtedly had important implications for post-Beaker chronologies (*e.g.* Needham 1996; Needham *et al.*1997) but a sceptic might say (albeit somewhat unfairly) that such a strategy also served to confirm that many of our Early Bronze Age burials, pots and artefacts were undoubtedly Early Bronze Age in date. With the advances in dating cremated bone, the suite of Bronze Age urn burials became available for dating but, once again, it was artefact-rich grave groups that were usually targeted (see, for example, Sheridan forthcoming and references therein). Unaccompanied burials, whether by cremation or inhumation, tended not to be dated because their value was perceived as low in terms of what they could contribute to artefact-based sequences.

There were, however, some very obvious and well-known exceptions or contradictions to these well-trusted rules of thumb. Firstly, for example, not all Neolithic long barrows covered large numbers of burials. There were, for example, only the fragmentary remains of three individuals (possibly deposited in a bag) below Giants Hills II in Lincolnshire (Evans and Simpson 1991) and there were no burials at all beneath the South Street long barrow in Wiltshire (Ashbee *et al.* 1979). Secondly, the absence of burials in some passage graves was always attributed to later robbing; an explanation that was as difficult to argue against as it was to prove. Thirdly, there were also Neolithic and therefore pre-Beaker round barrows that had been excavated in the late 19th and early 20th centuries. The round barrow of Duggleby Howe in Yorkshire, for example not only covered burials associated with earlier Neolithic pottery and other early to middle Neolithic grave goods such as a macehead (Loveday *et al.* forthcoming), a ground-edged axe and a polished flint knife, but also covered unaccompanied

Figure 7.1 How it probably wasn't. The reconstruction of the burial of a man with a beaker and dagger (from Bateman 1848).

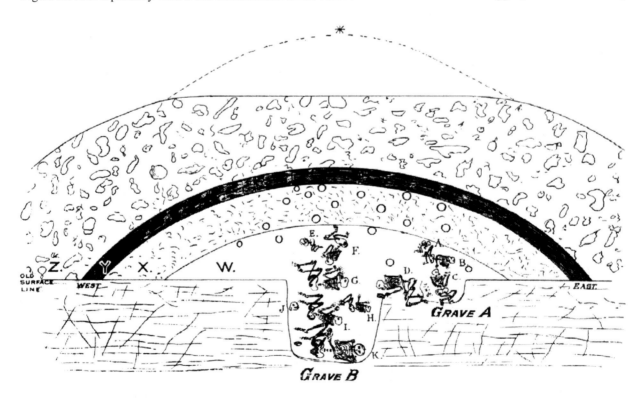

Figure 7.2 Section through the Neolithic round barrow of Duggleby Howe (from Mortimer 1905).

individual inhumations and cremations (Mortimer 1905: Kinnes *et al.* 1983; Loveday 2002) (Figure 7.2). Admittedly, these burials were often in large numbers (or at least multiples) but they nevertheless comprised discrete burials and certainly not the jumbles of disarticulated bones that were more common in long barrow or 'Neolithic' contexts.

The long barrow and chambered tomb burials also demonstrated that the Neolithic populations practised a pre-depositional rite of excarnation. The burial deposits in these monuments were generally composed of disarticulated, often fragmentary sometimes weathered and occasionally butchered and/or gnawed bones. There was, furthermore, evidence for the selection and sorting of skeletal material and probably also for the removal (i.e. absence) of some bones. The finding of partly articulated human remains in the ditch of the causewayed enclosure at Hambledon Hill in Dorset seemed to provide at least one location for this excarnation process and latterly the timber structures at, for example, Balfarg and Ballynahatty have also been interpreted as exposure platforms (Barclay and Russell White 1993; Hartwell 1998) though there are other equally plausible explanations (*e.g.* Loveday 2006: 78-82).

Sub-rectangular 'mortuary enclosures' were also interpreted as reserved areas where bodies were allowed to decompose prior to their incorporation in long barrows or chambered tombs. The distinct paucity of human remains from excavated examples of these sites, however, was either attributed to the local soil conditions or to the fact that the remains had been removed to the long barrows; another circular argument that still persists in some of the literature. However, contracted inhumations within the Nutbane long barrow, Hampshire (Morgan 1959) and an extended but complete burial in the passage of the chambered tomb at Hazelton, Gloucestershire (Saville 1990) seemed to suggest that some of the excarnation process may actually have taken place within the tombs. The rearrangement of a composite burial in such a way as to resemble a contracted inhumation at Fussell's Lodge, Wiltshire (Ashbee 1966), also suggests that Neolithic populations were not altogether unfamiliar with the foetal position of burial. This observation is further supported by the crouched inhumations from the ditches of causewayed enclosures such as Windmill Hill, Wiltshire (Smith 1965: plate VIIIa), or Whitehawk, Sussex (Curwen 1934), or indeed the flint mines of Sussex (Russell 2002: fig. 32).

Despite the enduring 'Neolithic=multiple, Bronze Age=individual' distinction, it has, of course, been recognised for some time that, despite its simplicity, this tenet of dichotomy can no longer be so rigorously sustained. Firstly, the wide application of radiocarbon dates, even discounting those with uncertain integrity, has served to demonstrate that the Neolithic in Britain now occupies some one and a half to two thousand years (depending on when one considers the Bronze Age to 'start'). This is clearly a much longer time-span that had been previously envisaged and it is worth remembering that, in his seminal work based on detailed and still largely accurate relative chronologies, Piggott had estimated only some 500 years for the Neolithic, from c.2000-c.1500 BC (Piggott 1954: fig. 64). Secondly, there would now appear to have been a gap of over five hundred years between the end of the construction of long barrows and the introduction of Beakers. Thirdly, the Beaker presence at some chambered tombs and passage

graves as well as their presence in the ditches and mounds of some long barrows suggest continued interest in the 'old ways' or at least old monuments. Fourthly, radiocarbon dating of unaccompanied inhumations is disproving the early Bronze Age affinity of many and we are now aware that there was a complexity of burial practices throughout the Neolithic and Bronze Age far more intricate or multifarious than had previously been envisaged.

Discussion of the complexity of Neolithic and Bronze Age burial practices has already been undertaken most notably by Petersen (1972), but also by, *inter alia*, Kinnes (1979), Thomas (1999) and Woodward (2000). Other authors such as Brodie (1994) and van der Linden (undated) have demonstrated how so-called 'Beaker' burial practices were already established in the indigenous later Neolithic. However, the post-Beaker Early Bronze Age has been given less attention and there is evidence to suggest that both multiple and individual burials continued to be made and that the process of excarnation continued to be practiced. This paper is not intended to be a definitive review, but rather to give some instances of the complexity of burial types during this period, to illustrate that collective burial, individual burial, token burial, and excarnation all continued to be practiced throughout the Beaker period in Britain and, finally, to highlight a major avenue for future research. Furthermore, it is my opinion that the 'Beaker burial', with its all-too-familiar pottery and artefact package, might therefore be regarded as a veneer which catches the eye and draws attention away from the chipboard beneath. The chipboard in this instance is the practice of a variety of modes of burial throughout the third and earlier second millennia BC. Indeed, it may be more accurate and less subjective to avoid the term 'burial' but rather to talk in terms of the great variation in the treatment and ultimate deposition of human remains since 'burial' has so many modern overtones and implications.

There are various strands of interrelated evidence and burial practices that we might consider. The first is individual burial; the second is multiple burial; the third examines cremation and inhumation; and the fourth considers exposure and articulation/disarticulation. Finally, the question of the absence or presence of grave goods is relevant to all these other issues. Before embarking on this review, however, it is first necessary to define some terms of reference. By individual burial, I mean the deposition of a single discrete corpse. By multiple burial I mean the deposition in the same context of the remains of more than one individual. By sequential burial, I mean burials in the same grave, but not in the same context, for example a burial in the fill or re-cut of an earlier grave or feature.

Individual inhumations

Individual crouched (Figure 7.3) or flexed inhumations in graves or cists and associated with a Beaker or Food

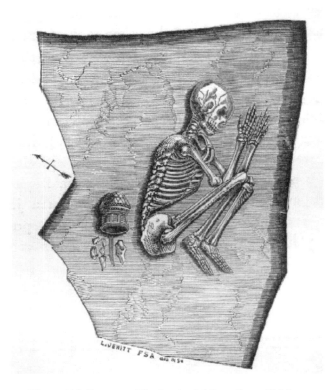

Figure 7.3 Contracted Beaker burial from Smerrill Moor (from Bateman 1861).

Vessel have come to almost typify the burial record of the final Neolithic and earlier Bronze Age. Such graves are abundant in the reports of both the early barrow diggers and recent excavators alike. However, and as mentioned above, circular arguments are often at play and because an inhumation is flexed, it is therefore generally assumed to be Bronze Age. This obviously need not be the case.

Mention has already been made of the individual burials in the tombs of Hazelton (Saville 1990) and Nutbane (Morgan 1959) above. At the former site, an extended inhumation was placed in the passage to the northern chamber. At the latter site, the crouched inhumations of three adult males and an adolescent were placed within the mortuary structure (Figure 7.4). The interpretation of the mortuary structures beneath earthen long barrows is a continuing debate, however, the sorting of bones within some of these structures combined with the reconstructed evidence from Street House (Vyner 1984) and the remarkable preservation at Haddenham (Evans and Hodder 2006) suggests that they were accessible for at least part of their existence and operated in a pre-mound environment. Once again, these individuals may have been left to decay prior to the intended sorting of the defleshed bones. Both these examples suggest periodic or episodic individual burials but that the importance of the integral individual was radically altered once it had been transformed from the corporeal to the skeletal state.

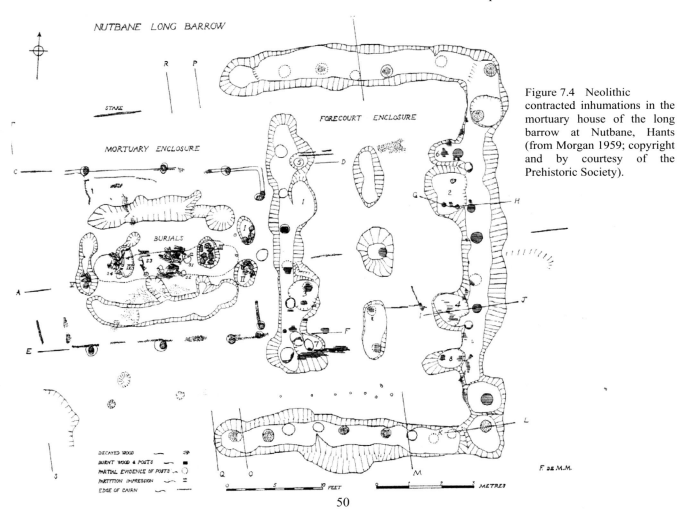

Figure 7.4 Neolithic contracted inhumations in the mortuary house of the long barrow at Nutbane, Hants (from Morgan 1959; copyright and by courtesy of the Prehistoric Society).

Figure 7.5   The grave group from Liffs Low, Derbyshire
(from Bateman 1861).

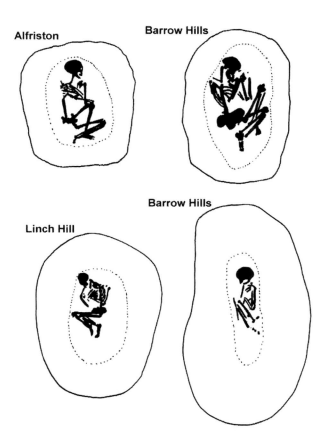

Figure 7.6   Neolithic contracted inhumations from graves. 1 -
Alfriston, Sussex (after Drewett 1975); 2 - Radley, Oxfordshire
(after Barclay and Halpin undated); 3 - Linch Hill, Oxford (after
Barclay *et al.* 1995).

In the ditches of the middle Neolithic causewayed enclosure at Windmill Hill, burials were placed within the silts (Smith 1965). The graves of two children at this site as well as child and adult crouched inhumations from the main causewayed enclosure ditch at Hambledon Hill (Frances Healy pers. comm.) in broad association with the deposition of 'domestic rubbish' has led some to consider that this demonstrates that a more cavalier attitude towards infant mortality was held in the Neolithic. However, given the importance now attached to the ritual deposition of apparently everyday objects (the elevation of the mundane; Thomas 1999; Gibson 1999: 160–162), this older view may be simplistic, and the fact that these burials were placed in contexts where other ritually charged structured depositions were also made suggests that they are not casual disposals: the burials cannot be divorced from their contexts.

Returning to the giant round barrow of Duggleby Howe in Yorkshire, a central pit c. 2.7m deep below the ground surface sealed by the barrow mound contained at its base the articulated body of an adult male (burial K) associated with fragments of round-based bowl of early to middle Neolithic date. Two further adult males and a child were buried in an articulated state in the fill of this pit. The lower of the two males (Burial I) [check burial] was associated with a lozenge-shaped arrowhead, also of early to middle Neolithic date and an antler macehead which has produced a radiocarbon date of c.3500-3100 Cal BC (Loveday * et al. in prep.). The skull of a second individual (Burial J) was also associated with Burial I and this skull has traces of extensive peri-mortem trauma: it may have been a ritual killing (sacrifice or execution) and which subsequently became a trophy (Kinnes et al. 1983: 95; Gibson and Ogden in prep.).

At Liffs Low in Derbyshire (Bateman 1861) a contracted inhumation lay below a round barrow and was associated with a package of artefacts which included an antler macehead and also edge-polished Seamer-type flint axes and boars' tusks as well as a small, round-based flask (Figure 7.5) so far unique in Britain but with similarities to the Corded Ware ceramics of northern Europe. Unfortunately the macehead failed to produce sufficient collagen for a radiocarbon date but is, by analogy, likely to date to before 3000 BC. The burial of an adult male at Whitegrounds, North Yorkshire, associated with a jet belt slider and a Seamer-type axe also produced a Middle Neolithic date of c. 3300-3000 cal BC (Brewster 1984).

Further south, at Alfriston in Sussex (Figure 7.6), a contracted burial of a young female was found below an oval mound (Drewett 1975) broadly contemporary with Carinated Bowl pottery recovered from the primary ditch silts. Below a similar monument in the Thames Valley at Radley the crouched inhumations of an adult male and female (Figure 7.6) were associated with a flint arrowhead, knife and jet 'belt slider' of Middle Neolithic date around 3000 BC (Barclay and Halpin 1998). At Linch Hill Corner at Stanton Harcourt in Oxfordshire a contracted inhumation of a female (Figure 7.6) was associated with an edge-polished knife and jet belt slider of middle Neolithic affinity (Barclay *et al.* 1995). At Dorchester I, also in Oxfordshire, a crouched inhumation was central to a segmented ring-ditch (Atkinson *et al.* 1951). These graves are clearly a part of a developing Middle Neolithic prestige goods package: a concept which perhaps made easier the adoption of the Beaker package some 500 years later.

There was also a flat grave cemetery at Barrow Hills, Radley, in which was found the contracted burials of a child, adult female and adult male, all in individual graves. The male and the child both had associated grave goods in the form of flint flakes of undiagnostic type (1 with the child, 3 with the male). These burials might have been attributed to the Beaker or Bronze Age periods according to conventional wisdom but a radiocarbon date from each burial placed the group in the mid to late fourth millennium BC. These inhumations clearly illustrate the benefit of dating unaccompanied burials or burials with undiagnostic artefacts and illustrate the fact that contracted inhumations in discrete graves pre-date Beakers by over 500 years.

Multiple inhumations

Multiple burials, the perceived burial rite of the Neolithic, occur in both an articulated and disarticulated state. The burials encountered within long barrows and chambered tombs are well known and have already been mentioned above. However, such burials also occur in other contexts. For example, in the Severn Valley, at Four Crosses in northern Powys, a large pit lay beneath the centre of a round barrow and covered the contracted inhumations of three individuals (Figure 7.7); one in the centre and one each at the head and foot of the central burial (Warrilow *et al.* 1986). Though poorly preserved, the individual burials appeared crouched, were radiocarbon dated to c. 3300-2900 cal BC and were associated with a small undecorated round-based bowl with a sinuous 'S' profile.

Burials directly associated with Peterborough Ware pottery from the Middle Neolithic are rare. The Impressed Ware affinities of the vessel from Whitton Hill, Northumberland (Miket 1985) can be discounted on the grounds of its greater similarity to Food Vessel Urns, its relative stratigraphy and the unreliability of the radiocarbon date (Gibson 2002). Nevertheless a cist burial containing multiple disarticulated burials was found in a rock shelter at Church Dale in Derbyshire

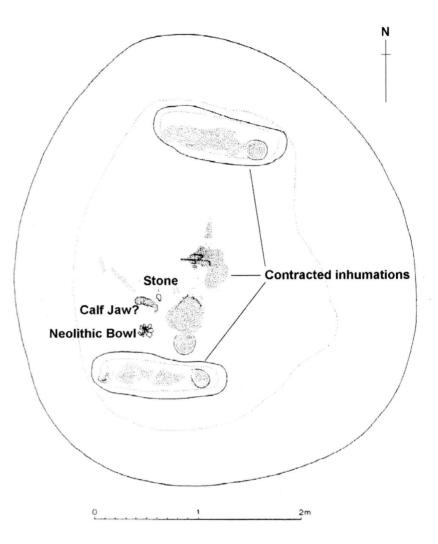

Figure 7.7   Multiple central burial from a ring-ditch at Four Crosses, Powys (copyright and by courtesy of the Clwyd-Powys Archaeological Trust).

(Burgess 1980) and was associated with a decorated Mortlake style bowl. This has sometimes been taken to represent a transitional phase between the multiple burials of the Neolithic and the cist burials of the early Bronze Age.

A pit burial containing the remains of seven individuals and associated with Beaker pottery was found at South Dumpton Down in Kent (Perkins undated). The sequence of burial was difficult to determine given the overlapping and intricate nature of the skeletons (Figure 7.8) but radiocarbon dates from the top and bottom of the deposit are statistically indistinguishable at c. 2000-1750 cal BC. Also in Kent, during the excavations at Monkton-Mount Pleasant on Thanet, Grave 751 contained four individuals: the crouched inhumation of a mature male with an S1 Beaker and, over his legs, the fragmentary remains representing the incomplete skeletons of three individuals – likely to be a woman and two children. In

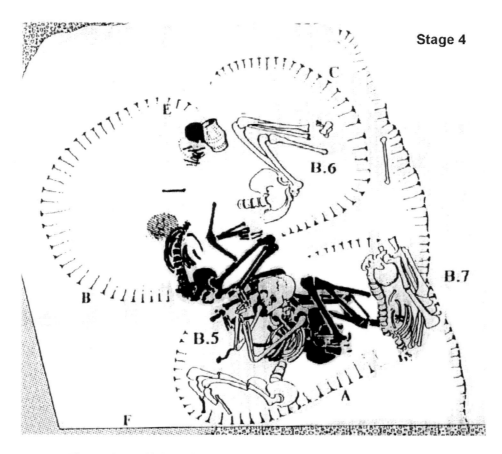

Figure 7.8   Multiple Beaker inhumations from South Dumpton Down, Kent
(copyright and by courtesy of the Trust for Thanet Archaeology).

the same area, Grave 6371 contained the skeletons of two young girls with an N3 Beaker and two copper alloy bracelets (P. Clark pers. comm.; Gibson 1996). The richly furnished grave of the 'Boscombe Bowmen' contained the relatively unweathered and unabraded remains of three adult males, a teenage male and three children, one of whom had been cremated (Fitzpatrick 2004). The bones were quite fragmented, there were relatively few small skeletal elements and only one male appears to have been articulated but it would appear that perhaps the males at least were related (Jacqui McKinley pers. comm.; Fitzpatrick 2004: 13).

At Bee Low, in Derbyshire, the disarticulated remains of seven individuals (Figure 7.9) were associated with an All Over Cord decorated Beaker (Marsden 1970). In the top of a natural mound at Hendre, in North Wales, a pit contained the fragmentary and disarticulated remains of a 25 year-old male and three children of approximately 8, 6 and 4 years old (Brassil and Gibson 1999). This deposit was radiocarbon dated to c. 1890-1680 cal BC. Another example of this practice is a cist discovered at Linlithgow in West Lothian (Cook 2000) where the skeletal remains of at least one adult and 5 children were radiocarbon dated to just before c. 2000 cal BC. The adult was represented by the skull and a fragment of femur and, given that the immature bones survived moderately well, it seems either that the entire adult skeleton was not

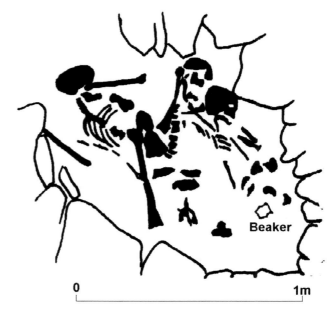

Figure 7.9   Multiple Beaker inhumations from Bee Low,
Derbyshire (after Marsden 1970).

deposited or else substantial parts were subsequently removed. This is exactly comparable with the arguments used to explain the fragmentary remains at earlier long barrows and chambered tombs but if bones had indeed

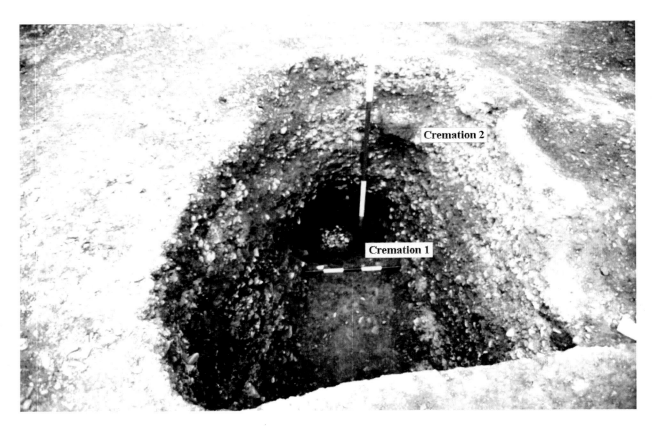

Figure 7.10 Middle Neolithic cremations *in situ* at Sarn-y-bryn-caled Site 2. Cremation 1 is primary and cremation 2 is from the upper silts, dated to *c.* 3000 cal BC (copyright and by courtesy of the Clwyd-Powys Archaeological Trust).

been removed, one might have expected the skull to have been amongst those taken.

Numerous other instances of multiple inhumations exist in the Beaker and early Bronze Age periods (Petersen 1972) and a comprehensive review is beyond the scope of this paper. However it is also worth noting Petersen's observation that there are, in addition and particularly in Yorkshire, instances of burials apparently accompanied by cremations, and the rite of cremation can also be dated to the late fourth millennium BC at, for example, Trelystan and Lower Luggy, Powys (Britnell 1982; Gibson 2006). The mixture of cremation and inhumation at Duggleby Howe has already been mentioned above and instances of cremations within the fills of graves will be outlined below.

Cremations

Cremation deposits in the earlier Neolithic are rare though crematoria have been identified below some long and round barrows (though the burning may be an act of closure rather than a burial rite – see Street House (Vyner 1984)). Certainly by the Middle Neolithic, however, the practice had become more common. The cremations within the mound of Duggleby Howe, for example, are well-known though their precise dating remains uncertain. The cremation deposits in the Aubrey Holes at Stonehenge are likely to date to the 3rd millennium BC as are the cremations from the ring-ditches in the cursus

complex at Dorchester on Thames (Atkinson *et al.* 1951). Secondary cremation deposits in a penannular ring-ditch at Sarn-y-bryn-caled in Powys (Figure 7.10) were from a phase of the monument associated with Peterborough Ware and dated to c. 3000 cal BC (Gibson 1994) which is in close agreement for the mixed inhumation and cremation burial at nearby Trelystan and the cremation of a mature female at Lower Luggy mentioned above. This date also acts as a *Terminus Ante Quem* for the cremation of a female in the basal silts of the same monument at Sarn-y-bryn-caled.

Later Neolithic cremations are more difficult to identify largely due to a lack of associated datable artefacts but there are occasional associations of Grooved Ware with cremations at, for example, Winhill and Eddisbury (Kinnes 1979). The association of Beakers with cremations, particularly in northern Britain, suggests that it was a predominant burial rite before the arrival of Beakers and, of course, cremation continued to be widely practised in the earlier Bronze Age accompanied by a variety of Food Vessel and urn forms suggesting an unbroken practice continuing behind the Beaker veneer. As with unaccompanied inhumations above, however, few cremations have been dated as they tend to lack diagnostic artefacts and therefore there may well be a large number of 'Neolithic' cremations that have, hitherto, been assumed to be Bronze Age. Now that cremated bone can be radiocarbon dated, such unaccompanied cremations may hold some surprises as has been found at North Mains, Perthshire, where the 'Neolithic' cremation beneath the henge bank (Barclay 1983, Burial A) has produced an early Bronze Age date forcing a reassessment of the entire site sequence (Barclay 2005).

Information regarding the age(s), gender(s) and pathology of cremated remains can be difficult depending heavily on the fragment size. The identification of sex, age and the number of individuals represented relies on the size, shape and duplication of diagnostic skeletal elements (see McKinley 1997). This raises some interesting questions regarding perceived wisdoms, questions which may not actually be answerable. For example, if no body parts are duplicated in a cremation deposit, are we necessarily correct in assuming that only one individual is present?

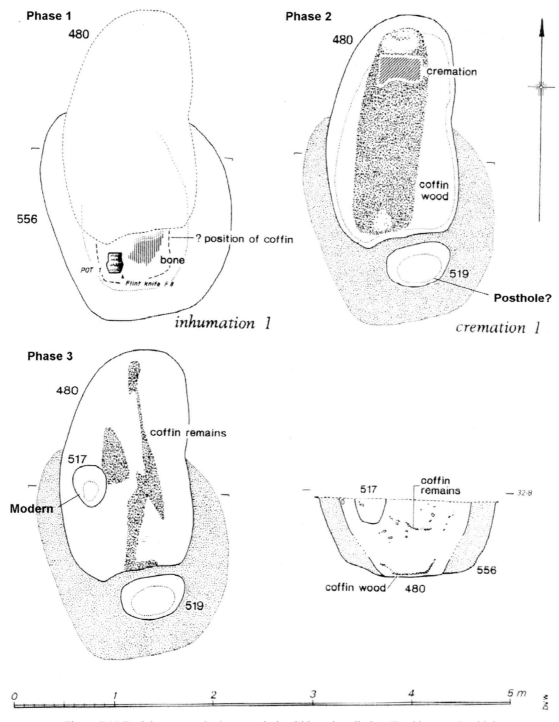

Figure 7.11 Burial sequence in the central pit within a ring-ditch at Tandderwen, Denbigh (copyright and by courtesy of the Clwyd-Powys Archaeological Trust).

55

Possibly - indeed probably. But, if bones were being selected for inhumation burial, as discussed below, why not for cremation too?

Certainly there are multiple cremations in the Bronze Age. At the Sarn-y-bryn-caled timber circle in Powys, fragments of two individuals comprised the primary burial (Gibson 1994) as evidenced by a duplicated left petrous temporal bone. The easy and obvious explanation for this is the re-use of a pyre site and the accidental recovery of a fragment from an earlier cremation. However, how many of the other bone fragments were from this second individual but cannot be identified because they are not duplicated or age or gender-indicative? In other instances, the evidence is not so contentious. At Trelystan, on Long Mountain and virtually overlooking Sarn-y-bryn-caled on the floor of the Severn Valley to the west, the cremated remains of a mature male and female were contained in the same Food Vessel Urn (Britnell 1982). A pit cut into the subsoil beneath a cairn at Carneddau, also in Powys contained the cremated remains of two children.

On the other side of the country at Weasenham Lyngs, Norfolk, a central grave associated with a Collared Urn contained the cremated remains of three or four adults, likely to have been three male and one possible female (Petersen and Healy 1986). The remains of an adult male and female plus two children were found within a Collared Urn at Hunstanton, Norfolk, (Longworth 1984: No. 948) and a similar vessel was inverted over 3 adults and a child at Hepple, Northumberland (*ibid*: No. 1054). At Barrow 5, West Cotton, Northamptonshire, a Collared Urn covered the remains of three adults (Allan *et al.* in Healy and Harding forthcoming).

At Tandderwen in Denbighshire (Figure 7.11), the central burial in the ring ditch had originally been an inhumation in a wooden coffin and it had been associated with a Beaker. Subsequently this burial had been partially disturbed by the insertion of a second coffin burial, this time containing the cremated remains of five individuals (two adult males, an adult female and two children; Brassil *et al.* 1991). Cremation 2 at the same site, associated with a Food Vessel Urn, comprised the remains of an adult male, an adolescent and a young child. Cremation 8 from the unenclosed part of the Tandderwen cemetery comprised the remains of two adults and, though the burial was unaccompanied, it produced a radiocarbon date of c. 1600 cal BC.

Articulation/disarticulation

Disarticulated remains are abundant in the Neolithic period and the process of excarnation, whether natural (exposure) or assisted (mechanical excarnation), is widely accepted amongst archaeologists. However, there would also appear to be a growing amount of evidence to suggest that excarnation was just as commonplace in the Bronze Age and a regionalised re-assessment of Bronze

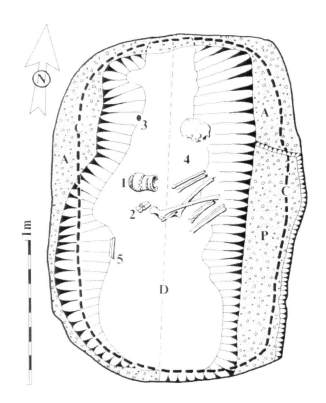

Figure 7.12 Disarticulated and incomplete burial from Manston, Kent (copyright and by courtesy of The Trust for Thanet Archaeology).

Age burials is overdue. The best evidence will come from inhumation burials where the ground conditions are favourable for the preservation of bone.

At Hemp Knoll, near Avebury, for example, a child inhumation lacked hand and foot bones. A Beaker burial from Manston in Kent (Figure 7.12), though arranged to resemble a crouched inhumation, lacked vertebrae, pelvis, both upper arms and mandible (Perkins and Gibson 1990). At Aldwincle in Northamptonshire, the Beaker burial in barrow 2 was disarticulated and the bones had been lightly burnt but not cremated (Jackson 1976). At Grendon, in the same county, an area of Bronze Age pits produced an adult and child inhumation in Pit 9 with the pelvis and lower limbs missing from the adult. From Pit 6 at the same site, the complete burial record comprised only a fragment of rib and a tibia and fibula with some attached foot bones: in other words a lower leg burial (Gibson and McCormick 1985). In Northumberland, a dagger grave at Newborough contained what appeared to have been a contracted inhumation but analysis of the bones proved that only the lower part of the body was represented. The 'head' was in fact the pelvis and the 'arms' and 'legs' comprised one leg each (Newman and Miket 1973). A similar scenario was encountered at Chealamy, Strathnaver, in northern Scotland where the beaker was associated with only the lower half of a body (Gourlay 1984). At Dalgetty, in Fife, it seems, from the size of the pits and from the dental evidence (the only skeletal material to survive), that heads (perhaps severed)

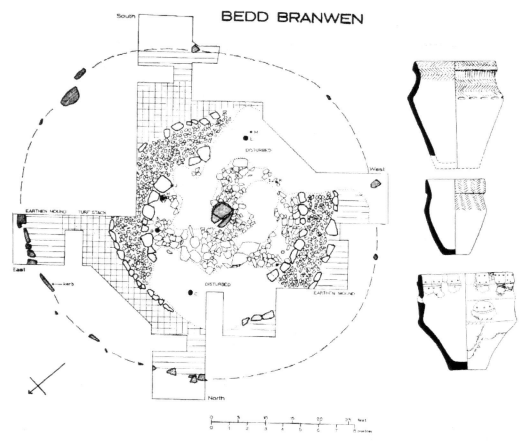

Figure 7.13 Bedd Branwen, Anglesey, and pots J, M and E which contained infant ear-bones
(from Lynch 1991; copyright and by courtesy of Frances Lynch).

may have been the only body parts to have been buried (Watkins 1982). If this is correct, then the practice can be seen to have had a long Neolithic ancestry as the practice has already been noted above at Duggleby Howe (burial J) and, of course, in the base of the causewayed enclosure ditch at Hambledon Hill (Healy 2006: 17; Healy and Mercer forthcoming).

Even ostensibly complete burials may occasionally provide evidence for exposure or excarnation. At Bredon Hill in Worcestershire, for example, a central pit beneath a barrow contained the remains of two individuals, a male first and a female added later, both associated with Beakers. The later, female, skeleton was the more complete but within the skull were found shells of the carnivorous snail Oxychilus as well as the pellet from a bird of prey such as a kite or buzzard (Thomas 1965). Even one of the woman's toe bones was found in the skull! These remains were found during the cleaning of the skull in the laboratory and could not have found their way into the skull after burial or during excavation. That the corpse was exposed prior to burial is the only explanation for all these observed phenomena. Thomas and his specialists not only conclude that the completeness of the skeleton does not suggest a lengthy period of exposure but they also observe that the only way the pellet could have entered the skull was through the foramen magnum at the base. They therefore suggest

that it is very likely that the corpse had been decapitated and that the brain had been removed prior to burial. It seems, therefore, that the process of excarnation may have been mechanically accelerated by human agency. Even the ostensibly complete skeleton of the 'Amesbury Archer' was subsequently found to have been lacking a rib; he could have lived with his damaged leg, but not the thoracic omission (Fitzpatrick 2002; McKinley pers. comm.). The rib may well have been removed during a post-burial visit to the grave, perhaps as a trophy or talisman but there may have also been associated deposition episodes which may account for the differing heights of some of the artefacts in this unusually well provisioned Beaker grave.

The completeness of cremations is often difficult to judge and complete combustion and/or a cavalier approach to the collection of cremated remains may be invoked to account for examples with less than expected bulk. A modern cremation of an adult might produce in the region of 3kg of bone (McKinley 1989). Allowing a fairly arbitrary amount for complete combustion and for collection difficulties in prehistory, we might expect at least 1.5kg-2kg from a complete adult cremation. However, many Bronze Age cremations weigh far less than this. A cremation from Hemp Knoll in Wiltshire, for example, associated with a Food Vessel of the early Bronze Age weighed only 72g. The individual was adult

57

and therefore the cremation cannot represent the whole body (Robertson-Mackay 1980). At Meldon Bridge, in Peebles the Neolithic and Bronze Age cremations produced a maximum of 1325g of bones and the smallest deposits comprised just a few fragments (Speak and Burgess 1999). Of the 14 documented adult or youth cremations, only three are recorded as producing more than 1kg of bone and 9 are recorded as weighing under 150g. There are also instances of cremations where substantial body parts have been found to be missing. At Welsh St Donats 3, in South Glamorgan, for example, burial E had been poorly cremated but lacked a tibia and humerus while cremation 6 at the same site lacked an arm (Ehrenberg *et al.* 1982).

Overwhelming evidence for the selection of human bone in the Bronze Age comes from three Bronze Age cremation deposits at Treiorwerth and Bedd Branwen on Anglesey (Figure 7.13) (Lynch 1991) where the only bone present comprised the ear bones of children. While these small bones may be resilient to cremation, it seems unlikely that no other skeletal elements would have survived.

It is clear that far from entire bodies were being deposited. There may be several scenarios at play here. For example, it may be that selected body parts, perhaps selected from an ossuary of some kind, were cremated. Alternatively, it may be that the cremated remains of a single individual were buried in more than one location. It may even be that we are not looking at burials at all but rather the ritual (or structured) deposition of transformed (disarticulated and cremated) human remains.

The incompleteness and/or disarticulation of some Bronze Age inhumations clearly suggests exposure or mechanical excarnation prior to final deposition. This may also be detected in some cremations. Occasionally (and, again, re-assessment is badly needed) the pits in which cremations have been found have been reddened by the action of fire. This has sometimes been interpreted as proving that the cremations were still hot when deposited but this is clearly erroneous (contra Longworth 1984: 47). Cremations cool quickly and only fire as opposed to hot items will be sufficient to burn the sides of the pit; the degree of reddening will depend on the intensity of the fire and the ferrous content of the soil and it is worth noting how little the sub-soil was affected by heat in some experimental pyre cremations (McKinley 1997). It therefore seems likely that some pits may actually have been the site of the cremation itself. This is especially so at Carneddau in Powys, where the sides of Pit 21-23, located beneath a small addition to Cairn I, were heavily burnt and the pit was filled with a mixture of charcoal and the cremated remains of an adult female and a child. At a maximum of 0.8m across, a complete body could not have been cremated in this pit nor was there burning around the feature to suggest that a pyre had been built over it. Logic dictates therefore that defleshed bones had been dropped into a raging fire set

within the pit. The fact that the bone and charcoal was thoroughly mixed further suggests that the fire was being stoked throughout the process (Gibson 1993) in order to introduce oxygen into the coals to ensure the complete combustion of the bone. This was also the case at pit 29 beneath cairn II at the same site, where the calcined bones of two children were thoroughly mixed with charcoal in a fire-reddened pit.

The ethnographic evidence (largely from colonial India) and the classical texts (the cremation of Misenus in Virgil's *Aeneid* [book VI] and the funeral of Patroklos in Homer's *Iliad* [book XXIII] with its associated rites including artefact, animal and human sacrifice) have made us familiar with constructed, sometimes elaborate, pyres and clearly actual pyre sites have been found below round barrows (Grinsell 1941; McKinley 1997). These pyre sites are, however, comparatively rare and, given the evidence from Carneddau mentioned above, we must conclude that the typical picture of a pyre site as a structured pile of wood onto which the complete body (or bodies) is/are laid may not have been the Bronze Age norm.

In her analysis of Bronze Age burials in Yorkshire excavated since 1950 (1950 was chosen to maximise the reliability of human bone reports), Armstrong (2002) noted that only 9% of cremations and 13% of inhumations could be regarded as complete (from a total corpus of 147 burials – 77 cremations and 70 inhumations). Of the complete deposits, 62% were cremation burials and 38% inhumations. The age profiles of both the complete and incomplete inhumations and cremations show no appreciable difference between the two sepulchral processes. There are also no appreciable differences between the body parts represented in cremations or inhumations (*ibid* graph 11) with skulls being most commonly represented (69% of all burials). Vertebrae, femora, thoracic elements, tibiae, fibulae and pelvic elements are each only represented in about one third of all burials. Even allowing for taphonomic processes and the vagiaries of cremation, this is a very small percentage.

Toots (1964) identified five stages in the natural decomposition of a human corpse. Meanwhile, Haglund *et al.* (1989) have undertaken research on dog scavenging of human remains and both authorities have postulated a staged disarticulation sequence for cadavers. These two observations have been summarised by Armstrong (2002) and can be compared in Table 7.1.

It has been noted in Bronze Age burials from Yorkshire that the cranium is present in 69% of the burials, the vertebra is present in only 36% of cases and the lower limbs, thoracic and pelvic regions are only represented in 30% of cases. This might be seen as a reversal of Haglund *et al.*'s observations and may suggest that, if excarnation by scavenging had been practised in Bronze Age Yorkshire, then the body parts were being selected

Natural (after Toots)	Scavenged (after Haglund *et al.*)
Skull and some limbs become disconnected	Removal of skin from the neck and face and removal of neck organs and soft tissue.
Ribs become disconnected	Feeding on the thoracic inlet leading to destruction of the thoracic vertebral area including sternum.
Limbs progressively disarticulate until isolated bones remain	Destruction of the sternal ends of ribs and clavicle.
Vertebral column disarticulates	Removal of scapulae and remaining clavicles.
Splintering and weathering of bone before the above is complete.	Removal of lower limbs.
Total disarticulation and bone fragmentation.	Removal of complete pelvic girdle and remaining lumbar and thoracic vertebrae
	All bones disarticulated

Table 7.1 Disarticulation sequences for cadavers (from Armstrong 2002).

for burial as they became cadaverous but before their removal by larger carnivores (Armstrong 2002: 47). The figures do not seem best suited to Toots' sequence: as the spine is the last element to become skeletal presumably it might be expected to be one of the better represented skeletal areas but instead it is one of the poorer represented elements. We are left with the conclusion that body parts were being selected but not with the answers to the questions of 'which' or 'why'.

In a similar, if more in depth study, of Scottish Bronze Age burials, Nash (2004) noted that, in the 116 cases where age and sex could be determined, male and female burials were more or less equal in numbers up to the 18-25 age range but a greater number of females died in the 26-35 age group (26 female against 7 males) while the picture is reversed in the 35-45 age group (24 males to 7 females). Numbers even out again but also greatly decrease in the 46+ range (3 male, 2 female). Assuming that the burial population is a true demographic indicator (and it may not be when, for example, the evidence for violent deaths is taken into account) it seems that fewer females were reaching old age and that people surviving to real old age were few. There seems to be no appreciable difference in the populations represented by cremations or inhumations. Nevertheless, some 50% of the cremations contained less than half the amount of bone expected from the age, sex and stature of the burials. The completeness of inhumations was more difficult to determine due to the taphonomic processes related to the acidic soils of Scotland but the incorrect anatomical order and the absence of cranial and pectoral regions in a burial from Horsbrugh Castle Farm, Peebleshire was highlighted as an example of incomplete and disarticulated inhumation (Peterson *et al.* 1974). Both multiple crouched and disarticulated burials were recorded in significant numbers (Nash 2004: fig. 5.3).

Therefore, in the Beaker and post-Beaker Bronze Age, there is a growing amount of data for the burial of incomplete corpses either by cremation or inhumation. The process of excarnation, well accepted in Neolithic contexts, clearly continued through into the second

millennium BC. Once more the Beaker veneer can be pulled away.

Sequential burial

As has been mentioned above, it would appear that, at both megalithic tombs as well as within the mortuary structures of earthen long barrows, there was a time or times when access (albeit probably restricted) was allowed to the human remains as for example at Haddenham, Cambridgeshire (Evans and Hodder 2006), and South Street, Cleveland (Vyner 1984). Thus some bones were sorted into piles while others were doubtless removed. In contrast to our modern understanding of burial (whether by inhumation or cremation) as the final deposition of a discrete individual, Neolithic and Bronze Age burial (i.e. deposition of human remains) does not seem to have been a final act but rather part of a process, perhaps involving one or more rites of passage, concerning death, laying out, excarnation, sorting of the skeletal remains, perhaps initial burial and, ultimately, final deposition. With each stage, the deceased (and, progressively, the remains of the deceased) may have been endowed with different meanings or significances. These significances may have increased with the age of the bones and the mythologies that might have been attached to them or they may have decreased in importance as they became further removed from the individual and/or human memory. Once again this might also be seen to be happening in the Beaker period and earlier Bronze Age and this aspect has recently been discussed by Woodward (2000).

A case has already been made for the extension of 'Neolithic' burial practices of multiple burial, excarnation and skeletal selection into the Bronze Age. We need now to look at the practice of burial replacement or disturbance. Mention has already been made of the Bredon Hill Beaker burial where the burial of an adult male was replaced with the burial of an adult female causing disturbance to the original. Clearly the grave pit was still visible when the second burial was made. This is also the case at Amesbury G71 (Christie 1967) where the

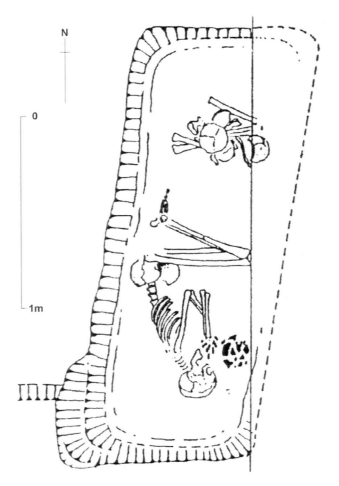

Figure 7.14 The Beaker contracted inhumation and disarticulate burial from Monkton-Minster, Kent (copyright and by courtesy of the Trust for Thanet Archaeology).

At Barrow 9 at Irthlinborough the contracted inhumation of a 4-6 year old child was deposited in F741 towards the edge of the barrow and associated with a rusticated Beaker. The grave was backfilled and the burial of a neonate inserted into this fill (Boyle in Healy and Harding forthcoming). At Bowthorpe, Norfolk, there was a complex sequence of recutting graves and pits (Lawson 1986). Grave 39, for example, cut grave 28. Both had held contracted inhumations though the bone preservation was very poor. Beaker sherds were found in the fill of the lower grave. At Shrewton 5k in Wiltshire, an adult male was buried with a Beaker and copper alloy dagger in a pit 2.25m deep (Green and Rollo-Smith 1984). Into the upper fill of this pit was inserted the contracted inhumation of a second adult male, also associated with a Beaker. These burials, like the other examples quoted are clearly sequential. At Monkton-Minster, in Kent (Figure 7.14), a Beaker inhumation had been placed in a grave with a pile of disarticulated bones representing another adult. Was this a simultaneous deposit or were the bones from an earlier burial pushed aside to make room for the later one? Depending on soil conditions, it might take a burial between five and fifteen years to deflesh and this suggests that, if sequential, the grave may have been marked for a considerable time. However, the possibility that the first corpse was defleshed before burial and as discussed above must also be considered.

At Gravelly Guy (site X, 6-8) in Oxfordshire (Barclay et al. 1995) there had been five successive burials in the centre of a ring ditch (Figure 7.15). The primary burial had been dug out by the later insertions and an original inhumation is inferred. The second inhumation, of a male adult, was accompanied by a bronze dagger, beaker, wristguard, scraper, copper alloy awl, whetstone, antler rod and two flint flakes. He had probably been buried in a coffin. The third burial was cut into the second at a higher level and contained the crouched inhumation of a young adult female. She was associated with a beaker, copper alloy awl and a flint scraper. Comparatively little time seems to have elapsed between these burials. Two cremation pits were then dug into the backfill of the third grave. The first contained the remains of an infant with a few unburnt and disarticulated adult bones. The second comprised the remains of an adult female. Clearly there was a sequence of use and reuse at this site. The grave was being revisited much as chambered tombs and long barrows were although the manner in which the graves were revisited is clearly different in detail given the obvious physical differences between pits and chambers or mortuary structures.

A similarly complex sequence was recorded at Tandderwen in Denbighshire (Brassil et al. 1991). Here, within the central grave complex of a ring-ditch, an inhumation had been interred in a coffin with a Beaker and a flint knife (the bone was too decayed for analysis). A second grave was dug into the first and into this was inserted a dug-out coffin containing the multiple cremation already discussed above. This grave may have

burial of an adult had been deposited in a pit. This was then dug out and the body of an adult male was deposited in the same pit. Below a round barrow (Barrow 6) at West Cotton, Northants, a pit containing a disarticulated burial, representing the incomplete remains of two individuals and dated to c. 3300-3000 cal BC, was dug into a millennium later and a Beaker contracted inhumation placed within this enlarged grave. The similar orientations of the two features led the excavators to believe that the earlier grave had been marked in some way (Windell 1989; Chapman et al. in Healy and Harding forthcoming). It also remains a possibility that the date between the two features was not that great but that old bones had been deposited in the earlier pit. The curation of artefacts had been demonstrated at nearby Irthlingborough Barrow 1 where a Beaker inhumation (described as 90% complete (!) – Allan et al. in Healy and Harding forthcoming) was associated with a range of artefacts including a boar's tusk which was dated to as much as 600 years earlier than the Beaker (Beaker burial 2200-1920 cal BC; tusk 2890-2460 cal BC; Healy 2004: 188). Some of the aurochs skulls which acted as a cairn over this burial also seem to have had a similar antiquity (Healy 2004) and may be derived from ancient bucrania.

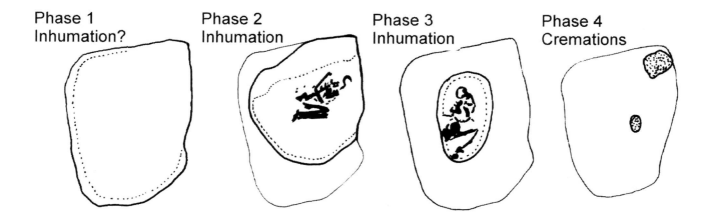

Figure 7.15 The recut grave sequence at Gravelly Guy, Oxford (after Barclay *et al.* 1995).

been marked by a standing post. The coffin stain measured 2.2m long yet the cremation deposit occupied a discrete rectangular area to the northern end of the coffin. The excavators therefore considered it likely that this grave had also held an inhumation burial but that this had not survived in the acid soil. The multiple cremation deposit is also interesting because it appeared to be layered; the remains of each individual (2 adult males, adult female, adolescent, child) were broadly restricted to these individual layers. It is possible, therefore, that this too was a sequential deposit, perhaps in a box or other organic container.

Conclusion

This brief review of the complexity of burial practices during the third and early second millennia BC in Britain indicates that the perceived split between the multiple inhumations of the Neolithic and the individual burials of the Early Bronze Age is no longer tenable. Instead, practices involving the deposition of complete, incomplete, articulated, disarticulated, inhumations and cremations were practiced throughout the period. The process of excarnation, so commonly observed in the Neolithic, seems to have been equally common in the Early Bronze Age. This is evidenced by both incomplete and complete inhumations as well as by small and token cremation deposits: cremation pits could not have coped with complete corpses. This important aspect of Early Bronze Age burial ritual has not really received the attention it deserves and regional syntheses are clearly needed. Contracted inhumations appear in the archaeological record well before the advent of Beakers and the only distinguishing feature about the 'Beaker burial' would be the presence of the pot itself and distinctive 'Beaker package' artefacts. Grave goods in general, however, start to appear from before the middle of the fourth millennium as witnessed by the recent dates from maceheads (Loveday *et al.* forthcoming.) and increased in complexity into the Early Bronze Age (see Kinnes 1979; Thomas 1999; and Loveday 2006: 172–9, for discussions of this). The presence of a Beaker and its

associated package of artefacts may simply be a logical extension of this grave good development. After all, the Beaker artefact package must initially have been regarded as exotic with links to Europe and foreign histories. Furthermore, the 'Beaker inhumation' is itself, at least in part, a myth since both complete and incomplete skeletons are found as well as articulated and disarticulated remains. The burial practices of this period, therefore, may be like cheap furniture - it's not the veneer that is important but rather what is happening underneath.

What seems certain from the above review is that the sentiment of 'Rest in Peace', generally wished upon the deceased of modern times, does not seem to have been a sentiment widely understood by our Neolithic and Bronze Age forebears. It appears that the dead did not rest easy. It might also be time to stop talking about Neolithic and Bronze Age 'burials' with all the modern inferences that this term implies, but rather to write in rather more vague terms such as the manipulation and deposition of human remains.

Acknowledgements

I would like to thank John McIlwaine for providing information on natural defleshing processes and Alison Sheridan for prompting some references. I am also grateful to Dave Perkins of the Trust for Thanet Archaeology, Bill Britnell of the Clwyd-Powys Archaeological Trust, Julie Gardiner of the Prehistoric Society and Frances Lynch for permission to use illustrative material.

References

Armstrong, J. A. 2002. *Bronze Age Excarnation.* Unpublished BSc thesis, Department of Archaeological Sciences, University of Bradford.

Ashbee, P. 1966. The Fussell's Lodge long barrow excavations, 1957. *Archaeologia* 100: 1-80.

Ashbee, P., Smith, I.F. and Evans, J.G. 1979. Excavation of three long barrows near Avebury. *Proceedings of the Prehistoric Society* 45: 207-300.

Atkinson, R., Piggott, C.M. and Sandars, N. 1951. *Excavations at Dorchester, Oxon*. Oxford: Ashmolean Museum.

Barclay, A. and Halpin, C. 1998. *Excavations at Barrow Hills, Radley, Oxfordshire. Volume I: The Neolithic and Bronze Age Monument complex*. Oxford: Oxford Archaeological Unit.

Barclay, A., Gray, M. and Lambrick, G. 1995. *Excavations at the Devil's Quoits, Stanton Harcourt, Oxfordshire, 1972-3 and 1988*. Oxford: Oxford Archaeological Unit.

Barclay, G. 1983. Sites of the third millennium BC to the first millennium AD at North Mains, Strathallan, Perthshire. *Proceedings of the Society of Antiquaries of Scotland* 113: 122-281.

Barclay, G. 2005. The 'Henge' and 'Hengiform' in Scotland. In V. Cummings and A. Pannett (eds) *Set in Stone: new approaches to Neolithic monuments in Scotland*. Oxford: Oxbow. 81-94.

Barclay, G. and Russell White, C.J. 1993. Excavations at the ceremonial complex of the Fourth to Second Millennium BC at Balfarg/Balbirnie, lenrothes, Fife. *Proceedings of the Society of Antiquaries of Scotland* 123: 43-210.

Bateman, T. 1848. *Vestiges of the Antiquities of Derbyshire*. London: John Russell Smith

Bateman, T. 1861. *Ten Years' Diggings in Celtic and Saxon Grave Hills in the Counties of Derbyshire, Stafford and York*. London: John Russell Smith.

Brassil, K. and Gibson, A. M. 1999. A Grooved Ware pit group and Bronze Age multiple inhumation at Hendre, Rhydymwyn, Flintshire. In R Cleal and A MacSween (eds) *Grooved Ware in Britain and Ireland*. Oxford: Oxbow. 89-97.

Brassil, K., Owen, G. and Britnell, W.J. 1991. Prehistoric and early medieval cemeteries at Tandderwen, near Denbigh, Clwyd. *Archaeological Journal* 148: 46-97.

Brewster, T.C.M. 1984. *The Excavation of Whitegrounds Barrow 1, Burythorpe, North Yorkshire*. Malton: East Riding Archaeological Research Committee.

Brodie, N. 1994. *The Neolithic-Bronze Age Transition in Britain*. Oxford: BAR (British Series) 238.

Burgess, C. 1980. *The Age of Stonehenge*. London: Dent

Christie, P.M. 1967. A barrow cemetery of the second millennium BC in Wiltshire. *Proceedings of the Prehistoric Society* 33: 336-366.

Clarke, D.L. 1970. *The Beaker Pottery of Great Britain and Ireland*. Cambridge: Cambridge University Press.

Cook, M. 2000. An early Bronze Age multiple burial cist from Mill Road industrial estate, Linlithgow, West Lothian. *Proceedings of the Society of Antiquaries of Scotland* 130: 77-91.

Curwen, E.C. 1934. Excavations in Whitehawk Neolithic camp, Brighton, 1932-3. *Antiquaries Journal* 14: 99-133.

Drewett, P. 1975. The excavation of an oval burial mound of the third millennium BC at Alfriston, East Sussex. *Proceedings of the Prehistoric Society* 41: 119-152.

Ehrenberg, M., Price, J. and Vale, V. 1982. The excavation of two bronze age round barrows at Welsh St Donats, South Glamorgan. *Bulletin of the Board of Celtic Studies* 29(4): 776-842.

Evans, C. and Hodder, I. 2006. *A Woodland Archaeology. Neolithic sites at Haddenham*. Cambridge: McDonald Institute Monographs.

Evans, J.G. and Simpson, D.D.A. 1991, Giants Hill 2 long barrow, Skendleby, Lincolnshire. *Archaeologia* 109: 1-45.

Fitzpatrick, A. 2002. The Amesbury Archer: a well-furnished early Bronze Age burial in southern Engand. *Antiquity* 76: 629-30.

Fitzpatrick, A. 2004. The Boscombe Bowmen: builders of Stonehenge? *Current Archaeology* 193: 10-16.

Gibson, A.M. 1993. The excavation of two cairns and associated features at Carneddau, Carno, Powys, 1898-90. *Archaeological Journal* 150: 1-45.

Gibson, A.M. 1996. *The Neolithic and Early Bronze Age Pottery from Monkton-Minster, Kent*. Report No39 prepared for the Canterbury Archaeological Trust.

Gibson, A.M. 1999. *The Walton Basin Project: Excavation and Survey in a Prehistoric landscape 1993-7*. Report 118. York: Council for British Archaeology.

Gibson, A.M. 2002. A matte of pegs and labels: a review of some of the prehistoric pottery from the Milfield Basin. *Archaeologia Aeliana* 30: 176 – 80.

Gibson, A.M. 2006. Excavation at a Neolithic enclosure at Lower Luggy, near Welshpool, Powys, Wales. *Proceedings of the Prehistoric Society* 72: 163-92.

Gibson, A.M. and McCormick, A. 1985. Archaeology at Grendon Quarry, Northamptonshire, Part 1: Neolithic and Bronze Age sites excavated in 1974-5. *Northamptonshire Archaeology* 20: 23-44.

Gibson A. M. and Ogden, A. R. In preparation. Burial J from Duggleby Howe.

Gibson, A.M. and Sheridan, A.S. (eds) 2004. *From Sickles to Circles: Britain and Ireland at the time of Stonehenge*. Stroud: Tempus.

Gourlay, R. 1984. A short cist Beaker inhumation from Chealamy, Strathnaver, Sutherland. *Proceedings of the Society of Antiquaries of Scotland* 114: 567-71.

Grinsell, L.V. 1941. The Bronze Age round barrows of Wessex. *Proceedings of the Prehistoric Society* 7(3): 73-113.

Hagland, W.D., Reay, D.T. and Swindler, D.R. 1989. Canid scavenging/disarticulation sequence of human remains in the Pacific Northwest. *Journal of Forensic Sciences* 34(3): 587-606.

Hartwell, B. 1998. The Ballynahatty complex. In A. Gibson and D. Simpson (eds) *Prehistoric Ritual and Religion*. Stroud: Sutton Publishing. 32-44.

Healy, F. 2004. Reading a burial: the legacy of Overton Hill. In Gibson and Sheridan (eds) *From Sickles to Circles: Britain and Ireland at the Time of Stonehenge*. Stroud: Tempus. 176-93.

Healy, F. 2006. Pottery deposition at Hambledon Hill. In Gibson, A.M. (ed.) *Prehistoric Pottery: Some Recent Research*. Prehistoric Ceramics Research group

Occasional Paper 5. Oxford: BAR (International Series) 1509. 11-38.

Healy, F. and Harding, J. forthcoming. *Raunds Area Project: the Neolithic and Bronze Age landscapes of West Cotton, Stanwick and Irthlingborough, Northamptonshire.* London: English Heritage.

Jackson, D.A. 1976. The excavation of Neolithic and Bronze Age sites at Aldwincle, Northants, 1967-71. *Northamptonshire Archaeology* 11: 12-70.

Kinnes, I., Schadla-Hall, T., Chadwick, P. and Dean, P. 1983. Duggleby Howe reconsidered. *Archaeological Journal* 140: 83-108.

Lawson, A. J. 1986. The excavation of a ring-ditch at Bowthorpe, Norwich, 1979. In A.J. Lawson (ed.) *Barrow Excavations in Norfolk, 1950-82.* Gressenhall: East Anglian Archaeology 29. 20-49.

Linden, M. van der, undated. Perpetuating traditions, changing ideologies: the Bell Beaker culture in the British Isles and its implications for the Indo-European problem. In M.E. Huld, K. Jones-Bley, A. Della Volpe and M.R. Dexter (eds) *Proceedings of the 12th Annual UCLA Indo-European Conference, Journal of Indo-European Studies Monograph* 40. Washington: Journal of Indo-European Studies. 269-286.

Longworth, I.H. 1984. Collared *Urns of the Bronze Age in Great Britain and Ireland.* Cambridge: Cambridge University Press.

Loveday, R. 2002. Duggleby Howe revisited. *Oxford Journal of Archaeology* 21: 135-46.

Loveday, R. 2006. *Inscribed Across the Landscape. The Cursus enigma.* Stroud: Tempus.

Loveday, R., Gibson, A.M. Marshall, P.D., Bayliss, A., Bronk-Ramsey, C., and van der Plicht, H. Forthcoming. Antler maceheads - radiocarbon results. *Proceedings of the Prehistoric Society* 1997.

Lynch, F. 1991. *Prehistoric Anglesey.* Second edition. Llangefni: Anglesey Antiquarian Society.

Marsden, B.M. 1970. The excavation of the Bee Low round cairn, Youlgreave, Derbyshire. *Antiquaries Journal* 50: 186-215.

McKinley, J. 1989. Cremations: expectations, methodologies and realities. In C.A. Roberts, F. Lee and J. Bintliff (eds) *Burial Archaeology: current research, methods and developments.* Oxford: BAR (British series) 211. 65-76.

McKinley, J. 1997. Bronze Age 'barrows' and funerary rites and rituals of cremation. *Proceedings of the Prehistoric Society* 63: 129 – 145.

Mercer, R. and Healy, F. forthcoming. *Hambledon Hill, Dorset, England. Excavation and survey of a Neolithic monument complex and its surrounding landscape.* Swindon: English Heritage.

Miket, R.F. 1985. Ritual Enclosures at Whitton Hill, Northumberland. *Proceedings of the Prehistoric Society* 51: 137–48.

Morgan, F. de M. 1959. The excavation of a long barrow at Nutbane, Hants. *Proceedings of the Prehistoric Society* 25: 15-51.

Mortimer, J.R. 1905. *Forty Years' Researches into British and Saxon Burial Mounds of East Yorkshire.* London: Brown and Sons.

Nash, E.F. 2004. An *Investigation of Burial Practices in Scotland, 2500-1500BC.* Unpublished BSc thesis, Dept of Archaeological Sciences, University of Bradford.

Needham, S. 1996. Chronology and periodisation in the British Bronze Age. In K. Randsborg (ed.) Absolute Chronology: archaeological Europe 2500-500 BC. *Acta Archaeologia Supplementa* 1: 121-140.

Needham, S., Bronk Ramsay, C., Coombs, D., Cartwright, C. and Pettitt, P. 1997. An independant chronology for British Bronze Age metalwork: the results of the Oxford radiocarbon accelerator programme. *Archaeological Journal* 154: 55-107.

Newman, T.G. and Miket, R.F. 1973. A dagger grave at Allerwash, Newborough, Northumberland. Archaeologia Aeliana 1(5th ser.): 87-95.

Perkins, D. undated. Two Evaluations: Dumpton Gap and South Dumpton Down, Broadstairs. Broadstairs: Thanet Trust for Archaeology.

Perkins, D. and Gibson, A., 1990. A Beaker burial from Manston, near Ramsgate. *Archaeologia Cantiana,* 108, 11-27.

Petersen, F. 1972. Traditions of multiple burial in later Neolithic and Early Bronze Age Britain. Archaeological Journal 129: 22-55.

Petersen, F. and Healy, F. 1986. The excavation of two round barrows and a ditched enclosure on Weasenham Lyngs, 1972. In A.J. Lawson (ed.) *Barrow Excavations in Norfolk, 1950-82.* Gressenhall: East Anglian Archaeology, 29. 70-103.

Petersen, F., Shepherd, I.A.G. and Tuckwell, A.N., 1974. A short cist at Horsburgh Castle Farm, Peebleshire. *Proceedings of the Society of Antiquaries of Scotland* 105 (1972 – 4): 43–62.

Piggott, S. 1954. *The Neolithic Cultures of the British Isles.* Cambridge: Cambridge University Press.

Robertson-Mackay, M.E. 1980. A 'head and hoofs' burial beneath a round barrow with other Neolithic and Bronze Age sites on Hemp Knoll, near Avebury, Wiltshire. *Proceedings of the Prehistoric Society* 46: 123-176.

Russell, M. 2002. *Prehistoric Sussex.* Stroud: Tempus.

Saville, A. 1990. *Hazelton North. The Excavation of a Neolithic Long cairn of the Cotswold-Severn Group.* London: English Heritage.

Sheridan, A. Forthcoming. Dating the Scottish Bronze Age: 'there is clearly much that the material can still tell us'. In C. Burgess, P. Topping and F. Lynch (eds) *Beyond Stonehenge.* Oxford: Oxbow. 162 – 85.

Smith, I.F. 1965. *Windmill Hill and Avebury. Excavations by Alexander Keiller 1925-1939.* Oxford: Clarendon Press

Speak, S. and Burgess, C. 1999. Meldon Bridge: a centre of the third millennium BC in Peeblesshire. *Proceedings of the Society of Antiquaries of Scotland* 129: 1-118.

Thomas, J. 1999. *Understanding the Neolithic.* London: Routledge.

Thomas, N. 1965. A double Beaker burial on Bredon Hill, Worcestershire. *Birmingham Archaeological Society Transactions and Proceedings* 82: 58-76.

Toots, H. 1965. Sequence of disarticulation in mammalian skeletons. *University of Wyoming Contributions to Geology* 4: 37-39.

Vyner, B. 1984 The Excavation of a Neolithic Cairn at Street House, Loftus, Cleveland. *Proceedings of the Prehistoric Society* 50: 151-96.

Warrilow, W., Owen, G. and Britnell, W. 1986. Eight ring-ditches at Four Crosses, Lalndyssilio, Powys, 1981-85. *Proceedings of the Prehistoric Society* 52: 53-88.

Watkins, T. 1982. The excavation of an Early Bronze Age cemetery at Barns Farm, Dalgetty, Fife. *Proceedings of the Society of Antiquaries of Scotland* 112: 48-141.

Windell, D. 1989. A late Neolithic 'ritual focus' at West Cotton, Northamptonshire. In A.M. Gibson (ed) *Midlands Prehistory. Some Recent and Current Researches into the Prehistory of Central England.* Oxford: BAR (British Series) 204. 85-94.

Woodward, A. 2000. *British Barrows: a matter of life and death.* Stroud: Tempus.

Chapter 8

Foragers, farmers or foreigners?
An assessment of dietary strontium isotope variation in
Middle Neolithic and Early Bronze Age East Yorkshire

Janet Montgomery[‡], Rachel E. Cooper[‡] and Jane A. Evans[+]

[‡]Department of Archaeological Sciences, University of Bradford, Bradford, West Yorkshire BD7 1DP, UK
[+]NERC Isotope Geosciences Laboratory, British Geological Survey, Keyworth, Nottinghamshire, NG12 5GG, UK

Introduction

One of the aims of the Beaker People Project is to address the question of whether the Beaker phenomenon involved a large-scale migration of people to the British Isles. However, there are still many unanswered questions concerning the mobility of *indigenous* peoples at this time and the advent of sedentary agriculturalism in Britain. Whittle (1997: 15) contrasts the *"attention which has been paid to modelling mobility in hunter-gatherer societies with the lack of discussion of kinds of settlement mobility and sedentism in the British ...Neolithic and Early Bronze Age"*. When, for example, did settlement in permanent houses and subsistence on farm-sized areas of land become the predominant economic practice and did this change take place at different times in different regions? Did it, as Thomas (1999) has argued, only become fully established in the middle to late Bronze Age? The aim of this pilot study was to investigate whether subsistence strategies based on different dietary and mobility practices (as distinct from simply trying to identify people originating from elsewhere), can be identified using multiple isotope analysis. The pilot study was carried out in the Yorkshire Wolds, one of the Beaker People Project's main areas of focus, on individuals excavated by J.R. Mortimer in the 19th century (Mortimer 1905) from Middle Neolithic and Early Bronze Age barrows (Figure 8.1). The Middle Neolithic burials, from Duggleby Howe (Towthorpe 273) and Callis Wold 275, date to the late 4th millennium BC whilst the Early Bronze Age burials (including those of the Beaker period) date to *c.* 2400-1700 cal BC. Here we present only the strontium isotope results of a multi-isotope pilot study.

In recent years there have been a burgeoning number of studies that have successfully used strontium isotope analysis (Bentley *et al.* 2004; Cox and Sealy 1997; Ezzo and Price 2002; Grupe *et al.* 1997; Montgomery *et al.* 2000, 2003; Price *et al.* 2000; 2004; Schweissing and Grupe 2003a and b) to demonstrate differences between ancient human individuals and populations that we assume arose through eating food sourced from different geological (and hence geographical) regions. Tooth enamel appears to be the material of choice as it is a highly mineralized, acellular, biogenic apatite that is particularly resistant to post-mortem contamination and thus preserves the integrity of lifetime signatures (Budd *et al.* 2000; Hoppe *et al.* 2003; Montgomery 2002; Trickett *et al.* 2003). The $^{87}Sr/^{86}Sr$ value of enamel is a weighted average derived from the food and water ingested when the tissue was mineralizing in childhood.

The isotope ratio of strontium in different types of rocks varies considerably in a known manner dependent on age and lithology (Faure 1986). Geological strontium enters the biosphere through soil, water and plants and is ingested by animals; the majority of the body's burden is deposited in the teeth and bones. The relative amounts of the isotopes of strontium do not alter in any measurable way as the element is transferred through this chain (Blum *et al.* 2000; Graustein 1989; Graustein and Armstrong 1983) and this provides the mechanism by which we can link a human to the place where they obtained their food and drink. It is, however, important to remember that this type of analysis is an exclusive one; that is, it can rule out places but there will most likely be many possible homelands that fit the isotope profile obtained from an archaeological skeleton. Some will be nearer than others and some may make no archaeological sense but, on its own, strontium isotope analysis cannot discriminate between them. Moreover, for a skeleton that is consistent with the local population, the most parsimonious explanation would suggest a local origin but the result cannot exclude origins on similar geology in distant places.

In archaeological populations, we are more inclined to infer that people moved from one food source to another either by a permanent or temporary change in residence. An alternative explanation, and one that happens to a very great extent for some modern populations, is that the food was transported to them. Clearly, if the natural link between where a person lives and the place they obtained the bulk of their food and drink is severed in this way, strontium isotope analysis is not going to give the 'right' answer. If large amounts of grain were exported from Orkney to Iceland, for example, indigenous Icelanders who may never have set foot in a boat, would become 'isotopic aliens' in their own land. Of course, in regions of highly variable geology, it is possible to exploit food resources with different strontium values without having to travel very far at all. It may, as illustrated in Figure 8.2, be possible to have a permanent base and grow crops on

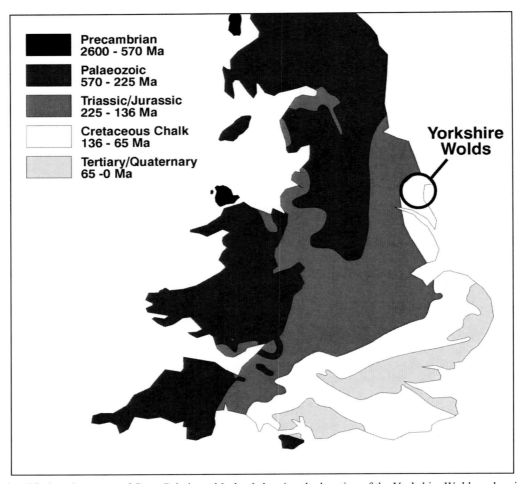

Figure 8.1. Simplified geology map of Great Britain and Ireland showing the location of the Yorkshire Wolds and major geological divisions pertinent to this study.

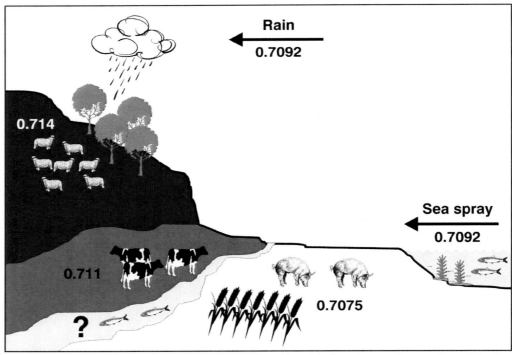

Figure 8.2. Schematic model of the possible sources of strontium that, if exploited, could contribute to the weighted average ratio of human enamel in Yorkshire.

one type of rock whilst grazing animals on one quite different, and at the same time exploiting marine or coastal resources.

Although it has changed over geological time, the $^{87}Sr/^{86}Sr$ value of modern seawater in the world's oceans is ~0.7092 (McArthur et al. 2001): the result of both the long residence and consequent thorough mixing of strontium in the oceans (Libes 1992). Hence, anything that comes out of the sea - for example, fish, mammals, seaweed, seaspray, seasplash and shell-sand such as machair - has a strontium isotope value of ~0.7092 (Figure 8.2). In coastal maritime regions, rainwater will have a similar strontium isotope ratio to seawater, its source. This, however, does vary in regions further from the coast because dust becomes incorporated in clouds as they travel over land and the ratio of the rain can decrease or increase depending on the land mass over which it travels (Åberg 1995; Capo et al. 1998; Land et al. 2000; Negrel and Roy 1998). It can also change seasonally given rain patterns and wind speeds. For example, rainwater in the Central Massif region of Southern France varies throughout the year from 0.7091 to 0.7106 but has a weighted annual mean value of 0.7094 (Negrel and Roy 1998).

The Yorkshire Wolds are formed of Cretaceous Chalk and have virtually no drift deposits and one, intermittent, water source: the Gypsey Race. Chalk is a notably homogeneous rock (Ager 1961) composed of the shells of sea-creatures that inhabited the oceans during the Late Cretaceous and records $^{87}Sr/^{86}Sr$ ratios between 0.7075 and 0.7078 (McArthur et al. 2001). Direct analyses of Chalk, Chalk-derived soils and water from Chalk aquifers in England have provided $^{87}Sr/^{86}Sr$ ratios from 0.7075 to 0.7077 (Evans et al. 2006; Montgomery 2002; Montgomery et al. 2005; Montgomery et al. 2006). According to a simple two-component model for maritime islands such as Britain (Montgomery et al. 2004; Montgomery and Evans 2006), a community subsisting entirely on food sourced from a Chalk substrate plus an input from rainwater should have strontium isotope ratios that fall between ~0.7075 to ~0.7092. In Figure 8.2, the lowlands have a strontium ratio of 0.7075, the lowest value recorded for Cretaceous Chalk. People living and farming on the Wolds could grow crops that are watered by rain and perhaps keep some domestic animals close by. They may have access to a spring water source and its strontium isotope ratio would reflect the host rocks and be likely to remain constant through time (Negrel et al. 1997). For example, 'Hildon' mineral water sourced from the Cretaceous Chalk in Hampshire has a $^{87}Sr/^{86}Sr$ ratio of 0.7077 (Montgomery et al. 2006).

Moving further inland in Figure 8.2, there is a region with a higher strontium ratio of 0.711 and, beyond that, uplands with a strontium ratio of 0.714. If these were heterogeneous rocks such as sandstones or granites, this ratio could indicate the weighted average value obtained

from dissolving a piece of rock or, of arguably more use when attempting to characterise biosphere values (Price et al. 2002), the value of the strontium released from the rock into the soil by weathering, which is likely to be dominated by the more soluble calcite and feldspar (Åberg 1995; Bau et al. 2004; Blum et al. 1993; Evans and Tatham 2004; Jacobson and Blum 2000). Although Figure 8.2 is somewhat simplistic, a similar sequence of progressively older and more radiogenic (higher $^{87}Sr/^{86}Sr$) rocks are found moving westwards from the Wolds to the Pennines, passing through sedimentary Jurassic and Permo-Triassic formations into the Palaeozoic rocks of the Coal Measures and the Carboniferous Millstone Grits of the Pennine hills (British Geological Survey 2001). Mineral waters hosted in these rocks show such a progressive increase in $^{87}Sr/^{86}Sr$ with increasing age (Montgomery et al. 2006) as do archaeological populations excavated from these lithologies (Bentley et al. 2004; Evans et al. 2006; Evans and Tatham 2004; Montgomery 2002; Montgomery et al. 2000; Price et al. 2001; 2002; 2004).

The strontium isotope ratio of river water depends on the rocks it is draining, what run-off reaches it, how fast it is running and how much it is raining; these parameters may vary throughout the year and over longer periods of time, if, for example, a river course has changed (Åberg 1995; Capo et al. 1998; Negrel et al. 1988). It is possible that animals and humans may have exploited it as both a source of drinking water and to irrigate crops, and clearly this is a mechanism for introducing 'alien' strontium into the region and thus into the local food chain, although its actual impact on local human strontium ratios may be insignificant.

Thus, in the wider Yorkshire area surrounding the Wolds, we have effectively four main sources of strontium (or end-members) that can contribute to diet:

- the lowest value of 0.7075 from the Chalk;
- higher values of 0.711 to 0.714 depending how far people ranged at the other extreme;
- values of ~0.7092 from the sea and rainwater.

The amount of strontium each of these provides to the biosphere, the amount of food sourced from each place and what types of food these are, will control how much each source region contributes to the strontium in tooth enamel. For example, meat – either terrestrial or marine – does not appear to be a rich source of strontium for several reasons (Burton and Wright 1995; Elias 1980) and, if even a small amount of plant food is eaten, the signal from the meat-derived strontium may be all but invisible. So we could hypothesise that people growing arable crops, grazing animals and living on the Wolds would have enamel strontium ratios dominated by Chalk. If the only other strontium source they exploited was rain or, indeed, marine and coastal resources, such as seaweed – a potentially rich source of plant strontium - for fertilizer, they would have a restricted range of ratios that fall between ~0.7075 and 0.7092.

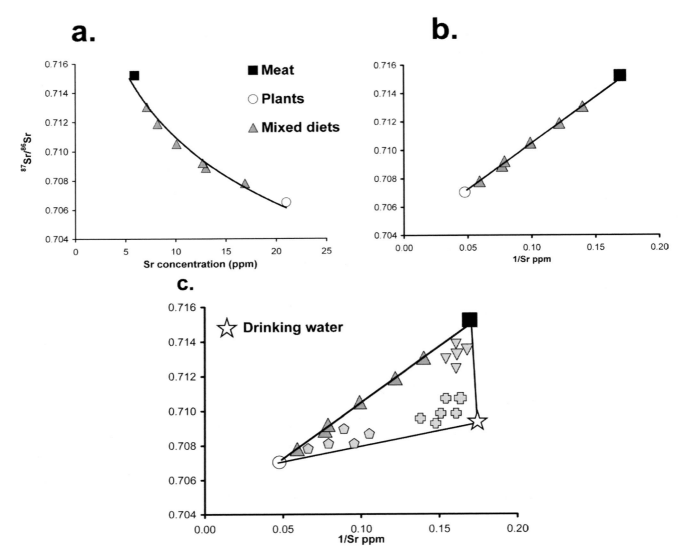

Figure 8.3. Theoretical mixing models for two and three-component diets with known end-members: (a.) shows a mixing curve of a two-component diet of meat and plants; (b.) shows this same diet converted to a straight line by using the inverse of the strontium concentrations; (c.) illustrates the effect of adding a third component, in this case drinking water, which will pull the diets off the line into a triangular field. Diets dominated by meat (inverted triangles), plants (pentagons) and water (crosses) are illustrated. Note these are diets *not* enamel values.

Figure 8.3 presents a model of how the combination of several sources of strontium may affect the isotope ratio and the concentration of the resulting diet. A simple two-component diet of meat and plants sourced from very different types of rock is plotted in Figure 8.3a. The meat has a high ratio and a low concentration, and plants a low ratio and a high concentration. Diets composed of different amounts of the two foods will define a mixing curve which can be converted into a linear array by plotting the inverse (1/Sr) of the concentration (Figure 8.3b). If a third dietary end-member is added (Figure 8.3c) this will have the effect of pulling the diets off the line. The proportions of the three end-members in different diets will control where they plot in this triangular field and Figure 8.3c illustrates diets dominated by meat, plants and water. If more dietary sources are added with different ratios and concentrations they would alter the field and could for example, produce one that is

more circular. We could go on to imagine mono-isotopic diets composed of varying amounts of strontium which would define a horizontal line (such as one based solely on marine foods), or diets of limited variability in either ratio or concentration which would define a tight cluster (e.g. sedentary, highly specialised feeders such as a domestic flock of grass-grazed sheep), or highly eclectic and variable diets that would result in a very diffuse cloud (e.g. mobile, far-ranging opportunistic foragers such as hunter-gatherers). It is, however, difficult to imagine a diet from isotopically varied sources that would nonetheless contribute identical amounts of strontium, so a vertical line would be much less likely.

It is important to note, of course, that these are not the measured enamel values but the values of the food and water that are ingested and imbibed. If a bag of grain and a haunch of beef are mixed together and divided unequally amongst a group of people, no strontium is going to be lost; but we are measuring tooth enamel and, before we can do that, strontium has to be transported from the mouth into the enamel. We know that, contrary to light stable isotopes, there is no measurable change in the *isotope ratio* of strontium in the human body but, when all the metabolic processes strontium is subject to prior to deposition in the skeleton are considered, it is very hard to understand how the relationship between the ratio and the amount of strontium ingested is maintained. A further complication is that the bioavailability of dietary strontium is not the same for all types of food. For example, meat and milk are not only very low in strontium but strontium uptake is suppressed in protein- or calcium-rich diets, whereas a vegetarian diet is strontium-rich, and strontium uptake is enhanced by high-fibre diets (Aufderheide 1989; Burton and Wright 1995; Ezzo 1994; Underwood 1977). Consequently, omnivores such as humans will obtain the majority of their strontium from plants, with a smaller input being derived from animal sources (Burton and Price 2000; Elias 1980). Omnivores may eat more meat than plants, but it is likely to be the plants that will contribute more strontium to the skeleton, and the skeletal isotope ratio will, therefore, be more sensitive to this part of the diet. Moreover, we cannot assume that the amount of strontium that is eaten from different food groups is reflected in any *linear* way in the amount measured in tooth enamel although it does appear to be the case that bone-strontium concentrations are dose-dependent (Boivin *et al.* 1996; Price *et al.* 1986). In foodwebs there is a decrease in skeletal strontium concentrations with increasing trophic level, if for no other reason than that most of the body's strontium is in the bones and not the meat (Blum *et al.* 2000; Burton and Wright 1995). There is thus no reason to suppose that, if the percentage proportion of strontium *ingested* from meat : plants : water is 30:60:10, this will be directly reflected in the skeleton. However, for linear dietary mixing relationships, such as that modelled in Figure 8.3b, to be seen in the measured enamel of a group of individuals, both the ratio *and* the concentration of the original diet must be at least *reflected* in the tissue (Montgomery and Evans 2006).

Method and materials

Samples were of core enamel only. Once childhood tooth mineralization is complete, core enamel is resistant to subsequent isotopic or elemental changes either during an individual's lifetime or during burial, whereas dentine equilibrates with the burial environment (Bocherens *et al.* 1994; Budd *et al.* 2000; Glimcher *et al.* 1990; Hoppe *et al.* 2003; Montgomery 2002). To remove soil-derived particulate on the tooth surface, all enamel surfaces were abraded to a depth >100μm with acid-cleaned, tungsten carbide dental burrs. All adhering dentine and enamel-dentine junction tissue were also removed entirely.

All samples were transferred in sealed containers to the Class 100, HEPA-filtered laboratory at the NERC Isotope Geosciences Laboratory (NIGL), Keyworth, UK. Enamel chips were washed ultrasonically in water (Millipore Alpha Q, <1ppb total heavy metal content) to remove adhering particulate. No chemical decontamination was carried out as, due to the high resistance of enamel to post-mortem contamination, changes in the bulk $^{87}Sr/^{86}Sr$ ratio of enamel samples following the use of such procedures has been negligible (Horn *et al.* 1994; Trickett *et al.* 2003). The laboratory procedure used ion exchange chromatography and Teflon-distilled reagents to isolate the strontium prior to instrumental analysis. The full method of preparation and analysis is reported in Cooper (2004). Strontium concentrations and compositions were obtained by thermal-ionisation mass spectrometry (TIMS) using a Finnigan Mat 262 multi-collector mass spectrometer. $^{87}Sr/^{86}Sr$ was normalized to a NBS 987 value of 0.710250. The strontium contribution from within-run laboratory blanks was negligible. External reproducibility was estimated at ±0.004% (2σ).

Results

The Neolithic and Early Bronze Age samples show almost total overlap in both strontium concentration and $^{87}Sr/^{86}Sr$ ratios (Figure 8.4). Some individuals from both periods have ratios that fall between the Chalk and rainwater end-members, conforming to a simple two-source model of a Wolds-based diet. The range of the Wolds dataset is very similar to the spread of data obtained from individuals dating from the Neolithic to the 7th century AD from West Heslerton (Montgomery 2002; Montgomery *et al.* 2005) on the northern edge of the Wolds (Figure 8.5). This suggests they are consistent with the strontium signatures of humans inhabiting this region. However, the structure of the Neolithic and Bronze Age data sets differs markedly. The Bronze Age individuals split into two groups, both of which form discrete linear arrays (or mixing lines), labelled A and B in Figure 8.4. As illustrated in Figures 8.3a and 8.3b, such arrays occur when the samples contain various combinations of just two sources of strontium which have different ratios and concentrations (Faure 1986). In contrast, the Neolithic individuals form a diffuse cloud of data points with $^{87}Sr/^{86}Sr$ values ranging between 0.7079 and 0.7102. In other words, not all the individuals conform to our model of a simple two-source, Wolds-based diet sourced from Chalk and rainwater. The lack of a direct linear relationship between the samples implies the presence of more than two end-members as shown in Figure 8.3c.

The Early Bronze Age skeletons
The individuals that form the Bronze Age mixing line B conform to the model of a simple two-source diet, with Chalk and rainwater end-members, and these individuals are consistent with a group who lived and farmed on the Wolds. An alternative upper end-member would be the Permo-Triassic and Jurassic sedimentary rocks to the north and west of the Wolds (Figure 8.1) as terrestrial $^{87}Sr/^{86}Sr$ ratios >0.7086 have been obtained from the

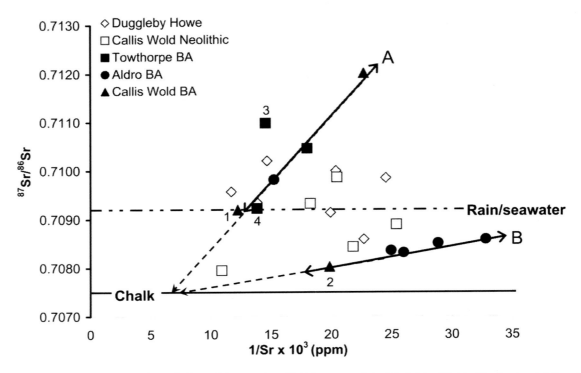

Figure 8.4. Human enamel data from Neolithic and Bronze Age (BA) barrows of the Yorkshire Wolds. The horizontal lines indicate possible end-members: the dashed line is seawater and an approximation for rainwater (~0.7092); the solid line on which both mixing lines may converge is the value for English Cretaceous Chalk (Evans *et al.* 2006; McArthur *et al.* 2001; Montgomery 2002; Montgomery *et al.* 2005). Solid mixing lines link all but one (symbol 3) of the Bronze Age individuals and the dashed extensions appear to converge on a Chalk end-member. For the upper mixing line (A), $r^2 = 0.9789$, for the lower mixing line (B), $r^2 = 0.9364$. Symbols 1 and 2 are early (1), and late (2), forming teeth from the same individual. Symbols 3 and 4 are the only individuals analysed identified by Mortimer (Mortimer 1905) as being of possible female sex. 2σ errors are within symbol.

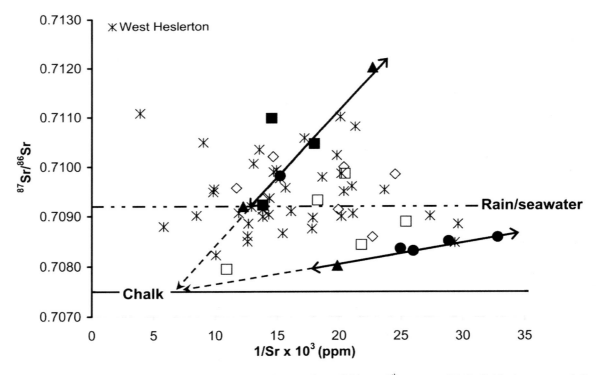

Figure 8.5. Comparison between the Yorkshire Wolds dataset and Neolithic to 7th century AD individuals excavated from the northern edge of the Wolds at West Heslerton. 2σ errors are within symbol. Data from Montgomery *et al.* 2005.

plants, soils and mineral waters in these regions (Evans and Tatham 2004; Montgomery 2002; Montgomery *et al.* 2005; Montgomery *et al.* 2006). Marine strontium would also provide such a value but this is not supported by the carbon and nitrogen isotope data (Mandy Jay pers. comm.). This group contains four individuals from Aldro 116, together with the later-forming third molar tooth from a male skeleton excavated at Callis Wold 23. The earlier-forming canine tooth from this individual falls on line A, suggesting a change in dietary source, and possibly group affiliation, sometime between the ages of 6 and 12 (Hillson 1996). The central, and possibly primary (Mortimer 1905), male burial from Aldro 116 falls on Line A, in contrast to the other individuals excavated from this barrow.

Line A requires an upper end-member greater than 0.712. To date, there is little evidence that such values can be obtained from the biosphere overlying the Permo-Triassic and Jurassic sedimentary deposits immediately to the north and west of the Chalk but there is some evidence that such values may be obtained from the Palaeozoic Carboniferous rocks which lie further to the west (Evans and Tatham 2004; Montgomery 2002; Montgomery *et al.* 2005; 2006). Contenders for the lower end-member for Line A are rainwater or Jurassic sedimentary rocks as noted above. However, given that this lower end-member is associated with high enamel concentrations, it is probably more likely to be the plant component of the diet that provides it, rather than simply drinking water. It is possible that, as suggested by the dashed line in Figure 8.4, the lower end-member for both Line A and Line B is Chalk, particularly as both lines appear to converge on such a value and if, given the fact that the barrows were located on the Wolds, we can assume the excavated individuals had some childhood connection with the region. Another explanation for the presence of converging linear arrays is that they were produced by differential *post mortem* incorporation of strontium from the Chalk burial environment, although it would be difficult to argue that diagenesis would only affect the Bronze Age samples in this manner. Evidence that they are not diagenetic artefacts is presented elsewhere (Montgomery *et al.* 2004; Montgomery and Evans 2006; Montgomery *et al.* in press).

Tooth enamel contains strontium that was ingested over a specific and restricted period of time during childhood when the tooth analysed was mineralizing. It is, therefore, unlikely that either of these two Bronze Age groups represent the arrival of a single wave of 'immigrants' to the Wolds from a region of higher strontium values because, by coincidence, they would all have had to have made the move whilst the specific tooth chosen for analysis was mineralizing. If they were immigrants, we would expect to see a discrete cluster of individuals all with high strontium ratios. In human terms, therefore, the Early Bronze Age data is consistent with each group procuring resources *from only two* sources of strontium and a different mix of these two strontium inputs has

resulted in enamel samples which contain various mixtures of the two sources (Figure 8.3). Such variation could arise in a sedentary population, moving through necessity with the seasonal availability of resources, personal food preferences or restrictions or, given the imprecision inherent in archaeological dating, due to gradual change over longer timescales. It could also indicate seasonal or shorter-term relocation of a group of individuals between two localities: the precise timing and duration of human enamel mineralization, as distinct from whole tooth crown formation, is not currently well established but strontium may well be incorporated over months to years depending on which tooth is analysed (Montgomery and Evans 2006).

The Middle Neolithic skeletons
No linear relationship between the Neolithic individuals sampled seems to be present and the distribution of the data is indicative of resources having been procured from more than two strontium sources (Figure 8.6). This would be consistent with many forms of mobility such as circulating, residential or tethered (Whittle 1997), and suggests that the Neolithic population of the Wolds were eclectic and opportunistic in their exploitation of resources and that they foraged over a wider geographical area beyond the Wolds. Conversely, it could simply indicate diverse origins and a lack of group affiliation between the individuals analysed from Duggleby Howe and Callis Wold 275. However, whether they have group affiliation or not, Figure 8.6 suggests it would be difficult to conclude that their strontium compositions are inconsistent with other Neolithic and Bronze Age individuals excavated from Chalk burial sites elsewhere in England. Although one individual from West Heslerton is clearly different, the rest appear to define a triangular field of data with three end-members as illustrated theoretically in Figure 8.3c, with the Bronze Age individuals restricted to two sides of the triangle. Figure 8.6 suggests that Chalk (providing a higher concentration of strontium) and rain/seawater (providing a lower concentration of strontium) constitute two of the three end-members with an unknown radiogenic third end-member.

Discussion and conclusions

For the Yorkshire Wolds study, the archaeological dating and funerary evidence accords well with the strontium isotope evidence; the types of evidence independently separate the individuals into the same two period-based groups. Although the *range* of strontium ratios and concentrations are similar, the *structure* within the two datasets is very different. The Early Bronze Age individuals separate into two linear arrays whilst, in complete contrast, the Middle Neolithic individuals form a loose cluster of points. Linear arrays indicate that the isotope ratio and the concentration of strontium in enamel was very closely controlled by the two geological sources providing the dietary strontium. From a geochemical perspective, linear arrays are highly unlikely to arise from

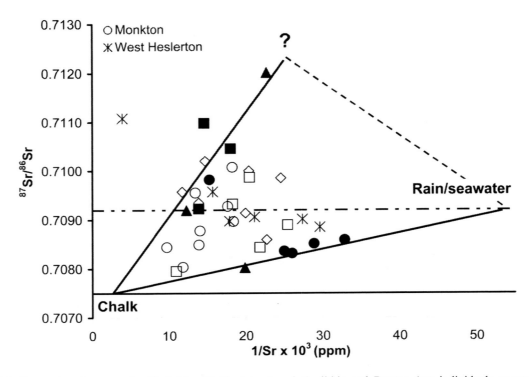

Figure 8.6. Comparison between the Yorkshire Wolds dataset and Neolithic and Bronze Age individuals excavated from West Heslerton and the Chalk site at Monkton-up-Wimborne, Dorset. A triangular field of data is indicated with Chalk and rainwater end-members. The upper end-member is unknown. 2σ errors are within symbol. Data from Montgomery *et al.* 2005 and Montgomery *et al.* 2000.

Barrow	Period	Burial	Age[1]	Sex[1]	Tooth
Towthorpe 273	Middle Neo	72/G	Adult	M	second incisor
(Duggleby Howe)		73/I	Adult	M	second molar
		69/C	Adult	M	first premolar
		74/K	Adult	M	first premolar
		76/M	Adult	M	second premolar
		72/H	Juvenile	n/k	dec. second molar
		75/L	Adult	M	first premolar
Callis Wold 275	Middle Neo	7	Adult	M	second premolar
		9	Adult	M	second molar
		8?	Adult	M	first premolar
		3	Adult	M	first premolar
		?	Adult	M	first premolar
Mixing line A					
Callis Wold 23	EBA		Adult	M	canine
Callis Wold 100	EBA	2	Adult	M	first premolar
Towthorpe 3	EBA		Adult	F?	second molar
Towthorpe 72	EBA		Adult	M	second premolar
Towthorpe 73	EBA		Adult	F?	canine
Aldro 116	EBA	6	Adult	M	second premolar
Mixing line B					
Aldro 116	EBA	2	Adult	M	first premolar
Aldro 116	EBA	5	Juvenile	n/k	first molar
Aldro 116	EBA	3	Adult	M	second premolar
Aldro 116	EBA	4	Juvenile	M	canine
Callis Wold 23	EBA		Adult	M	third molar

Table 8.1. Skeletons analysed for this study. Source of ageing and sexing information: Mortimer (1905).

co-incidence. As Faure (1986: 143) asserts: *"The goodness of fit of the data points to a straight line is a test for the validity of the mixing hypothesis and of the assumption that neither the Sr concentrations nor the $^{87}Sr/^{86}Sr$ ratios were modified after mixing had occurred"*. He is not writing about biological organisms, but the Bronze Age individuals do indeed appear to be strongly related in such a simple binary relationship that can be explained through access to food and water that derives from two, and only two, sources of strontium. Given the discrepancy we might expect between the strontium concentration in the diet of an individual and the resulting concentration in their enamel, the extremely good fit of the human samples on the mixing lines is very interesting and suggests some degree of control and rigidity in the food procurement strategy, whether based on subsistence or culture, by the individuals on a line. It must, however, be remembered that quite different sources of strontium (e.g. sedimentary rock and modern seawater) may have the same $^{87}Sr/^{86}Sr$ ratio and that, whilst geochemically these may be identical, archaeologically the difference may be important. Nonetheless, given the controls that must be exerted over not only the isotope ratio but also the concentration in order to obtain such a linear array, it seems likely that individuals who define such an array were following a rigid, formalized dietary strategy. It also suggests group affiliation, particularly in the case of the four individuals from Aldro 116. Moreover, the movement from one group to another around or prior to puberty by the male individual excavated from Callis Wold 23 (Symbols 1 and 2 in Figure 8.4), could indicate that these two Bronze Age groups were roughly contemporary.

The data for Line A are consistent with the group visiting the Wolds, either regularly or seasonally, as children, perhaps as a family group. It would support the continued use in the Early Bronze Age of such ceremonial complexes as 'social glue' to: *"hold communities together, and to provide people with regular opportunities to gather, meet potential wives or husbands, exchange livestock and prestige goods…"* (Pryor 2003: 256). However, such a linear array may also be produced by a controlled food procurement strategy. The group could, for example, have eaten grain grown on the Wolds, a region of fertile arable land (Kinnes *et al.* 1983), whilst grazing animals on higher land to the west either all year round or following a strategy of fixed, as opposed to nomadic, transhumance. Such long distance movement of livestock in the Early Bronze Age is likely to have preceded the development of the extensive networks of droveways which dominate large areas of the British landscape in the Middle and Late Bronze Age (Pryor 2003).

Whittle (1997:19) has suggested that we should: *"envisage a very long sequence encompassing the Early and Late Neolithic and the Early Bronze Age, characterised by mobility throughout, declining perhaps in certain foci in the Late Neolithic and becoming more formalised in some areas in the Early Bronze Age"*. We believe that the isotope data presented here support the model of greater restriction and formalisation of mobility, and perhaps landscape, in the Early Bronze Age.

Acknowledgements

We are grateful to Martin Foreman, Graham Myers, Craig Barclay and Bryan Sitch at the Hull and East Riding Museum for providing permission to sample the Mortimer collection and Mike Parker Pearson and Alex Gibson for enlightening discussions. JM acknowledges the support of the NERC through the award of a Fellowship NER/1/S/2002/00691.

References

Åberg, G. 1995. The use of natural strontium isotopes as tracers in environmental studies. *Water, Air and Soil Pollution* 79: 309-322.

Ager, D.V. 1961. *Introducing Geology*. London: Faber and Faber.

Aufderheide, A.C. 1989. Chemical analysis of skeletal remains. In M.Y. Iscan and K.A.R. Kennedy (eds) *Reconstruction of Life from the Skeleton*. New York: Alan R. Liss, Inc.

Bau, M., Alexander, B., Chesley, J.T., Dulski, P. and Brantley, S.L. 2004. Mineral dissolution in the Cape Cod aquifer, Massachusetts, USA: I. Reaction stoichiometry and impact of accessory feldspar and glauconite on strontium isotopes, solute concentrations, and REY distribution. *Geochimica et Cosmochimica Acta* 68: 1199-1216.

Bentley, R.A., Price, T.D. and Stephan, E. 2004. Determining the 'local' Sr-87/Sr-86 range for archaeological skeletons: a case study from Neolithic Europe. *Journal of Archaeological Science* 31: 365-375.

Blum, J.D., Erel, Y. and Brown, K. 1993. Sr-87/Sr-86 Ratios of Sierra-Nevada Stream Waters - Implications for Relative Mineral Weathering Rates. *Geochimica et Cosmochimica Acta* 57: 5019-5025.

Blum, J.D., Taliaferro, E.H., Weisse, M.T. and Holmes, R.T. 2000. Changes in Sr/Ca, Ba/Ca and $^{87}Sr/^{86}Sr$ ratios between trophic levels in two forest ecosystems in the northeastern U.S.A. *Biogeochemistry* 49: 87-101.

Bocherens, H., Brinkman, D.B., Dauphin, Y. and Mariotti, A. 1994. Microstructural and geochemical investigations on Late Cretaceous archosaur teeth from Alberta, Canada. *Canadian Journal of Earth Sciences* 31: 783-792.

Boivin, G., Deloffre, P., Perrat, B., Panczer, G., Boudeulle, M. Mauras, Y., Allain, P. Tsouderos, Y. and Meunier, P.J. 1996. Strontium distribution and interactions with bone mineral in monkey iliac bone after strontium salt (S 12911) administration. *Journal of Bone and Mineral Research* 11: 1302-1311.

British Geological Survey. 2001. *Solid Geology Map UK South Sheet*. Southampton: Ordnance Survey/NERC.

Budd, P., Montgomery, J., Barreiro, B. and Thomas, R.G. 2000. Differential diagenesis of strontium in archaeological human dental tissues. *Applied Geochemistry* 15: 687-694.

Burton, J.H. and Price, T.D. 2000. The use and abuse of trace elements for palaeodietary research (trans.) M.J. Aitken, E.V. Sayre and R.E. Taylor. In S. Ambrose and M.A. Katzenberg (eds) *Biogeochemical Approaches to Palaeodietary Analysis*. Advances in Archaeological and Museum Science. New York: Kluwer Academic/Plenum.

Burton, J.H. and Wright, L.E.. 1995. Nonlinearity in the relationship between bone Sr/Ca and diet: paleodietary implications. *American Journal of Physical Anthropology* 96: 273-282.

Capo, R.C., Stewart, B.W. and Chadwick, O.A.. 1998. Strontium isotopes as tracers of ecosystem processes: theory and methods. *Geoderma* 82: 197-225.

Cooper, R.E. 2004. *An Assessment of Dietary Strontium Isotope Variation in Neolithic and Bronze Age East Yorkshire*. M.Sc.: University of Bradford.

Cox, G. and Sealy, J.C. 1997. Investigating identity and life histories: isotopic analysis and historical documentation of slave skeletons found on the Cape Town Foreshore, South Africa. *International Journal of Historical Archaeology* 1: 207-224.

Elias, M. 1980. The feasibility of dental strontium analysis for diet-assessment of human populations. *American Journal of Physical Anthropology* 53: 1-4.

Evans, J., Stoodley, N. and Chenery, C. 2006. A strontium and oxygen isotope assessment of a possible fourth century immigrant population in a Hampshire cemetery, southern England. *Journal of Archaeological Science* 33: 265-272.

Evans, J.A. and Tatham, S. 2004. Defining "local signature" in terms of Sr isotope composition using a tenth-twelfth century Anglo-Saxon population living on a Jurassic clay-carbonate terrain, Rutland, UK. In K. Pye and D.J. Croft (eds) *Forensic Geoscience: principles, techniques and applications*. London: Geological Society of London Special Publication.

Ezzo, J.A. 1994. Putting the "Chemistry" Back into Archaeological Bone Chemistry Analysis - Modeling Potential Paleodietary Indicators. *Journal of Anthropological Archaeology* 13: 1-34.

Ezzo, J.A. and Price, T.D. 2002. Migration, regional reorganization, and spatial group composition at Grasshopper Pueblo, Arizona. *Journal of Archaeological Science* 29: 499-520.

Faure, G. 1986. *Principles of Isotope Geology*. New York: John Wiley and Sons Inc.

Glimcher, M.J., Cohen-Solal, L., Kossiva, D. and de Ricqles, A. 1990. Biochemical analyses of fossil enamel and dentin. *Paleobiology* 16: 219-232.

Graustein, W.C. 1989. [87]Sr/[86]Sr ratios measure the sources and flow of strontium in terrestrial ecosystems (trans.) W.D. Billings, F. Golley, O.L. Lange, J.S. Olson and H. Remmert. In P.W. Rundel, J.R. Ehleringer and K.A. Nagy (eds) *Stable Isotopes in Ecological Research*. Ecological studies. New York: Springer.

Graustein, W.C. and Armstrong, R.L. 1983. The use of strontium-87/strontium-86 ratios to measure transport into forested watersheds. *Science* 219: 289-292.

Grupe, G., Price, T.D., Schröter, P., Söllner, F., Johnson, C.M. and Beard, B.L. 1997. Mobility of Bell Beaker people revealed by strontium isotope ratios of tooth and bone: a study of southern Bavarian skeletal remains. *Applied Geochemistry* 12: 517-525.

Hillson, S. 1996. *Dental Anthropology*. Cambridge: Cambridge University Press.

Hoppe, K.A., Koch, P.L. and Furutani, T.T. 2003. Assessing the preservation of biogenic strontium in fossil bones and tooth enamel. *International Journal of Osteoarchaeology* 13: 20-28.

Horn, P., Hölzl, S. and Storzer, D. 1994. Habitat determination on a fossil stag's mandible from the site of Homo erectus heidelbergenius at Mauer by use of [87]Sr/[86]Sr. *Naturwissenshaften* 81: 360-362.

Jacobson, A.D. and Blum, J.D. 2000. Ca/Sr and Sr-87/Sr-86 geo-chemistry of disseminated calcite in Himalayan silicate rocks from Nanga Parbat: Influence on river-water chemistry (vol 28, og 463, 2000). *Geology* 28: 672-672.

Kinnes, I.A., Schadla-Hall, T., Chadwick, P. and Dean, P. 1983. Duggleby Howe Reconsidered. *Archaeological Journal* 140: 83-108.

Land, M., Ingri, J., Andersson, P.S. and Öhlander, B. 2000. Ba/Sr, Ca/Sr and [87]Sr/[86]Sr ratios in soil water and groundwater: implications for relative contributions to stream water discharge. *Applied Geochemistry* 15: 311-325.

Libes, S.M. 1992. *An Introduction to Marine Biochemistry*. Chichester: John Wiley and Sons.

McArthur, J.M., Howarth, R.J. and Bailey, T.R. 2001. Strontium isotope stratigraphy: LOWESS version 3: best fit to the marine Sr-isotope curve for 0-509 Ma and accompanying look- up table for deriving numerical age. *Journal of Geology* 109: 155-170.

Montgomery, J. 2002. *Lead and Strontium Isotope Compositions of Human Dental Tissues as an Indicator of Ancient Exposure and Population Dynamics*. Ph.D.: University of Bradford.

Montgomery, J., Budd, P. and Evans, J. 2000. Reconstructing the lifetime movements of ancient people: a Neolithic case study from southern England. *European Journal of Archaeology* 3: 407-422.

Montgomery, J., Evans, J. and Cooper, R.E. 2004. Resolving archaeological populations with strontium mixing diagrams. Paper presented to the EGU General Assembly, Vienna, 2004.

Montgomery, J. and Evans, J.A. 2006. Immigrants on the Isle of Lewis - combining traditional funerary and modern isotope evidence to investigate social differentiation, migration and dietary change in the Outer Hebrides of Scotland. In R. Gowland and C. Knüsel (eds) *The Social Archaeology of Funerary Remains*. Oxford: Oxbow.

Montgomery, J., Evans, J.A. and Cooper, R.E. In press. Resolving archaeological populations with Sr-isotope mixing models. *Applied Geochemistry*, (2007), doi:10.1016/j.apgeochem.2007.02.009.

Montgomery, J., Evans, J.A. and Neighbour, T.. 2003. Sr isotope evidence for population movement within the Hebridean Norse community of NW Scotland. *Journal of the Geological Society* 160: 649-653.

Montgomery, J., Evans, J.A., Powlesland, D. and Roberts, C.A. 2005. Continuity or colonization in Anglo-Saxon England? Isotope evidence for mobility, subsistence practice, and status at West Heslerton. *American Journal of Physical Anthropology* 126: 123-138.

Montgomery, J., Evans, J.A. and Wildman, G. 2006. ^{87}Sr/^{86}Sr isotope composition of bottled British mineral waters for environmental and forensic purposes. *Applied Geochemistry* 21: 1626-1634.

Mortimer, J.R. 1905. *Forty Years Researches in British and Saxon Burial Mounds of East Yorkshire*. London: A. Brown and Sons.

Negrel, P., Fouillac, C. and Brach, M. 1997. A strontium isotopic study of mineral and surface waters from the Cezallier (Massif Central, France): Implications for mixing processes in areas of disseminated emergences of mineral waters. *Chemical Geology* 135: 89-101.

Negrel, P. and Roy, S. 1998. Chemistry of rainwater in the Massif Central (France): a strontium isotope and major element study. *Applied Geochemistry* 13: 941-952.

Negrel, P., Seimbille, F. and Allegre, C.J. 1988. Quantitative Modelization of Differential Erosion between Crystalline and Sedimentary Area of a French Basin by Isotopic Analysis of Strontium in River Waters. *Chemical Geology* 70: 13-13.

Price, T.D., Bentley, R.A., Lüning, J., Gronenborn, D. and Wahl, J. 2001. Prehistoric human migration in the Linearbandkeramik of Central Europe. *Antiquity* 75: 593-603.

Price, T.D., Burton, J.H. and Bentley, R.A. 2002. The characterization of biologically available strontium isotope ratios for the study of prehistoric migration. *Archaeometry* 44: 117-135.

Price, T.D., Knipper, C., Grupe, G. and Smrcka, V.. 2004. Strontium isotopes and prehistoric human migration: the Bell Beaker Period in Central Europe. *European Journal of Archaeology* 7: 9-40.

Price, T.D., Manzanilla, L. and Middleton, W.D. 2000. Immigration and the ancient city of Teotihuacan in Mexico: a study using strontium isotope ratios in human bone and teeth. *Journal of Archaeological Science* 27: 903-913.

Price, T.D., Swick, R.W. and Chase, E.P. 1986. Bone chemistry and prehistoric diet: Strontium studies of laboratory rats. *American Journal of Physical Anthropology* 70: 365-375.

Pryor, F. 2003. *Britain BC: Life in Britain and Ireland before the Romans*. London: Harper Collins.

Schweissing, M.M. and Grupe, G. 2003a. Stable strontium isotopes in human teeth and bone: a key to migration events of the late Roman period in Bavaria. *Journal of Archaeological Science* 30: 1373-1383.

Schweissing, M.M. and Grupe, G. 2003b. Tracing migration events in man and cattle by stable strontium isotope analysis of appositionally grown mineralized tissue. *International Journal of Osteoarchaeology* 13: 96-103.

Thomas, J. 1999. *Understanding the Neolithic*. London: Routledge.

Trickett, M.A., Budd, P., Montgomery, J. and Evans, J. 2003. An assessment of solubility profiling as a decontamination procedure for the Sr-87/Sr-86 analysis of archaeological human skeletal tissue. *Applied Geochemistry* 18: 653-658.

Underwood, E.J. 1977. *Trace Elements in Human and Animal Nutrition*. London: Academic Press.

Whittle, A.W.R. 1997. Moving on and moving around: Neolithic settlement mobility. In P. Topping (ed.) *Neolithic Landscapes*. Oxford: Oxbow. 15-22.

Chapter 9

The Beaker People Project: progress and prospects for the carbon, nitrogen and sulphur isotopic analysis of collagen

Mandy Jay and Michael P. Richards

Department of Human Evolution, Max Planck Institute for Evolutionary Anthropology, Deutscher Platz 6, 04103 Leipzig, Germany and Department of Archaeology, University of Durham, Durham, UK

Introduction

This paper discusses the analysis of the organic bone and dentine collagen fraction of the Beaker People Project skeletal material and the interpretation of the resultant data for dietary and environmental reconstruction. The project involves the extraction of collagen from both bone and tooth dentine for stable isotopic analysis of the elements carbon, nitrogen and sulphur. These isotopic data are mainly useful for dietary reconstruction, but are also helpful in the consideration of local environmental background. This environmental element to the interpretation makes a contribution to the discussion of the data obtained for the purpose of investigating mobility of groups and individuals at this period in time, these latter involving the isotopic analysis of strontium and oxygen from the inorganic tooth enamel. Separate papers in this volume discuss the analysis of the inorganic material for the project. The collagen extracted for the purpose of isotopic analysis is also being used to radiocarbon date around half of the individuals being investigated, adding considerably to the corpus of available dates for this material in Britain.

Stable Isotope Analysis

The carbon and nitrogen from which bone and dentine collagen are formed are thought to originate mainly in the protein content of the foods consumed by the human or animal involved (DeNiro and Epstein 1978; Ambrose and Norr 1993; Tieszen and Fagre 1993). This is why their analysis is useful for dietary reconstruction, the major interpretational value being in terms of trophic level (what degree of animal protein is in the diet?) and position within the marine food chain (were marine fish or mammals being consumed?). Freshwater and estuarine resources can also be identified, as can the inclusion of C_4 plants in the food chain. The latter, however, are not likely to be relevant to this project, since such plants (which originate in warm, dry environments and include tropical grasses and millet) were not available in prehistoric Britain. Although millet is thought to have been available in parts of continental Europe as far back as the Neolithic (Renfrew 1973: 99; Zohary and Hopf 2000: 83), it is not expected that it will show a significant presence in the Beaker People Project material, even if mobility is identified for analysed individuals.

The different chemical elements investigated in a study such as this have more than one isotope. The analysis compares the ratio of two *stable* isotopes for each element. Since these isotopes, by definition, are not radiogenic (as, for instance, ^{14}C is), the ratio obtained should reflect that seen in the collagen at the time of its formation. This assumes that the collagen is not seriously degraded, or affected by contamination or diagenesis. In fact, collagen is a remarkably robust skeletal fraction and there are a number of indicators that can be used to 'weed out' those few data which might have been adversely affected by these factors (DeNiro 1985; Ambrose 1993; van Klinken 1999).

Whilst carbon and nitrogen have been used for this kind of analysis for several decades, there are relatively few studies involving sulphur in archaeological material and its consideration in this context is in its infancy (Richards *et al.* 2001; Richards *et al.* 2003a; Craig *et al.* 2006). This is largely due to difficulties involved in the analytical techniques, both in the area of mass spectrometry and also due to the fact that there is very little sulphur in collagen in comparison to the much more prevalent carbon and nitrogen. These problems are being overcome with advances in available equipment, allowing, in particular, the analysis of smaller samples. Since sulphur, like the other two elements, comes from ingested foodstuffs, the relationship of the sulphur, carbon and nitrogen in the environment with the plants at the base of the food chain is the important factor. Whilst the carbon in plants is from the atmosphere (from carbon dioxide taken up during the process of photosynthesis), the nitrogen usually comes from the soil and the same is true for the sulphur. The results of this analysis, therefore, not only allow some consideration of what is being eaten (level of animal protein, aquatic resources), but they also reflect environmental factors affecting the chemistry of the plants at the base of the food chain.

In addition to the terrestrial environment, all three isotopic systems will cause variations in the data to be seen where aquatic, and particularly marine, resources are being consumed. This is because the elements obtained from a marine environment are significantly different in their isotopic ratios to those found in terrestrial ecosystems.

The collagen in bone is built up over a long period of time, so that the analysis of a bone sample from an adult

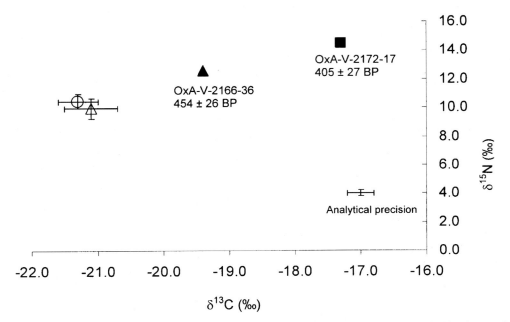

Figure 9.1. Average of Early Bronze Age samples from Scotland (open circle, *n* = 37) and East Yorkshire (open triangle, *n* = 58), with 1 standard deviation error bars. The filled square and triangle represent the Scottish Seaview Crescent and near the House of Binns samples respectively, these being consumers of marine resources, now dated to the 15th to 17th centuries AD.

will give results which reflect dietary protein over at least a decade. The collagen from the tooth dentine, in contrast, is formed over a more limited period of time, in the early life of an individual, and there is little subsequent turnover of material in this source during adulthood. This project concentrates on the analysis of permanent second molars, both for the analysis of the collagen and for the inorganic enamel fraction (the latter discussed elsewhere in this volume). These start to form at 2½ to 3 years of age, with the completion of the root occurring at around 14 years. This means that the timing of the data from the two sources is different. The dentine will give information about diet and environment from childhood, whilst the bone collagen will provide data relating to a later period in the individual's life. A comparison of the data from the two periods may allow the identification of a change in dietary sources across these periods. If this occurs, then it will either relate to an alteration in the types of foodstuffs present at different times in life, or it may also reflect a change in the sources of those foodstuffs, thus adding to the discussion on the possibility of mobility amongst people at this time in prehistory.

Progress

The project aims to analyse 250 individuals from the Early Bronze Age in Britain, these being taken from four general geographical regions. At the time of writing, bone collagen has been analysed for carbon and nitrogen from over 100 individuals from two of these regions (Scotland and East Yorkshire). The Scottish burials are all from different sites, excavated at various times over the last century and mainly originating from along the east coast of the Scottish mainland. They have been curated by the National Museums of Scotland and by the Marischal

Museum of the University of Aberdeen. The East Yorkshire material is more tightly defined in geographical terms and has been taken from the J. R. Mortimer collection, curated at the Hull and East Yorkshire Museum, all of which was excavated from barrows on the Yorkshire Wolds.

Acidic Scottish soils do not generally facilitate the preservation of bone in that region and the individuals from there analysed for this project were largely protected by the stone cists in which they were buried. Animal bone assemblages, however, have not been identified from anywhere in mainland Scotland for the appropriate period. The Yorkshire Wolds is better in this regard, although no Early Bronze Age animal results are available for discussion at the time of writing.

Results

The results so far have produced some interesting data for interpretation. The general picture for both the Scottish and East Yorkshire populations indicates a diet which includes high levels of animal protein. This is, perhaps, unsurprising for British prehistoric material of this date. However, there are some more particular points which are of interest within this overall view.

The Scottish group originally included two individuals with relatively high levels of marine food in their diets (Figure 9.1). This was an unexpected finding, since the consumption of marine resources in significant quantities on the British mainland appears to have been present during the Mesolithic, after which it is rarely found in prehistoric material, reappearing again when Roman influences become apparent (Richards *et al.* 1998; Richards *et al.* 2003b; Müldner and Richards 2005; Jay and Richards 2006; Richards *et al.* 2006). The majority of the individuals from the Scottish group are not consuming marine foods at a level at which it is visible in the isotopic data, but the two for whom the signal is present showed very significant quantities in the diet.

As part of the radiocarbon dating programme for this project, these two individuals have now been dated. They were included in the study based on burial form (they were from stone cists), but had no ceramic associations or other grave goods. In both cases, this showed that the inclusion of these burials within the group for this period was incorrect, since they date to the 15th to 17th centuries AD. The two individuals concerned were from sites in West Lothian and Aberdeenshire, formerly Kincardineshire (near the House of Binns and Sea View Crescent, Gourdon, respectively). It is of interest to note that the only two individuals which showed any indication of the consumption of marine resources actually conformed to expectation, in that they are not from the prehistoric period during which such resources are apparently rarely used in significant quantities in Britain.

A second point for further discussion relates to sex differences. In most cases so far, the skeletal material being analysed for this project have been quite fragmentary and sexing is difficult. However, where probable sexes have been attributed to this group by Patrick Mahoney for this project, the pattern of nitrogen isotopic values is interesting, since the Scottish males generally show lower values than the females (Figure 9.2), whilst the East Yorkshire situation is reversed (Figure 9.3). Looking at the Scottish values first, the female value for Ardachy (Isle of Mull) appears significantly different to the other females in having a much lower $\delta^{15}N$ value. It would be reasonable to remove this value from a statistical comparison of the sexes, since this is from an island to the west of Scotland, rather than the eastern coastal mainland where all of the other sexed samples originate. This difference in environmental background may make a significant difference to the nitrogen values in itself. If this sample is removed, a *t*-test comparing male and female $\delta^{15}N$ values shows them to be significantly different ($t(22) = 2.81$; $p < 0.05$). If the sample is retained and the Mann Whitney test applied on the basis that the distribution is not normal, they remain significantly different ($z = -2.10$; $p < 0.05$). It should be remembered here, however, that sexing is problematic and some of the individuals may not be in the correct category.

Moving on to East Yorkshire, the reverse situation is apparent, with the identified males apparently having higher $\delta^{15}N$ values than the females (see Figure 9.3). Again, a *t*-test comparing them shows a significant difference ($t(22) = -3.90$; $p < 0.001$). Most of the Mortimer skeletal collection consists of crania, so that sex attributions are once again better considered as probable rather than conclusive.

This possible sex differentiation for two separate locations would be a very interesting finding, if it related to dietary protein intake, since such a difference in prehistoric British material has not previously been noted, the first such distinction apparently occurring in the Roman period (Richards *et al.* 1998). These data might suggest that males in East Yorkshire were consuming more animal protein than females, with the reverse true in Scotland. However, there is a chance that this differentiation is not related to the types of food being consumed, at least for the Scottish group, but occurs because of the relationship between the individual and the location of the resources obtained (but see Mahoney this volume).

Nitrogen isotopic values at the base of the food chain will alter according to the local environment, so that plant values will be dependent on factors affecting the soil such as aridity, salinity, acidity and manuring. Even within mainland Britain, these values can vary noticeably for different sites. It is generally noted that bone collagen values from coastal sites appear elevated in this respect, which may well relate to salinity issues. In the case of the Scottish group, it may be relevant that the majority of the females have been buried close to the coast (10 out of 13 are within 7.5 km), whilst the majority of the males have been buried within a much wider range (4 out of 12 range with the females, but the other 8 range up to 30 km from the coast, which is only true for 2 of the females).

These distances from the coast relate to burial sites, not to settlements, so that it is not clear that the positions are necessarily related to where resources were obtained. However, if males were ranging further inland on a long-term and/or regular basis, then their consumption of resources found further inland is likely to have led to lower nitrogen isotopic values being seen in their collagen than for females for whom resources were regularly obtained in coastal areas. It is important to be clear here that the discussion relates to differences in the locations of *terrestrial* resources, and that none of the individuals concerned were consuming significant amounts of *marine* resources.

It is hoped that when the sulphur data are available, these will help to clarify the position. Sulphur isotopic values will vary for resources which have been obtained from very close to the coast, as compared to further inland, because of a 'sea-spray' effect on the local environment which contributes to the values found in the local plants. If it is true that the Scottish females were generally eating foods obtained close to the coast, whilst the males were getting theirs from further inland, then it might be expected that a distinction in the sulphur isotopic values will be seen.

It may also be of relevance that the four males with $\delta^{15}N$ values above 10.5‰, making them equivalent to the higher female values, have all now been dated to the period prior to 2200 BC. The Scottish nitrogen values

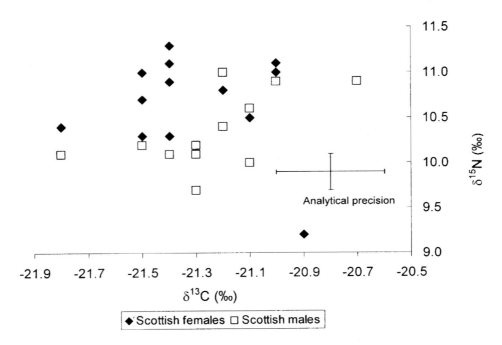

Figure 9.2. Scottish samples for which probable sex has been attributed by Mahoney for this project based on skeletal evidence. Other than Ardachy (Isle of Mull), only samples attributed to the possibly male group show nitrogen values below 10.3‰.

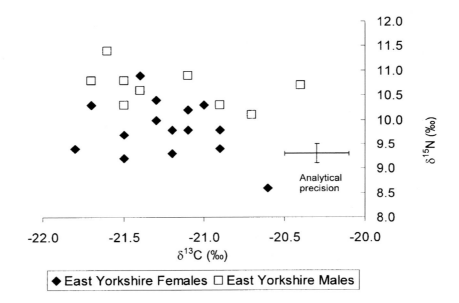

Figure 9.3. East Yorkshire samples for which probable sex has been attributed by Mahoney for this project based on skeletal evidence. Males have elevated $\delta^{15}N$ values compared to females, with only the latter showing values below 10.0‰.

appear to increase for males at this earlier date (see Figure 9.4), which coincides with Needham's 'fission horizon' for Beaker period artefacts and pottery (Needham 2005). Unfortunately, there are only currently seven Beaker period individuals from East Yorkshire for which both dates and probable sex are available; only three of these are male and none of them date to before 2200 BC, so that a comparison of the situation is not possible.

Another point of interest arising from the data obtained so far relates to the carbon isotopic values seen for material

across Britain at different points in time. Middle Iron Age data collected from across mainland Britain, from Cornwall to East Lothian (Jay, unpublished data) is remarkably consistent in terms of the range of carbon data to be seen for both humans and animals. For humans considered to have very similar dietary regimes, they are restricted to a range of 1.5‰ and do not display statistically significant (or visually noticeable) differences between sites. When Early Bronze Age material from two of these sites (Wetwang in East Yorkshire and Ferry Fryston in West Yorkshire) were compared with the Middle Iron Age, it was noted that there was a distinct

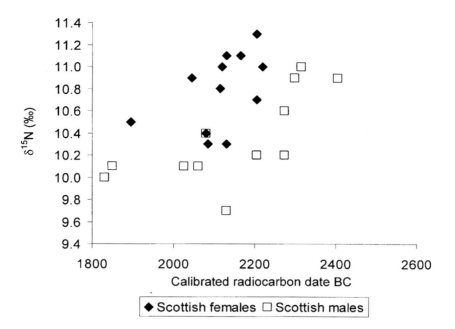

Figure 9.4. δ^{15}N values for Scottish samples where both probable sex and date are available. The nitrogen values for the males appear to become elevated after 2200 BC and it is only during this earlier period that there is significant overlap between the sexes.

shift towards more negative carbon values, although there continued to be significant overlap. It was interesting, therefore, to compare the Scottish and East Yorkshire carbon values from the Beaker People Project with these existing data.

The observed shift in the carbon values is maintained in these groups. Since the Middle Iron Age data-set includes material from East Lothian and from East Yorkshire, it is possible to compare like-with-like in geographical terms. Whilst there continues to be some overlap, it is clear that the Early Bronze Age material has generally more negative carbon values and that this difference is statistically significant.

Since the nitrogen isotopic values do not differ noticeably and it is thought likely that, in terms of animal protein input, the diets for these time periods may well have been very similar, the carbon shift is probably caused by environmental factors. Possibilities may well include deforestation and climate changes between these two periods, both of which are known to have occurred. In order to test the hypotheses available, it will be necessary to check animal bone values for the earlier period against those already available for the Middle Iron Age. If climate change were responsible, for instance, then the shift in values should be visible in domesticated herbivores from the two periods.

Prospects

At the current stage in the project, we now have a significant data-set for carbon and nitrogen isotopic values on human bone collagen from two British regions. Other regions (Southern England (including Wessex), Wales and the Peak District) will be added to this and

sampling arrangements are currently being made for this material. Overall, these will make a very significant contribution to the isotopic picture available for this period in prehistory, for which only minimal data currently exist. As such, they will allow comparison with earlier and later prehistoric data and contribute significantly to the picture we have for diet and environment in the Early British Bronze Age.

Data from the dentine are not yet available, since the recording of the teeth prior to destruction takes priority and this is still underway at the time of writing. However, processing will commence soon and the comparison of the carbon and nitrogen results between bone and dentine will be of particular interest in the discussion of mobility during this period, given the timing difference between the formation of these different tissues in an individual's life.

The sulphur data will also become available soon. Whilst their interpretation is not as routine as that for carbon and nitrogen, it is expected that they will give a picture of the possibility of short-distance mobility between coastal and inland areas, thus elucidating the situation described above for which the Scottish males and females appear to have distinct nitrogen values. It is also expected that the sulphur values will make a contribution to the discussion relating to aquatic and marine resource consumption patterns.

References

Ambrose, S. H. 1993. Isotopic analysis of paleodiets: methodological and interpretive considerations. In M. K. Sandford (ed.) *Investigation of Ancient Human*

Tissue: Chemical analyses in anthropology. Langhorne (Pennsylvania): Gordon and Breach Science Publishers. 59-130.

Ambrose, S. H. and Norr, L. 1993. Experimental evidence for the relationship of the carbon isotope ratios of whole diet and dietary protein to those of bone collagen and carbonate. In J. B. Lambert and G. Grupe (eds), *Prehistoric Human Bone: archaeology at the molecular level.* Berlin: Springer-Verlag. 1-37.

Craig, O. E., Ross, R., Andersen, S. H., Milner, N. and Bailey, G. N. 2006. Focus: sulphur isotope variation in archaeological marine fauna from northern Europe. *Journal of Archaeological Science* 33: 1642-1646.

DeNiro, M. J. 1985. Postmortem preservation and alteration of *in vivo* bone collagen isotope ratios in relation to palaeodietary reconstruction. *Nature* 317: 806-809.

DeNiro, M. J. and Epstein, S. 1978. Influence of diet on the distribution of carbon isotopes in animals. *Geochimica et Cosmochimica Acta* 42: 495-506.

Jay, M. and Richards, M. P. 2006. Diet in the Iron Age cemetery population at Wetwang Slack, East Yorkshire, UK: carbon and nitrogen stable isotope evidence. *Journal of Archaeological Science* 33: 653-662.

Müldner, G. and Richards, M. P. 2005. Fast or feast: reconstructing diet in later medieval England by stable isotope analysis. *Journal of Archaeological Science* 32 (1): 39-48.

Needham, S. 2005. Transforming Beaker culture in north-west Europe; processes of fusion and fission. *Proceedings of the Prehistoric Society* 71: 171-217.

Renfrew, J. M. 1973. *Palaeoethnobotany.* London, Methuen and Co.

Richards, M. P., Fuller, B. T. and Hedges, R. E. M. 2001. Sulphur isotopic variation in ancient bone collagen from Europe: implications for human palaeodiet, residence mobility, and modern pollutant studies. *Earth and Planetary Science Letters* 191(3-4): 185-190.

Richards, M. P., Fuller, B. T. and Molleson, T. I. 2006. Stable isotope palaeodietary study of humans and fauna from the multi-period (Iron Age, Viking and Late Medieval) site of Newark Bay, Orkney. *Journal of Archaeological Science* 33: 122-131.

Richards, M. P., Fuller, B. T., Sponheimer, M., Robinson, T. and Ayliffe, L. 2003a. Sulphur isotopes in palaeodietary studies: a review and results from a controlled feeding experiment. *International Journal of Osteoarchaeology* 13 (1-2): 37-45.

Richards, M. P., Hedges, R. E. M., Molleson, T. I. and Vogel, J. C. 1998. Stable isotope analysis reveals variations in human diet at the Poundbury Camp cemetery site. *Journal of Archaeological Science* 25: 1247-1252.

Richards, M. P., Schulting, R. J. and Hedges, R. E. M. 2003b. Sharp shift in diet at onset of Neolithic. *Nature* 425: 366.

Tieszen, L. L. and Fagre, T. 1993. Effect of diet quality and composition on the isotopic composition of respiratory CO_2, bone collagen, bioapatite, and soft tissues. In J. B. Lambert and G. Grupe (eds), *Prehistoric Human Bone: archaeology at the molecular level.* Berlin: Springer-Verlag. 121-155.

van Klinken, G. J. 1999. Bone collagen quality indicators for palaeodietary and radiocarbon measurements. *Journal of Archaeological Science* 26: 687-695.

Zohary, D. and Hopf, M. 2000. *Domestication of Plants in the Old World.* Oxford: Oxford University Press.

Chapter 10

Microwear studies of diet in Early Bronze Age burials from Scotland

Patrick Mahoney

Department of Archaeology, University of Sheffield, Sheffield, UK

Introduction

The consumption of food can leave a characteristic signature on the human skeleton. For archaeologists this is of interest because it can provide insights into prehistoric human diet. These insights are important because they can help to identify patterns of consumption in the past, or changes to those patterns over time (*e.g.* Moore and Corbett 1971; 1973). Such changes are of interest because they can reflect important stages in human economic evolution (*e.g.* Childe 1928).

Direct insights into diet can sometimes be gained from archaeological samples of modern humans. If the burial environment has preserved soft tissue then, occasionally, direct examination of the gut contents is possible. More usually, only hard tissue survives, and this can be studied using a range of techniques, such as dental microwear. Data from microwear allows inferences to be made about the type of food consumed.

The aim in this study is to infer two aspects of diet - hardness and abrasiveness - from dental microwear in Early Bronze Age (EBA) burials from Scotland. This study was undertaken as part of the Beaker People Project.

Background

Microscopic dental pits and scratches form on the surface of teeth during chewing. These pits and scratches - dental microwear - are caused as hard particles are driven into (compression) or dragged between (shear) opposing enamel surfaces as the jaw moves through the chewing cycle. Two types of particle commonly ingested are thought to be hard enough to cause microwear. Silica bodies (phytoliths) are present in some plant leaves, stems, and seed coats, and have a hardness that exceeds dental enamel (Baker *et al.* 1959; Piperno 1988). The quartz inclusions present in some soils, and plant-grinding stone tools are also harder than enamel, and could therefore cause microwear if present on food as contaminants (Cook and Kirk 1995; Pough 1996).

Based on these causal agents, increases and decreases in compression and shear during chewing have been inferred from the frequency and size of microwear. A diet high in compression and low in shear should produce large and/or frequent dental pits (Gordon 1982; Mahoney 2006a, b and c). Scratches should become longer as shear increases and narrower as compression decreases

(Gordon 1982; Mahoney 2006a, b and c). Studies on extant species support some of these ideas. Harder diets produce more and larger pits (Teaford and Oyen 1989; Teaford and Runestad 1992; Teaford and Walker 1984), which might sometimes reflect increases in compression as more hard particles are driven deeper into enamel (*e.g.* Ryan, 1979). More folivorous species have longer microwear features than more frugivorous species (Teaford and Walker 1984; Ungar *et al.* 2006), because a diet rich in plant foods requires opposing teeth to shear past each other as the mandible moves through the chewing cycle, producing more slicing actions and thus reducing the food. Another consistent correlation occurs as dietary abrasiveness increases, which generates more scratches (Covert and Kay 1991; Teaford and Lytle 1996; Walker *et al.* 1978).

The adoption of an agricultural economy in Britain is still poorly understood. Cereal production was a component of the prehistoric diet during the Neolithic period, though its relative importance for the economy, together with mobile pastoralism, is uncertain (*e.g.* Budd *et al.* 2003; Richards 2000; Rowley-Conwy 2000; Thomas 1991; 1999). Large-scale cereal production is thought to have intensified in the Middle Bronze Age, and domesticated animals were present on some archaeological sites from the Neolithic onwards (*e.g.* Chamberlain 2001). A continuation of a mobile lifestyle is also a possibility for the Early Bronze Age (see Montgomery *et al.* this volume).

Materials and Methods

The skeletal and dental sample

The second mandibular molar was selected from 14 adult skeletons from 13 previously excavated archaeological sites. The burials date to the EBA and are mainly from the east coast of Scotland, though one site was from the Western Isles (Figure 10.1; Table 10.1).

The comparative sample

Microwear from four human groups in the Southern Levant (Natufian, pre-pottery Neolithic A, pre-pottery Neolithic B, Late Bronze-Iron Age), and two human groups from North America were selected as a comparative sample (Table 10.2).

Natufian hunter-gatherers exploited a diverse range of animal and plant foods from both sedentary and more mobile settlements (*e.g.* Bar Yosef, 1998). Animal foods included mainly gazelle, while wild cereals were ground

Figure 10.1 Map of Early Bronze Age archaeological sites in Scotland.

Site	Date (BP)[1]
Dalmore, Halkirk, cist 1. Caithness[2]	Ox. 3562 ±30
Skateraw Farm, E. Lothian (1950 exc.)[3]	Ox. 3846 ±29
Thurston Mains, E. Lothian[4]	Ox. 3721 ±33
Holm Mains Farm, Inverness, cist 1[5]	Ox. 3743 ±33
Holm Mains Farm, Inverness, cist 2[5]	Ox. 3755 ±32
Park Quarry, Durris, cist 1. Aberdeen[6]	Ox. 3769 ±32
Pitdrichie 2, Keabog Quarry. Mearns[7]	Ox. 3910 ±33
Sandhole, Fettergus. Buchan[8]	Ox. 3845 ±32
Lochend, Highland[9]	Ox. 3534 ±31
Ardachy, Bunessan, Mull[10]	Ox. 3584 ±28
Clashfarquhar, Aberdeenshire[11]	Ox. 3506 ±32
Tealing Hill, Angus[12]	Ox. 3683 ±32
Priory Park, Kirkcaldy, Fife[13]	Ox. 3652 ±32
Boatbridge Quarry, Thankerton, cist 2[14]	Ox. 3824 ±32

[1]All dates provided by the Beaker People Project, except Thurston Mains. [2]MacCuallum 1962. [3]Cruden 1958. [4]Stevenson 1940. [5]Brown 2003. [6]Shepherd and Grieg 1989. [7]Shepherd and Bruce 1987. [8]Ralston 1981. [9]Childe 1944. [10]Mitchell 1896. [11]Thomson 1831. [12]Neish 1871. [13]Yeoman 1992. [14]Clarke and Ritchie 1985.

Table 10.1 The Early Bronze Age sample

Culture	n[1]	Date
Natufian[2]	30	12,500-10,000 BP
PPNA[3]	12	10,300-9,300 BP
PPNB[2]	30	9,400-8,100 BP
LBA-Iron Age[4]	10	3570–3000 BP
Arikara[5]	5	AD 1600-1700
Aleut[5]	5	AD 1700

[1]Number of individuals. [2]Mahoney 2006a. [3]Mahoney 2007. [4]Mahoney 2006b. [5]Ungar et al. 2006 .

Table 10.2 The comparative sample

Site	Pits			Scratches	
	%	length	width	length	width
Dalmore 1, Halkirk. Caithness.	37.10	3.86	1.97	34.23	1.02
Thurston Mains, E. Lothian.	32.00	3.11	1.43	49.16	1.15
Holm Mains Farm, Inverness, cist 1.	48.80	3.75	2.13	47.14	1.39
Holm Mains Farm, Inverness, cist 2.	32.70	2.50	1.57	37.75	1.00
Park Quarry, Durris 1. Aberdeen.	26.00	2.24	1.17	52.25	0.82
Pitdrichie 2, Keabog Quarry. Mearns.	35.80	6.22	2.93	30.81	1.32
Sandhole, Fetterangus. Buchan.	60.00	3.29	1.96	28.40	1.18
Lochend, Highland.	28.50	2.90	1.43	30.50	1.09
Skateraw farm, E. Lothian (1952 exc.).	9.30	3.02	2.31	31.24	1.14
Ardachy, Bunessan, Mull.	35.00	2.51	1.46	60.98	1.30
Longhillock Cottages, Clashfarquhar, Aberdeenshire.	7.14	1.79	.91	53.39	1.41
Tealing, Angus.	27.00	4.43	2.42	50.48	1.25
Priory Park, Kirkcaldy, Fife.	11.31	2.87	1.93	57.80	1.46
Boatbridge Quarry, Thankerton, cist 2.	14.94	3.15	1.74	47.48	0.91
Mean	28.97 ±14.97	3.26 ±1.09	1.81 ±0.53	43.68 ±11.16	1.17 ±0.19

Table 10.3   Microwear measurements for the EBA sample with stone tools before consumption (Martin 1994; Willcox 1999).

Human group	n	Pits						Scratches			
		%		length		width		length		width	
		X[1]	sd[2]	X	sd	X	sd	X	sd	X	sd
Natufian[3]	30	51.0	15.1	4.71	1.84	2.46	0.21	23.80	8.61	1.46	0.18
PPNB[3]	30	49.02	15.69	5.24	2.28	2.56	0.17	26.14	8.85	1.59	0.24
Aleut[4]	5	45.84	10.00	8.08	2.17	6.34	1.06	26.62	4.38	1.54	0.19
PPNA[5]	12	36.52	13.86	2.36	1.42	1.42	0.21	41.89	16.26	0.87	0.19
Scottish EBA[6]	**14**	**28.98**	**14.97**	**3.26**	**1.09**	**1.81**	**0.53**	**43.68**	**11.16**	**1.17**	**0.19**
Arikara[4]	5	30.80	19.38	6.52	2.14	4.92	1.30	33.48	9.78	1.20	0.24
LBA-Iron Age[7]	10	28.68	7.32	7.77	2.32	3.73	1.64	24.47	6.47	1.58	0.13

[1]Mean. [2]Standard deviation. [3]Mahoney 2006a. [4]Ungar et al 2006. [5]Mahoney 2007. [6]**This study**. [7]Mahoney 2006b.

Table 10.4 Microwear measurements for the comparative sample

Pre-pottery Neolithic A (PPNA) sites suggest an increasingly sedentary lifestyle with a broad spectrum economy, similar to that of the Natufians (Bar Yosef 1998; Martin 1994; Willcox 1999). At the sites in this study, abundant remains of fish, molluscs, crab, water mole, and avifauna, indicate that aquatic foods were an important dietary component (Bar Yosef et al. 1991; Ronen and Lechevallier 1993).

Pre-pottery Neolithic B (PPNB) sites in this study focused on hunting and farming (Garfinkel 1987). Like the Natufians, animal foods included mainly gazelle. Unlike the earlier hunter-gatherers' diets, pulses and cereals may have been cultivated and prepared for consumption using plant grinding tools (Gopher 1997;

Wright 1993). Farming was also a component of the Bronze-Iron Age economy in the Southern Levant (e.g. Clapham, 1988).

The Aleut economy relied almost exclusively on animal foods, such as fresh and dried fish, molluscs, and sea mammals (Ungar et al. 2006). The Arikara exploited plant foods such as maize, beans, squash, and sunflowers, and large quantities of bison meat, which was cut into strips and dried (Meyer 1977).

The microwear procedure
Contaminants were removed from the occlusal surface of each molar using ethanol and cotton wool. An impression was taken using a rubber-based, addition-curing silicone

(Colte`ne President Jet, lightbody). Facet nine (Maier and Schneck 1982) was excised from each impression using a scalpel and surrounded with Colténe President Putty to create a depression. A cast of the facet was produced using an epoxy resin (Araldite MY 753, hardener HY 956, Ciba-Geigy). Each cast was mounted on an aluminium stub after its base had been coated with an electrode paint (Electrodag1415 M). The base (towards the intercuspal fissure) of each facet was marked on each stub to help orient the facet in the scanning electron microscope (SEM) specimen chamber. The base of facet nine was chosen to try and standardize the dental locations between individuals and because this location can maximize microwear variations in some human populations (Mahoney 2006a, b and c).

Each SEM stub was placed into a sputter coating unit (EMSCOPE; SC500) for 3 minutes, and coated with 20-nm of gold-paladium. Digitized micrographs were taken at a magnification of 500x, using a SEM (CAMSCAN) at the Sorby Centre for Electron Microscopy and Microanalysis, University of Sheffield. The CAMSCAN was operated in the secondary electron emission mode, with a resolution of 3.0 and an accelerating voltage of 15kV. Dental casts were orientated perpendicular (tilt angle $0°$) to the primary beam. Each digitized micrograph (1004 x 744 pixels) represented approximately 0.04 mm^2 of the tooth surface.

Data collection
Pits and scratches were measured and counted using a semi-automated image analysis computer program (Microware Version 3; Ungar 1997). A resolution of 0.254 microns per pixel (DPI 200) was selected. Five variables representing the size and frequency of microwear were created from each micrograph: percent pits, mean length and width of pits, and mean length and breadth of scratches. A 4:1 length-to-width ratio was used to distinguish between pits and scratches. All micrographs were recorded and a mean value produced for each individual.

Analyses
Multiple comparisons using a Tukey test in a one-way Analysis of Variance Analysis were undertaken to examine the microwear variation between the Scottish EBA and the comparative sample.

A Discriminant Function Analysis (DFA) was chosen to assess how each microwear variable contributed to the variation between the samples For a DFA statistical methodology see Mahoney (2006a). All statistical tests were conducted using SPSS 12 for Windows. The significance level was set at $P \leq 0.05$.

Results

Microwear measurements are shown in Table 10.3 (Scottish EBA) and Table 10.4 (comparative sample). Inferential statistics are given in Table 10.5 (multiple

comparisons). A representative micrograph is shown in Figure 10.2. A plot of the DFA is shown in Figure 10.3.

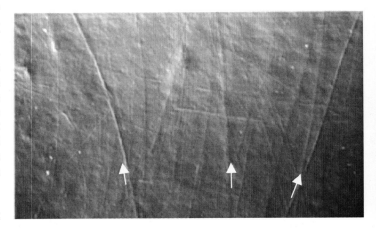

Fig 10.2. Representative micrograph of Early Bronze Age microwear

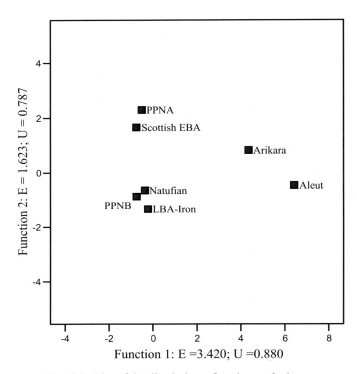

Fig 10.3. Plot of the discriminant function analysis

mean discriminant score for each group, illustrates the good visual separation between the smaller pits of the Scottish EBA and the larger pits of the Aleut and Arikara (Figure 10.3). Even though less variance was accounted for by the second function, there is still good visual separation between the long narrow scratches of the Scottish EBA and the short wide scratches of the PPNB and LBA-Iron Age farmers, the Natufian hunter-gatherers, as well as the Aleut. This latter interpretation is supported by the multiple comparisons of the individual ANOVAs (Table 10.5), which show significant differences in scratch size between the EBA and these comparative groups. Overall, the proximity of Scottish

| | | | | Pits | | | | | | Scratches | | | | | | |
| | % | | | length | | | width | | | length | | | width | | | |
Group	MD[1]	SE[2]	P[3]	MD	SE	P	MD	SE	P	MD	SE	P	MD	SE	P
Natufian	**-16.145**	**4.860**	**0.021**	-1.481	0.597	0.178	-0.652	0.300	0.321	**19.876**	**3.250**	**0.000**	**-0.292**	**0.090**	**.027**
PPNA	-11.213	5.783	0.460	0.776	0.710	0.929	0.337	0.357	0.964	2.957	3.868	0.988	0.271	0.107	.166
PPNB	**-18.350**	**4.811**	**0.004**	**-1.981**	**0.591**	**0.019**	-0.749	0.297	0.164	**17.795**	**3.218**	**0.000**	**-0.422**	**0.089**	**.000**
Aleut	-16.869	7.822	0.329	**-4.820**	**0.961**	**0.000**	**-4.528**	**0.483**	**0.000**	**17.066**	**5.232**	**0.025**	-0.365	0.146	.169
Arikara	-1.829	7.822	1.000	**-3.260**	**0.961**	**0.017**	**-3.108**	**0.483**	**0.000**	10.206	5.232	0.453	-0.025	0.146	1.000
LBA-Iron	0.289	7.326	1.000	**-4.511**	**0.900**	**0.000**	**-1.925**	**0.453**	**0.001**	**19.216**	**4.900**	**0.003**	**-0.409**	**0.116**	**.045**

1 = Mean difference between each culture in the comparative sample and the Scottish EBA. 2 = Standard error. 3 = p value (significance). Significant differences are in bold.

Table 9.5 Multiple comparisons between the Scottish EBA and the comparative sample

EBA to the PPNA in the plot of the DFA implies similarities in their microwear signatures.

Discussion

The dental pits on the Scottish EBA molars were small, compared to either the Aleut or Arikara (Figure 10.3; Table 10.4-5). The smaller pits suggest a comparatively softer diet, which did not focus on particularly hard foods. For instance, the diet of the Aleut and the Arikara included foods such as dried meat, which can require great compressive forces while chewing, producing large dental pits. The results for the EBA also contrast with preliminary findings for the Neolithic period at Whitwell Quarry, and the Bronze-Iron Age at Carsington Pasture Cave, both in Derbyshire, where dental pits were much larger (width = 3.0µm ±0.8, 3.1µm ±0.7 respectively; Nystrom and Cox 2003). The variation in pit size within the British samples suggests temporal or regional variation in dietary hardness.

The long and narrow scratches on the Scottish EBA molars contrasted mainly with the Natufians, the PPNB, and LBA-Iron Age farmers, as well as the Aleut (Figure 10.3; Table 10.4-5). The short, wide scratches on the molars from the Southern Levant were likely to be due to a great reliance upon foods contaminated by hard stone grit from processing procedures (Mahoney 2006a). This implies that the diet of the Scottish sample may not have relied much on stone-ground foods. Some support for this idea is provided by the proximity of the Scottish EBA to the PPNA in the plot of the DFA (Fig. 10.3.). Plant foods were an important dietary component at the PPNA sites in this study, but their preparation for consumption may not have relied very much upon stone grinding equipment (Mahoney 2007).

The comparatively low frequency of dental pits, and therefore high frequency of (long narrow) scratches on the Scottish EBA molars suggest an abrasive diet that required more shearing rather than compressive forces. This microwear signature is seen in humans and non-human primates with a diet rich in plant foods (Teaford and Walker 1984; Lalueza et al. 1996; Ungar et al. 2006). Alternatively, a diet rich in aquatic foods seems to produce a similar effect in Inuit populations (Gordon 1986). The overall similarity in the microwear signature between the Scottish EBA and the PPNA, where aquatic foods were also a dietary component, and the proximity of all EBA sites to the coast suggest this might have been a contributing agent to the microwear signature. However, a diet rich in marine foods is not indicated by either the carbon or nitrogen signals (Jay and Richards this volume).

Conclusion

Microwear from the Scottish EBA burials was characterised by a few small pits and a high frequency of long fine scratches. The microwear pattern suggests an abrasive diet that did not focus on particularly hard foods. It was inferred that the diet of the Scottish Early Bronze Age was most probably rich in plant foods that were not always prepared with stone grinding equipment.

References

Baker, G., Jones, L.H.P. and Wardrop, I.D. 1959. Cause of wear in sheep's teeth. *Nature* 184: 1583-1584.

Bar Yosef, O. 1998. The Natufian culture in the Levant: threshold to the origins of agriculture. *Evolutionary Anthropology* 6: 159-77.

Bar Yosef, O. Gopher, A. Tchernov, E. and Kislev, M.E. 1991. Netiv Hagdud: an early Neolithic village site in the Jordan Valley. *Journal of Field Archaeology* 18: 405-424.

Brown, G. 2003. Holm Mains Farm, Inverness, short cists. *Discovery and Excavation in Scotland* 87.

Budd, P., Chenery, C., Montgomery, J. and Evans, J. 2003. You are where you ate: Isotopic analysis in the reconstruction of prehistoric residency. In M. Parker Pearson (ed.) *Food, Culture and Identity in the Neolithic and Early Bronze Age*. BAR International Series 1117. 69-78.

Callander, J. and Low, A. 1929. Two short cists at Kilspinddie golf-course, Aberlady, East Lothian. *Proceedings of the Society of Antiquaries of Scotland* 64: 191-99.

Chamberlain, A.T. 2001. Radiocarbon dates from Carsington Pasture Cave, Brassington, Derbyshire. *Capra 3*.

Childe, V. G. 1928. *The Most Ancient Near East*. Routledge and Kegan Paul: London.

Childe, V.G. 1944. Newly discovered short cist burials with beakers. *Proceedings of the Society of Antiquaries of Scotland* 78: 106-9.

Clapham, A. 1988. The plant remains from Tell es-Sa'idiyeh. *Levant 20*: 82-83.

Clarke, D.V. and Ritchie, A. 1985. Two cists from Boatbridge Quarry, Thankerton, Lanarkshire. *Proceedings of the Society of Antiquaries of Scotland* 114: 557-60.

Cruden, S. 1958. Skateraw, East Lothian. *Discovery and Excavation, Scotland* 39.

Close-Brooks, J., Clark, D.V. and Ritchie, A. 1972. Dunbar, Skateraw, short cist. *Discovery and Excavation, Scotland* 22.

Cook, D. and Kirk, W. 1995. *Rocks and Minerals*. Paris: Larousse.

Covert, H.H. and Kay, R.F. 1981. Dental microwear and diet: implications for determining the feeding behaviours of extinct primates, with a comment on the dietary pattern of Sivapithecus. *American Journal of Physical Anthropology* 55: 331-336.

Garfinkel, Y. 1987. Yiftahel: a Neolithic village from the seventh millennium B.C. in lower Galilee, Israel. *Journal of Field Archaeology* 14: 199-212.

Gordon, K.D. 1982. A study of microwear on chimpanzee molars: implications for dental microwear analysis. *American Journal of Physical Anthropology* 59: 195-215.

Jones, G. 2000. Evaluating the importance of cultivation and collecting in Neolithic Britain. In A.S. Fairbarn (ed.) *Plants in Neolithic Britain and Beyond*. Neolithic Studies Group Seminar Papers 5. Oxford: Oxbow. 79-84.

Lalueza, C., Pérez-Pérez, A. and Turbon, D. 1996. Dietary inferences through buccal microwear analysis of middle and upper Pleistocene human fossils. *American Journal of Physical Anthropology* 100: 367-87.

MacCuallum, R.E. 1962. Dalmore, Halkirk. *Discovery and Excavation, Scotland* 24.

Mahoney, P. 2006a. Dental microwear from Natufian hunter-gatherers and early Neolithic farmers: comparisons between and within samples. *American Journal of Physical Anthropology* 130: 308-19.

Mahoney, P. 2006b. Inter-tooth and intra-facet dental microwear variation in an archaeological sample of modern humans from the Jordan Valley. *American Journal of Physical Anthropology* 129: 39-44.

Mahoney, P. 2006c. Microwear and morphology: functional relationships between human dental microwear and the mandible. *Journal of Human Evolution* 50: 452-459.

Mahoney, P. 2007. Human dental microwear from Ohalo II (22,500-23,500 cal. bp), Southern Levant. *American Journal of Physical Anthropology* 132: 489-500.

Maier, W. and Schneck, G. 1982. Functional morphology of hominoid dentitions. *Journal of Human Evolution* 11: 693-696.

Martin, L. 1994. Hunting and herding in a semi-arid region: an archaeological and ethnological analysis of the faunal remains from the epi-Palaeolithic and Neolithic of the eastern Jordan steppe. *Ph.D. dissertation, University of Sheffield.*

Meyer, R.W. 1977. *The Village Indians of the Upper Missouri*. Lincoln: University of Nebraska Press.

Mitchell, A. 1896. Scottish burials and skulls probably belonging to the Bronze Age. *Proceedings of the Society of Antiquaries of Scotland* 31: 115-21.

Moore, W.J. and Corbett, M.E. 1971 Distribution of dental caries in ancient British populations: I Anglo-Saxon period. *Caries Research* 5: 151-168.

Moore, W. J and Corbett, M. E. 1973 Distribution of dental caries in ancient British populations: II Iron Age, Romano-British and Medieval periods. *Caries Research* 7: 139-153.

Neish, J. 1871. Notice of the discovery of a cist with overlying urns at Tealing, Forfashire. *Proceedings of the Society of Antiquaries of Scotland* 8: 381-3.

Nystrom, P. and Cox, S. 2003. The use of dental microwear to infer diet and subsistence patterns in past human populations: a preliminary study. In M. Parker Pearson (ed.) *Food, Culture and Identity in the Neolithic and Early Bronze Age*. BAR (International Series) 1117. 59-67.

Nystrom, P., Phillips-Conroy, J.E. and Jolly, C.J. 2004. Dental microwear in anubis and hybrid baboons (*Papio hamadryas*, sensu lato) living in Awash National Park, Ethiopia. *American Journal of Physical Anthropology* 125: 279–291.

Organ, J.M., Teaford, M.F., Larsen, C.S. 2005. Dietary inferences from dental occlusal microwear at mission San Luis de Apalachee. *American Journal of Physical Anthropology* 128: 801-11.

Piperno, D.R. 1988. *Phytolith analysis: an archaeologicaland geological perspective*. San Diego: Academic Press.

Pough, F.H. 1996. *Rocks and Minerals*. Houghton Mifflin Company: New York.

Ralston, I. 1981. Sandhole Fetterangus, short cist. *Discoveryand Excavation in Scotland* 13.

Richards, M.P. 2000. Human consumption of plant foods in the British Neolithic: direct evidence from bone stable isotopes. In A.S.Fairbairn (ed.) *Plants in Neolithic Britain and Beyond*. Neolithic Group Seminar Papers 5. Oxford: Oxbow. 123-35.

Robinson, M.A. 2000. Further consideration of Neolithic charred cereals, fruits and nuts. In A.S. Fairbairn (ed.) *Plants in Neolithic Britain and Beyond*. Neolithic

Studies Group Seminar Papers 5. Oxford: Oxbow. 85-90.

Ronen, A. and Lechevallier, M. 1993. Hatula. In A. Lewinson-Gilboa and J. Aviram (eds) *The New Encyclopaedia of Archaeological Excavations in the Holy Land, I.* New York: Simon and Schuster. 120-122.

Rowley-Conwy, P. 2000. Through a taphonomic looking glass darkly: the importance of cereal cultivation in Neolithic Britain. In J.P. Huntley and S. Stallibrass (eds) *Taphonomy and Interpretation.* Oxford: Oxbow. 43-53.

Ryan, A. 1979. Wear striation direction on primate teeth. *American Journal of Physical Anthropology* 50: 155-68.

Shepherd, I. and Grieg, M. 1989. *Discovery and Excavation in Scotland* 22.

Shepherd, I.A.G. and Bruce, M.F. 1987. Two beaker cists atKeabog, Pitdrichie, near Drumlithie, Kincardine and Deeside. *Proceedings of the Society of Antiquaries of Scotland* 117: 33-40.

Stevenson, R.B.K. 1940. Short cists in the Parish of Innerwick, East Lothian. *Proceedings of the Society of Antiquaries of Scotland* 74: 138-45.

Teaford, M.F. and Lytle, J.D. 1996. Brief communication:diet-induced changes in rates of human tooth microwear: a case study involving stone-ground maize. *American Journal of Physical Anthropology* 100: 143.

Teaford, M.F. and Oyen, O.J. 1989. Differences in the rate of molar wear between monkeys raised on different diets. *Journal of Dental Research* 68 (110): 1513-1518.

Teaford, M.F. and Runestad, J.A. 1992. Dental micowear and diet in Venezualan primates. *American Journal of Physical Anthropology* 88: 347-364.

Teaford, M.F. and Walker, A. 1984. Quantitative differences in dental microwear between primate species with different diets and a comment on the presumed diet of sivapithecus. *American Journal of Physical Anthropology* 64: 191-200.

Thomas, J. 1991. *Rethinking the Neolithic.* Cambridge: Cambridge University Press.

Thomas, J. 1999. *Understanding the Neolithic.* London: Routledge.

Thomson, A. 1831. Account of a grave discovered in the parish of Banchory-Devenick. *Archaeology, Scotland* 3: 45-7.

Turner W. 1917. A contribution to the craniology of the people of Scotland. *Transactions of the Royal Society of Edinburgh* 51: 190.

Ungar PS. 1997. Microware 3. http://comp.uark.edu/_pungar

Ungar, P.S., Grine, F.E., Teaford, M.F. and El Zaatari, S. 2006. Dental microwear and diets of African early Homo. *Journal of Human Evolution* 50: 78-95.

Walker, A., Hoeck, H.N. and Perez, L. 1978. Microwear of mammalian teeth as an indicator of diet. *Science* 201 (8): 908-910.

Willcox, G. 1998. Archaeobotanical evidence for the beginnings of agriculture in Southwest Asia. In A.B. Damania, J. Valkoun, G. Willcox, and C.O. Qualset (eds) *The origins of agriculture and crop domestication.* Aleppo, Syria: ICARDA. 25–38.

Woodham, A.A. and Mackenzie, J. 1959. Two cists at Golspie, Sutherland. *Proceedings of the Society of Antiquaries of Scotland* 90: 234-8.

Wright, K. 1993. Early Holocene ground stone assemblages in the Levant. *Levant* 25: 93-111.

Yeoman, P. 1992. Priory Park (Kirkcaldy and Dysart parishes): cist burial. *Discovery and Excavation, Scotland* 30.

Chapter 11

Scottish Beaker dates: the good, the bad and the ugly

Alison Sheridan

Department of Archaeology, National Museums Scotland, Edinburgh, Scotland, UK

Introduction

As Stuart Needham's recent review of British Beaker typochronology has demonstrated (Needham 2005), the establishment of a firm chronological base for the study of Beakers – as for any archaeological phenomenon – is of crucial importance. It is only by building up a substantial body of high-quality dating evidence that overall trends can be discerned, individual anomalous dates can be spotted, and more interesting interpretative issues can start to be addressed (as seen, for example, in Jay and Richards' review of the Beaker People Project dietary results in the light of the newly-obtained dates, this volume).

The Beaker People Project (BPP), which used north-east Scotland as its first study region, has made a significant contribution to the study of Scottish Beakers (and also to the study of Scottish short cist graves in general: see Sheridan *et al.* 2007), and the 18 new high-quality Scottish Beaker radiocarbon dates that it has furnished brings the number of currently-available dates which are associated – directly, indirectly or allegedly – with Scottish Beakers to over 100. However, not all of those dates are of the same high quality, with some being determined many years ago and others suffering various problems relating to sample selection, processing, and other factors as outlined below.

In seeking to promote rigour in the creation and use of radiocarbon dates, and as part of an independent, National Museums Scotland (NMS)-run initative to improve the dating of Scottish Chalcolithic and Bronze Age artefacts (Sheridan 2002; 2004; 2005; 2007; Sheridan and Shortland 2004), a critical review of the available radiocarbon dates relating to Scottish Beakers was undertaken by the author immediately before the BPP commenced. This review included the 16 radiocarbon dates that had recently been obtained for NMS (with funding assistance from various bodies, as detailed below) as part of its dating programme. This paper presents the updated results of that review, setting the new BPP-obtained dates within their broader context. It includes details of *all* the currently-available radiocarbon dates for Scottish Beakers known to the author as of June 2007. It is hoped that by differentiating these into 'the Good, the Bad and the Ugly', archaeologists might agree to focus their discussions of Scottish Beakers on the 'Good'; to avoid the unconditional use of any 'Bad' dates; and henceforth to cease using 'Ugly' dates altogether.

This contribution will start with a brief review of the history of British Beaker dating, followed by a description of developments since the British Museum's attempt at a systematic dating programme in 1991 (Kinnes *et al.* 1991). The ranking of the available Scottish dates will then be outlined, and ways of approaching the interpretation of the 'Good' dates will be considered. The resulting narrative of Scottish Beaker development – and its goodness of fit with Needham's scheme – will then be sketched, and an agenda for future dating requirements set out. Finally, Marischal Museum's current 'Beakers and Bodies' project, which builds on the BPP's work in north-east Scotland, will be introduced.

A brief history of British Beaker dating

In Britain, the task of establishing a chronological framework and sequence for Beaker pottery has occupied antiquarians and archaeologists for over a century, with Thurnam's work in 1871, and Abercromby's *corpus* of Bronze Age pottery (1912), representing the first systematic attempts in this direction (see Clarke 1970 and Needham 2005 for a fuller history of this research). Until the establishment of radiocarbon dating as a routine technique, typology remained the main method of ordering the material, with stratigraphy and associations providing additional clues. This was the basis on which David Clarke established his highly influential scheme in 1970, weighing consideration of formal variability against that of decorative technique, motifs and schemes, to produce a number of stylistic groups. Some of these groups are extensively distributed, others less so, and Clarke interpreted this patterning in terms of a series of episodes of colonisation from continental Europe, followed by regional adoption and adaptation (summarised in Clarke 1970, fig VII). This scheme was pertinently criticised by Lanting and van der Waals (henceforth L&vdW) in 1972, who offered their own, regionally-ordered, step-based typochronology for British Beakers. (Graham Ritchie and Ian Shepherd were the first to adopt this L&vdW scheme to describe Scottish Beakers: see Ritchie and Shepherd 1973.) Other typochronologies were to follow, with Ian Shepherd offering a modified version of the L&vdW scheme for north-east Scotland (Shepherd 1986), and Humphrey Case proposing an 'Early–Middle–Late' scheme for Britain and Ireland, making use of the limited number of radiocarbon dates then available to provide some chronological anchorage (Case 1977; 1993; cf Case 2001). Meanwhile, in 1982, Alex Gibson published the first (and still the only) comprehensive review of Beaker pottery from non-funerary contexts in Britain, reminding us of the need to look beyond funerary beakers in order to build a rounded account of the development of the Beaker ceramic tradition (Gibson 1982).

In the late 1980s, Ian Kinnes and colleagues set out to establish the absolute chronology of British Beaker pottery on a firmer basis by undertaking a programme of new radiocarbon dating, along with a roundup of the published radiocarbon dates that already existed (Kinnes *et al.* 1991). This British Museum programme, which focused on human bone from Beaker graves, produced 20 new dates (including seven for Scottish Beakers) and considered a further 100 dates which had been obtained from various materials and contexts (of which eleven were rejected outright, on grounds such as insecurity of association). The results, presented in various formats including plots featuring the Clarke, L&vdW and Case schemes (*ibid.:* figs 2–7), came as a depressing surprise. Kinnes and his colleagues concluded that no clear chronological pattern emerged to support any of these schemes and that, although a certain degree of chronological patterning in some associated artefacts was suspected, all that could be said for certain was that 'Beaker currency falls in a time band approximately 2600 to 1800 cal BC' (*ibid.:* 39). Various archaeologists' reactions to this gloomy conclusion were published in the same volume of *Scottish Archaeological Review* and although it was agreed that radiocarbon dating was unlikely to provide the fine chronological resolution needed to detect short-term design shifts, it was nevertheless also agreed that further dating should be undertaken; as Kinnes *et al.* put it, 'Clearly it remains worthwhile to increase the database. Direct associations of human bones with Beakers are undoubtedly the most reliable archaeological means to do this and every opportunity should be taken to continue such dating' (*ibid.:* 39).

In the sixteen years since that article was published, much has happened in the world of archaeological dating in general, and in the dating of Scottish Beakers in particular. Before outlining those developments, the most recent attempt at a Britain-wide Beaker typochronology needs to be introduced. Stuart Needham's magisterial article, 'Transforming Beaker Culture in North-West Europe: processes of fusion and fission' (2005), resulted from a thorough reassessment of all types of Beaker dating evidence: not just radiocarbon dates, but also stratigraphy and patterns of artefactual associations. It also took into account the latest Beaker dating evidence from Continental Europe, and set the British developments within this necessary broader perspective. A broad three-phase scheme emerged, as follows:

- Period 1 (during the third quarter of the third millennium BC): introduction of the 'primary Beaker package': Beaker as exotic novelty, and as 'circumscribed, exclusive culture'. Graves with Beakers are relatively rare, and the Beakers are basically of Continental types, in use in specific parts of north-west Europe.
- Period 2 (by the 23rd century, probably between 2250 and 2150 BC, until 1950 BC): the 'fission horizon'; Beaker as 'instituted culture', whereby it became '*de rigeur* to "buy into" Beaker cultural values' (*ibid.:* 207). The use of Beaker pottery now increasingly popular, with marked diversification and regionalisation both in Beaker design and in the associated grave goods and funerary practices. 'Much of the detail of this fascinating transition during the fission horizon has yet to be worked out..' (*ibid.:* 208).
- Period 3 (*c* 1950–1700/1600 BC): 'Beaker as past reference'. Beaker-associated 'graves are almost universally "poor"..While..a minority of communities were still potting in a tradition continued from earlier Beaker ones, the overall picture is of a complex cultural mix of varied Urn, Food Vessel, and [non-Beaker-associated] "rich" burial rites' (*ibid.:* 210).

Needham's scheme, prepared in June 2004, was of course informed by the radiocarbon dating evidence then available for Scottish Beakers; Scottish dates figure prominently in his lists. Since then, more Scottish Beaker dates – including those obtained by the BPP – have emerged, and we can now assess the currently-available evidence against his model.

Developments in the dating of Scottish Beakers since 1991

The following four main developments have shaped our current understanding of Scottish Beaker pottery since the British Museum Programme:

1. Methodological advances made by radiocarbon dating laboratories, working individually and in collaboration. The key advances have been: i) a significant reduction of sample size, thanks to the advent of accelerator-mass spectrometry (AMS) radiocarbon dating in 1985, and its widespread use from the 1990s; ii) improvements in the accuracy and precision of determinations; iii) an improved understanding of the factors that can affect the reliability of the results (*e.g.* bone diagenesis as a result of groundwater leaching: Hedges 2002), and hence improvements in sample preparation and processing, and in the calibration of dates; and iv) the recent advent of a new AMS technique, allowing the dating of cremated bone on the basis of its structural carbonate (Lanting *et al.* 2001). These advances mean that, for around £300 per determination at current rates, it is possible to obtain dates with a precision of ±25–40 radiocarbon years, from samples of under 5g, from a wide variety of materials.

2. Increasing rigour in archaeologists' approaches to sample selection and to the interpretation of results. In Scotland, much credit for this goes to Patrick Ashmore, formerly of Historic Scotland (HS), who imposed strict criteria of acceptability for the submission of any samples to be dated at HS' expense; gone are the days of bulk charcoal samples of mixed (and sometimes unidentified) species. This rigorous approach to sample selection is now the norm in Scotland – as it is south of the Border – irrespective of who funds the dates. Ashmore also initiated a database of all Scottish radiocarbon dates obtained to May 1996 (*www.historic-scotland.gov.uk*); as part of this work, he critically evaluated these dates in terms of their reliability (Ashmore *et al.* 2000). Following the recommendations of the International Study Group on Radiocarbon Dating, Ashmore increased the standard deviation of dates obtained before the mid-1980s, to allow for any methodological shortcomings that may have affected these dates' reliability. As a consequence, many of the dates that had been included in the British Museum's review of existing determinations now have adjusted standard deviations above the maximum acceptable level of ±100.

Regarding the interpretation of radiocarbon dates, two approaches have recently been advocated as a way of enhancing rigour when assessing sets of dates: the application of Bayesian statistical analysis, favoured by Alex Bayliss and colleagues (*e.g.* Bayliss *et al.* 2007b, in discussing dates for Early Neolithic monuments in southern England); and the use of 'wiggle-matching', as used by Anna Brindley in creating a typochronology for Irish Early Bronze Age pottery (see Brindley 2007 for details). Both Bayliss *et al.* and Brindley have called for an end to the traditional (but much less complicated) practice of 'eyeballing' sets of dates. While wiggle-matching has not yet been applied to the study of Scottish Beaker dates, Bayliss *et al.* have recently analysed the Scottish (and English) Beaker dates using the Bayesian approach, and they concluded that Beakers appeared in Scotland marginally later than in England, between 2385 and 2235 BC as opposed to 2475–2315 BC (Bayliss *et al.* 2007a, 50 and fig. 10). Whether that claim is actually correct will be discussed below.

3. An increase in the number of radiocarbon dates for Scottish Beakers. The current total of 116 Scottish Beaker dates (including many that are unacceptable for various reasons), up from the 29 (of similarly variable quality) listed by Kinnes *et al.* in 1991, is due partly to the now-routine use of the technique by excavators, and partly to targeted programmes of Beaker dating, the latter focusing exclusively on funerary contexts. The aforementioned BPP, funded by the Arts and Humanities Research Council, has produced 18 high-quality dates for Scottish samples, with a couple more still to come. A further 18 high-quality dates have now been produced through the NMS programme (with funding assistance from the National Environmental Research Council, Historic Scotland, the Society of Antiquaries of Scotland and Aberdeenshire Archaeology), while Aberdeenshire

Archaeology have sponsored six more dates in their own right (Shepherd 2005). Figure 1 shows the geographical distribution of those currently-available Scottish Beaker dates that fulfil the criterion for ranking as 'Good', as detailed below. Its strong easterly bias is due partly to the original distribution of Beakers in Scotland, partly to the availability of datable material and funds, and partly to the desire to build regionally-robust, inter-comparable datasets, especially for the North East – the first target area for the BPP.

4. An improved understanding of the chronology of Beaker pottery across Europe. This has come about thanks to parallel advances in Beaker radiocarbon dating in different countries (*e.g.* Müller and van Willigen 2004) and to careful reconsideration of associated artefacts (some of which are independently dated) and of relative stratigraphy in Britain and abroad (*e.g.* Case 2001; Needham 2005). All these factors make it easier to detect chronological patterns where they exist (*e.g.* the apparent primacy of Iberia in the emergence of the ceramic style: Harrison and Martín 2001; Kunst 2004), and to spot anomalies (*e.g.* a claimed Beaker presence in Scotland, at Dunragit, Dumfries & Galloway, dating to *c* 2800–2500 BC: Thomas 2004. Here the pottery in question was in fact Late Neolithic Grooved Ware, not Beaker).

Radiocarbon dates for Scottish Beakers in 2007: the Good, the Bad and the Ugly

The 116 currently-available dates for Scottish Beaker pottery can be ranked qualitatively against the following criteria:

- the dated material is closely and unequivocally associated with the Beaker/s that one wishes to date;
- the dated material has a short own-life;
- the dated material is a single-entity sample (*e.g.* a single bone fragment or cereal grain)
- the date has been determined since the mid-1980s, and preferably much more recently than that;
- the standard deviation is less than ±100 (in the current survey, this correlates with the old dates);
- the dated material is not obviously contaminated or of poor quality (*e.g.* poorly-preserved unburnt bone).

The 50 dates listed in Appendix 1, determined using human remains, fulfil most or all of these criteria; almost all of these have been produced as part of a targeted dating programme. These can be regarded as 'Good' dates, and they are shown in calibrated form in Fig. 11.2. The geographical distribution of the findspots in question

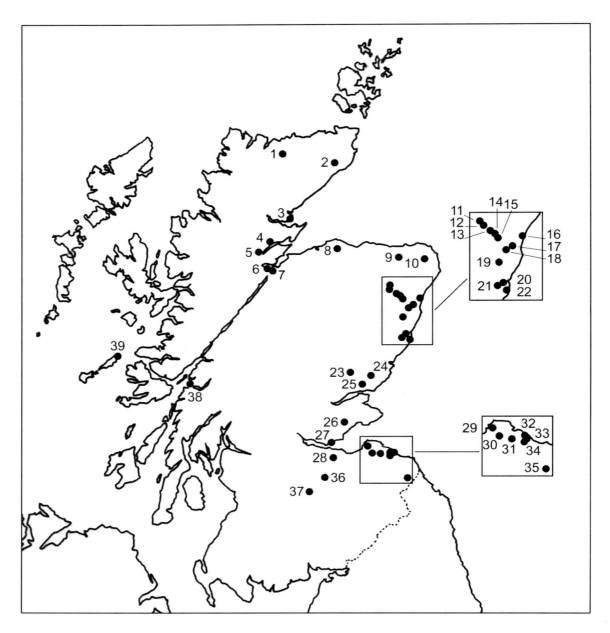

Fig. 11.1   Findspots of Scottish Beakers associated with the 'Good' dates as listed in Appendix 1. Key: 1. Chealamy; 2. Achavanich; 3. Dornoch Nursery; 4. Fyrish; 5. Fodderty; 6. Lochend; 7.Holm Mains Farm; 8. Lesmurdie; 9. Slap; 10. Sandhole; 11. Old Rayne; 12. Newlands; 13. nr. Manar House, Inverurie; 14. Broomend of Crichie; 15. Tavelty; 16. Keir; 17. Stoneywood; 18. Borrowstone; 19. Park Quarry, Durris; 20. Nether Criggie; 21. Keabog; 22. Uppermains; 23. Cookston; 24. Bractullo; 25. Middle Brighty; 26. Balfarg; 27. Barns Farm; 28. Juniper Green; 29. West Fenton; 30. Abbey Mains Farm, Haddington; 31. Ruchlaw; 32. Dryburn Bridge; 33. Skateraw; 34. Thurston Mains; 35. Doons Law; 36. West Water Reservoir; 37. Boatbridge Quarry, Thankerton; 38. Achnacreebeag; 39. Sorisdale.

is shown in Fig. 11.1; and Figs. 11.3–7 show images of the Beakers in question, where illustrations already exist.

Appendix 2 lists potentially 'Good' dates, from non-funerary contexts where there is a reasonably good chance that the dated material was contemporary with the Beakers, but where the closeness of association is not as good as with the Appendix 1 specimens. The dated samples are all of short-life material (*e.g.* cereal grains), and in most cases single entity samples have been used. Their relationship with the Beakers in question includes

cases where they had been found in the fill of a pit, and no obviously later material had been found in that pit fill. Figure 11.8 shows the calibrated dates, the geographical distribution of the findspots, and images of the more complete or reconstructable of the Beakers concerned.

Now for the 'Bad' dates, which should not be cited in discussions of Beaker dating unless their shortcomings are clearly stated. Appendices 3 and 4 present dates for funerary and non-funerary contexts respectively where the closeness of association with the Beakers concerned

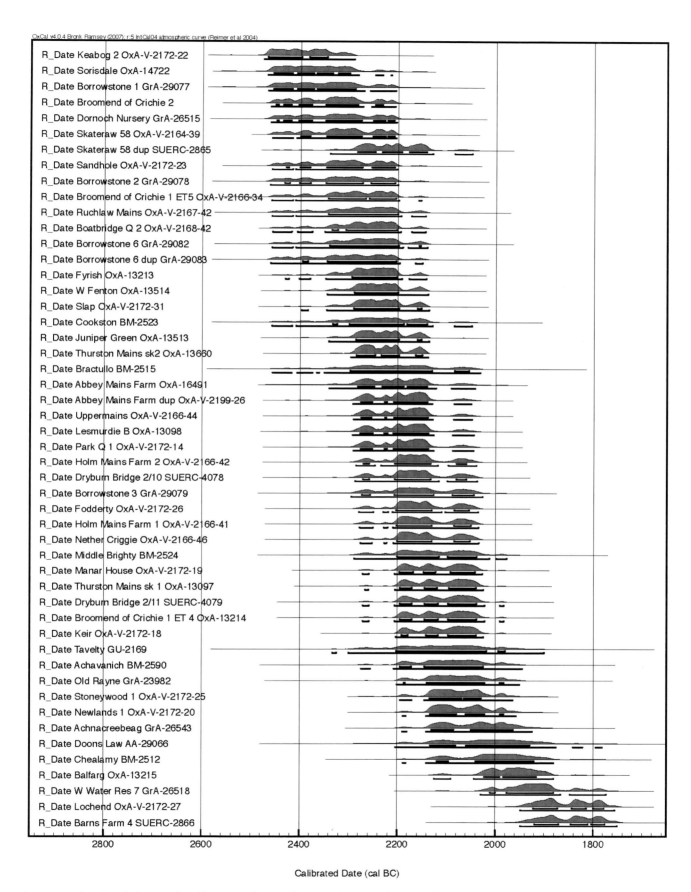

Fig. 11.2 The 'Good' dates as listed in Appendix 1, calibrated using OxCal v.4; results normalised. Note: although OxCal v.3.10 has been used to calibrate the dates in the Appendices, the results are effectively identical to those shown here.

leaves more to be desired. In some cases, the dates in question have other shortcomings (such as the use of oak charcoal, or non-single-entity samples).

Finally, the 'Ugly' dates – that is, ones that should not be cited any more in discussions of Beaker dating (even though some are perfectly sound in other respects, and for other purposes) – are listed in Appendices 5–7. Appendix 5 deals with old dates from funerary contexts, whose standard deviation has had to be increased to over ±100. In several cases, the skeletons in question have been re-dated recently. With some of these the new determination is closely comparable with the original date (*e.g.* Boatbridge Quarry, Thankerton, cist 2: originally dated to 3835±75 BP (GU-1117) during the early 1980s, now re-dated for the BPP to 3824±32 BP (OxA-V-2168-42)); while with others, the difference is significant (*e.g.* Sandhole, Fetterangus: original 1980s date 3650±50 BP (GU-2100), new BPP date 3845±32 BP (OxA-V-2172-23)). Appendix 6 lists dates from non-funerary contexts that suffer both from standard deviations in excess of ±100 and from insufficiently-close association with the Beakers in question. Finally, Appendix 7 rounds up dates that can be rejected for a variety of reasons, including residuality of pre-Beaker material or intrusion of post-Beaker material; misidentification of the pottery; use of a non-single entity sample; insecure or mis-association; insufficient collagen; and contamination. Three dates for bone samples – from Broomend of Crichie cist 2; Abbey Mains Farm, Haddington; and Holm of Papa Westray North – have been deleted from the Oxford Radiocarbon Accelerator Unit datelist because of a contamination problem at that laboratory, affecting ultrafiltration equipment used to pretreat bone specimens, between 2000 and 2002 (Bronk Ramsey *et al.* 2004). Two of these have been re-determined and the results are given in Appendix 1. Re-dating may be a solution with some of the other 'Ugly' dates, and this has indeed been attempted, twice, with the human remains from the 1972 Skateraw cist; unfortunately these failed due to insufficient collagen being present, and this might account for the anomalous nature of the initial SRR-453 date, obtained during the 1970s.

It cannot be guaranteed that the Appendices cover *every* date that has been obtained for the purposes of dating Beaker pottery in Scotland, since not all dates have been published, and Historic Scotland's practice of publishing an annual datelist in *Discovery and Excavation in Scotland*, alongside the NMS' own list, has apparently ceased. Nevertheless the list presented here is as comprehensive as possible, and it certainly gives a good impression of the overall number of dates involved, the range of material that has been dated, and the various issues involved in interpreting the dates.

Interpreting the results: a coherent narrative of Scottish Beaker development?

If one considers the 50 'Good' dates in Appendix 1 (plus the potentially 'Good' dates listed in Appendix 2), what do these tell us about Scottish Beaker chronology? And how are we to approach their interpretation? Two important initial comments need to be made. The first is that the existing body of dates does not tell us the full story – especially as far as the earliest Scottish Beakers are concerned. The second is that, for all the claims made about the ability of Bayesian statistical analysis and wiggle-matching to achieve relatively fine-grained chronological resolution, their application is not a wholly objective exercise, nor are these techniques able to overcome entirely the chronological uncertainties inherent in radiocarbon dates.

Regarding the earliest Scottish Beakers – the ones which, according to Needham's persuasive scheme, should be very close to their Continental forerunners – it seems that, while Needham is indeed correct in arguing that these are relatively rare, they are also clearly under-represented in the radiocarbon dating record. The simple, non-cist grave at Sorisdale on Coll, with its All-Over-Cord-decorated Beaker of Needham's Low Carinated (LC) type (Fig. 3.2), is unusual in having preserved bone that could be dated. Beaker-associated non-cist graves are very rare in Scotland, and normally all traces of their original occupants have decayed away. Amost invariably, however, they are orientated E-W and are associated with Continental-style, LC Beakers, whose technique of manufacture shows strong links with Continental practices (Hammersmith 2005). Examples are described and discussed below (see 'Conclusions'). Perhaps the most striking of these is the all-over herringbone-decorated LC Beaker found at Newmill, Perth & Kinross (Fig. 11.9; Watkins and Shepherd 1980; Shepherd 1986: 4). This Dutch-style Beaker was found in a Dutch-style grave, with a penannular ditch and a central rectangular grave-pit, the grave being covered by a small, low mound of large pebbles (see Watkins and Shepherd 1980 for details.) The acid soil had destroyed all traces of the associated, E-W-orientated body, which had been buried in a very thin coffin, possibly of bark. On current reckoning against dated Dutch *comparanda*, this pot should date to around the 25th century BC (Lanting pers. Comm.) and should therefore be one of Britain's earliest Beakers; the grave's orientation, as its excavators pointed out (Watkins and Shepherd 1980: 41), is reminiscent of that associated with Protruding Foot Beakers in the Netherlands.

If, on the basis of this observation, one accepts that Beaker use could have started in Scotland as early as the 25th century BC – and this is not contradicted by the Sorisdale date of 2460–2300 cal BC (at 95% probability) – then this calls into question Bayliss *et al*'s claim that it started as late as 2385–2235 BC, and was later than initial

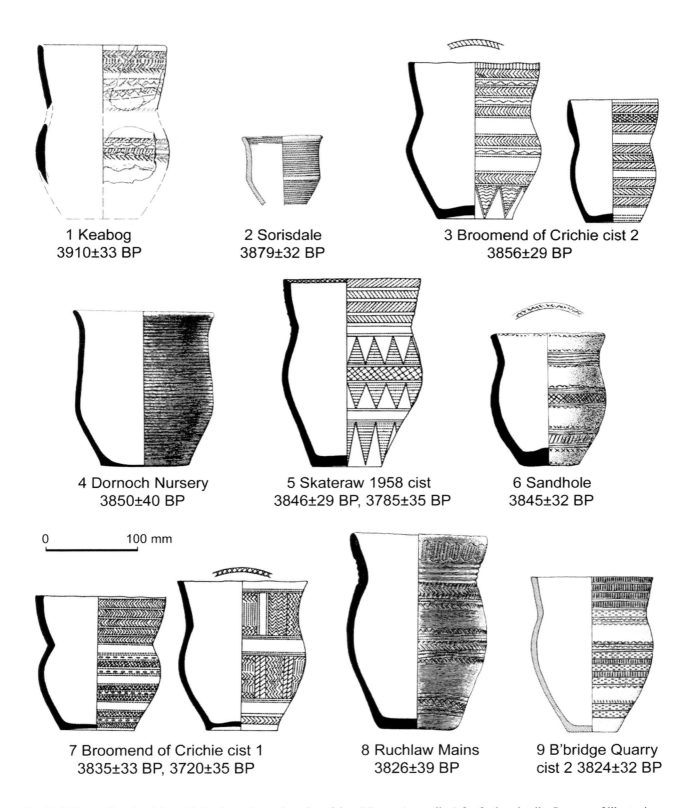

Fig. 11.3 The earliest dated Scottish Beakers, shown in order of date BP; see Appendix 1 for further details. Sources of illustrations: 1: Shepherd and Bruce 1987; 2: Ritchie and Crawford 1978; 3,5,7: Clarke 1970; 4: Ashmore 1989; 6: Ralston 1996; 8: Ashmore *et al.* 1982; 9: Clarke *et al.* 1984. For illustration of Beakers from Borrowstone that fall within the date range shown here, see Fig. 11.4.

Borrowstone cist 1
3865±40 BP

Borrowstone cist 2
3845±40 BP

Borrowstone cist 3
3750±45 BP

Nr Manar House
3725±33 BP

Fig. 11.4 Dated Beakers from Borrowstone and from near Manar House, Aberdeenshire. (Note: image of dated Beaker from Borrowstone cist 6 not available.) Copyright University of Aberdeen, reproduced courtesy of Marischal Museum.

Beaker use in England. The reason for this discrepancy is that Bayliss *et al.* were relying solely on the existing set of Scottish radiocarbon dates, almost all of which derive from cist graves (which were evidently *not* the earliest type of Beaker-associated grave in Scotland). The Bayesian treatment of radiocarbon dates – which works best with date sets relating to a single, stratigraphically-differentiated site rather than to those such as the Scottish Beaker dates – tends, for good reasons, to narrow the overall range of dates for a given set of events (Bayliss *et al.* 2007b). Key to the success of the method is the making of subjective value judgements regarding the reliability and significance of individual dates, and to the identification and weeding-out of 'outliers'. By not factoring in the possibility that Beakers *may* have been in use in Scotland as early as the 25th century, the statistical programme compressed the existing dates into a range that may well turn out to be too narrow. Similar problems are likely to pertain to the use of wiggle-matching, as a

close reading of Brindley's recent study of Irish Bronze Age ceramic typochronology (2007) can reveal. Brindley's claims, for instance, that many dates for Scottish Food Vessels seem 'too young' (*ibid.:* 304) arguably stem not from any problem with the dates in question, but from an attempt to impose an Irish ceramic typochronology on a Scottish ceramic tradition that could genuinely have had a longer duration than its Irish congener.

If one sets aside concerns about the application of Bayesian statistics and wiggle-matching – which are both techniques that require skills that the present author does not yet possess – and examine the Scottish radiocarbon dates at face value, warts and all, then what picture emerges?

To cut a long story short, it appears that the evidence generally fits Needham's model well. The overall currency for Scottish Beaker use, taking on board the aforementioned shortage of dates for the earliest material, would seem to span the 25th century BC to *c* 1800 BC (ie *c* 3900/3875–3550 BP). The vast majority of dates fall within the last three centuries of the third millennium BC (ie *c* 3850–3650 BP); this, and the diversity of designs represented, fit with Needham's model of a 'fission horizon'. However, if one considers the totality of dates covering the diverse designs that characterise this phase of Beaker-related activity, it appears that this 'fission horizon' may have started slightly earlier in Scotland than in southern England – perhaps as early as *c* 2350 BC (with the Keabog cist 2 date seeming to be a markedly early example). Here, arguably, is a case where the careful use of Bayesian statistics and/or wiggle matching might help to clarify matters.

The end of the Beaker tradition in Scotland, which on current evidence seems to have occurred during the first two centuries of the second millennium BC (i.e. *c.* 3650–3550 BP), does indeed seem to be marked by the changes in design identified in Needham's 'Beaker as past reference' period, with Beaker/Food Vessel hybrid forms and handled Beakers in use. (See also Manby 2004 on the use of handled Beakers, and note that there is one Scottish 'hybrid' Beaker/Food Vessel handled pot that is likely to be earlier than the other 'hybrid' and handled vessels: the unique specimen from Mains of Craichie, Angus (Coutts 1971: no. 83a), which combines Beaker motifs with a bipartite Irish Bowl Food Vessel shape, and can be dated to the last two centuries of the third millennium on the basis of its shape, decoration, and associated flat bronze dagger: Sheridan 2007, fig. 14.12.) The question of the duration of the overlap between the Food Vessel and Beaker traditions in Scotland, and indeed of the Urn traditions as well, is another area where the current author disagrees with Brindley's reading of the Scottish evidence (Brindley 2007, 297–325). If one uses the much-maligned 'eyeballing' technique, it appears that there was at least a two century overlap in the use of Beakers and Food Vessels (see Sheridan 2004 and 2007 for further discussion); but again, the future use of Bayesian statistics and/or wiggle-matching on the Scottish date sets may change this impression. What is clear is that Food Vessels were in use in Scotland by the 22nd century – some three centuries after the appearance of Beaker pottery – and the directly dated Beaker/Food Vessel 'hybrids' suggest that pottery relatable to the Beaker tradition was still being made around 1800 BC. Of particular interest in this regard is the distibution pattern for Beakers and Food Vessels in north-east Scotland, with Aberdeenshire having many Beakers and very few Food Vessels, while in Angus the opposite is the case. The chronological aspect of this phemonenon is something that the new radiocarbon dating programme led by Marischal Museum (see below) is currently addressing.

What else can be said about Scottish Beaker use from the evidence currently available? Given the inherent imprecision of the radicarbon dating technique, it is a moot point whether a fine-grained (and preferably regionally-specific) typochronology can be developed, especially given the 'plateau' in the radiocarbon calibration curve around 3700 BP (Müller and van Willigen 2004, fig 2): this produces a 'bunching' of the calibrated results, making it hard to tease out details of design changes within the date range. No doubt there will in future be attempts to undertake the kind of detailed stylistic seriation as used by Brindley for Irish Early Bronze Age pottery, and judicious use of wiggle-matching and/or Bayesian statistical analysis may well help to improve the chronological resolution for at least parts of the period of Beaker use. In the meantime, certain specific observations can be offered.

The first concerns the currency of the All-Over-Cord-decorated (AOC) variant of LC Beakers, one of the types of beaker with clear Continental ancestry. The two dates from Sorisdale and Dornoch Nursery Cist (Appendix 1) suggest that it is likely to have been in use by the 24th, if not the 25th century BC; and the dates from the non-funerary contexts at Eweford and Fox Plantation (Appendix 2) suggest that it was still being made during the 23rd or 22nd century. A similar impression is gained from the other dates that are ostensibly associated with AOC pottery, from Sligeanach on South Uist and Machrie North on Arran (Appendix 2). A comparable currency for these and other kinds of Beaker with strong and widespread Continental parallels is evident elsewhere in Britain and Ireland (Brindley 2004; Needham 2005).

The second is that the dating evidence now available confirms earlier suspicions (as expressed, for example, by Ian Shepherd in 1986) that there had been a design influence from the Netherlands to north-east Scotland during the last three centuries of the third millennium – *in addition* to any previous Dutch (or other Continental) influence on Scottish/British Beaker design. This is evident, for example, in the fact that the dated Beaker from Fyrish (Fig. 11.5.1) bears at least a passing resemblance to Dutch Veluwe Beakers (*e.g.* Kalbeck: Lanting and van der Waals 1976: fig 26), and is comparable with them in date. Similarly, Dutch influence has been detected in the design of the Chealamy Beaker (Fig. 11.7.3), and in the very similar example – unfortunately associated with an anomalously late date – from Mains of Balnagowan (Appendix 7; Shepherd *et al.* 1984). Furthermore, such influence was not limited to ceramics, as the Dutch-style copper diadems or neck rings from Lumphanan, Aberdeenshire, indicate (Shepherd 1986: 9; Needham 2004: 237–8). Nor, indeed, is the area of contact limited to north-east Scotland. For all their faults, Clarke's stylistic groupings (Clarke 1970) highlight widespread and regionally-variable design links across the North Sea; Clarke and Case (*e.g.* Case 2004) have argued for a possible lower Rhine conduit for the ultimately north European fashion of using battle axeheads as grave goods; and Needham has argued for the presence of a Veluwe-style Beaker, along with a

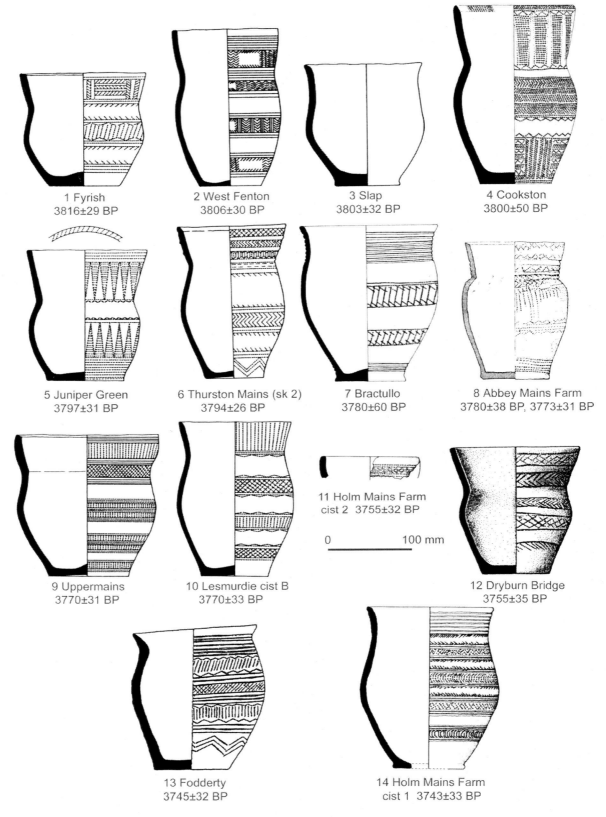

Fig. 11.5 Dated Scottish Beakers, continued. Sources of illustrations: 1–3,5,6,9,10: Clarke 1970; 4,7: Coutts 1971; 8: Lawson *et al.* 2002; 11,14: Headland Archaeology; 12: CFA Archaeology (A. Dunwell); 13: Robin Hanley. Note: i) other Beakers dating to within this range but not shown here: Borrowstone cist 3 (see Fig. 4), Park Quarry Durris, cist 1 (no illustration available); ii) Thurston Mains: other skeleton from same cist dated to 3721±33 BP; iii) Dryburn Bridge: other skeleton from same cist dated to 3720±35 BP; see Appendix 1 for discussion.

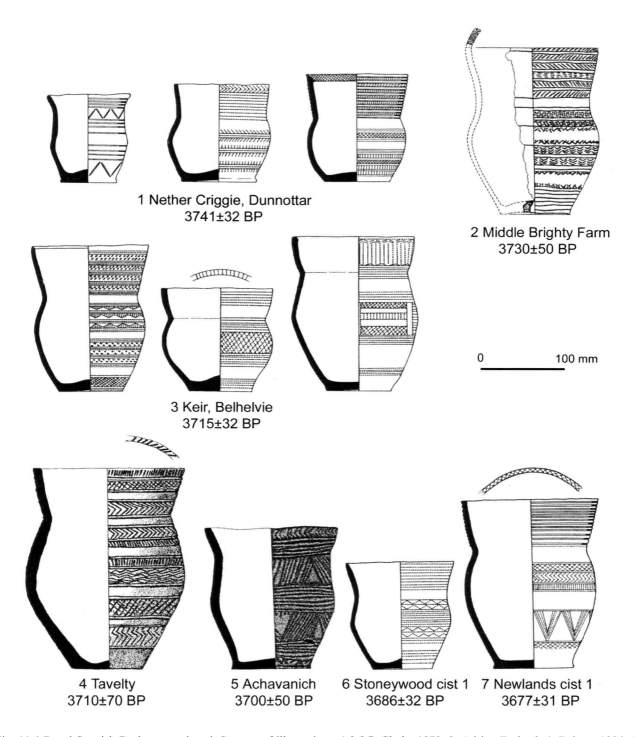

Fig. 11.6 Dated Scottish Beakers, continued. Sources of illustrations: 1,3,5,7: Clarke 1970; 2: Adrian Zealand; 4: Ralston 1996; 5: Tricia Weeks. See Figs. 11.3–5 for illustrations of other Beakers with dates falling within the range shown here (and see Appendix 1 for further details), and note there is no illustration of the lost Beaker from Old Rayne.

tanged copper knife closely comparable with Dutch examples, at Shrewton (5K, Wiltshire: Needham 1976: table 3; 2005). As far as Scottish Beakers are concerned, it would be useful to re-compare them with Dutch Beakers to assess the likely strength of the Dutch influence – and to interpret what it signifies (c.f. Clarke 1970: chapter 13; Lanting and van der Waals 1972).

Conclusions, and the future of Scottish Beaker studies

This brief review of the radiocarbon dating evidence for Scottish Beakers has not set out to offer a thorough-going reassessment of all the strands of evidence for Beaker typochronology that are currently available; to a degree, that task has already been tackled by others (principally

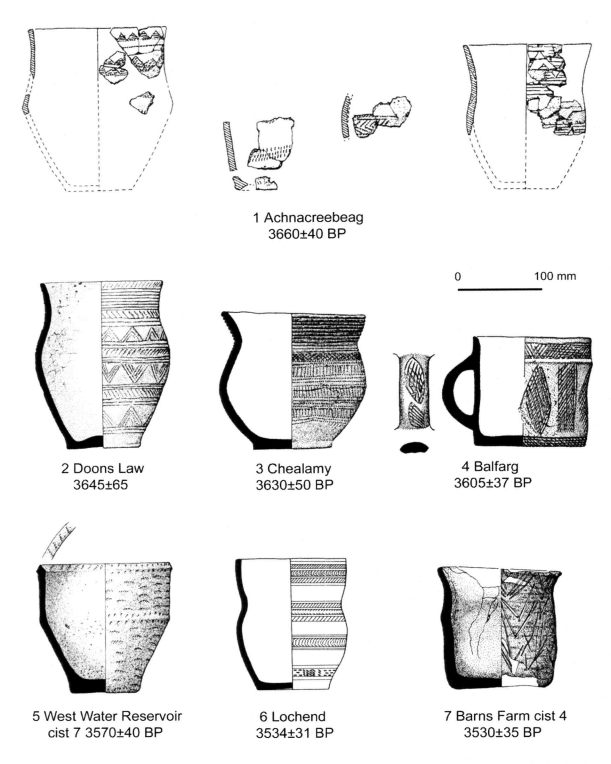

1 Achnacreebeag
3660±40 BP

0 ⊢————⊣ 100 mm

2 Doons Law
3645±65

3 Chealamy
3630±50 BP

4 Balfarg
3605±37 BP

5 West Water Reservoir
cist 7 3570±40 BP

6 Lochend
3534±31 BP

7 Barns Farm cist 4
3530±35 BP

Fig. 11.7 Dated Scottish Beakers, continued. Sources of illustrations:1:Ritchie 1970; 2: Clarke and Hamilton 1999; 3: Gourlay 1984; 4: Mercer 1981; 5: Hunter 2000; 6: Clarke 1970; 7: Watkins 1982. Note: i) it is unclear to which of the Achnacreebeag Beakers the date relates; the two most complete pots could be earlier; ii) the West Water Reservoir date is a *terminus ante quem* for the illustrated vessel.

Case 2001 and Needham 2005). Its completion, through a detailed study of context, associations and stratigraphy, is best pursued separately. Nor has it addressed vital questions such as how and why Beaker pottery started to be used in Scotland; whether the process/es involved were the same as the ones that brought Beaker use to elsewhere in Britain; or what is signified by its widespread adoption and eventual abandonment. However, it does offer a way of assessing the radiocarbon evidence that is currently available; it builds the

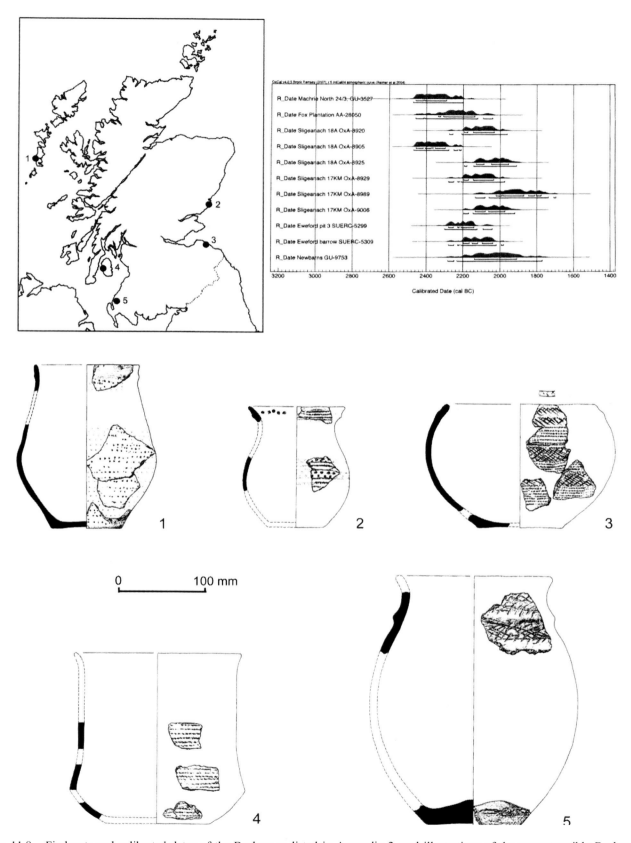

Fig. 11.8   Findspots and calibrated dates of the Beakers as listed in Appendix 2, and illustrations of the reconstructible Beakers from Eweford (nos. 1–4: from pit; no. 5: from cairn built on long barrow). Key to map: 1. Sligeanach, S. Uist; 2. Newbarns, Angus; 3. Eweford, East Lothian; 4. Machrie North, Arran; 5. Fox Plantation, Dumfries & Galloway. Note: although dates are calibrated here using OxCal v.4, they are effectively identical to those calibrated using OxCal v.3.10 as listed in Appendix 2. Beaker illustrations by Jill Seivewright, reproduced by courtesy of Gavin MacGregor.

Fig. 11.9 Fig 9 The Dutch-style Beaker (of All-Over-Ornamented, Low-Carinated type), with its associated flint artefacts, from a Dutch-style grave at Newmill, Perth & Kinross. Photo: National Museums Scotland.

foundations for an overall chronological picture; and it helps to set the agenda for future radiocarbon dating work.

Obvious agenda issues include the following:

- the need for a critical mass of dates (and, if possible, a better geographical spread of dated material to counteract the current east Scottish bias: Fig. 11.1), so that any regionally-specific trends, or trends relating to specific techniques of Beaker manufacture, can be distinguished from the overall picture;
- the need for more dates relating to the earliest Beakers in Scotland, so that the repertoire of designs can be defined more clearly, and the relationship (chronological, geographical and contextual) between Beaker use and the use of Grooved Ware and any other Late Neolithic pottery can be clarified. This will probably depend on the discovery of new material, as the existing dating opportunities relating to early-style Beakers are rapidly being exhausted;
- the need for more dates relating to the last few centuries of Beaker use, so that the geographical and contextual relationship between the various ceramic traditions current at the beginning of the second millennium BC can be explored further;
- re-dating of the skeletal material whose existing dates have unacceptably large standard deviations or which seem anomalous (and

indeed re-dating of any potentially promising, well-contexted material to which the same applies). The anomalies might arguably include the dates from Keabog and Lochend which, if one compares them with other dates for similar-looking Beakers, appear to be rather early and late respectively.

Some idea of the specific questions that might usefully be addressed by targeted radiocarbon work in Scotland in the future has been offered above. In particular, an enhanced set of dates for our earliest beakers might help us to examine the mechanisms involved in the appearance of Beaker pottery, especially given that the recent discoveries at Amesbury and Boscombe Down in Wiltshire (and indeed at the Ross Island copper mine in south-west Ireland: O'Brien 2004: 557–573) have rekindled debate on the degree to which small-scale immigration from the Continent could have been a key factor. At present, two interesting and different (though not necessarily mutually exclusive) contextual patterns can be detected among the Beakers that are likely to be Scotland's earliest examples, as follows:

Pattern 1: Early Beakers in Continental-style graves, raising the intriguing possibility of possible immigrants, analogous to the 'Amesbury Archer' and 'Boscombe Bowmen'. As discussed above, inhumation in a simple grave (with or without a wooden 'coffin'), rather than a stone cist, is a rare occurrence in Scotland and, when associated with early-type Beakers, is likely to reflect Continental practice (*pace* Gibson 2004 and this volume). A small number of such graves can be identified in disparate parts of Scotland, of which the aforementioned, Dutch-style example from Newmill in east-central Scotland (with its ?bark coffin, encircling ring ditch and LC All Over Ornamented Beaker) is one. The recently re-dated grave from Sorisdale on the Hebridean island of Coll, with its LC AOC Beaker, is another; a third is the shallow oval grave edged by a stone kerb, dug into a non-megalithic long barrow, on Biggar Common, South Lanarkshire, in southern Scotland (Johnston 1997, 194–5). This had contained a LC Beaker with zones of comb impressions (in otherwords, a Bell Beaker of Clarke's E, and of L&vdW step 2 type), aong with a small cord-decorated pot reminiscent of (but later than) Corded Ware, and a small undecorated dish with Continental *comparanda* (Sheridan 1997: 215–7). Like the Newmill and Sorisdale examples, this grave was orientated E-W. A fourth, once more featuring a shallow, oval, E-W orientated pit which is most likely to have been a grave, has recently been excavated at Beechwood Park, Inverness, Highland, in north-east Scotland (Suddaby and Sheridan 2006); this contained an undecorated LC Beaker. A fifth probable example has just come to light at Upper Largie, Argyll & Bute (Cook pers. Comm.): here, three Continental-style Beakers including one AOC example were found in a pit encircled by a ring-ditch, dug into gravel. Two AOC Beakers from a sand quarry at Bathgate, West Lothian, in the Central Belt of Scotland, are also likely to have come from simple graves, unrecognised at the time of the pots' discovery (Mann 1906, 369–71; *Proceedings of the Society of Antiquaries of Scotland* 55 (1920–1), 12). Unfortunately, only one of these findspots (Sorisdale) has produced human remains. (A further pit containing an undecorated LC Beaker at Boghead, Aberdeenshire (Burl 1984, 39–40), is excluded from this list of possible non-cist graves as it is smaller than them and, rather than being a grave, may have been associated with non-funerary ceremonies held in the vicinity of a much earlier, Early Neolithic monument. The same is true of the pit at Eweford, with its LC AOC Beaker: see Appendix 2. And, unfortunately, too little is known about a cemetery of 17 round barrows with east-west-orientated central graves at Newton on Islay (McCullagh 1989) to tell whether this might have been a Beaker-period cemetery, although this remains a possibility and further investigation would be worthwhile.)

Pattern 2: AOC Beakers, in a variety of intriguing contexts, perhaps suggesting complex mechanisms for the adoption of this style of Beaker. This is a particularly widely-distributed style of Beaker, with a possible example being found as far north as Shetland (Calder 1950: 194). A North British bias to AOC Beaker distribution – allied with a dense concentration in Wessex – has long been recognised (*e.g.* Clarke 1970, 529–30, map 1; Case 2001: Group C), as has its coastal bias. In Scotland it has been found in a number of non-funerary contexts, mostly on or near the coast (including the aforementioned Eweford pit; for other findspots, see Gibson 1982, Ritchie 1970 and Ritchie and Shepherd 1973), and in a variety of funerary contexts. These range from the by-now familiar grave at Sorisdale (Ritchie and Crawford 1978), to an Orkney-Cromarty passage tomb at Kilcoy South, Highland; to definite and possible ring-cairns at Sundayswells, Aberdeenshire (Henshall 1963: 255, 399) and Muirkirk, East Ayrshire respectively (Ritchie 1970; Ritchie and Shepherd 1973); and, rarely, to the stone cist format that constitutes the commonest form of Beaker-associated grave type in Scotland (*e.g.* at Dornoch Nursery Cist, Highland: Ashmore 1989). This interesting distributional range and contextual variety – which, as we have seen, may cover two or three centuries' activity – invites further investigation and explanation. This is particularly important given the considerable skill with which many of the vessels in question have been manufactured: specific technical parallels with Continental Beaker manufacturing technique (Hammersmith 2005 and pers comm, and cf. van der Leeuw 1976) suggest that *some* of these pots *may* have been manufactured by immigrant specialist potters.

Clearly there is much more that needs to be understood about Scotland's Beakers. It is hoped that many more radiocarbon dates will be obtained in the future, and in this respect the aforementioned new programme of radiocarbon dating and isotope-based dietary research recently initiated by Neil Curtis of Marischal Museum

(with Leverhulme funding) is warmly welcomed. This 'Beakers and People' project, inspired by and building on the BPP, aims to obtain some 40 new dates for Beaker and contemporary short cist burials in north-east Scotland. Not only will it be able to address the question of the chronological relationship between Aberdeenshire's Beakers and Angus' Food Vessels; it will also, arguably, make north-east Scotland the best-dated region of Chalcolithic and Early Bronze Age Britain. The future of Scottish Beaker studies is therefore bright.

Acknowledgements

Many institutions and individuals have provided invaluable help and support for the NMS Beaker Dating programme. For funding, the author thanks the National Environmental Research Council, Historic Scotland (especially Patrick Ashmore), the Society of Antiquaries of Scotland, and Aberdeenshire Archaeology (especially Ian Shepherd). Tom Higham at the Oxford laboratory, Gordon Cook at the SUERC laboratory, East Kilbride and Jan Lanting (University of Groningen) have provided expert advice on the dating results. The author also thanks Patrick Ashmore, Stuart Needham, Ian and Lekky Shepherd and David Clarke for their comments on previous drafts of this paper, Hattie Hammersmith for her observations on AOC Beaker manufacture, and Gavin MacGregor and Niall Sharples for pre-publication information on the radiocarbon dates from Eweford and Fox Plantation, and from Sligeanach, respectively. Beaker illustrations are reproduced by kind permission of the Society of Antiquaries of Scotland, Cambridge University Press, the University of Aberdeen (with thanks to Neil Curtis and Neil Wilkin) and individual artists; others who have provided illustrations are named in the figure captions. Craig Angus is thanked for his Photoshop assistance. Finally, Mike Parker Pearson and Rajka Makjanic are thanked for their patience.

References

Abercromby, J. 1912. *The Bronze Age Pottery of Great Britain and Ireland*. Oxford: Clarendon Press.

Ashmore, P. J., Brooks, M., Maté, I. and Strong, P. 1982. A cist at Ruchlaw Mains, East Lothian. *Proceedings of the Society of Antiquaries of Scotland* 112: 542–548.

Ashmore, P. J. 1989. Excavation of a beaker cist at Dornoch Nursery, Sutherland. *Proceedings of the Society of Antiquaries of Scotland* 119: 63–71.

Ashmore, P. J., Cook, G. T. and Harkness, D. D. 2000. A radiocarbon database for Scottish archaeological samples. *Radiocarbon* 42(1): 41–48.

Atkinson, J. A. 2002. Excavation of a Neolithic occupation site at Chapelfield, Cowie, Stirling. *Proceedings of the Society of Antiquaries of Scotland* 132: 139–92.

Barber, J. 1997. *The Archaeological Investigation of a Prehistoric Landscape: Excavations on Arran 1978–*

1981. Edinburgh: Scottish Trust for Archaeological Research.

Bayliss, A., McAvoy, F. and Whittle, A. 2007a. The world recreated: redating Silbury Hill in its monumental landscape. *Antiquity* 81: 26–53.

Bayliss, A., Bronk Ramsey, C., van der Plicht, J. and Whittle, A. 2007b. Bradshaw and Bayes: towards a timetable for the Neolithic. *Cambridge Archaeological Journal* 17:1 (supplement): 1–28.

Brindley, A. 2004. Prehistoric pottery. In W. O'Brien, *Ross Island. Mining, Metal and Society in Early Ireland*. Galway: National University of Ireland, Galway. 316–38.

Brindley, A. 2007. *The Dating of Food Vessels and Urns in Ireland*. Galway: National University of Ireland, Galway.

Bronk Ramsey, C., Higham, T., Bales, A. and Hedges, R. E. M. 2004. Improvements in the pretreatment of bone at Oxford.. *Radiocarbon* 46(1): 155–163.

Burl, H. A. W. 1984. Report on the excavation of a Neolithic mound at Boghead, Speymouth Forest, Fochabers, Moray, 1972 and 1974. *Proceedings of the Society of Antiquaries of Scotland* 114: 35–73 & fiche 1: A2–C10.

Calder, C. S. T. 1950. Report on the excavation of a Neolithic temple at Stanydale in the parish of Sandsting, Shetland. *Proceedings of the Society of Antiquaries of Scotland* 84 (1949–50): 185–205.

Case, H. J. 1977. The Beaker culture in Britain and Ireland. In R.J. Mercer (ed.), *Beakers in Britain and Europe: Four Studies*. Oxford. British Archaeological Reports, International Series 26. 71–101.

Case, H. J. 1993. Beakers: deconstruction and after. *Proceedings of the Prehistoric Society* 59: 241–268.

Case, H. J. 2001. The Beaker Culture in Britain and Ireland: groups, European contacts and chronology. In: Nicolis F. (ed.), *Bell Beakers Today. Pottery, People, Culture, Symbols in Prehistoric Europe*. Proceedings of the International Colloquium at Riva del Garda 11–16 May 1998. Trento: Servicio Beni Culturali, Provincia Autonoma di Trento. 361–77.

Case, H. J. 2004. Bell Beaker and Corded Ware Culture burial associations: a bottom-up rather than top-down approach. In A. M. Gibson and J. A. Sheridan (eds.), *From Sickles to Circles: Britain and Ireland at the Time of Stonehenge*. Stroud: Tempus. 201–14.

Clarke C. and Hamilton, J. 1999. Excavation of a cist burial on Doons Law, Leetside Farm, Whitsome, Berwickshire. *Proceedings of the Society of Antiquaries of Scotland* 129: 189–201.

Clarke, D. L. 1970. *Beaker Pottery of Great Britain and Ireland*. Cambridge: Cambridge University Press.

Clarke, D. V., Ritchie, A. and Ritchie, J. N. G. 1984. Two cists from Boatbridge Quarry, Thankerton, Lanarkshire. *Proceedings of the Society of Antiquaries of Scotland* 114: 557–560.

Coutts, H. 1971. *Tayside Before History*. Dundee: Dundee Museum and Art Gallery.

Davidson, C. B. 1868. Notice of further stone kists found at Broomend near the Inverurie paper-mills. *Proceedings of the Society of Antiquaries of Scotland* 7 (1866–8): 115–118.

Gibson, A. M. 1982. *Beaker Domestic Sites. A Study of the Domestic Pottery of the late Third and early Second Millennia B.C. in the British Isles*. Oxford: British Archaeological Reports 107.

Gibson, A. M. 2004. Burials and beakers: seeing beneath the veneer in Late Neolithic Britain. In J. Czebreszuk (ed.), *Similar but Different: Bell Beakers in Europe*. Poznan: Adam Mickiewicz University. 173–92.

Gourlay, R. B. 1984. A short cist beaker inhumation from Chealamy, Strathnaver, Sutherland. *Proceedings of the Society of Antiquaries of Scotland* 114: 567–571.

Hammersmith, H. 2005. *British Beaker Construction Technologies*. Unpublished MSc dissertation, University of Edinburgh.

Harrison, R. J. and Martín A. M. 2001. Bell Beakers and social complexity in Central Spain. In F. Nicolis (ed.), *Bell Beakers Today. Pottery, People, Culture, Symbols in Prehistoric Europe*. Proceedings of the International Colloquium at Riva del Garda 11–16 May 1998. Trento: Servicio Beni Culturali, Provincia Autonoma di Trento. 111–24.

Hedges, R. E. M. 2002. Bone diagenesis: an overview of processes. *Radiocarbon* 44(3): 319–328.

Henshall, A. S. 1963. *The Chambered Tombs of Scotland. Volume I*. Edinburgh: Edinburgh University Press.

Hunter, F. J. 2000. Excavation of an Early Bronze Age cemetery and other sites at West Water Reservoir, West Linton, Scottish Borders. *Proceedings of the Society of Antiquaries of Scotland* 130: 115–182.

Johnston, D. A. 1997. Biggar Common 1987–93: an early prehistoric funerary and domestic landscape in Clydesdale, South Lanarkshire. *Proceedings of the Society of Antiquaries of Scotland* 127: 185–253.

Kinnes, I. A., Gibson, A. M., Ambers, J., Bowman, S., Leese, M. and Boast, R. 1991. Radiocarbon dating and British Beakers: the British Museum programme. *Scottish Archaeological Review* 8: 35–68.

Kunst, M. 2004. Invasion? Fashion? Social rank? Consideration concerning the Bell Beaker phenomenon in Copper Age fortifications of the Iberian Peninsula. In: F. Nicolis (ed.), *Bell Beakers Today: Pottery, People, Culture, Symbols in Prehistoric Europe*. Proceedings of the International Colloquium at Riva del Garda 11–16 May 1998. Trento: Servicio Beni Culturali, Provincia Autonoma di Trento. 81–90.

Lanting J. N., Aerts-Bijma, A. T. and Plicht, J. van der 2001. Dating of cremated bones. *Radiocarbon* 43(2): 249–254.

Lanting, J. N. and van der Waals, J. D. 1972. British beakers as seen from the Continent: a review article. *Helinium* 12: 20–46.

Lanting, J. N. and van der Waals, J. D. 1976. Beaker culture relations in the Lower Rhine Basin. In J.N. Lanting and J.D. van der Waals (eds.), *Glockenbechersymposion Oberried, 18–23 März 1974*, Bussum/Haarlem: Fibula-van Dishoeck. 1–80.

Lawson, J., Henderson, D. and Sheridan, J. A. 2002. An Early Bronze Age short-cist burial at Abbey Mains Farm, Haddington, East Lothian. *Proceedings of the Society of Antiquaries of Scotland* 132: 193–204.

Leeuw S. van der 1976. Neolithic Beakers from the Netherlands: the potter's point of view. In J.N. Lanting and J.D. van der Waals (eds.), *Glockenbechersymposion Oberried, 18–23 März 1974*, Bussum/Haarlem: Fibula-van Dishoeck. 81–139.

Lelong, O. and MacGregor, G. in press. *Ancient Lothian Landscapes: the Archaeology of the A1*. Edinburgh: Society of Antiquaries of Scotland.

McCullagh R. P. J. 1989. Excavations at Newton, Islay. *Glasgow Archaeological Journal* 15 (1988–89): 23–51.

McCullagh R. P. J. and Tipping, R. 1998. *The Lairg Project 1988–1996. The Evolution of an Archaeological Landscape in Northern Scotland*. Edinburgh: Scottish Trust for Archaeological Research.

McGill, C. 2004. Excavations of cropmarks at Newbarns, near Inverkeilor, Angus. *Tayside and Fife Archaeological Journal* 10: 94–118.

MacGregor, G. 2005. Eweford, Dunbar. In P. J. Ashmore, A list of archaeological radiocarbon dates. *Discovery and Excavation in Scotland* 6:169–170.

MacLean, I., Shepherd, I. A. G. and Shepherd, A. 1978. Paible. *Discovery and Excavation in Scotland 1978*: 35.

Manby, T. G. 2004. Food Vessels with handles. In A. M. Gibson, and J.A. Sheridan (eds.), *From Sickles to Circles: Britain and Ireland at the Time of Stonehenge*. Stroud: Tempus. 215–42.

Mann, L. McL. 1906. Notes on – (1) a drinking-cup urn, found at Bathgate; (2) a prehistoric hut in Tiree; (3) a cairn containing sixteen cinerary urns, with objects of vitreous paste and of gold, in Stevenston, Ayrshire; and (4) prehistoric beads of coarse vitreous paste. *Proceedings of the Society of Antiquaries of Scotland* 40 (1905–6): 369–402.

Mercer, R. J. 1981. The excavation of a late Neolithic henge-type enclosure at Balfarg, Markinch, Fife, Scotland, 1977–78. *Proceedings of the Society of Antiquaries of Scotland* 111: 63–171.

Müller, J. and Willigen, S. van 2004. New radiocarbon evidence for european Bell Beakers and the consequences for the diffusion of the Bell Beaker Phenomenon. In: F. Nicolis (ed.), *Bell Beakers Today: Pottery, People, Culture, Symbols in Prehistoric Europe*. Proceedings of the International Colloquium at Riva del Garda 11–16 May 1998. Trento: Servicio Beni Culturali, Provincia Autonoma di Trento. 59–80.

Needham, S. P. 1976. Chronology and periodisation in the British Bronze Age. *Acta Archaeologica* 67: 121–140.

Needham, S. P. 2004. Migdale-Marnoch: sunburst of Scottish metallurgy. In I. A. G. Shepherd and G. J. Barclay (eds.), *Scotland in Ancient Europe. The Neolithic and Early Bronze Age of Scotland in their European Context*. Edinburgh: Society of Antiquaries of Scotland. 217–45.

Needham, S. P. 2005. Transforming Beaker Culture in North-West Europe: processes of fusion and fission. *Proceedings of the Prehistoric Society* 71: 171–217.

O'Brien, W. 2004. *Ross Island. Mining, Metal and Society in Early Ireland*. Department of Archaeology, National University of Ireland, Galway, Bronze Age Studies 6. Galway.

Parker Pearson, M., Sharples, N. M. and Symonds, J. 2004. *South Uist. Archaeology and History of a Hebridean Island*. Stroud: Tempus.

Ralston, I. 1996. Four short cists from north-east Scotland and Easter Ross. *Proceedings of the Society of Antiquaries of Scotland* 126: 121–155.

Ritchie, J. N. G. 1970 Excavation of the chambered cairn at Achnacreebeag. *Proceedings of the Society of Antiquaries of Scotland* 102 (1969–70): 31–55.

Ritchie, J. N. G. 1970 Beaker pottery in south-west Scotland. *Transactions of the Dumfriesshire and Galloway Natural History and Antiquarian Society* 3rd series, 47: 123–46.

Ritchie, J. N. G. and Crawford, J. 1978. Recent work on Coll and Skye: (i) Excavations at Sorisdale and Killunaig, Coll. *Proceedings of the Society of Antiquaries of Scotland* 109 (1977–8): 75–84.

Ritchie, J. N. G. and Shepherd, I.A.G. 1973. Beaker pottery and associated artefacts in south-west Scotland. *Transactions of the Dumfriesshire and Galloway Natural History and Antiquarian Society* 3rd series, 50: 18–36.

Robertson, A. 1854. Notes of the discovery of stone cists at Lesmurdie, Banffshire, containing primitive urns, &c., along with human remains. *Proceedings of the Society of Antiquaries of Scotland* 1 (1851–4): 205–11.

Shepherd, I. A. G. 1986. *Powerful Pots: Beakers in North-East Prehistory*. Aberdeen: Anthropological Museum, University of Aberdeen.

Shepherd, I. A. G. 2005. Radiocarbon dates sponsored by Aberdeenshire Archaeology in 2004. *Discovery and Excavation in Scotland* 6: 184–185.

Shepherd, I. A. G. and Bruce, M. F. 1987. Two beaker burials from Keabog, Pitdrichie, near Drumlithie, Kincardine and Deeside. *Proceedings of the Society of Antiquaries of Scotland* 117: 33–40.

Shepherd, I. A. G., Shepherd, A.and Bruce, M. 1984. A beaker burial at Mains of Balnagowan, Ardesier, Inverness District. *Proceedings of the Society of Antiquaries of Scotland* 114: 560–566.

Shepherd, I. A. G. and Tuckwell, A. 1977. Traces of beaker-period cultivation at Rosinish, Benbecula. *Proceedings of the Society of Antiquaries of Scotland* 108 (1976–7): 108–113.

Sheridan, J. A. 1997. Pottery. In: Johnston D. A. Biggar Common 1987–93: an early prehistoric funerary and domestic landscape in Clydesdale, South Lanarkshire. *Proceedings of the Society of Antiquaries of Scotland* 127: 202–223.

Sheridan, J. A. 2002. The radiocarbon dating programmes of the National Museums of Scotland. *Antiquity* 76: 794–796.

Sheridan, J. A. 2003. New dates for Scottish Bronze Age cinerary urns: results from the National Museums' of Scotland *Dating Cremated Bones Project*. In: Gibson A. M. (ed.), *Prehistoric Pottery: People, Pattern and Purpose*. Oxford: British Archaeological Reports, International Series 1156. 201–226.

Sheridan, J. A. 2004. Scottish Food Vessel chronology revisited. In A.M. Gibson and J.A. Sheridan (eds.), *From Sickles to Circles: Britain and Ireland at the Time of Stonehenge*. Stroud: Tempus. 243–267.

Sheridan, J. A. 2005. Dating Scotland's past: the National Museums' of Scotland C14 dating programmes. *The Archaeologist* 56: 38–40.

Sheridan, J. A. 2007. Dating the Scottish Bronze Age: 'There is clearly much that the material can still tell us'. In: C. B. Burgess, P. Topping and F. M. Lynch (eds.), *In the Shadow of the Age of Stonehenge*. Oxford: Oxbow. 162–185.

Sheridan, J. A. in press. Beaker pottery from Eweford. In O. Lelong and G. MacGregor, *Ancient Lothian Landscapes: the Archaeology of the A1*. Edinburgh: Society of Antiquaries of Scotland.

Sheridan, J. A. and Shortland, A. 2004. '...beads which have given rise to so much dogmatism, controversy and rash speculation': faience in Early Bronze Age Britain and Ireland. In I.A.G. Shepherd and G.J.

Barclay (eds.), *Scotland in Ancient Europe. The Neolithic and Early Bronze Age of Scotland in their European Context*. Edinburgh: Society of Antiquaries of Scotland. 263–279.

Sheridan, J. A., Parker Pearson, M., Jay, M. and Curtis, N. 2007 Radiocarbon dating results from the *Beaker People Project*: Scottish samples. *Discovery and Excavation in Scotland* 7: xx–xx.

Spriggs, M. J. and Anderson, A. J. 1993. Late colonisation of East Polynesia. *Antiquity* 67: 200–217.

Suddaby, I. and Sheridan, J.A. 2006. A pit containing an undecorated Beaker and associated artefacts from Beechwood Park, Raigmore, Inverness. *Proceedings of the Society of Antiquaries of Scotland* 136: 77–88.

Thomas, J. 2004. Dunragit. In: P.J. Ashmore, A list of archaeological radiocarbon dates. *Discovery & Excavation in Scotland* 5: 160–161.

Thurnam, J. 1871. On ancient British barrows especially those of Wiltshire and the adjoining counties. Part II: round barrows. *Archaeologia* 43: 285–544.

Watkins, T. 1982. The excavation of an Early Bronze Age cemetery at Barns Farm, Dalgety, Fife. *Proceedings of the Society of Antiquaries of Scotland* 112: 48–141.

Watkins, T. and Shepherd, I. A. G. 1980. A beaker burial at Newmill, near Bankfoot, Perthshire. *Proceedings of the Society of Antiquaries of Scotland* 110 (1978–80): 32–41.

Appendices: Datelists of Scottish Beaker Dates – the Good, the Bad and the Ugly

Introduction

These lists have been collated from the following principal sources of information: the NMS and BPP dating programmes; Kinnes *et al.* 1991; the on-line Historic Scotland list of Scottish C14 dates obtained to May 1996 (www.historic-scotland.gov.uk); datelists published in *Discovery & Excavation in Scotland* from 1996 onwards; and personal communications from colleagues. Although extensive, the lists do not purport to be exhaustive. All the dates have been calibrated using OxCal v3.10, with atmospheric data from Stuiver *et al.* 1998. Under 'References', in order to save space, the National Monuments Record for Scotland (NMRS) reference number has been cited wherever possible. By accessing CANMORE, the on-line NMRS database (www.rcahms.gov.uk) and entering the findspot name, further details (warning: not always 100% correct!) and bibliographic references can be accessed. (Where the findspot name differs from that given here under 'Findspot', the NMRS version is given after the NMRS number.) Beaker types are cited, wherever possible, in terms of the schemes devised by Needham (2005), Clarke (1970) and Lanting & van der Waals (1972), with the Shepherd 1986 version of the L&vdW scheme used for north-east Scottish Beakers. The identifications are given in that order. Collagen yields and $\delta^{13}C$ values are not cited here, because all the 'Good' dates cited have been cleared by the laboratories in question as having had sufficient collagen in the samples to produce a reliable date, and as having had no need for correction of any marine effect. Where there has been an issue with low collagen yield or with the marine effect (in the case of shell dates for the Udal and for Rosinish), this is clearly stated.

APPENDIX 1: Beaker-associated dates that fulfil most or all of the criteria for quality and reliability as set out in the text.

Unless specified otherwise, all dates have been obtained from unburnt human bone from crouched inhumations in cists. Dates obtained for the NMS project are indicated by using *italics* for the laboratory code; dates obtained for the BPP are indicated by using **bold** for the laboratory code. Age and sex identifications: for skeletons included in the BPP (which include some that had previously been dated, not as part of that Project), as per BPP identifications. Otherwise, as per original publications, where identifications given.

Findspot	Beaker type	Beaker context, associations	Laboratory code	Date BP	Cal BC (1σ values in bold, 2σ plain)	Comments; current location and (where known) registration number of Beaker, and/or of human remains, in brackets	References
Keabog, Pitdrichie Farm (cist 2), Aberdeenshire	Uncertain/ intermediate; N3(L); step 6 (Fig. 3.1)	Adult (26–35), probably male, on L side, facing N; flint knife	**OxA-V-2172-22**	3910±33	**2470–2340** 2480–2290	Supersedes date obtained in 1980s, GU-1123, as discussed in Appendix 5; is significantly earlier than GU-1123. (Marischal Museum, bones: ABDUA 90006)	NO78SE 17
Sorisdale, Coll, Argyll & Bute	LC; AOC; step 1–2 (Fig. 3.2)	In pit grave, orientated E-W, adult (17–25), sex indeterminate (but in original publication thought probably to be female); no other grave goods	*OxA-14722*	3879±32	**2460–2300** 2470–2230	Date virtually identical to that obtained in the 1970s (BM-1413, 3884±46 BP, std dev increased by Ashmore to ±110). (NMS, bones unreg)	NM26SE 8
Borrowstone (cist 1), Aberdeenshire	SN; N3; step 5 (Fig. 4)	Sub-adult female; cist floor covered with black organic material, which might have been an ox-hide.	GrA-29077	3865±40	**2460–2280** 2470–2200	(Marischal Museum, Beaker ABDUA 15639, bones 14237)	NMRS NJ80NE 28
Broomend of Crichie (cist 2), Aberdeenshire	SN x 2; N2 x 2; step 4 x 2 (Fig. 3.3)	Adult male & infant; 2 Beakers; horn spoon; 2 flint flakes; 'a small quantity of black earth'; pieces of 'charcoal'; bodies covered by ox-hide.	*OxA-15056*	3856±29	**2460–2230** 2470–2200	Supersedes *OxA-11243* (3932±35), which has now been deleted by the Oxford laboratory (see Appendix 7). (Inverurie Museum)	NJ71NE 11
Dornoch Nursery Cist, Highland	LC; AOC; step 1–2 (Fig. 3.4)	Adult with wristguard, 5 arrowheads, strike-a-light, iron ore nodule; cremated remains of young adult *may* have been deposited at same time	*GrA-26515*	3850±40	**2450–2200** 2460–2200	Cremated bone dated. (Inverness Museum, INVMG-DNC)	NH79SE 18 (Hilton of Embo)
Skateraw (1958 cist), East Lothian	SN; N3; step 5 (Fig. 3.5)	Adult male	i) **OxA-V-2164-39** ii) *SUERC-2865*	i) 3846±29 ii) 3785±35	i) **2400–2200** 2460–2200 ii) **2290–2140** 2340–2040	SUERC date had been obtained in 2004; OxA-date obtained 2006. There is no obvious reason for the discrepancy in the dates, although the	NT77NW 7

Site	Context	Individual / finds	Lab code	Date BP	Calibrated	Notes	NMRS ref
Sandhole, Fetterangus, Aberdeenshire	SN; N1D with N/NR features; step 3/4 (Fig. 3.6)	Adult, probably male (age cited as 20–25 in original publication); piece of flint; organic material on cist floor	OxA-V-2172-23	3845±32	**2430–2200** 2460–2200	Supersedes GU-2100, 3650±50, which had been determined during the 1980s. (Marischal Museum, ABDUA 14300)	NJ95SE 25
Borrowstone (cist 2), Aberdeenshire	SN; N2; step 4 (Fig. 4)	Senior adult male (40+); 3 flint flakes; 6 pebbles	GrA-29078	3845±40	**2440–2200** 2470–2200	(Marischal Museum, Beaker ABDUA 15640, bones 14236)	NMRS NJ80NE 28
Broomend of Crichie (cist 1), Aberdeenshire	SN; N2(L); step 5 & SN; N3; step 5 (Fig. 3.7)	One of 2 adult males in cist, prob buried simultaneously; flint flake, bone belt ring, prob ox hide	OxA-V-2166-34	3835±33	**2350–2200** 2460–2190	See also *OxA-13214* for the other individual in the cist (NMS, Beakers X.EQ 23–4; skull X.ET 5)	NJ71NE 11
Ruchlaw Mains, East Lothian	SN; N2 or N3; step 4 (Fig. 3.8)	Senior adult (46+ years), probably male	OxA-V-2167-42	3826±39	**2350–2200** 2460–2140	Supersedes GU-1356 (3720±80 (increased to ±110), see Appendix 5) (NMS, Beaker X.EG 124, bones unreg)	NT67SW 14; Ashmore *et al.* 1982
Boatbridge Quarry (cist 2), Thankerton, S Lanarkshire	SN; N1; step 4 (Fig. 3.9)	Unusually tall adult (described as adolescent in original report), indeterminate sex	OxA-V-2168-42	3824±32	**2340–2200** 2460–2140	Supersedes GU-1117 (3835±75 (increased to ±110), see Appendix 5 (NMS, Beaker X.EG 106, bones unreg)	NS93NE 27
Borrowstone (cist 6), Aberdeenshire	SN; N2(L); step 4 (not ill.)	Adult (25–35 years), male; sinew, poss from a bow; wristguard; bone belt ring: 1 flint flake; 4 other flints; quartz pebble. Cist of massive slabs	i) GrA-29082 ii) GrA-29083	i) 3820±40 ii) 3835±40	**i) 2340–2150** 2460–2150 **ii) 2410–2200** 2460–2140	(Marischal Museum, Beaker ABDUA 17948, bones 14742)	NMRS NJ80NE 73
Fyrish, Highland	SN; N4; step 5 (Fig. 5.1)	Adult male; wristguard	*OxA-13213*	3816±29	**2295–2200** 2410–2140	(NMS, Beaker X.EQ 131, bones unreg)	NH66NW 5
West Fenton, East Lothian	SN; N3; step 5 (Fig. 5.2)	Youth (11–12, indeterminate sex)	*OxA-13514*	3806±30	**2290–2200** 2350–2130	Dentine dated. (NMS, Beaker X.EG 78, bones unreg)	NT48SE 14 (Park Hills)

relevant laboratories state that it is insignificant, given the degree of overlap at 1σ. (NMS, Beaker & bones unreg; Clarke 1970 fig. 648)

Site	Pot type / step	Skeletal remains	Lab code	BP date	Calibrated date	Notes	NGR
Slap, Turriff, Aberdeenshire	SP; Undecorated cf. N1; step 1 or 2 (Fig. 5.3)	Young adult (16–25 years), indeterminate sex	*OxA-V-2172-31*	3803±32	**2290–2150** 2400–2130	(NMS, Beaker X.EQ 140, bone unreg)	NJ75SE 3
Cookston, Airlie, Angus	SN; N3(L); step 6 (Fig. 5.4)	No published identification of age and sex of skeletal remains. Decorated bone button with 2 straight perforations	BM-2523	3800±50	**2340–2140** 2460–2040	Replaced earlier, unreliable date N-1239 (3550±85, increased to ±120) BP (Dundee Museum, Beaker DUNMG 1971-144-1)	NO34NW 14
Juniper Green, Midlothian	LN; N3(L); step 5 (Fig. 5.5)	Adult male, 40–55	*OxA-13513*	3797±31	**2290–2150** 2350–2130	Dentine dated (NMS X.EG 3)	NT16NE 4
Thurston Mains (skeleton 2), East Lothian	SN; N3; step 4 (Fig. 5.6)	Adult female: one of two bodies buried in cist simultaneously, with one Beaker (see below) and flint flake	*OxA-13660*	3794±26	**2290–2150** 2300–2130	Dentine dated (NMS EQ 479)	NT77SW 16
Bractullo, Perth & Kinross	SP; N/N4; step 4 (Fig. 5.7)	Adult; pebble 'burnisher', plano-convex flint knife & 2 other knife frags; axehead fragment; 2 flint scrapers, several pieces struck flint	BM-2515	3780±60	**2300–2050** 2460–2030	(DUNMG 1969-244.1)	NO54NW 18
Abbey Mains Farm, East Lothian	SN; N2 or N3; step 4 (Fig. 5.8)	Adult (17–25 years), probably female; had been accompanied by a joint of pork	i) *OxA-16491* ii) **OxA-V-2199-26**	i) 3780±38 ii) 3773±31	i) **2290–2140** 2340–2040 ii) **2280–2130** 2300–2040	These dates supersede the now-deleted – and anomalously early –date OxA-10254 (see Appendix 7), and are effectively identical to each other (E Lothian Museums Service)	NT57NW 115; Lawson et al. 2002
Uppermains, Catterline, Aberdeenshire	SN; N4; step 6 (Fig. 5.9)	Adult (36–45 years), prob female; one piece quartzite	**OxA-V-2166-44**	3770±31	**2280–2130** 2290–2040	(Marischal Museum, bones ABDUA 14793)	NO87NE 2
Lesmurdie (cist B), Moray	SN; N3; step 4 (Fig. 5.10)	Adult (40–60), prob male. 3 flint chips and iron-rich substance (poss a fire-making kit), poss in pouch	*OxA-13098*	3770±33	**2280–2130** 2300–2040	(NMS, Beaker X.EQ 30)	Robertson 1854
Park Quarry (cist 1), Durris, Aberdeenshire	SN; N/NR or N2; step 4 or 5 (not ill.)	Adult (26–35 years), prob male; 7 flints and perforated stone disc	**OxA-V-2172-14**	3769±32	**2280–2130** 2290–2040	(Marischal Museum, Beaker ABDUA 17929, bones ABDUA 14752)	NO89NW 31
Holm Mains Farm (cist 2),	SN/;	Adult (17–25 years), prob	**OxA-V-2166-**	3755±32	**2270–2060**	c/o Headland	NH64SE

Site	Context	Skeletal / Associations	Lab code	Date BP	Calibrated date	Archaeology	NMRS
Inverness, Highland	N2/N3; step 5 or 6 (Fig. 5.11)	female	42		2290–2030		356
Dryburn Bridge (cist 2, burial 10), East Lothian	SN; N2; step 5 (Fig. 5.12)	Plano-convex knife & thumbnail scraper of flint, associated with either burial 10 or burial 11	SUERC-4078	3755±35	**2280–2050** 2290–2030	Beaker (NMS unreg) found above cist in grave pit; uncertain whether it had originally been associated with this body (which was a secondary addition to the cist) or with burial 11, but will definitely date to one or the other. Note: this date supersedes previous dates obtained for this body: the old date GU-1408, 3620±85 (increased to ±120) and AA-53715 (GU-10823), 3660±55, rejected because of low collagen yield. See Dunwell in press, 5	NT77NW 18
Borrowstone (cist 3), Aberdeenshire	SN; N; step 4 (Fig. 4)	Adult (25–35), male; flint knife, quartz pebble; token charcoal deposit beneath floor and traces of burning on capstone	GrA-29079	3750±45	**2280–2040** 2300–2020	(Marischal Museum, Beaker ABDUA 15641, bones 14740)	NMRS NJ80NE 72
Fodderty, Highland	SN (not classic) – more like SP (high-bellied); N4; step 5 (Fig. 5.13)	Adult (36–45 years), indeterminate sex; 6 flint flakes	OxA-V-2172-26	3745±32	**2210–2050** 2280–2030	Supersedes BM-2514 (3770±50); the two results overlap at 1σ range (Inverness Museum, bones INVMG 980.1.8)	NH55NW 31
Holm Mains Farm (cist 1), Inverness, Highland	SP; N/NR or N2; step 4 or 5 (Fig. 5.14)	Adult (26–35 years), probably male; 2 barbed-and-tanged arrowheads and 10 other pieces of flint	OxA-V-2166-41	3743±33	**2210–2050** 2280–2030	c/o Headland Archaeology	NH64SE 356
Nether Criggie, Dunnottar, Aberdeenshire	i) WC; N/NR; step 5 ii) SN; N3(L); step 5 iii) LN; N3(L); step 5	Adult (17–25 years), prob female; also new-born child; 2 flint scrapers; other stone objects found nearby prob also from the cist	OxA-V-2166-46	3741±32	**2210–2050** 2280–2030	(Marischal Museum, bones ABDUA 14247; artefacts 19758–60 and 233/25)	NO88SW 6

Site	Details	Description	Lab code	Date BP	Calibrated	Comments	NMRS no.
Middle Brighty Farm, Angus	(Fig. 6.1) SN or SP; N3(L); step 6 (Fig. 6.2)	No details available	BM-2524	3730±50	**2200–2030** 2290–1970	Excavated by Professor D R Dow 1947 (Dundee Museum. DUNMG 1973-993)	Zealand pers comm
Manar House, Inverurie, Aberdeenshire	SP or SN; N2 or N3; step 4 or 5 (Fig. 4)	Adult (17–25 years), prob female; 11 flints	**OxA-V-2172-19**	3725±33	**2200–2040** 2280–2020	Supersedes GrA-29084 (3760±45: Shepherd 2005) for which the collagen yield had been less than desirable. (Marischal Museum, bones ABDUA 14765, artefacts 17914–6)	NJ72SW 50
Thurston Mains (skeleton 1), East Lothian	(N3; step 4) (Fig. 5.6)	Adult female: one of two bodies buried in cist simultaneously, with one Beaker (see above)	*OxA-13097*	3721±33	**2200–2030** 2210–2020	(NMS, Beaker X.EQ 479)	NT77SW 16
Dryburn Bridge (cist 2, burial 11), East Lothian	(SN; N2; step 5) (Fig. 5.12)	Plano-convex knife & thumbnail scraper of flint, associated with either burial 10 or burial 11	SUERC-4079	3720±35	**2200–2030** 2280–2020	See above. The remains of burial 11, the original 'occupant' of the cist, had decomposed by the time burial 10 was added. This date supersedes previous dates obtained for this body: old date GU-1409, 3550±80 (increased to ±110) and AA-53716 (GU-10824), 3765±60, rejected because of insufficient collagen yield. For further details, see Dunwell in press, 5.	NT77NW 18
Broomend of Crichie (cist 1), Aberdeenshire	SN; N2(L); step 5 & SN; N3; step 5 (Fig. 3.7)	One of 2 adult males in cist, prob buried simultaneously; flint flake, bone belt ring, prob ox hide	*OxA-13214*	3720±35	**2200–2030** 2280–2020	See also **OxA-V-2166-34** for the other individual in the cist (NMS, Beakers X.EQ 23–4; skull X.ET 4)	NJ71NE 11
Keir, Belhelvie, Aberdeenshire	i) SN; N3(L); step 5 ii) SN; N4; step 5 iii) SN; N4;	Adult (17–25 years), prob female	**OxA-V-2172-18**	3715±32	**2200–2030** 2210–2020	(Marischal Museum, bones ABDUA 14226)	NJ91NE 3

113

Site	Context/step	Description	Lab code	BP	Cal BC	Notes	Grid ref
Tavelty, Aberdeenshire	step 5 (Fig. 6.3) SN; N2; step 4 (Fig. 6.4)	Young adult male, late teens/early 20s, fairly tall; copper dagger (Needham pers comm), 2 barbed & tanged flint arrowheads, flint flake, chunk, spall and pebble core	GU-2169	3710±70	2210–1980 2300–1890	(Marischal Museum, ABDUA 14475)	NJ71NE 72
Achavanich, Highland	SN; N4; step 6 (Fig. 6.5)	Young adult female 18–22; 2 flint flakes, flint thumbnail scraper	BM-2590	3700±50	2200–2020 2280–1940	Excavated by Robert Gourlay 1987; unpublished (Northlands Viking Centre)	White & Weeks pers comm
Old Rayne, Aberdeenshire	Indet; lost	Central pit in recumbent stone circle; fragment of wristguard	GrA-23982	3690±45	2140–1980 2200–1940	Cremated bone dated; pottery known only from antiquarian description, but clearly Beaker (NMS, bones unreg)	NJ62NE 1
Stoneywood (cist 1), Newhills, Aberdeenshire	SN; N2; step 4 (Fig. 6.6)	Adult (36–45 years), prob female	OxA-V-2172-25	3686±32	2140–2020 2200–1960	(Marischal Museum, Beaker ABDUA 19703, bones 14222)	NJ81SE 14
Newlands (cist 1), Oyne, Aberdeenshire	SN; N3; step 4 (Fig. 6.7)	Adult (possibly 36–45 years), prob male	OxA-V-2172-20	3677±31	2140–1980 2150–1950	(Marischal Museum, bones ABDUA 14248; Beaker NMS X.EG 65)	NJ62NE 24
Achnacreebeag, Argyll	Various, including TMC; ?N4; steps 5–6 (Fig. 7.1)	Found among material blocking Neolithic passage tomb; cannel coal/shale disc beads, flint scrapers, flakes, blade and chip	GrA-26543	3660±40	2130–1960 2190–1920	Cremated bone from among the blocking material dated; very likely to be contemporary with one or more of the Beakers, although cannot say which one/s (NMS, Beakers X.EO 1018–21)	NM93NW 4
Doons Law, Whitsome, Scottish Borders	SP N/NR; step 4 (Fig. 7.2)	Adult female; 4 pieces of flint; copper awl; charcoal	AA-29066	3645±65	2140–1920 2210–1820	(Dunbar Museum)	NT85SE 7
Chealamy, Highland	SN; N/NR; step 4 (Fig. 7.3)	Adult male over 30	BM-2512	3630±50	2120–1920 2150–1880	(Strathnaver Museum, Bettyhill)	NC75SW 67
Balfarg henge, Fife	Unusual/ uncertain/ intermediate; handled; step	?Male, 14–18; flint knife. Cist inside henge	OxA-13215	3605±37	2030–1910 2130–1880	(NMS X.EPB 273)	NO20SE 5

	7 (Fig. 7.4)							
West Water Reservoir (cist 7), Scottish Borders	WC; Beaker/ Food Vessel 'hybrid' (Fig. 7.5)	Beaker/FV hybrid pot associated with crouched inhumation in cist; also present was secondary deposit of cremated remains, with FV, a burnt flint tool and 2 burnt bone beads	GrA-26518	3570±40	2010–1880 / 2030–1770		Cremated bone from the secondary burial was dated, so provides *tag* for the Beaker/FV hybrid (NMS, bones X.EQ 1040)	NT15SW 37
Lochend, Highland	SN; N3; step 5 or 6 (Fig. 7.6)	Adult (17–25 years), prob male; flint nodule	OxA-V-2172-27	3534±31	1930–1770 / 1950–1750		(Inverness Museum, bones INVMG 978.38)	NH53NE 2
Barns Farm (cist 4), Fife	WC; Beaker/ Food Vessel 'hybrid' (Fig. 7.7)	Adult female; cannel coal or shale disc-bead necklace, 2 broken 'jet' pendants	SUERC-2866	3530±35	1920–1770 / 1950–1750		(NMS, Beaker X.EQ 908)	NT18SE 8

APPENDIX 2: Potentially 'Good' dates, from non-funerary contexts where there is a reasonably good chance that the dated material had been contemporary with the Beakers, but where the closeness of association is not as good as with the Appendix 1 specimens

Findspot	Beaker type	Context of Beaker, associations	Lab. code	Date BP	Date cal BC (1σ value in bold)	Material dated	Comments	References
Machrie North (site 24/3), Arran, N Ayrshire	Prob SP; probably AOC; step 1–2	Pit; charred plant remains, thought to represent domestic refuse	GU-3527	3870±50	2460–2290 / 2480–2200	Hazel & alder charcoal	Sherds from 6 vessels, including one, allegedly of Grooved Ware, but more likely to be Beaker	NR93SW 113 Barber 1997, 80–87
Fox Plantation, Dunragit, Dumfries & Galloway	Uncertain/ intermediate; AOC; step 1–2, plus sherd with horizontal? incised lines and 2 other sherds	In pit in probable settlement site. Pit had 4 fills, including struck flint, burnt bone, stone scraper and carbonised cereal grains	AA-28050	3795±55	2340–2130 / 2460–2040	Burnt hazelnut shell	Precise stratigraphic relationship between dated material and Beaker sherds to be confirmed but may well be contemporary	NX15NW 16; MacGregor pers comm
Sligeanach (mound 18, trench A), Cill Donnain, South Uist	?LC; AOC; step 1–2 plus incised and indeterm-inate	Small sherds and fragments in occupation horizons sealed in mound: sherds of	i) OxA-8920 ii) OxA-8905 iii) OxA-	i) 3710±45 ii) 3875±35 iii) 3655±45	i) 2200– 2030 2280–1960 ii) 2460– 2290	i) cattle bone ii) sheep bone iii) barley grains	Material is from sealed horizons and so there is a reasonable chance that the dated material is contemporary with the	NF72NW 37; Sharples pers comm

Site	Pottery	Context	Lab code	Date BP	Cal date	Material	Comments	References
		indeterminate type from layer 71, dated by OxA-8920; AOC, incised and indeterminate sherds from layer 18, associated with OxA-8905 and OxA-8925	8925		2470–2200 iii) 2130–1950 2200–1900		pottery; but note the difference between dates ii) and iii), from the same context. No evidence for any potential marine effect with animal bone dates	NF72NW 37; Sharples pers comm
Sligeanach (mound 17, trenches K and M), Cill Donnain, South Uist	Incised and indeterminate	Small fragments sealed in occupation horizons in mound	i) OxA-8929 ii) OxA-8989 iii) OxA-9006	i) 3715±45 ii) 3565±70 iii) 3665±45	i) 2200–2030 2280–1970 ii) 2030–1770 2140–1730 iii) 2140–1970 2200–1910	i) barley grains ii) cattle bone iii) cattle bone	Trench K: in occupation horizon sealed between layers dated by OxA-8929 (*tpq* for the pottery) and OxA-8989 (*taq*). Trench M: pottery from layer above dated layer, so OxA-9006 gives *tpq*. No evidence for any potential marine effect with animal bone dates	
Eweford (pit 3), East Lothian	i) LC; AOC; step 1–2; ii) SP; generalised similarity to E Anglian & FN; step 3; iii) indet but cf SP; bowl of type found with W/MR Beakers; step 3; iv) LC; AOC; step 1–2 (Fig. 8.1–4)	In fill of pit, prob connected with ceremonies relating to a nearby Early Neolithic non-megalithic long barrow	SUERC-5299	3775±35	2280–2130 2300–2040	Carbonised barley grain	Grain probably contemporary with Beakers. For further details, see MacGregor 2005; Lelong & MacGregor in press; Sheridan in press	NT67NE 474; MacGregor 2005 and pers comm; MacGregor and Lelong forthcoming
Eweford (on long mound), East Lothian	Sherds from 3 Beakers including one SP; cf. E Anglian/ FN/BW; step 3 (Fig. 8.5)	Part of deliberate deposit on surface of re-shaped Early Neolithic long barrow	SUERC-5309	3725±40	2200–2030 2280–1980	Carbonised barley grain	Grain probably contemporary with Beakers. Note: there are a further 10 contemporary radiocarbon dates for single carbonised barley grains from other contexts at Eweford (namely code nos. EWE 3, 11, 12, 19, 21 and 23–27 in	NT67NE 474;

Findspot	Beaker type/description	Context of Beaker, associations	Material dated	Laboratory code	Date BP	Cal BC (1σ in bold)	Comments	References
Newbarns, Angus	SN; N4; step 4	In pit, with flint artefact; heat-cracked stones in upper fill. Sherds possibly from same vessel in adjacent pit	Beech charcoal	AA-47749 (GU-9753)	3645±85	**2140–1900** 2300–1750	MacGregor 2005). Two of these (EWE 26–7, SUERC-5316–7, 3650±35 and 3680±40 respectively) are from contexts loosely associated with Beakers. For further details, see MacGregor 2005; Lelong & MacGregor in press; Sheridan in press; Dated charcoal may well be contemporary with the Beaker	NO64NE 17; McGill 2004

APPENDIX 3: C14 dates pertaining to Beaker-associated funerary activity, whose standard deviation has not had to be increased (by Patrick Ashmore) to take account of factors such as possible old laboratory errors, but whose relationship to the Beaker is indirect (eg as *termini ante* or *post quos*, less close to the Beaker than those cited in Appendix 1), or uncertain.

Findspot	Beaker type/description	Context of Beaker, associations	Material dated	Laboratory code	Date BP	Cal BC (1σ in bold)	Comments	References
Curriestanes, Dumfries & Galloway	'decorated with lines of impressed twisted cord and rows of fingernail impressions'	In small pit (truncated) inside a cursus monument; small fragments of burnt bone (species unidentified)	Oak charcoal	AA-53171	3875±45	**2460–2290** 2470–2200	Might not be a grave. Dated material 'possibly from a large timber' and may well have 'old wood' effect	NX97NE 85
Kilpatrick (cairn 16/3), Arran, N Ayrshire	Sinuous profile, with comb- and nail-impressed and incised decoration; claimed as ?step 7 in publication but this ID uncertain	From disturbed cist; sherds found among soil cover of cairn	Charcoal (hazel & willow)	GU-1562	3790±65	**2340–2060** 2460–2030	Original publication cites date as 3810±65. From soil sealed by main body of cairn; chronological relationship with Beaker uncertain	NR92NW 27, Barber 1997, 46, fig 22 bottom left

117

APPENDIX 4: Dates from non-funerary contexts, where the closeness of the association between the dated material and the date of Beaker manufacture and use cannot be guaranteed (or where the dates provide only *termini ante* or *post quos*)

Note: full details of the recently-excavated material from a house at Crossiecrown, Orkney (*Discovery and Excavation in Scotland* 1998, 70–1 and volume 4 (2003), 162), are not yet available.

Findspot	Beaker type	Context of Beaker, associations	Lab. code	Date BP	Date cal BC (1σ value in bold)	Material dated	Comments	References
Chapelfield, Cowie, Stirling (pit 4)	Indeterminate; horizontal lines of comb impressions	In fill of pit; according to HS datelist, 'from upper fill of pit 4; [dated charcoal] appears to be deposited in single event with potsherds within the matrix'	GU-7204	4210±90	**2910–2630** 3050–2450	Oak charcoal	Charcoal probably from old wood or residual material; contemporaneity of deposition of charcoal and pottery probably not as secure as claimed	NS88NW 43; Atkinson 2002, 149, 159, illus 16 (4A)
Tommaverie, Aberdeenshire	One indet; one ?SN; N3/4; step 5/6	On OGS, sealed by (and therefore predating) platform	AA-49279–84 (6 dates)	Range between 3985±45 (49280) and 3740±60 (49283)	Range between **2580–2460** 2630–2340 and **2280–2030** 2340–1950. Combined result of 5 dates suggests 25th century BC	Alder charcoal	Dates relate to other pre-platform activity from elsewhere on the monument; chronological relationship with Beakers uncertain but could be contemporary	NJ40SE 1
Northton, Harris, Western Isles	Various, incl SN, LN and SP; 'North British'; step 4–5	In 2 stratified midden deposits; no stylistic or technical differences between pottery from the two deposits	i)BM-706 ii) BM-707	i)3604±70 ii)3481±54	i) **2130–1880** 2150–1750 ii) **1880–1740** 1950–1660	Both animal bone (species unspecified)	Cited as 3610±70 and 3480±60 respectively in Kinnes *et al.* 1991. i) from lower, Beaker I horizon, ii) from Beaker II horizon. Recently-obtained AMS dates for human remains from corbelled cist dug into upper Beaker midden provide *taq* for this Beaker-associated activity, the earliest of which is AA-50316, 3395±50 BP (*Discovery & Excavation in Scotland 3*, 2002, 153)	NF99SE 2.00
Callanish (Calanais), Lewis, Western Isles	Not closely comparable with any of Clarke's styles; likely	In cultivation soil with ard marks, from time of dilapidation of chambered cairn ;	i) AA-29462 ii) AA-24968	i) 3555±50 ii) 3575±45	i) **1980–1770** 2030–1750 ii) **2020–1880** 2040–1770	i) Birch charcoal ii) Willow charcoal	i)from cultivation soil; ii) from under cultivation soil; nature of activities that produced this charcoal is unknown, and may not be related at all to the activities	NB23SW 1

to 'post-date' step 2	originally associated with the Beaker pottery. Note also: other dates from cultivation soil (AA-29460–1, 29463) clearly relate to residual Neolithic charcoal; residual Neolithic pottery also present in this cultivation soil
	this material rich in Beaker sherds. Beakers probably originally deposited with burials inside the chamber tomb, then cleared out onto this soil

APPENDIX 5: Dates relating to Beaker graves, where standard deviation has had to be increased

All from unburnt human bone, from crouched inhumations in cists, unless specified otherwise. Calibration not worth attempting with such large adjusted standard deviations. See Appendix 1 for details of the old dates from Sorisdale, Cookston and Dryburn Bridge that fall within this category, and for details of their recent replacements. See also Appendix 7 for other dates from Beaker graves

Findspot	Beaker type	Context of Beaker, associations	Laboratory code	Date BP (adjusted std dev in brackets)	Comments	References
Boatbridge Quarry (cist 2), Thankerton, S Lanarkshire	SN; N1; step 4	Unusually tall adult (described as adolescent in original report), indeterminate sex	GU-1117	3835±75 (110)	Now superseded by **OxA-V-2167-42**. There had been confusion over the GU-1117 date: version cited here is as listed in HS on-line datelist; but in publication (Clarke et al. 1984), date and code given as 3730±60 BP, GU-1122. See below for Keabog cist 1, GU-1122	NS93NE 27
Kilpatrick (cairn 16/2), Arran, N Ayrshire	LC; AOC; step 1–2	From disturbed cist in kerbed earthen mound covered with stones; inhumation in cist totally decayed	GU-1177	3835±55 (110)	Mixed hazel, oak, birch, willow & beech charcoal from sand mound (according to Barber 1997, 40; HS datelist says charcoal found under mound). Either tpq for, or contemporary with, burial.	NR92NW 27; Barber 1997, 40
Keabog (cist 1), Pitdrichie Farm, Aberdeenshire	SN; N3; step 5	Adult male at least 35–45, with possible ante-mortem skull fracture	GU-1122	3725±60 (110)	There is confusion over date: date cited is as listed in HS on-line datelist; but in publication (Shepherd and Bruce 1987), date and code given as 3730±60 BP, GU-1122 – the same as that cited in the Boatbridge Quarry publication (see above).	NO78SE 18

Ruchlaw Mains, East Lothian	SN; N2 or N3; step 4	Senior adult (46+ years), probably male	GU-1356	3720±80 (110)		Now superseded by **OxA-V-2167-42** (see Appendix 1)	NT67SW 14; Ashmore et al. 1982
Keabog (cist 2), Pitdrichie Farm, Aberdeenshire	Uncertain/ intermediate; N3(L); step 6	Adult (26–35), probably male, on L side, facing N; flint knife	GU-1123	3675±95 (135)		Now superseded by **OxA-V-2172-22** (see Appendix 1). GU-1123 date cited is as listed in HS on-line datelist; but in Shepherd and Bruce 1987, date given as 3695±95 BP	NO78SE 18
Dalladies, Aberdeenshire	WC; S4; step 7	Cremated remains (no bone report) in cist set into Early Neolithic non-megalithic long barrow; 3 thumbnail flint scrapers, 2 broken flint blades, egg-shaped pebble	SRR-553	3630±90 (125)		Date obtained (in 1970s) from carbonised 'burnt') oak plank – possibly a cist cover – lying over cremated remains	NO66NW 27

APPENDIX 6: Dates from non-funerary contexts, where the closeness of the association between dated material and Beakers cannot be guaranteed and where the standard deviation has either had to be increased, or already exceeds 100

Findspot	Beaker type	Context of Beaker, associations	Laboratory code	Date BP (adjusted version in brackets)	Material dated	Comments	References
Rosinish, Benbecula, W Isles	'Early Northern', step 5	In stratified midden and in contemporary ard furrows	i) GU-1065 ii) GU-1064	i) 3920±60 (3515±140) ii) 3850±80 (3445±140)	Limpet shell	Whole dates revised to take into account the marine reservoir effect. Carbonised cereal grain from midden due to be AMS dated (Shepherd pers comm)	NF85SE 4; Shepherd and Tuckwell 1977
Boghead, Moray	LN; AOC, probably also All Over Ornamented, and plain; steps 1–2	In fill of pit (70 cm long, 60 cm deep, NNE-SSW, its mouth covered by flat stones); uniform earth filling, some charcoal	SRR-687	3867±70 (110)	Charcoal (species unspecified)	Pit seems too small to have been a grave; may relate to ceremonies connected with nearby Early Neolithic mound. The fact that the pit was sealed, and the date is in line with other dates for step 1–2 pottery, suggests that the charcoal and the Beaker may well have been contemporary.	NJ35NE 5
Links of Noltland (central area, Trench C), Orkney	Closest to SN; 'Northern British'; step 4–5	Sherds of 2 or 3 Beakers in midden overlying a wall and a deer butchering area	i) GU-1693 ii) GU-1690 iii)GU-1432	i) 3990±85 (not adj) ii)3760±85 (not adj) iii) 3722±60 (110)	i) cattle & red deer bone ii) red deer bone iii) red deer bone	Dates provide *tpq* for Beaker pottery: i) from below the wall; ii) and iii) from deer butchery area	HY44NW 33

Findspot	Beaker type	Context of Beaker, associations	Laboratory code	Date BP	Material	Comments	References
Lairg, Achany Glen (burial cairn 1), Highland	Indet but comparable with SN; 'North British'; step 4–5 type	Thought to relate to domestic activity pre-dating erection of burial cairn	GU-3322	3700±130	Charcoal (species unspecified)	Date is as cited in HS datelist; in publication (McCullagh and Tipping 1998, variously cited as 3630±130 (p 36) and 3700±150 (p 87)	NC50SE 8
The Udal, N Uist, Western Isles	Includes ?LC; AOC	Occupation layer in multi-period site	i)Q-1134 ii)Q-1133	i)3564±100 (140) ii)3466±120 (3061±140)	i)Animal bone ii) Marine shell	Shell date revised to take into account the marine reservoir effect.	NF87NW 1
Tormore, Arran	Indet; AOC; step 1–2 & banded comb-decorated (type unspecified)	In earliest bank of a hut-circle	GU-1176	3485±60 (110)	Charcoal (birch, willow, hazel, ash)	Dated charcoal is from latest phase of the same hut, so *taq* for Beaker	NR83SE 21
Berrybrae, Aberdeenshire	?SN; N3; step uncertain (according to Shepherd 1986, 34)	From enclosed cremation cemetery post-dating recumbent stone circle	i)HAR-1849 ii) HAR-1893	i) 3450±80 (110) ii) 3310±90 (125)	Charcoal (species unspecified)	Dated charcoal from plank overlying the Beaker	NK05NW 2

APPENDIX 7: Dates that can be rejected (as pertaining to the dating of Scottish Beakers) for a variety of reasons, as specified below

Findspot	Beaker type	Context of Beaker, associations	Laboratory code	Date BP	Comments	References
Linlithgow Friary, West Lothian	Indet	Pit: one of a cluster of prehistoric pits and gullies	GU-1875	5265±55	Mixed charcoal (mainly oak, with 5% hazel); not from the pit containing the Beaker sherds, and clearly wholly unconnected with the Beaker phase of activity	NT07NW 7.00
Balnahanaid, Ben Lawers, Perth & Kinross	LC; AOC; step 1–2	Pit: one of a group of pits and scoops	OxA-8973	5055±45	Hazel charcoal from upper fill of pit with Beaker; evidently residual	NN63NE 78
Skateraw (cist found 1972), East Lothian	SN; N2; step 4	Crouched inhumation of adult, possibly female, in cist	SRR-453	4420±130	Old date, obtained from poor condition bone. Two other attempt to re-date other samples from same skeleton in 2004 and 2006 failed due to insufficient collagen	NT77NW 14
Dunragit, Dumfries & Galloway	See comment	In pit near innermost ring of Late Neolithic	SUERC-2109, 2107, 2104,	i) 4175±45 ii)4150±35	Dates actually relate to Grooved Ware: pottery had originally been	NX15NE 69.01; Thomas 2004

Site	Type / Step	Context	Lab no.	Date BP	mis-identified as Beaker!	Reference
Loch Paible, N Uist, W Isles	'cord-decorated'	enclosure; dated material consisted of oak charcoal (i), burnt hazelnut (ii) and hazel charcoal (iii–iv)	2106 respectively	iii) 4085±35 iv) 4055±35		Maclean et al 1978
		In midden on exposed machair edge; pieces of quartz and animal bones recovered from same exposure	GU-1088	4060±135 (whole date adjusted to 3655±195)	Date determined on sea shell (hence total revision, to compensate for marine effect). Association between dated shell and pottery insecure	
Abbey Mains Farm, East Lothian	SN; N2 or N3; step 4	Adult (17–25 years), probably female; had been accompanied by a joint of pork	OxA-10254	3945±40	Sample contaminated during ultrafiltration pretreatment process (see Bronk Ramsey et al. 2004 for details). Date now deleted by Oxford laboratory; see Appendix 1 for 2 replacement dates	NT57NW 115; Lawson et al. 2002
Broomend of Crichie (cist 2), Aberdeenshire	SN x 2; N2 x 2; step 4 x 2	Adult male & infant; 2 Beakers; horn spoon; 2 flint flakes; ' a small quantity of black earth'; pieces of 'charcoal'; bodies covered by ox-hide.	OxA-11243	3932±35	Sample contaminated during ultrafiltration pretreatment process (see Bronk Ramsey et al. 2004 for details). Date now deleted by Oxford laboratory; see Appendix 1 for replacement date	NJ71NE 11
Holm of Papa Westray North, Orkney	Indeterminate coarse Beaker	Red deer bone from midden that is believed to have accumulated after chamber tomb went out of use; Grooved Ware also present in the midden	OxA-9872	3855±40	Sample contaminated during ultrafiltration pretreatment process (see Bronk Ramsey et al. 2004 for details). Date now deleted by Oxford laboratory and is being redetermined, but in any case, association with the Beaker pottery is not sufficiently close for one to be sure that the dated material had been associated	HY55SW 2
Mains of Balnagowan, Highland	SP N/NR; step 4	Crouched inhumation of mature adult male in cist; flint flake	GU-1121	3505±85 (120)	Excavators noted close similarity between Beaker and cist construction with dated Beaker from Chealamy (see Appendix 1); both Beakers may show Dutch influence. Date appears anomalously late	NH85SW 15; Shepherd et al. 1984
Boysack Mills, Angus	SN; N3; step 5	Crouched inhumation of adult female, 25–30, in cist	BM-2513	3460±50	Date appears anomalously late	NO64NW 23
Knockenny, Glamis, Angus	SN; N3; step 4	Crouched inhumation in cist; no detail about skeleton	N-1240	3390±90 (125)	Associated pot (DUNMG 1969-246) is an N3 Beaker, not a Beaker-Food Vessel hybrid as stated in the HS datelist. Date appears anomalously late	NO34SE 7

Site		Description	Lab code	Date BP	Comments	NGR
Balbirnie, Fife	WC; S4; step 6	Beaker and disc bead of jet-like material found with charred wooden planks on surface of subsoil under cairn; thought to be disturbed contents of a cist	GaK-3425	3280±90 (270)	Insecure association beneath cairn; and GaK determination of dubious reliability (cf Spriggs and Anderson 1993)	NO20SE 4
Mains of Scotstown, Aberdeen	SN; N4; step 4	Crouched inhumation of fairly tall adult male, 40–45, in cist; 2 flint flakes; traces of copper or copper alloy artefact	UB-2097	3140±70	Unspecified 'carbonised material' from cist floor dated. Anomalously late	NJ91SW 13
Ashgrove (Methilhill), Fife	WC; S4; step 6–7	Crouched inhumation of senior adult male (c 55) in cist; dagger in scabbard; plant remains over body	Q-764	2950±150 (210)	Mixed organic material found in chest area of body dated. Anomalously late	NT39NE 3
Limefield, South Lanarkshire	WC; S4; step 6–7	Cremated human remains from central burial pit under cairn; jet V-perforated button also present in grave	*GrA-23404*	2940±50	Date echoes that obtained before mid-1980s for charcoal from same deposit (BM-451, 2761±85) and confirms that the cremated remains must be from a secondary, Late Bronze Age burial, inserted into pit of a Beaker-associated inhumation grave. Date therefore does not relate to the Beaker or button	NS93SW 6
East Barns, Dunbar, East Lothian	SN; N/MR; step 3	Crouched inhumation, male 'of large proportions', in cist; also present in same storage box in NMS are bones of a juvenile and a ?cattle tooth, but not known whether originally associated (and see comment)	*OxA-13212*	688±25	Date obtained from the human bone which had allegedly been found with the Beaker in 1900; evidently much younger bone has accidentally become associated with this vessel since its discovery	NT77NW 3

Samples of unburnt human bone from the following graves failed to produce dates due to insufficient collagen being present: Dornoch Nursery Cist, Highland; Skateraw (1972 cist), East Lothian (see above); Collessie, Fife; Kilspindie, Aberdeenshire; West Castlehill, Aberdeenshire; Whitestone, Aberdeenshire; and Kintore, Aberdeenshire. All but the last were submitted as part of the NMS or BPP dating programmes; the Kintore date was submitted as part of a developer-funded excavation (Cook pers comm). A probable *tag* for the Collessie burial is provided by dates of 3690±80 BP (OxA-4510) and 3695±45 BP (GrA-19054) for a cist, under the same cairn, containing cremated remains and a dagger with gold hiltband. Finally, material from a probable ox-hide from Broomend of Crichie cist 2 also failed to produce a result, but bone from this cist was successfully dated (see Appendix 1).

Chapter 12

The Stonehenge Riverside Project: excavations at the east entrance of Durrington Walls

Mike Parker Pearson

Dept. of Archaeology, University of Sheffield

The Stonehenge Riverside Project was begun in 2003 as a 7-year field investigation into the purpose and context of Stonehenge, to examine its role as just one monument within a larger complex of 3rd millennium BC monuments linked by the River Avon. The project aims to investigate the chronology and context of other prehistoric monuments within the Stonehenge World Heritage Site and more widely across Salisbury Plain. In particular, certain key monuments such as the Greater Cursus and the Stonehenge Palisade remain undated whilst the internal chronology of Stonehenge itself is not yet fully established.

Background

The impetus for the project came from an observation by Ramilisonina that the stones of Stonehenge might have been erected to commemorate the ancestors whilst the timber circles of Woodhenge and the Southern Circle at Durrington Walls were built for the living (Parker Pearson and Ramilisonina 1998a). This juxtaposition of eternal stones and perishable timber was mediated by the monuments' relationships to the River Avon (Figure 12.1) which was proposed as an intermediate zone into which the remains of the dead were cast.

In 1998 this theory appeared a little unlikely to many prehistorians. In terms of chronology alone, the stone phase (Phase 3) at Stonehenge was reckoned to date to several centuries after the henge enclosure of Durrington Walls. There were also theoretical misgivings about the likelihood and nature of ancestor commemoration in the Late Neolithic (Whitley 2002) and the unlikelihood of a planned, large-scale architectural ordering of life-death dichotomies in the landscape as opposed to their development occurring within a more randomly constituted sequence of contingencies and unforeseen consequences of human agency (Barrett and Fewster 1998). For others, the practical implementation of a project to explore this theory was simply too speculative.

Aims

The Stonehenge Riverside Project was designed to establish four important points which may shed light on the viability - or not - of the wood/stone hypothesis:

1. Do the wood and stone monuments of Durrington Walls and Stonehenge date to the same period, to be established as closely as might be possible through radiocarbon dating?

2. Was there a ceremonial avenue linking Durrington Walls to the river in the same way that the 30m-wide Stonehenge Avenue linked Stonehenge to the Avon?

3. Can the dichotomy of a monument for the dead and a monument used by the living be properly justified in terms of evidence for the dead and for the living at the two different sites?

4. Are there complementarities between Durrington Walls and Stonehenge which strengthen the case for their being planned and executed as components of a single grand scheme?

Durrington Walls: a brief history of research

Durrington Walls is Britain's largest henge, some 18ha in size and over 400m in diameter (Figure 12.2). Yet it has suffered considerably from ploughing over the last two millennia and the earthworks of its bank and ditch are barely noticeable in many places. As OGS Crawford wrote in 1929, '[p]robably not one in ten thousand of those who pass through the middle of Durrington Walls is aware of its existence' (1929: 49). This super-henge was first recorded by Sir Richard Colt Hoare in 1812 and he even dug into a barrow-sized mound on the south side of Durrington Walls; he found no burial here but recorded a flat Beaker-period grave 'above Durrington Walls', presumably to the west of the henge (1812: 170-2). In 1917 Percival Farrer excavated a pipe trench into the southwest bank of the henge and discovered artefacts and bones underneath the henge bank, including Beaker pottery (Farrer 1918: 100). He interpreted the site as being the settlement for the priests who had officiated at Stonehenge.

Interest then moved to Durrington Walls' small annexe, Woodhenge. In 1926 Maud Cunnington excavated the post holes of this now more famous timber monument that had been newly revealed by aerial photography. Another aerial photographic discovery was made by OGS Crawford a couple of years later when he recorded the cropmark of a large circular enclosure within the western part of Durrington Walls (Crawford 1929; this was the one plotted as 'A' by David and Payne in 1996 [1997: fig. 11] and excavated in 2006; see Thomas this volume). In the winter of 1950/51, J.F.S. Stone recorded the sections of a utility trench dug alongside the old A345 running north to south through Durrington Walls (Stone *et al.* 1954). Unprepared for the massiveness of the site, he misinterpreted the huge henge ditches as natural valleys or coombes. On the outside of the bank on its

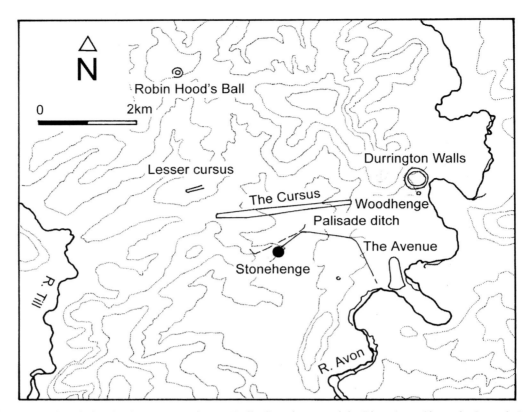

Figure 12.1 The relationship between Durrington Walls, Stonehenge and the River Avon (drawn by Irene de Luis)

south side near Woodhenge, Stone observed postholes in the trench section and, in 1952, he carried out an excavation to find out if these were part of a Neolithic house. These in fact formed a line of posts standing to the south of the henge bank but later engulfed by it. The posts and the henge bank were covered by midden deposits which are important because they are the only Late Neolithic deposit found so far which post-dates the henge. Unfortunately, Stone's co-author Stuart Piggott wrote up the pottery from this context without distinguishing it from Grooved Ware found beneath the henge bank in 1950/1951.

In the late 1960s Durrington Walls was the site of one of the most significant British excavations of the 20th century. The A345 was to be re-routed through the henge and 5% of its interior would be destroyed by the road. Between 1966 and 1968 Geoffrey Wainwright, then an Inspector of Ancient Monuments for the Ministry of Works, carried out the largest excavation yet seen in Britain (Wainwright with Longworth 1971). The story of his then controversial methods of large-scale machine stripping, and the furore this caused amongst academics and local archaeologists, is well told in Mike Pitts' *Hengeworld* (2000: 50-61); this excavation in fact set the standard for today's large-scale excavations in advance of roadlines and other major developments. The excavation was also significant in that more than half of the 100 workers on the project were paid diggers, breaking with traditional archaeological practice in which a director and his/her staff supervised a team of (archaeologically

untrained) workmen. Many of these excavators went on to pursue archaeological careers as rescue archaeology developed throughout the succeeding decades. Paid £1 per day, the volunteers worked hard and played hard, spending their money in the nearby Stonehenge Inn and creating the legendary spirit of drinking and mayhem that still remains part of the ethos of field archaeology today.[1]

The results of the excavation were stunning. Wainwright's fleet of machines removed up to 1.4m of colluvium from the valley bottom and exposed more than half of a 40m-diameter circle of post holes set within six concentric rings. These formed the second phase of a two-phase timber monument whose first phase was a post facade breached by an entrance which led to a 4-post structure. This two-phase structure is called the Southern Circle to distinguish it from the Northern Circle, another post circle around a 4-post setting with a façade and entrance. The Southern Circle lay close to the east entrance of the henge and Wainwright's team were able to excavate the adjacent terminal of the massive henge ditch, 5.5m deep and 10m wide. Immediately east of the Southern Circle, they discovered a terraced midden surrounded by the stakeholes of a fence; this terraced feature is likely to have been a house platform, by analogy with similar features found in 2006. To the north of the Northern Circle, they also excavated the henge

---

[1] Personal communications from several of the Wainwright team, especially Dave Buckley and Peter Drewett, as well as Geoff Wainwright himself.

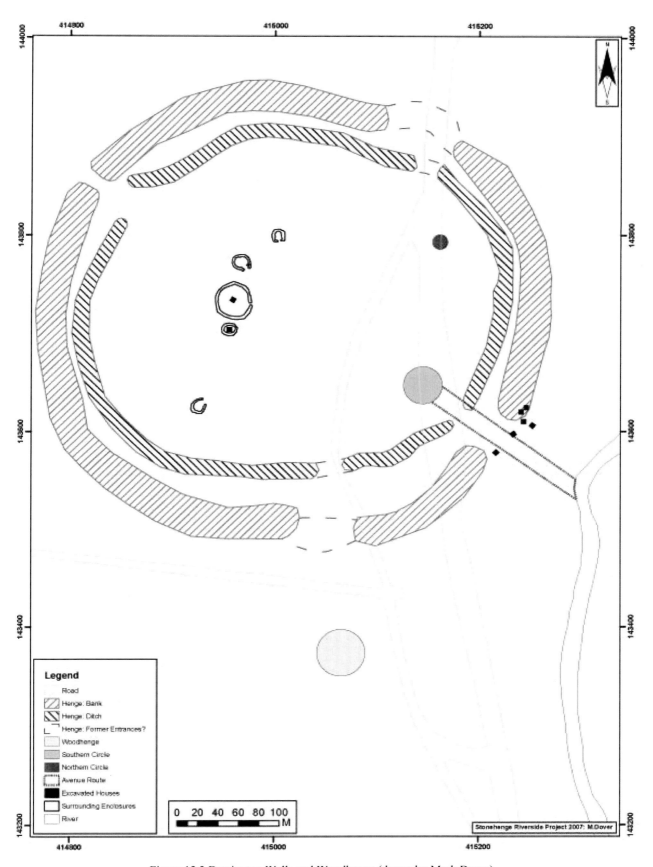

Figure 12.2 Durrington Walls and Woodhenge (drawn by Mark Dover)

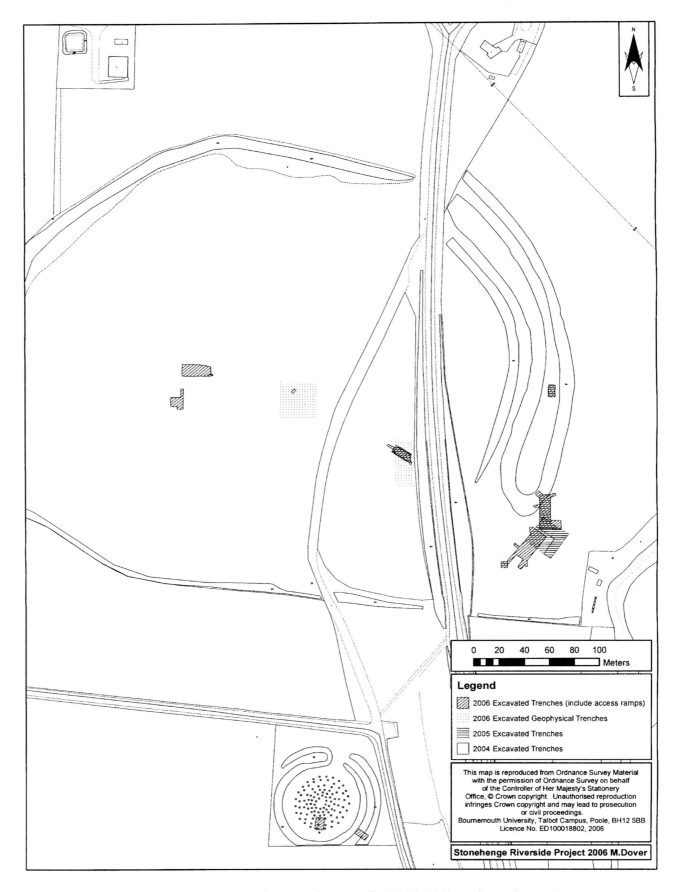

Figure 12.3 Excavation trenches at Durrington Walls, 2004-2006 (drawn by Mark Dover)

ditch in a section that we now know to have been a later blocking of the henge's north entrance.

Radiocarbon dating established Durrington Walls' construction within the 3rd millennium BC. In those days the error margins on radiocarbon dates were much greater than today, and cannot help our current attempts to gain more precise estimates of the monument's period of use. Two of the first radiocarbon determinations in Britain had been previously carried out on samples of charcoal from the pre-henge (and pre-Grooved Ware) ground surface under the south bank recovered in the 1952 excavations. These first Durrington Walls dates had a major impact on British archaeology, pushing back the antiquity of the British Neolithic into the 4th millennium BC and stirring Stuart Piggott to deliver the memorable if ungrammatical statement that these radiocarbon dates were 'archaeologically inacceptable' (Piggott 1959: 289).

The east entrance

The Stonehenge Riverside Project began in 2003 when a small team of local volunteers investigated the riverside at Durrington Walls, clearing vegetation to expose an incline which dropped from the hanging valley in which the henge is located down to the present course of the River Avon. Mike Allen carried out a programme of

coring within this incline and in two transects outside the henge's entrance to establish stratigraphic sequences beneath the deep colluvium which filled the valley. Neil Linford, Andy Payne and Louise Martin of English Heritage extended the 1996 magnetometry survey of the western half of Durrington Walls to cover its eastern half and the area outside the east entrance (Payne 2003). Between 2004 and 2006 a series of trenches were opened across the henge (Figure 12.3).

The coring results indicated that possible stratified layers survived in pockets beneath the colluvium outside the east entrance. The magnetometry survey identified a narrow linear feature running from in front of the east entrance to the riverside. In addition, there were two clusters of magnetic anomalies on either side of the entrance, close to or even under the henge bank. In 2004 an L-shaped trench (Trench 1) was excavated on the north side of the east entrance to investigate the west end of the linear anomaly (suspected to be an avenue ditch) and the southeast margin of the northern cluster of anomalies, as well as to discover whether traces of an avenue could be found running out of the henge towards the river. Three trenches were planned for the incline by the riverside; Trenches 2 and 4 were dug but their negative results made it clear that Trench 3 was not worth opening.

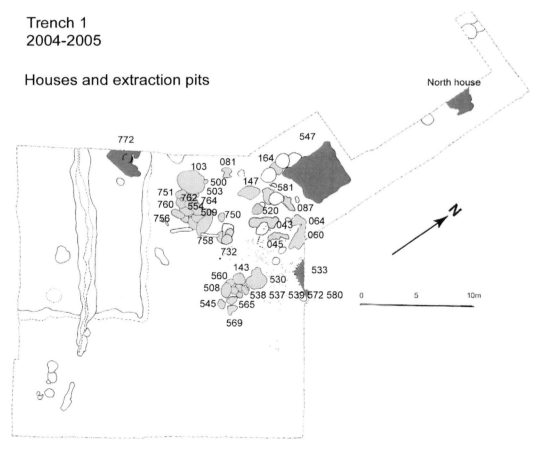

Figure 12.4 Trench 1, as excavated in 2004 and 2005, showing the northern half of the avenue, three of the house floors, and the pit complex (drawn by Mike Parker Pearson)

The 2004 excavation's results were, on one level, deeply disappointing. The riverside incline was entirely the product of post-Neolithic erosion. Within Trench 1, the linear anomaly was an Iron Age ditch which formed part of a larger fields system (see Bewley *et al.* 2005 for a Lidar plot of the Iron Age field boundaries on this side of the henge). Furthermore, Iron Age and later cultivation had removed all deposits from the area outside the east entrance except for the bases of a few Late Neolithic pits. Yet there were some encouraging results. The steep slope on the north side of the entrance was covered with over 50 Late Neolithic pits and, in the northwest corner of Trench 1, there was a platform of chalk-derived clay with burnt deposits on its surface (Figure 12.4). Was this a feasting platform akin to the flint and chalk surfaces outside and within the Southern Circle where a large, 5m-long fire pit had been found in 1967?

The 2005 season was the make-or-break year. If there was no trace of an avenue leading from the east entrance to the river then this part of the hypothesis could be abandoned. Trench 1 was extended northwards and southwards. To the north, resistivity survey had picked out a circular anomaly with a low resistance feature at its centre. To the south there was no indication of any anomalies in the geophysics results but we were determined to have one last look for traces of an avenue. Perhaps the Late Neolithic pit bases were part of a more extended formation leading to the henge entrance. The entire excavation was also to be filmed for a Time Team Special documentary – would the project fall flat on its face in front of over a million viewers or would it take us to a new level of understanding?

The Durrington Walls avenue

The decision to open up a large area outside the east entrance was fully vindicated. At the south end of the trench we discovered part of a large avenue, consisting of an embanked flint surface, running towards the Southern Circle. We had failed to locate it in the 2004 excavations because that part of it which crossed the excavation trench had been destroyed by cultivation; further west it survived on the uphill side of a lynchet which had formed from the Iron Age onwards. As we were to discover during the 2006 excavations, this avenue was 30m wide, composed of a 15m-wide trampled flint surface covered by a buried soil and flanked by shallow gullies inside low banks which were each 5m wide (Figures 12.5, 12.6 and 12.7). The flint surface did not extend to the banks but petered out at a gully on the northeast side and a lower flat area on the southwest side. The avenue's upper surface, protected beneath the buried soil, was composed of naturally weathered flints as well as lesser quantities of animal bones, burnt flint, sarsen lumps, pottery sherds and worked flint. It may well have been formed of materials lying on the exposed floor of the Durrington coombe but fractured flint from the base of the river cliff could also have been incorporated. A lower flint surface was largely devoid of cultural material and may have

formed naturally, being augmented by dumped flint, or was constructed as a road surface prior to the deposition of animal bones and cultural material which were later incorporated into the upper surface.

By the 2006 field season, it became apparent that the end of this avenue might be at the Southern Circle and that the flint platform excavated in 1967, inter-stratified with the post setting (on top of its Phase 1 posts and filling the post ramps but not the postholes of Phase 2), was the road surface. This was confirmed in 2006 when the avenue's width was found to be equivalent to that of the platform and, as closely as could be judged from the 1967 photographs, its composition was seen to be similar. In 2006 a further trench close to the edge of the river cliff demonstrated that the avenue's flint surface had not survived here although its southwest edge is visible as a slight earthwork. Charly French's coring of the Avon floodplain in 2006 also demonstrated that, where the avenue met the river, the prehistoric palaeochannel (deeper and wider than today's river channel) had flowed on the same course as today before curving eastwards off the river's current line. The avenue's approach to the river was thus along a gentle incline until it reached the near-vertical 4m-high river cliff. There was thus no easy descent to the river's edge, making this a place more suitable for deposition than for embarkation.

The avenue was thus 170m long and 30m wide, and ran from the Southern Circle to the bank of the Avon. Along its northeastern edge, the flint roadway had a set of three sarsen stoneholes but there was no trace of a similar arrangement on its opposite side. The Southern Circle is aligned on the midwinter sunrise yet the avenue's axis is *not* aligned on this solstice direction when looking down it from the timber circle towards the southeast. However, when looking in the opposite direction, uphill and northwestwards towards the henge, it is within 1° of midsummer sunset (Clive Ruggles pers. comm.). Given that the line of the avenue is slightly across the slope rather than following the Durrington coombe's natural incline, this is probably a deliberate rather than a coincidental orientation.

As every prehistorian knows, these two solstice orientations are the opposites of those embodied in the layout of Stonehenge and its avenue.[2] The comparison between the wooden Southern Circle and the sarsen Stonehenge is further strengthened by the newly revealed plan of the Southern Circle. In 2006 a magnetometry survey by English Heritage, combined with the 2005-2006 excavation (see Thomas this volume) and the results of the 1967 excavation, revealed that the six concentric rings of its Phase 2 arrangement were not all circular (Linford and Payne in preparation). The second innermost ring is in fact oval, with its long axis northeast-southwest. It thus forms a more precise wooden analogy

---

[2] Junior prehistorians looking for a clear demonstration of this observation are directed to *The Amazing Pop-up Stonehenge* (Richards 2005: 14-15).

Figure 12.5 The avenue in cross-section with its rammed flint surface and external banks, viewed from the northwest
(photographed by Mike Parker Pearson)

Figure 12.6 The avenue (cross-sectioned within the trench nearest the camera), viewed from the south
(photographed by Adam Stanford of Aerial-Cam)

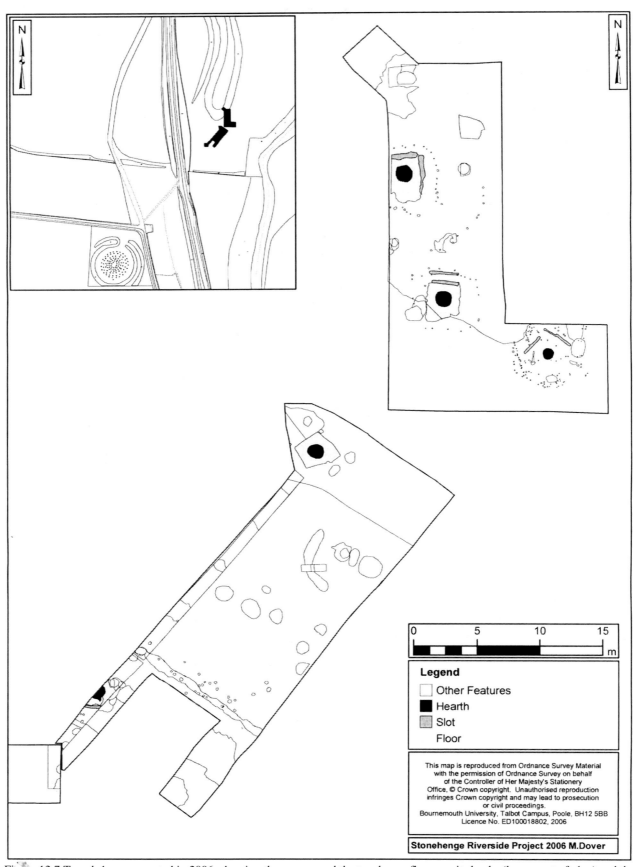

Figure 12.7 Trench 1, as excavated in 2006, showing the avenue and the two house floors on its banks (lower part of plan) and the midden area (593) with four houses (upper part of plan; drawn by Mark Dover)

for Stonehenge, with its near-oval setting of sarsen trilithons enclosing an oval arrangement of bluestones, both on a northeast-southwest axis. That the complementary and oppositional arrangement of these two complexes was a contemporaneous feature is supported by an initial radiocarbon date for an antler pick deposited within one of the Southern Circle's postholes. This dates to 2580-2400 cal BC at 89.1% probability (3966±33 bp; OxA-14976) and compares closely to the date of 2620-2480 cal BC at 92% probability (4023±21 bp; UB-3821) for an antler pick within one of the stone holes of Stonehenge's sarsen circle (Cleal *et al.* 1995). Further dating in 2007 should establish the chronology more firmly.

The living and the dead

The 20th century excavations at Stonehenge showed it to be probably the largest cremation cemetery known in Britain during the 3rd millennium BC, with an estimated 240 cremation burials in its ditch fill, Aubrey Holes and other parts of the monument as well as a good selection of unburnt disarticulated human bones (McKinley 1995; Pitts 2000). Durrington Walls, on the other hand, has proved to have surprisingly few human remains for a Neolithic ceremonial site. Farrer reckoned to have found some cremated bone beneath the bank in 1917 and there are a couple of Beaker-period burials (c. 2400-2000 BC) from outside the the banks of the henge (Stone *et al.* 1954; Wainwright with Longworth 1971: 5). During the 1967 excavations, skull fragments from two adults were found in Posthole 95 of the Southern Circle and various longbones from an adult, a sub-adult and an infant were found in the fill of the henge ditch south of the east entrance.[3] In 2004-2006 we found three human bones, each one to the south of a house and possibly placed there when each house went out of use. Given that these human bones are a tiny proportion of the estimated 50,000 animal bones from Durrington Walls, it is clear that people using this site had very different practices in comparison to the depositions at Stonehenge.

Our excavations at Durrington Walls have served to further emphasise the dichotomy of living and dead that was hypothesised in 1998. Furthermore, they have allowed us to gain a clearer understanding of this coombe as a 'domain of the living' which changed dramatically in character during the mid 3rd millennium BC. The bank of the henge lies over the bank of the avenue and is thus one of the latest features.

The Durrington Walls sequence
Our provisional and relative chronology for Durrington Walls is as follows.

- There was limited activity during the 4th millennium BC in the area subsequently to become the north

entrance to the henge (Wainwright with Longworth 1971: 14). Earlier Neolithic flintwork and pottery has also been recovered from buried turf outside the east entrance in 2004-2006 and a tree-throw hole under Woodhenge's bank produced Carinated Bowl pottery in 2006. Thereafter, there is no trace of any human presence until the mid 3rd millennium when the Southern Circle's first phase was constructed.

- The Southern Circle was partially terraced into the chalk slope on its southwest side. It may have been at this time that a terraced area of houses in the western enclosures higher up the coombe was built (see Thomas this volume). However, these could be contemporary with houses found beside the avenue (see below).

- The avenue was subsequently constructed to link the Southern Circle, probably during the circle's second phase (Wainwright with Longworth 1971: 32), to the river and to incorporate and integrate the solstice directions.

- On top of the banks of the avenue, a pair of houses was built, giving the appearance of opposed gatehouses. These were probably contemporary with four other houses terraced into the slope stretching northwards from the side of the avenue and separated from it by a zone of pits.

- The henge ditch and bank were then constructed. The bank covered the ground surface on which the houses were built. It also spread over the southwest bank of the avenue.

- A final phase of Grooved Ware and Beaker occupation is attested by the occupation layer deposited against the bank on the south side of the henge (Stone *et al.* 1954).

The houses

Five houses and a likely entrance area to a sixth house were found beside the avenue (Figures 12.7 and 12.8). Two of these were set upon opposite sides of the avenue's banks and the remainder were terraced into the slope rising to the northeast of the avenue, and separated from the avenue by a 10m-wide zone of pits (Figure 12.4; see below). The houses are square or sub-rectangular and vary in size from 5.8m x c.5.5m (House 851) to just 2.5m x 3m (House 772) with a roughly central hearth set within a chalk plaster floor. In Houses 851 and 547, this floor was edged by slots which presumably held footings for wooden beds and furniture. In these two houses, the micro-debris left on the floor by their occupants shows that activities took place in different parts of the house. For example, cooking debris was concentrated on the south side whilst flint tools such as scrapers, arrowheads and retouched flakes were mostly found in the northeast. Soot staining of the surfaces of these two floors also showed evidence of raking out of the hearth on their south sides.

---

[3] These are more than the two human bones from these two contexts reported in the excavation monograph by Powers (1971: 351).

Figure 12.8 Trench 1, as excavated in 2006, viewed from the north and showing the midden area with house floors in the foreground (photographed by Adam Stanford of Aerial-Cam)

Figure 12.9 House 851's floor, viewed from the east (photographed by Bob Nunn)

House 851

House 851 was the largest and best preserved house (Figure 12.9). It was 5.8m north-south and probably over 5m east-west (its western edge was not excavated in 2006). It lay east-southeast of the Southern Circle and northeast of the avenue, north of House 547 and consisted of a rectangular clay floor, 3.6m north-south by probably 2.5m east-west. The house was terraced into the sloping valley side so that its floor was level.

The hearth was not quite central to this floor or to the house but was slightly north of centre. It was slightly sunken and oval, 1.4m north-south x 1.3m east-west, and had been intensely used so that its contours had become well smoothed (in contrast to those of the hearth in House 547; see below). Another sign of wear on the floor was a shallow, double depression, 0.5m east-west x 0.3m north-south, immediately south of the hearth. This could be a kneeling spot where the cooking was organised and the hearth cleaned out. The clay floor was bounded by slots on its north and east sides. On the east side a 0.5m-long east-west slot was cut by a north-south slot, 2.5m long and 0.35m wide, placed against the edge of the clay floor. This delimited space between the floor and wall of 1.2m, adequate for a box bed. To the south of this slot, there was a second slot or cut in the edge of the clay floor, 0.7m long north-south. The abandonment layer on top of the floor here contained large quantities of sherds and hearth ash and this sunken area is thus interpreted as holding furniture associated with cooking. On the north side of the house, a further slot was at least 2m east-west and 0.45m wide. The space between floor and wall provided by this slot was only 0.8m north-south, suggesting that this was the footing for a dresser rather than a box bed.

The doorway was clearly marked towards the west end of the south side by a deeply worn hollow, 1.3m north-south, in the southern edge of the clay floor. This was slightly to the west of the doorway's centre as marked by two 0.5m-deep postholes spaced 0.9m apart. This suggests that the door was pivoted on the eastern stakehole and opened inwards, directing movement to the west side. In between the doorway stakeholes there was a small stakehole into the top of which a small pit, 0.2m in diameter, had been filled with animal bones and an arrowhead, possibly as a special deposit. The line of the wall was formed by 23 stakeholes, most of them appearing as voids. Unlike House 547 there was no concentration of daub fragments around the house's exterior. The doorway was recessed within a 'hornwork' which expanded eastwards to its full distance of 1m from the southern edge of the clay floor. There was then a 1.6m gap with no stakeholes before the east wall of the house which ran north-south and curved westwards in the northeast corner. The north wall ran just below the top of the terraced edge.

The wear caused by entering the doorway was so great that the clay floor in this part of the house was entirely

missing, exposing an orange and black layer beneath. It is very likely that this is the hearth area of an earlier house on which House 851 was subsequently built. If so, then this indicates a degree of longevity for dwelling in this spot.

House 848

On the level ground about 2m northeast of House 851 there was a concave, beaten surface of yellow clay which formed the floor of House 848 (Figure 12.10). It was 2.6m long east-west and 1.9m-2.1m wide north-south, with the east end 0.2m narrower than the west. Its sides are slightly curved rather than straight. Within this slightly trapezoidal structure, there was a central, circular hearth 0.6m in diameter, which was heavily eroded. Unlike the main houses, the hearth was not set within a hollowed-out bowl in the ground and was only 0.05m thick. The clay floor surface was discoloured around the hearth with black and dark orange ash but not to the extent seen in the larger houses.

Unlike Houses 547 and 851, House 848 had no appreciable spread of household debris over its surface other than a few sherds against the western edge of the house and a single sherd in a small depression southeast of the hearth.

The absence of daub or dissolved chalk plaster beyond the edges of the floor suggests that it may not have had daub walls. Nor was there any trace of postholes or stakeholes surrounding it. However, there was an irregular spread of small chalk lumps within half a metre of the floor's edge and thius could be the remains of a cobb-like wall matrix. Alternatively the walls were constructed not from earthfast posts or stakes but from beams laid upon the ground, out of which plank walls and corner posts might have been supported. The only evidence of an entrance was a worn-away area of floor at the east end of the south wall.

House 848's floor was different in composition from those of other buildings. It contained small pieces of chalk rubble, especially in the eastern half, within its clay matrix, giving the floor a rougher surface. This may, in part, relate to greater wear of the floor in the zone between the doorway and the hearth but, even so, it shows that chalk lumps were included in the mix of the floor matrix. The small size of this house floor suggests that this was very much smaller than a standard dwelling and that it might have been a temporary house or even an ancillary hut. The house's close spatial relationship with House 851, reinforced by their position within an arc of palisade posts, suggests that the latter interpretation is more likely.

House 547

At the break of slope about 10m northeast from the avenue, below and south of Houses 851 and 848, there was a house floor (547) which had been protected by a thin layer of Late Neolithic midden (layer 593; Figure

Figure 12.10 House 848's floor (left of centre), northeast of House 851 and north of the curving fence line which separates these two houses from the others (photographed by Bob Nunn)

12.11). It survived as a trapezoidal spread of dark orange and black ash resting on a chalk clay platform surrounded by a thin layer of grey-brown baked soil speckled with soot and decayed chalk plaster lumps (Figure 12.12). The house interior was 5m N-S x 5.2m east-west, broadly aligned on the cardinal points. The stakeholes of its walls were shallow and hard to detect and there were substantial stretches of wall line along the east and west sides where none could be found. In total, 23 stakeholes were identified around the edges of the house, but none were voids. There was a double row on the north side, with seven set 0.5m south of the outer line of three. This could represent an internal partition or a northward extension of the house in its later life.

The house's trapezoidal clay floor was 2.7m east-west x 3.2m-2.5m north-south. The hearth was set in this clay floor, so as to be precisely central within the house. It was slightly oval in plan (1.35m southeast-northwest x 1.3m northeast-southwest) and its edge was a 0.05m-deep lip down onto its slightly sunken surface. The clay of the hearth was baked hard from continuous and intense heat and its original surface had mostly cracked and flaked off during use; only a small section of the cracked surface still remained in place. Despite this evidence for long-term use, the sharper edges and contours of House 547's hearth surface are a marked contrast to those of House

851, whose smoother contours indicate a greater degree of wear and use.

House 547's features, other than the clay floor, were more ephemeral than those of House 851. The doorway could not be identified with certainty but is most likely to have been at the north end of the west wall. Here there was a 1.6m-wide gap in the line of stakeholes which corresponded with a plume of high magnetic susceptibility values leading out from the hearth, presumably caused by the tracking of hearth ash towards the doorway on the inhabitants' feet.

The only trace of interior furniture was a pair of shallow, parallel slots aligned east-west, 0.5m apart, along its north side. The northernmost slot was 2.4m x 0.25m and the southern one was 2.1m x 0.27m. These had presumably held beams or rough planks that served as the sides of a box bed or dresser. The southern slot lay against the northern edge of the clay floor and its east end was enveloped within its clay matrix, demonstrating that this beam was installed at the same point as the floor was laid during the floor's construction. To the east of this slot there was a 0.80m diameter patch of baked turf surface which may have served as a working area in the northeast corner of the house. Otherwise the only notable feature other than the clay floor was a small spread of ash

Figure 12.11 The midden area (593, viewed from the north (photographed by Adam Stanford of Aerial-Cam)

Figure 12.12 House 547, viewed from the northeast (photographed by Bob Nunn)

and burnt turf within the central eastern margin of the house.

The clay floor's surface had been heavily burnt over much of its extent. Concentrations of burnt flints, sherds and bone fragments lay on the surface. In one of the burnt areas on the south side there was a small group of burnt sarsen cobbles. Most of the pottery sherds were concentrated on the south side of the house floor, although a few large sherds lay in the northwest. Flint tools such as scrapers, retouched blades and arrowheads were concentrated in the northeast of the house. An articulated section of cattle vertebrae lay within the southwest edge of the hearth. An articulated pig's trotter was left on the central northern house floor beyond the clay floor between the two slots.

After abandonment, three intercutting Neolithic pits were dug into the southwest corner of the house. These were cut up to the edge of the clay floor and destroyed this corner of the floor surface as well as any stakeholes in the southwest corner. Evidence of a closing deposit comes from the centre of the hearth where a 0.2m-diameter hole was dug into it after the hearth had fallen into disuse; two cattle bones were inserted vertically into this small pit's fill. This mirrors a similar deposit within House 772's hearth (see below).

House 800

This was a complex group of stakeholes, slots, pits, hearth and floor debris set in and around a hollow (Figure 12.13) east of House 547. It is probably a multi-phased structure which may have been a house (without a clay floor) at some stage but is more likely to have been the compound in front of a house. There were seven major lines or arrangements of stakeholes within a sub-rectangular area. The most impressive of these was a northnorthwest-southsoutheast line of 14 on the west side. This may have continued in an east-turning arc of ten further stakeholes.

The hearth was located at the lowest part of the hollow, at its south end and was 0.9m in diameter. It was not a constructed feature like those in the other houses but was merely the result of repeated burning in the same spot directly on top of the subsoil. To its northwest and northeast there were two slots. That to the northwest was 1.85m northeast-southwest and 0.2m wide. Its fill contained a ground stone pounder and polisher. That to the northeast was 1.5m northwest-southeast and 0.2m wide. Together they formed a symmetrical funnel for movement north from the hearth.

The hollow was not a constructed house floor as in the other examples excavated in 2006 but was presumably formed through erosion from continuous use. Upon its surface, a thin layer of cultural debris accumulated. There were substantial numbers of sherds within its abandonment layer (856), mostly in the north and northwest parts of the hollow. There was also a small knapping cluster on the lip of the hollow east of the hearth.

The interpretation of this feature is problematic. The sub-rectangular arrays of stakeholes could be interpreted as one or more house walls and a case could be made for this to be a 5m x 5m house plan just like the others except that it does not have a formal floor. However, the angled slots do not fit with such an argument since they are set at an angle to the north-south axis of the structure; they give an impression of a funneled approach to a dwelling located further north.

An obvious parallel to House 800 is the terraced base of the midden north of the Southern Circle (Wainwright with Longworth 1971: 38-41). This has the same north-south orientation, the same concave cross-section which is also about 5m across (*ibid.*: fig. 16), and also the same 'nosed' terminal at its south end (*ibid.*: fig. 15). Of course, Structure 800 was not a midden although it lies just south of the centre of the midden (layers 787 and 593). On a different tack, the Southern Circle "midden" could be interpreted as a similarly terraced structure which later acted as a sediment trap: an extensive midden formed across a much wider area than the terrace and was then truncated so that only those midden deposits within the hollow survived.

House 772

The house floor 772 was visible as a surface of cream-coloured plaster on the northeast bank of the avenue (Figure 12.14), about 10m southwest of House 547 and about 100m from the Southern Circle. Its dimensions are 2.8m northeast-southwest and 2.8m southeast-northwest although its shape is trapezoidal with a narrower southwest side. The hearth is on a similar orientation to the walls, with a southeast-northwest axis (140°-320°) bisecting two arcs of burnt clay forming its southwest and northeast edges. The house floor had lost its uppermost surface during the Neolithic. At its northwest corner, the house was terraced into the subsoil, demonstrating that the wall of the house originally extended about 0.4m beyond the northeast and northwest edges of the plaster floor but there was no sign of any features forming its walls other than a shallow posthole in the north corner and a possible posthole in the west corner.

The house was well used in that its hearth showed evidence of heavy and intense heat, with the 0.12m-deep plaster beneath the hearth being thoroughly reddened. As with other houses, the floor plaster had been set into a prepared depression in which the central area of the hearth was hollowed out deeper into the ground as a circular-shaped bowl 1.3m in diameter. Two features were cut into the surface of the plaster. One of these was a stakehole placed symmetrically with the axis of the hearth, at its northwest end, and the other was a wider hole 0.2m in diameter, placed in the centre of the hearth and containing four cattle bones, deposited vertically.

Figure 12.13 Structure 800, viewed from the north (photographed by Bob Nunn)

Figure 12.14 House 772 on the north bank of the avenue (photographed by Mike Parker Pearson)

House 902

House 902 was located on the southwest bank of the avenue, directly opposite House 772 on the opposite bank. Prior to the building of House 902, the southwest avenue bank was cut through by a small pit. The clay floor of House 902 had been built on top of this pit soon after its filling and prior to its settling. The house's clay floor was only partially excavated in 2006 and so its dimensions cannot be ascertained. Unlike House 772, this house had a surviving layer of debris on its floor surface together with a deposit of hearth ash at its centre. There was also a 0.20m-wide slot along the floor's southern edge, beyond which there were two stakeholes which probably formed part of the south wall of the house.

After abandonment, a low flint and soil cairn was heaped over the ruins of House 902 and then the henge bank was deposited on top of it.

Summary

It is likely that most if not all of the houses were contemporary. The construction of a 10m-long curving fence line separating Houses 851 and 848 from Houses 547 and 800 does suggest that these four were in use at the same time. All were covered by the uppermost layers of midden which appears to pre-date the henge. The houses on the avenue banks were earlier than the henge but there is no other stratigraphic indication of their occupation with regard to Houses 851, 848, 547 and 800.

House 851 and its ancillary building 848 were set within a compound which was surrounded on its east and south sides by a fence line. They invite comparison with Houses 6 and 7 at Skara Brae in Orkney (Childe 1931) in shape, size and arrangement. House 851 compares closely in size and internal layout with House 7 at Skara Brae with its corner 'cupboard' and box bed on the right of the doorway when entering, and its dresser opposite the doorway. House 848 is also similar in size, shape and interior use of space to House 6, the ancillary structure that sits to the east of House 7's entrance passage. Of course, the Orcadian hearths are square rather than oval (see Richards 2004). Less well preserved parallels nearer to home are Wyke Down in Dorset (Green 2000: 74-5) and Trelystan in Powys (Britnell 1982).

The size of the Durrington Walls settlement is difficult to ascertain. Two of the six houses' hearths could be identified in retrospect as magnetic anomalies visible on the magnetometer survey plot (Payne 2003) whereas pits in this area tended not to be recognizable by this method. It is possible that a further twenty or so similar anomalies northeast of the avenue are further hearths and may represent a small proportion of a larger number of houses in this part of the valley, protected beneath the henge bank and its spread. The discovery of houses within the western part of the henge (Thomas this volume) raises the possibility that they may have filled the coombe.

The pit groups

Between the northeast bank of the avenue and Houses 547 and 800, there was a 10m-wide zone of pits (Figure 12.4). These were less than a metre in depth and mostly under 1.5m in diameter. Most of these pits were arranged in four inter-cutting clusters and are interpreted as extraction pits for chalky clay used in house walls and floors. Other pits were used for special deposits of animal bones, worked flints and pottery which differed in composition from the layer of midden covering the zone of houses by having greater proportions of pig mandibles and pottery. The likely contemporaneity of artefact pits and midden makes it likely that the deposition of special refuse in pits was motivated by reasons different to the disposal of waste on the midden. Their well-dug profiles, structured deposits and different shapes to the extraction pits mark these out as features which had more than a practical utility. One of them cut through the southwest corner of a house (House 547; this was the 'platform' whose corner was uncovered in 2004) and, in addition to the finds noted above, contained a battered human femur of a probable male with two projectile injuries. The two other human bones were a battered and toothless mandible from south of the house on the southwest bank of the avenue and the base of a skull of a probable female from south of the house on its northeast bank.

The construction of the henge ditch and bank

With the exception of the blockings of the north and south entrances to the henge and the deposition of occupation debris against the south bank (Stone *et al.* 1954), the henge bank and ditch were probably the final phase of construction at Durrington Walls. The banks of the east entrance covered the southwest bank of the avenue and also midden layers associated with the houses. Some of these had filled a pair of large postholes to the north of House 851, one of which was excavated and found to have been filled mostly with midden refuse. The spoilheaps of each posthole were still standing as positive features on the east sides of the holes. In the east entrance, the south terminal of the henge bank impinged slightly onto the avenue, covering its southwest bank. This partial slighting of a pre-existing access has been recognised by Josh Pollard at other Late Neolithic Wessex enclosures, notably Woodhenge, Avebury and Beckhampton (Joshua Pollard pers. comm.)

The henge ditch and bank appear to have been dug by separate gangs in the manner of the causewayed enclosures of the 4th millennium BC, except that the causeways separating each segment were broken through to form a continuous ditch circuit. The Durrington Walls ditch thus has the appearance in plan of a partially merged string of sausages, with each 'sausage' or segment being on average about 40m long, up to 10m wide and over 5m deep. There are probably about 22 of these segments and they are clearest on the northeast side of the henge where one particular segment is dug wider

Figure 12.15 Trench 6 through the centre of the henge bank, viewed from the north, showing the pit (lower right), the tree-throw hole (lower left) and the east-west demarcation gully (top; photographed by Mike Parker Pearson)

than its neighbours. Its bank is also heaped up to form a mound which stands out from the henge bank's otherwise uniform shape. A trench into the henge bank in 2005 and 2006 between this segment and the segment to its south revealed a complex pre-construction history on this boundary (Figure 12.15).

First of all, a large tree had fallen here long before the Neolithic occupation and its tree-throw hole then accumulated a deep Neolithic soil containing a leaf-shaped arrowhead. The disturbed base of the tree-throw had then been dug into, creating a flat-bottomed pit which was filled with ash and Grooved Ware pottery and re-cut a further two times. The pit was then buried beneath an east-west arc of heaps of ash and occupation debris against which chalk spoil was thrown from the digging of a shallow east-west gully to its north. This gully was dug immediately prior to the construction of the henge bank since it was filled with chalk blocks dug out of the henge ditch and forming the base of the henge bank. The line of ash pits and the adjacent gully appear to have formed the boundary between the two bank segments; the northerly segment was started first, with chalk rubble spilling

southwards over the boundary, and then both segments were continued at the same time.

If each segment of ditch and bank was dug by a single gang of workers, Wainwright's discovery of 57 antler picks lying on the base of the ditch segment forming the south terminal of the east entrance may provide some idea of the numbers involved. If each pick was held by a single person, it may have needed a second to hammer it into the chalk. There may also have been people collecting the fractured chalk, carrying it out of the ditch and heaping it up onto the bank. We might expect around 200 to be involved in this hard manual labour, not including those providing food and infrastructure.

There may be further clues to the methods of organisation. The distribution of curvilinear motifs on Grooved Ware pottery at Durrington Walls is spatially restricted, with examples being found only in the pits re-cut into the postholes of the southeast quadrant of the Southern Circle and in the southeast quadrant of the henge. In the latter case it occurs both in the fill of the henge ditch and in the buried midden which lies beneath the henge bank. Despite Wainwright's excavation of the northeast sector of the Southern Circle and our extensive excavations along the fringe of the henge's northeast sector, none of the copious pottery from these contexts has curvilinear motifs. It may be that this special design motif was restricted to a particular social group that was responsible over a lengthy period of decades or even centuries for the southeast sector both of the Southern Circle and of the entire coombe. House 902, from whose immediate vicinity curvilinear-decorated pottery has been found, may have been one of their many houses in the southeast. Placing of structured deposits into the pits of the southeast sector of the Southern Circle, and perhaps erection of the posts into whose decayed remains the pits were later dug, may have been their responsibility. They may also have been responsible for digging just the two segments of ditch within the unusually short southeast quadrant of the circuit.

If this group came from a geographically discrete region then it may be possible to identify it from the isotopic signatures of teeth from their cattle. A pilot study by Jane Evans of strontium isotopes in a single cattle mandible from the northeast sector shows that it was reared away from the chalklands. Secondly, the chronological range of contexts for curvilinear decoration at Durrington Walls hints at relatively long-term associations of certain groups with specific parts of the coombe. This is reinforced by the likely longevity of the boundary between segments on the northeast side. At some point in the Late Neolithic, an ancient tree-throw was chosen as a boundary marker, along which ash and debris were heaped; this was used later to divide work gangs involved in building the henge. An implication of this is that the coombe was already divided radially into sectors for different social groups who maintained rights to specific sectors. They were presumably lumped into four quadrants, each of which was initially involved in constructing a quadrant of the

Southern Circle (whose spatial division into quadrants had not been appreciated until the 2006 magnetometer survey). Perhaps the erection of the bluestones and sarsens at Stonehenge followed a similar organizational logic in which geographically and socially distinct work teams were divided by quadrant and sub-divided by sector.

Interpreting the Durrington Walls settlement

It has been recognised for some time that the 'Durrington zone' of the Stonehenge environs was likely to have been densely settled in the Late Neolithic (for example, Darvill 2006: 114; Richards 1990: 269-70). As mentioned above, Farrer considered Durrington Walls to be the settlement for priests officiating at Stonehenge (1918), a view echoed by Euan Mackie (1977) who proposed that the timber circles of Woodhenge, the Southern Circle and the Northern Circle were roofed buildings for astronomer-priests. Recently Darvill (2006: 114-15) has interpreted the post settings of the Northern Circle and Durrington 68 (a 4-post structure set within a sub-rectangular post setting; Cunnington 1928; Pollard 1995) as Late Neolithic houses. However, such interpretations can now be reconsidered in the light of new results.

Firstly, the evidence for roofing of the Southern Circle is considerably undermined by the results of the 2005-2006 excavations which demonstrate that the outer two circles of its posts did not continue around the entire circuit, leaving the back (northwest) open. No floor layer was found in either the 1967 or the 2005-2006 excavations except for a localised spread of rammed chalk which can now be interpreted as the surface of a path which led into the timber circle in a sunwise direction from its southeast entrance to its centre. The tiny hearth in the middle is also probably associated with Phase 1, the square post setting and post façade which pre-dated the concentric timber circle.

Secondly, the houses found in 2005-2006 at Durrington Walls are closely comparable to other confirmed domestic dwellings from Britain, notably Orkney. They are far smaller (generally under 30sq m) than the Northern Circle and Durrington 68 whose floor areas are in excess of 100sq m. The 2006 excavation of the houses in the western half of Durrington Walls indicate that their outer post circuits were probably fences rather than house walls (see Thomas this volume). We cannot rule out the possibility that the large four-posters within were houses but the great sizes of the posts suggest that they were monumental elaborations on the theme of the house.

Thirdly, we cannot rule out the possibility that the Durrington settlement – or at least part of it - was lived in by religious officiants. However, the internal organization of households is similar to that found in Orcadian villages where we assume that family groups lived their daily lives. The picture from the houses at Durrington Walls is more that of a large, bustling and mixed community of possibly thousands of people rather than a community of priests or shamans.

A radiocarbon date from articulated pig bones in a pit cutting the southwest corner of House 547 indicates that it was filled in 2630-2470 cal BC at 93.4% probability (4036±32 bp; OxA-14801). This coincides very closely with the date for erection of the sarsen circle at Stonehenge and raises the distinct possibility that this potentially very large settlement was occupied by the builders of Stonehenge. They seem not to have brought their work home with them – there is only one pounding stone and many small pieces of sarsen within the settlement – but they were well fed and not especially burdened by mundane daily activities. Not only were there many thousands of animal bones (principally pig and cattle) in the settlement but also they include largely intact longbones and well over a hundred articulated bones, many of which were not fully processed to their nutritional potential. The midden was effectively the ground surface, heaped with what must have been the rotting debris derived from consumption of meat in feasting quantities. In addition, the lithic assemblage is remarkably skewed in having very small proportions of scrapers and tools other than arrowheads. Nor is there much evidence for cereal processing despite considerable flotation sampling; there are no quern stones and carbonized plant remains are almost entirely absent except for a few barley grains in the buried soil on top of the avenue roadway. This appears to have been a 'consumer' settlement rather than a 'producer' site.

A variety of alternative interpretations are possible:

1. This was a military encampment in which an army of archers prepared for battle.
2. This was a seasonal encampment occupied by solstice revellers who lived and feasted here at midwinter and midsummer as part of their religious observances at Stonehenge.
3. This was a long-lived large village gathered around a timber circle and avenue which were not linked with Stonehenge.
4. This was a long-lived small village lived in by people who may or may not have been associated with the solstice comings and goings of itinerant visitors.

There are flaws with most of these interpretations although the second one could be close to the mark, especially when combined with the builders' settlement theory. The first interpretation puts an interesting focus on the large quantities of arrowheads but it may be that the number of pig bones with broken-off arrow tips embedded in them makes their presence explicable more in terms of sporting contests than martial engagement. Further research at Durrington Walls and elsewhere within the Stonehenge environs, as well as radiocarbon dating and isotopic analysis, may help to gain a closer understanding of who formed this community, when and why.

Acknowledgements

Permissions to carry out excavations and survey were kindly given by various landowners, tenants and statutory authorities. We are particularly grateful to Stan and Henry Rawlins for a third season of excavation on the east entrance of Durrington Walls.

English Heritage's support has been full and unwavering throughout the project. David Batchelor, Peter Carson, Amanda Chadburn, Kath Graham and Ann Snell are especially thanked for their help. We have greatly benefited from the encouragement and advice of members of the National Trust and its Archaeology Panel, notably Chris Gingell. The outreach team thank Phil Harding and Edwin Deady as well as the many re-enactors and guides who made the open days and other visits such a huge success. We also thank the Wiltshire Constabulary for keeping an eye on the security of the sites after hours.

Wessex Archaeology kindly lent equipment and provided consumables when needed. We are also grateful to Wiltshire County Council, particularly Helena Cave-Penny, for providing advice and help throughout the season. The Wiltshire Archaeological and Natural History Society are also thanked for co-ordinating volunteers to work on the excavations.

Reg Jury and machine operators Brian, Peter and Shane made the opening and backfilling of so many large areas possible within the time available, and their unstinting work ensured that the project's goals were fully met. Adam Stanford is thanked for his Aerial Cam photographs of the sites under excavation and for his good company while visiting. Thanks also to the many colleagues and friends who stayed over and even did some digging: Dave Bennett, Duncan Brown, Martin Green, Jake Keen, Helen Smith, Niall Sharples and Mick Tizzard. Back at base, landlord Paul Adams of the Woodbridge Inn is thanked for providing a campsite and adjacent public house.

The supervisory staff working on the East Entrance in 2004-2006 were Ben Chan, Mark Dover (computing), Ian Heath, Hugo Lamdin-Wymark (finds), Bob Nunn, Becca Pullen, California Dave Robinson, Ellen Simmons (flotation). Site assistants were Lizzie Carleton, Chris Caswell, Ralph Collard, Dave Shaw and James Thomson (outreach).

Funding for the 2006 season was provided by the Arts & Humanities Research Council and the National Geographic Society.

Bibliography

Barrett, J. and Fewster, K. 1998 Stonehenge: is the medium the message? *Antiquity* 72: 847-51.

Bewley, R.H., Crutchley, S.P. and Shell, C.A. 2005 New light on an ancient landscape: lidar survey in the Stonehenge World Heritage Site. *Antiquity* 79, 636-47

Britnell, W. 1982. The excavation of two round barrows at Trelystan, Powys. *Proceedings of the Prehistoric Society* 48: 133-201.

Cleal, R.M.J., Walker, K.E. and Montague, R. 1995 *Stonehenge in its Landscape: twentieth-century excavations*. London: English Heritage.

Childe, V.G. 1931. *Skara Brae: a Pictish village in Orkney*. London: Kegan Paul, Trench, Trubner & Co.

Colt Hoare, R. 1812 *The Ancient History of South Wiltshire*. Volume 1.

Crawford, O.G.S. 1929 Durrington Walls. *Antiquity* 3: 49-59.

Cunnington, M.E. 1929 *Woodhenge*. Devizes: Simpson.

Darvill, T. 2006 *Stonehenge: the biography of a landscape*. Stroud: Tempus.

David, A. and Payne, A. 1997 Geophysical surveys within the Stonehenge landscape: a review of past endeavour and future potential. In C. Renfrew and B. Cunliffe (eds) *Science and Stonehenge*. Proceedings of the British Academy 92. Oxford: Oxford University Press. 73-113.

Farrer, P. 1918 Durrington Walls, or Long Walls. *Wiltshire Archaeological and Natural History Magazine* 40: 95-103.

French, C. 2006 The geoarchaeological study. In M. Parker Pearson, Pollard, J., Richards, C., Thomas, J., Tilley, C., Welham, K., Allen, M., Field, D., French, C. and Robinson, D. Stonehenge Riverside Project: full interim report. Unpublished manuscript.

Green, M. 2000. *A Landscape Revealed: 10,000 years on a chalkland farm*. Stroud: Tempus.

Linford, N. and Payne, A. In preparation Durrington Walls Henge, Wiltshire. Report on Geophysical Surveys, August 2006. Centre for Archaeology Report Series. Portsmouth: English Heritage.

MacKie, E. 1977 *Science and Society in Prehistoric Britain*. London: Paul Elek.

McKinley, J. 1995 Human bone. In R.M.J. Cleal, K.E. Walker and R. Montague 1995 *Stonehenge in its Landscape: twentieth-century excavations*. London: English Heritage. 451-61.

Parker Pearson, M. and Ramilisonina. 1998 Stonehenge for the ancestors: the stones pass on the message. *Antiquity* 72: 308-26.

Payne, A. 2003. Durrington Walls Henge, Wiltshire. Report on Geophysical Surveys, January 1996 and April 2003. Centre for Archaeology Report Series 107/2003. Portsmouth: English Heritage.

Piggott, S. 1959 The radio-carbon date from Durrington Walls. *Antiquity* 33: 289-90.

Pitts, M. 2000 *Hengeworld*. London: Arrow Books.

Pollard, J. 1995 The Durrington 68 timber circle: a forgotten Late Neolithic monument. *Wiltshire Archaeological and Natural History Magazine* 88: 122-25.

Powers, R. 1971 Report on the human bones. In G.J. Wainwright with I.H. Longworth, *Durrington Walls:*

excavations 1966-1968. London: Society of Antiquaries. 351.

Richards, C. 2004. *Dwelling Amongst the Monuments: excavations at Barnhouse and Maes Howe*. Cambridge: McDonald Institute monographs.

Richards, J.C. 1990 *The Stonehenge Environs Project*. London: English Heritage.

Stone, J.F.S., Piggott, S. and Booth, A. St. J. 1954 Durrington Walls, Wiltshire: recent excavations at a ceremonial site of the early second millennium BC. *Antiquaries Journal* 34: 155-77.

Wainwright, G.J. with Longworth, I.H. 1971 *Durrington Walls: excavations 1966-1968*. London: Society of Antiquaries.

Whitley, J. 2002 Too Many Ancestors. *Antiquity* 76: 119-26.

Chapter 13

The internal features at Durrington Walls: investigations in the Southern Circle and Western Enclosures 2005-6

Julian Thomas

School of Arts, Histories and Culture, University of Manchester

Introduction

When a cutting 20m to 40m wide was opened across the Durrington Walls henge in advance of roadbuilding in 1966-67, two large posthole structures were revealed. The Northern Circle was located on the flank of the dry valley that runs north-west from the River Avon, through the eastern entrance of the henge and, as a consequence, its features had been severely truncated by erosion. The Southern Circle, however, lay immediately inside the eastern entrance, on the floor of the valley, and its preservation was enhanced by its burial beneath over a metre of colluvium. The information that Geoffrey Wainwright gleaned from these two structures has dominated our understanding of the henge and its use ever since. As the authors of *Stonehenge and its Environs* pointed out, 'beyond the area of excavation relatively little is known of the interior of Durrington Walls' (RCHM 1979: 17). One of the priorities of the Stonehenge Riverside Project has been to clarify the results of the 1967 work at the Southern Circle by selective excavation, and to explore other internal features within the Durrington henge. This contribution presents an interim account of the results of fieldwork conducted inside the henge monument in 2005 and 2006.

The re-excavation of the Southern Circle

It is arguable that alongside the Star Carr platform and the Glastonbury Lake Village, the southern timber circle at Durrington Walls is one of the most intensively interpreted structures in British prehistory. The circle was apparently a two-phase structure. While the first phase was composed of modestly sized posts forming six concentric rings with an associated post-avenue and façade, the second had massive, ramped uprights and a more elaborate plan. 105 second-phase postholes were found in the 60% of the circle that was excavated in 1967. Associated with the post-circle were a chalk and gravel platform, two rammed chalk surfaces, a midden apparently cordoned off by screens, and two hearths (Wainwright with Longworth 1971: 23-38). Wainwright clearly considered that the Southern Circle had been a roofed building, and compared it with the large council houses of certain Native American communities (see Wainwright 1989: 133).

The existence of such large roofed structures later formed a contributory element in Colin Renfrew's arguments concerning the existence of chiefdoms in Neolithic Wessex:

> "Wainwright has written of the wooden rotundas in several of the larger henges and very plausibly compared them with the council houses of the Creek and Cherokee Indians..... It is not stretching the limits of proper ethnographic comparison too far to suggest that their function may likewise have been as centres which coordinate social and religious as well as economic activity" (Renfrew 1973: 555).

Euan MacKie was to suggest that buildings like the Southern Circle had formed the residences of an astronomer-priesthood:

> "The great henges of Wessex were inhabited ceremonial centres on the Maya pattern in and near which lived a permanent population of non-agricultural specialists such as priests, astronomers, wise men, poets and all their attendant craftsmen and servants (as well, no doubt, as their womenfolk) – professional classes who were supported by tributes of food and labour by the peasant population" (MacKie 1977: 162-3).

By contrast, John Barrett maintained that the architecture of Durrington Walls had developed in a piecemeal fashion over a considerable period, and that it had formed the resource and locale for the construction of new forms of social authority:

> "By building Avebury and Durrington Walls new social realities were also constructed. These social realities did not lie behind the building of these monuments but emerged from their existence" (Barrett 1994: 28).

In another contribution, two of the members of the present project investigated the patterns of deposition of ceramics and faunal remains in and around the Southern Circle, and concluded that they were representative of ritual activity (Richards and Thomas 1984).

Each of these accounts of the circle has direct implications for the kinds of social practice and social organisation that we imagine in later Neolithic Wessex, so that the relationship between grand theory and the minutiae of on-site stratigraphy is here unusually close.

DURRINGTON WALLS

SOUTHERN CIRCLE: PHASES 2A AND 2B

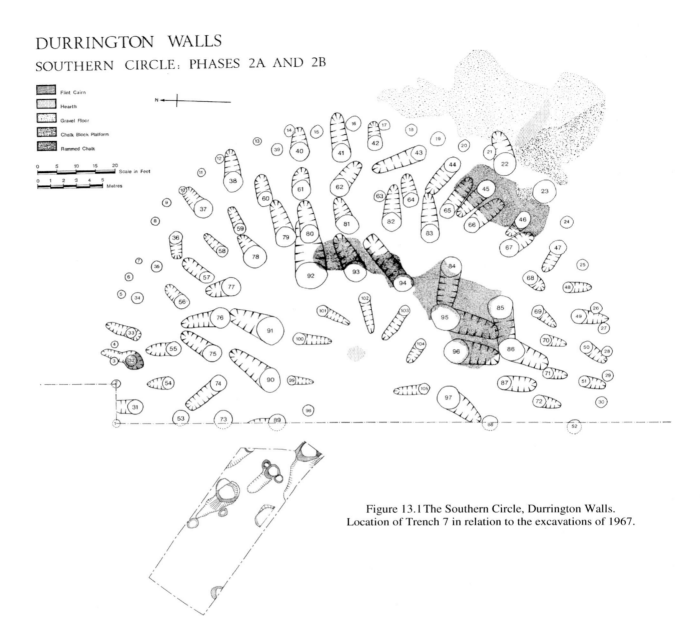

Figure 13.1 The Southern Circle, Durrington Walls.
Location of Trench 7 in relation to the excavations of 1967.

However, the 1967 excavations were undertaken under formidable time constraints and, although they can justly be claimed to have transformed our understanding of the later Neolithic in Britain, they left a series of questions unanswered (for an engaging account of the 1966-7 excavations, see Pitts 2000: 48-61). It was with this point in mind that a targeted, small-scale investigation was undertaken in the summer of 2005, and completed in 2006. This involved the opening of a trench on the far side of the circle from the entrance, cutting across the arcs of posts and was intended to sample the five outer rings (Figure 13.1). The location of the cutting was designed to determine whether there had been a second entrance opposite the first, and whether people passed through the structure and continued on up the dry valley through the interior of the enclosure, toward the western entrance. No such entrance was identified, but the position of the cutting was, despite this, a fortuitous one.

Returning to the site nearly forty years after Wainwright's excavation presented an unusual set of problems. Our expectations of what we might encounter had been generated by the combination of written accounts of the site and archaeological 'folk knowledge' (such an important site, which played a critical role in the development of publicly funded archaeology in Britain, has generated its fair share of anecdote and speculation). In practice, the features revealed in the western part of the Southern Circle were relatively straightforward to identify and excavate, although they were not without their complications (see below).

A further set of concerns had been raised by Pitts' recent re-excavation of the timber circle at the Sanctuary, on Overton Hill near Avebury (Pitts 2001). At the Sanctuary, Pitts was able to identify small patches of sediment in some of the postholes which had not been removed by the Cunningtons' excavation in 1930 (Cunnington 1931).

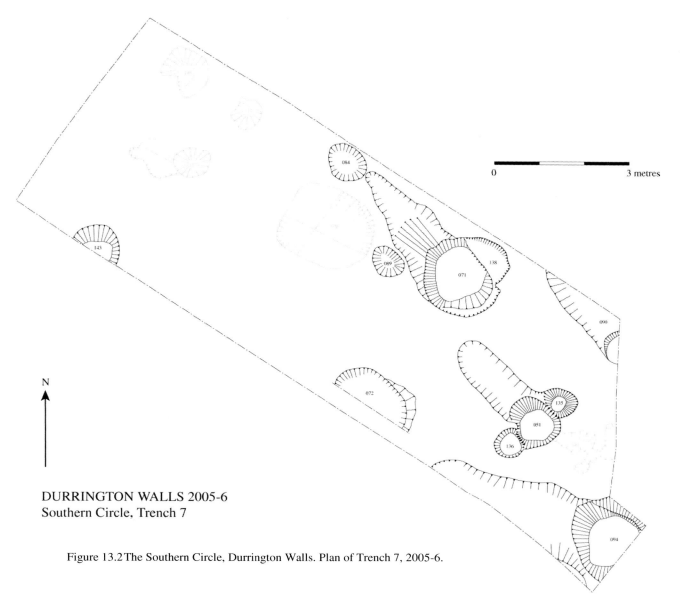

0   3 metres

DURRINGTON WALLS 2005-6
Southern Circle, Trench 7

Figure 13.2 The Southern Circle, Durrington Walls. Plan of Trench 7, 2005-6.

The multiple episodes of packing that these documented implied that each individual posthole had contained a series of timber uprights, which had been removed and replaced on a number of occasions. Pitts argued on this basis that particular timbers had been 'circulated' from place to place, either within the monument, or within the wider landscape. This raises the possibility that the posts of some of these later Neolithic timber structures had amounted to more than utilitarian building materials, and may have had distinct identities, and complex histories. Their places of origin (as trees) may have been remembered, and each may have been connected with particular persons or events. By contrast, at the later Neolithic enclosure at Dunragit in south-west Scotland, my excavations demonstrated that individual posts been deliberately withdrawn and replaced by a series of elaborate, placed deposits, although there was no evidence for the circulation and replacement of posts (Thomas 2004: 103-4). None the less, this again points to the importance of individual timbers, in that these

episodes of deposition suggest the commemoration of uprights following their removal.

Postholes of the Southern Circle: a fenced central area?
In the period since Wainwright's excavation, still larger late Neolithic timber circles have been identified at sites such as Balfarg (Mercer 1981) and Stanton Drew (David *et al.* 2004). The difficulty of roofing such enormous structures has swung opinion away from the council-house model and towards the image of rings of free-standing timbers (Gibson 1998: 106-8). This view is supported by the results of the 2005-2006 fieldwork. The cutting contained five large post-holes and one small one, all of which could be attributed to Wainwright's Phase 2 (Figure 13.2). Despite efforts to identify postholes in all of the appropriate places, it appears that ring 2B was incomplete and ring 2A was entirely missing in the area investigated. The unfinished character of the Southern Circle suggests both that it was unroofed (certainly that no ring-beam could have run around the outer edge of the

Figure 13.3 Reconstruction of the Southern Circle constructed for *Time Team* at North Newnton, Wiltshire, summer 2005 (Photo: author).

structure), and that its appearance from the back, opposite the entrance, was not of great consequence. This point is supported by Figure 13.3, a photograph of the reconstruction of the Southern Circle built for a *Time Team* television programme. At the time when the picture was taken, it too was incomplete on the far side, yet the visual effect is not impaired. This seems to indicate that the Southern Circle has a 'front' and a 'back', and that it was intended to be seen from the south-east, the direction of the henge entrance, the avenue and the river.

There was no evidence that postholes held sequences of uprights comparable to those at the Sanctuary. Each post was dug, inserted, and finally rotted away *in situ*. However, posthole 051 was quite unusual, in that the main large posthole appeared to be bracketed by two smaller features (135 and 136), to the northeast and southwest. Feature 051 was one of the postholes of Wainwright's Circle 2D, and many of the posts of this ring were associated with similar small features, particularly in the northern part of the circle (Wainwright with Longworth 1971: 23). These were evidently lesser postholes, which were generally identified in the sides of the 2D features after their excavation. For this reason no section survives from 1967 showing the relationship between the fills of the larger and smaller postholes in this ring. However, it is clear that some form of structure did exist. For instance, the section of Features 90 and 176

shows the latter to have been cut by the former (Wainwright with Longworth 1971: Fig. 129), and similar relationships are evident between Features 94 and 182, and 95 and 183 (*ibid.*: Fig. 131). However, the lesser features here in each case belong to Wainwright's Circle 1C (ibid: 26). The postholes that intersect with the Circle 2D posts are identified as Circle 1B, and it is notable that, in many cases, the 2D feature is neatly positioned between two 1B postholes. It is difficult to see how this could have been achieved had the smaller posts not still been standing when the larger ones were inserted. This suggests that large and small postholes alike formed parts of an integral structure.

In the case of Feature 051, the cuts of the main posthole, 135 and 136 intersected, and it was quite difficult to distinguish between the packing of the three features. Only on the basis of texture and feel was it possible to ascertain that the filling of 051 was probably distinct and later than that of 135 and 136. This implies an intimate relationship between the three features, and it seems probable that all three posts were standing at the same time. Such a picture could be interpreted in a number of different ways: either the development of the Southern Circle architecture was gradual and organic, with posts being added to a relatively simple primary structure as Barrett (1994) argues, or the 'Circle 1B' posts were actually part of the later manifestation of the circle. If so,

148

the smaller posts might have served to hold lintels, or may have provided the framework for some form of shuttering or screening. This would be similar to the arrangements at Dunragit and Meldon Bridge (Speak and Burgess 1999: 17), where large ramped posts were interspersed by smaller uprights to support a fence or palisade. If this were the case, the putative fence would have served to seclude the innermost area of the circle (the middle two rings). It is notable that the smaller posts are absent from the probable entrance passage on the southern side of the circle (features 22 and 23, 45 and 46, 66 and 67, 85 and 95, 86 and 96), and would therefore not have impeded movement toward the central area. Moreover, it is arguable that the scatter of small postholes in this area form an entrance 'funnel' for the passage-way.

If the 'Circle 1B' postholes were actually part of the mature architecture of the Southern Circle, the existence of Wainwright's Phase 1 is not denied, but it takes on a simpler and less substantial form. Removing features 156 to 172 from the plan, the Phase 1 structure now appears very similar to the Northern Circle: four relatively large, ramped posts at the centre, surrounded by a ring of posts linked by an avenue to a façade. The four posts surrounded by a ring have clear affinities to the small buildings excavated at the eastern entrance and the western enclosures (see Parker Pearson this volume, and below). Thus both the Northern Circle and the earliest structure at the Southern Circle can be seen as elaborations on the architectural themes implicit in contemporary house-building (a suggestion originally made by Joshua Pollard; see Pollard and Robinson this volume). All of this serves to mark the second phase of the Southern Circle as something strikingly different from the other structures at Durrington Walls. In the regional context, its concentric rings of massive ramped postholes invite comparison only with Woodhenge and the stone settings at Stonehenge. The radical change from a plan that evokes domestic space to a series of concentric rings arguably identifies the point at which the Southern Circle became a distinctive focal space. We will explore the significance of this development below.

Evidence of depositional practice
While the study of the Durrington Walls material by Richards and Thomas (1984) was instrumental in drawing attention to the phenomenon of structured deposition, more recent studies have often been able to consider the issue in a more detailed manner (e.g. Pollard 1995; 2001; Thomas 1999: 62-88). This is because it is difficult to unravel the spatial and contextual organisation of the material from the 1967 Durrington Walls excavation. Flints and potsherds in the site archive can be attributed to individual postholes, but cannot always be tied to precise layers within those features. More seriously, the faunal assemblage from the entire Southern Circle is internally undifferentiated, making comparison with the lithic and ceramic assemblages entirely impossible. This is unfortunate, as it has become clear

over the years that the patterns that characterise structured deposition are ones that involve the co-variation of different classes of cultural material. Over and above that, the precise configurations of objects as they were placed in the ground, which were clearly observed in the pit deposits excavated at the eastern entrance in 2004 (Parker Pearson this volume), went largely unremarked in the original investigation of the Southern Circle postholes. This is not intended as a criticism of the 1966-67 excavators, so much as a recognition that, as we refine the questions that we address to the archaeological evidence, we need to make fresh observations, as the information that we need may not be retrievable from the records of past excavations.

Very large quantities of animal bones, pottery sherds, flint and bone artefacts, and flint waste were recovered from the postholes of the Southern Circle in 1967. Wainwright's original interpretation for the concentration of finds in the upper parts of the posthole fills was that, within the roofed hall, cultural material had been placed as 'offerings' at the bases of the timber uprights. When the latter had rotted out, these objects had fallen into what he referred to as 'weathering cones' (Wainwright with Longworth 1971: 24-5). These he argued to have been formed by the erosion of the post-packing, following the decay of the posts. However, this interpretation is questionable on a number of grounds. If the Southern Circle had not been a circular roofed building, but a concentric setting of free-standing wooden uprights, it is unclear how objects that had been placed beside these posts could have come to be incorporated in the 'weathering cones' in a relatively unabraded condition, having presumably been exposed on the surface for a period of some decades. Most of the postholes that Wainwright identified as belonging to Phase 1 have no weathering cones and, if the formation of the latter was a natural product of post-decay, it is hard to imagine why they should be absent from the earlier features. Furthermore, some of the cones in Wainwright's sections appear to be off-centre from the post-pipe, suggesting a cut feature rather than an erosion product (for instance, Feature 76). In all of the post-holes that were excavated in 2005 and 2006, it was clear that the so-called 'weathering cones' were actually conical re-cuts, dug after the posts had rotted out. In the case of Feature 051, a single re-cut truncated the central post *and* the 'Phase 1' postholes 135 and 136. Just as Wainwright had observed, the finds from these recuts massively outnumbered those from the primary packing.

Within the post-holes excavated in 2005-6, the density of finds was meagre compared with certain areas of the original cutting, principally around the entrance (Figure 13.4). This confirms that deposition was highly spatially variable in its density. In the deposits of chalk packing surrounding the posts, finds consisted of sporadic, isolated, but well-preserved animal bones and flint flakes. Their distribution appears unstructured, and they may represent residual material incorporated into the post-

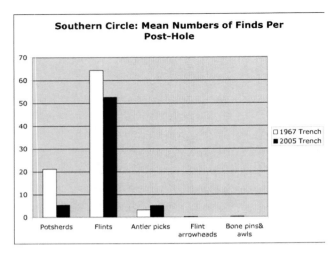

Figure 13.4 The Southern Circle: comparison of density of finds per posthole in 1967 and 2005.

packing by chance. If so, it is interesting that similar material was lacking from the large posts in Trench 14 in the western enclosures (see below). This may mean that the area of the Southern Circle had seen intense activity in the period before construction of the Phase 2 elements.

The exceptions to this pattern of deposition in the re-cut pits are the antler picks; in both 1967 and 2005-2006 the great majority of these were found in the primary post-packing. Arguably these were tools used in the digging of the post-holes, which then formed the principal deliberate deposits associated with the construction and initial use of the circle. Their overall distribution does not directly reflect the size or capacity of the postholes, but suggests instead that antler picks were preferentially deposited in those features that occupied significant locations within the overall structure (Figure 13.5). Thus, in particular, the pattern emphasises the 'entrance passage' to the structure.

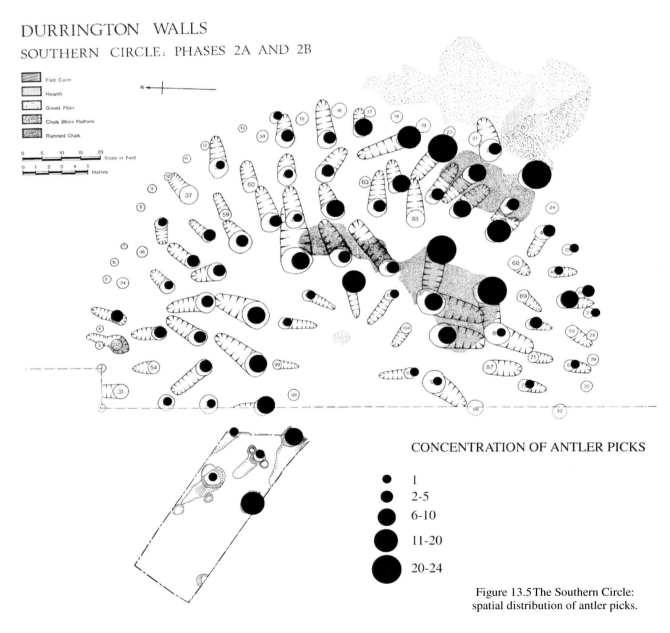

Figure 13.5 The Southern Circle: spatial distribution of antler picks.

However, one of the post-holes excavated in 2005 produced no fewer than 19 antler picks, after only having emptied half of the feature, and this *may* reflect its position directly opposite the entrance to the circle. Within this Feature (099), twelve of the antlers were from the packing, and the remaining seven were from the re-cut. What is not clear is whether this represents the continued deposition of a particular class of artefact in a given location over time, or whether *all* of the antlers originally constituted a single deposit, which may have been disturbed by the recutting, with the result that some picks were *redeposited* in the re-cut fills. Certainly, in some post-holes we do have clear examples of antler picks eroding out of the packing, cut across by the re-cut. This is of some significance, because one of the picks from the re-cut in 099 produced a radiocarbon date of 2574-2348 cal BC (at 2σ) (OxA-14976). It remains unclear at this stage whether this dates the construction or the recutting event, and a more detailed radiocarbon chronology will soon be established for the Southern Circle.

Within the re-cuts, the mode of occurrence of finds was strikingly different from that in the packing. Concentrations of flints and animal bones had clearly been placed, or at least dumped, rather than having fallen haphazardly into eroding post-pipes, as they often formed dense interlocking clusters of objects. Although the patterns of filling were individual and distinctive, they possessed a clear overall structure, composed of a series of discrete events. Animal bone predominated, but flint occurred as clusters of waste, often higher in the fill. Particularly dense dumps of animal bones were identified in post-holes 051 and 071, which almost suggested deposition in some kind of container, such as a bag. In all cases, pottery sherds were found almost exclusively in the upper part of the re-cut fill. This suggests a pattern in which sherds were being carefully placed into the tops of the re-cuts following the more summary deposition of flint and bone.

As argued above, if this material had been deposited into features that were cut at a time subsequent to the rotting of the posts, this must have post-dated the construction and initial use of the circle by one or two centuries, if not more. It is an open question whether the bones, flints and sherds concerned had been freshly generated in events of consumption immediately before deposition, or whether they had been retrieved from the colossal middens found elsewhere at Durrington Walls. Indeed, it may have been a combination of the two. In any case, the likelihood that the Southern Circle was ancient and ruinous by the time that the re-cutting took place reveals the depositional activity to have been essentially commemorative in character. That is to say, digging a hole and placing cultural materials into it was a means of venerating the Circle, its component elements, and the past activities that had taken place within it. The richness of the material deposited in the recuts reflected the relative significance of the different parts of the timber circle, even though the

structure was now ruinous. In other words, the architecture of the circle was now one of collapsed timbers, slumped post-holes, and memories that were brought to mind through acts of deposition. We have already argued that the individual posts would have had specific meanings and histories, and these now acquired a kind of afterlife by being commemorated in their absence. Deposition contributed to the construction of an 'architecture of memory'.

The context of the Southern Circle

The significance of the Southern Circle also needs to be re-evaluated in the context of the other discoveries at Durrington Walls in 2005-6. The identification of the avenue that connects the henge to the River Avon (see Parker Pearson, this volume) is of the greatest importance, since it demonstrates that Durrington and Stonehenge are effectively parts of a single structure, linked by the Stonehenge Avenue, the Durrington Avenue, and the river (Parker Pearson and Ramilsonina 1998). This challenges some of our implicit understandings of the character of monumentality for, rather than being a cultural imposition onto a natural landscape, the Stonehenge-Durrington complex threads together built elements and topography. It is arguable that both the Stonehenge and the Durrington Avenues were conceptually indistinguishable from the river, and the two enclosures were linked by flows and movements of a variety of kinds. This also encourages us to consider the relationship between the Southern Circle and the stone settings at Stonehenge. The mature phase of the Southern Circle and the sarsen structures were arguably both constructed in the 26th century BC, and they have a number of architectural similarities. Both are circular with oval centres, and yet each faces in a distinct direction, with an entrance opening on one side. Both were (eventually) set within an earthwork enclosure, and in each case the monument faced toward an avenue which connected it to the river, so that they effectively form the two ends of a single pattern of movement. This is perhaps comparable with the relationship between the Avebury henge and the Sanctuary, at either end of the West Kennet Avenue.

However, Stonehenge and the Southern Circle are better described as *complementary* structures. While composed of stone and timber respectively, they are remarkably similar in plan, much more so than Stonehenge and Woodhenge, which have more often been compared. The principal sarsen and bluestone settings at Stonehenge have much the same diameters as the four inner rings at Durrington (Figure 13.6), and Andrew Chamberlain has argued that the same units of measurement were used in the construction of each (Chamberlain and Parker Pearson this volume). Furthermore, subsurface radar survey of the unexcavated portion of the Southern Circle conducted by Neil Linford of English Heritage during 2006 suggests that Circle 2E (the ring with the largest post-holes, second from the centre) was an oval rather

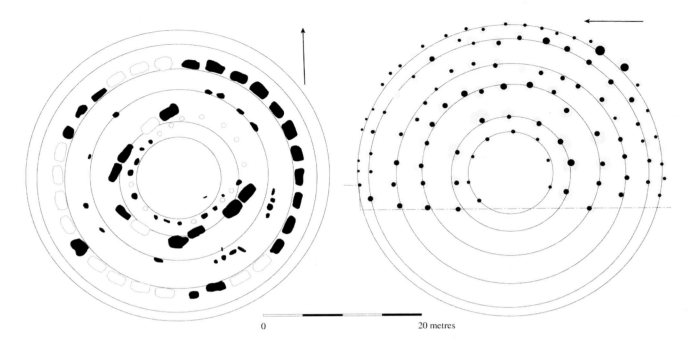

0   20 metres

Figure 13.6 Comparison of the layout of stone settings at Stonehenge and timber uprights at the Southern Circle, Durrington Walls.

than a true circle. This enhances the structure's similarity to Stonehenge, where the corresponding setting of five great trilithons is horseshoe-shaped. Significantly, the inner spaces of Stonehenge and the Southern Circle were much the same size, and would have admitted the same number of people, at either end of a journey – in whichever direction. My suggestion is that the successive phases of remodelling of the stone arrangements at Stonehenge would have had the effect of making them progressively more like a stone version of the Southern Circle.

Of course, these re-workings of the stone monument would have been played out against the background of the Southern Circle's gradual decay and rotting away. The different temporalities of the materials used will undoubtedly have been an explicit element in the linked relationship between the two structures, which is likely to have condensed a whole series of homologies and oppositions. However, if the digging of the Y and Z holes outside of the sarsen ring does represent the final phase of activity at Stonehenge, as the presently-accepted sequence indicates (Cleal *et al.* 1995: 256-65), it is probable that this will have happened at a time when the timbers of the Southern Circle had long rotted away. Speculating rather wildly, it may be that the final configuration of the central area at Stonehenge, as a structure composed of six concentric rings of features, may refer to the Circle in its derelict state. That is to say, the Y and Z holes may not refer to the uprights of the outer two rings of the Southern Circle, but the recuts that succeeded and commemorated them. What this would mean is that in its eventual form, Stonehenge was a static and changeless equivalent of a monument of a different

but complementary kind in the process of changing through time.

The Western Enclosures

While the work at the Southern Circle sought to clarify the results of the earlier excavation, investigations in the western interior of the Durrington henge in the summer of 2006 were rather more of a leap in the dark. Magnetometer survey conducted in this area by A.J. Clark in the 1970s revealed a series of anomalies, most strikingly a circular feature, roughly 35m in diameter, around 200m WNW from the Southern Circle (RCHM 1979: 16-17). Subsequent geophysical surveys have shown this enclosure to have a putative entrance facing to the east, and to be one of at least six penannular structures arranged in an arc around the western part of the henge interior (Figure 13.7). The other structures are smaller in size, being approximately 15-20m in diameter, and each having a single entrance. These entrances generally face eastwards down the dry valley towards the avenue and the river, but one structure immediately to the south of the large circle has an entrance facing in the opposite direction to the southwest. While these results were striking, they left open a number of possibilities: each enclosure might represent a funerary ring-ditch or the quarry-ditch of a barrow, a small henge monument, or an enclosed timber circle comparable with Site IV at Mount Pleasant in Dorset (Wainwright 1979: 9-34). In order to resolve the character of these structures, excavation was undertaken on the largest enclosure (Trench 14), and the smaller ring-ditch immediately to the south (Trench 15).

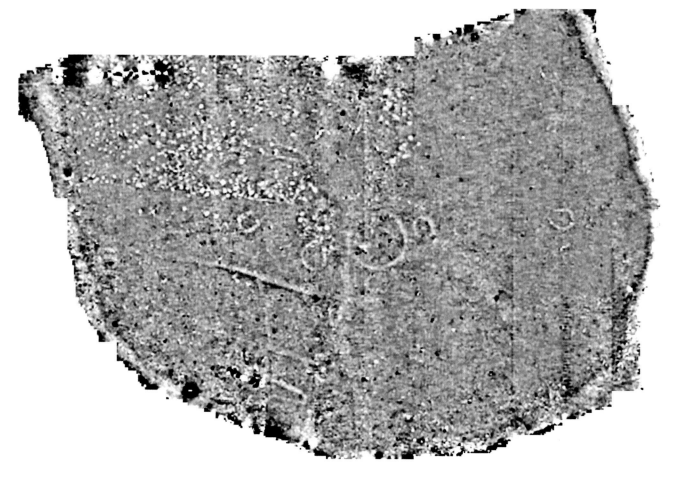

Figure 13.7 Magnetometer survey of the western part of the interior of Durrington Walls.

DURRINGTON WALLS 2006
Western Enclosures Trench 14

0   5 metres

N

Figure 13.8 Trench 14, Western Enclosures, Durrington Walls 2005.

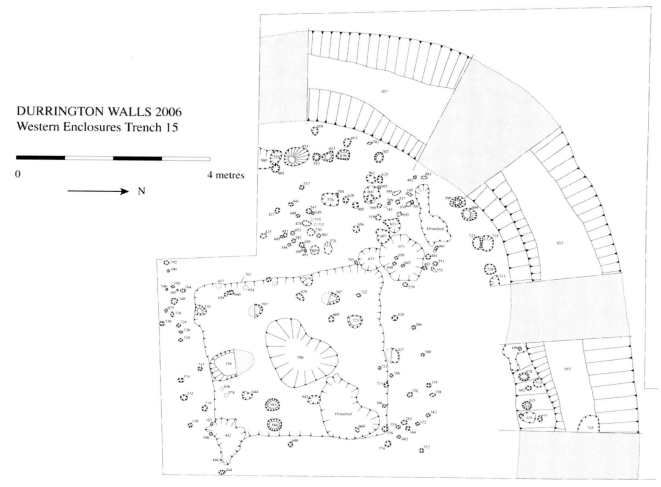

DURRINGTON WALLS 2006
Western Enclosures Trench 15

0   4 metres

⟶ N

Figure 13.9 Trench 15, Western Enclosures, Durrington Walls 2005.

Trench 14

An area 23m x 10m in extent was opened in the larger ditched enclosure, running westwards from its probable entrance into the interior (Figure 13.8). The most striking feature revealed was the cut floor hollow of a building, roughly 4m x 4m in extent, in the approximate centre of the enclosure. This structure was very similar to the late Neolithic houses identified at the eastern entrance (see Parker Pearson this volume), having lines of stakeholes indicating the position of an outer wall roughly a metre north and south of the floor area, and a slot containing further stakes on the eastern side. The floor cut was oriented west-southwest/north-northeast, respecting the entrances of the surrounding palisade and ditch, and was terraced back into the slope. However, unlike the eastern entrance houses, no floor layers were present, and no artefacts were found inside the building. This may be because, although the building was sealed beneath more than a metre of colluvium, the surface had been subject to erosion before its deposition. All that remained of the crushed chalk floor were those parts of it beneath the hearth where the fire had hardened it to a degree which made it more resistant to erosion than the unbaked areas of flooring in the rest of the house. This baked central area, beneath where the hearth once sat, formed a thick

deposit of fire-altered material, and was surrounded by a series of substantial post-holes, which suggest four roof-supports, some of which had been replaced. This evidence for repair indicates that the structure may have been in use for a considerable period of time.

Surrounding the building was a palisade or fence, approximately ten metres in diameter, and composed of postholes up to 40 cm deep. Two particularly deep post-holes, 085 and 240, bracketed an entrance on the eastern side, which appeared to have been blocked by a group of shallower post-holes, offset to the east. Immediately outside and to the south of the palisade entrance was a large, shallow pit, 506, which contained a dense and disordered scatter of animal bones and sherds of Grooved Ware. This deposit contrasted with pit 307, further to the east, a neatly-cut circular feature which contained the carefully placed remains of at least two pigs, which displayed numerous instances of articulation.

Between the palisade and the ditch there were three very large postholes, which apparently formed elements of some form of monumental façade. Time precluded the excavation of the southernmost of these features, 058, which had a clear post-ramp to the east. The two remaining posts, 090 and 361 were set close together and, although they were of comparable size, 361 was rather deeper at 1.95 metres. The disparity in depth may have been a device for levelling two timber uprights of differing lengths, and it is tempting to speculate that these two massive timbers, positioned so closely together, may have been capped by a lintel, making the equivalent in wood of the Stonehenge trilithons. The subsequent histories of the two posts were quite different, however. 090 was withdrawn from the south, while 361 was subject to an episode of recutting, similar to those recognised at the Southern Circle. As mentioned below, the packing of these two postholes was almost entirely devoid of finds.

Only one terminal of the surrounding ditch was revealed in the cutting, suggesting that the entrance was relatively wide. When first revealed it appeared to be a single wide feature, but it was eventually resolved into two separate cuts. The innermost of these (298) was apparently the earlier, and it seemed to have had an internal bank. This bank was slighted and returned to the ditch at the same time as spoil from the cutting of the outer ditch was being thrown in from the other side. This episode of slighting was marked by the placing of a deposit of knapped flint flakes and an exhausted core, together with several large pieces of cattle bone, on the base of the inner ditch. The outer ditch (401) was slighter than the inner, but its section suggests the presence of an external bank which eroded naturally. This sequence indicates that an enclosure with an internal bank was remodelled at a certain point in order to make it more characteristically 'hengelike'. In the regional context it may be pertinent to draw a comparison with Stonehenge I, the earliest local henge, which also had an internal bank and external ditch.

Trench 15
The lesser enclosure, more characteristic of the structures in the western interior as a whole, had an ovoid plan and was roughly 15m x 12m in extent. Its entrance opened to the south-west. A cutting 10m x 8m in extent, with an extension to the south-west was opened over the enclosure, revealing part of the ditch and the central part of the interior. Magnetometer survey had detected the presence of a small feature in the centre of the enclosure, and it was imagined in advance of excavation that this might represent a grave. Surprisingly, it was actually the hearth of a second building, similar in size and morphology to that in Trench 14 (Figure 13.8). Although the subsoil had suffered significantly from root disturbance, the floor hollow, wall stakes, hearth-pit and roof-posts were all present. Like the Trench 14 building, this structure lacked any trace of floor deposits. Yet the scatter of inter-cutting stake-holes and pits immediately to the west of the floor area and the potentially replaced roof posts argue for a lengthy period of occupation and use.

Just as the size of the building precisely matched that in Trench 14, so the surrounding palisade of postholes was similar in diameter to that in the other cutting. Yet the ditch enclosed a far smaller area – to such an extent that it had weathered back directly onto the palisade postholes. This need not indicate any particular chronological relationship between ditch and palisade, other than that the posts were probably already in place at the time when the ditch had been dug. The ditch itself was an impressive feature, around 1m deep and 1.4m wide. Animal bones and sherds of Grooved Ware were recovered from immediately above the primary silting, and the sections suggested the erosion of bank material from the outside of the ditch. In any case, there would have been no room for an internal bank while the building and palisade had been standing. This makes an interesting comparison with Trench 14, where there were two separate episodes of ditch-digging, only the later of which was associated with an external bank. One possibility is that the Trench 15 ditch was contemporary with this later ditch, and thus that the Trench 14 enclosure was earlier in its inception.

Discussion

The discovery of two buildings within the western part of Durrington Walls radically revises our understanding of the great henge monument. While Wainwright's and MacKie's interpretations of the Southern Circle as a huge circular building might have included some elements of a residential function, the shift of opinion toward free-standing rings of timber uprights as characteristic of later Neolithic ceremonial architecture has implicitly cast the interior of Durrington Walls as a space set aside for non-utilitarian activities. If the buildings inside the western enclosures were dwellings, we would have to revise this view. But were they houses, or something different?

Of course, the 'settlement' at the eastern entrance appears to pre-date the construction of the henge bank and ditch (see Parker Pearson this volume), and it is very probable that the western enclosure buildings were contemporary with this earlier phase of settlement activity. At this time the mettled avenue had already been constructed, leading up the valley from the river, and it is probable that the Northern and Southern Circles had already been constructed in some form. The pre-enclosure Durrington landscape (extending as far as the vicinity of Woodhenge) thus probably contained a variety of different forms of post-and-stake architecture, including variations on the themes of four-post settings, avenues, rings and palisades, constructed at different scales, and used for a variety of purposes (see Pollard, this volume). As we have noted above, the final form of the Southern Circle as a series of concentric rings of quite massive timbers stands out from this range of structures as something both colossal and unusually elaborate.

Aside from their surrounding ditches, the two buildings in the western interior of the henge registered on magnetometer survey as small anomalies marking the positions of the baked floors beneath their eroded hearths. Potentially similar anomalies can be identified throughout the western part of the monument (see Figure 13.7), and it is therefore potentially possible that the whole area is littered with Late Neolithic houses. On the other hand, only the 'midden' platform was identified as a possible house platform in the large area stripped in 1966-67 (Mike Parker Pearson and Geoffrey Wainwright pers. comm.), and even 'Structure A' located near Totterdown Clump bears little comparison with the houses around the avenue (Wainwright and Longworth 1971: 44). The small ditched enclosures appear to be ranged around a terrace running around the head of the dry valley enclosed by the henge and, if each one surrounded a building, they would appear to have been considerably more scattered than the relatively nucleated houses around the avenue. Their being enclosed by substantial timber palisades seems to mark them out as, in some way, special. Yet, if anything, the buildings themselves are more humble in scale than those around the avenue. The coincidence of the orientation of the floor hollow, palisade entrance and ditch entrance in Trench 14 might hint at contemporaneity, but the blocking of the palisade entrance demonstrates a need to render the building inaccessible at some point. In social terms, we can propose a series of alternative interpretations for the 'houses' in the western enclosures:

1. That these buildings represent part of a general scatter of houses throughout the Durrington Walls dry valley, including those around the avenue, and that the dwellings of particular important people (elders, chiefs or ritual specialists) were elaborated after their deaths by the addition of palisades and/or ditches. We should not necessarily expect social hierarchy to be reflected in the sizes of houses, and the larger buildings at the eastern entrance may be a reflection of household size rather than status.

2. That the six or more houses in the western interior were set apart from the more densely packed structures around the avenue, and this separation reflects the importance of the people who occupied them. Palisades and/or ditches were in place during the period of occupation, and further enhanced the distinction between the different elements of the community. The blocking of the palisade entrance in Trench 14 may have followed the death of the house's occupant, and may or may not have coincided with the digging of the first or the second ditch. If the ditch was dug while the house was in use, its greater diameter and its temporal priority over the enclosure in Trench 15 may indicate that the person concerned had a particular social pre-eminence.

3. The buildings in the western interior were not permanently occupied at all, and, while they were constructed using the same architectural style as the houses at the eastern entrance, their separation from the settlement, their scattered locations and their enclosure indicates that they were used for one or more non-domestic purpose (as places where rites of passage – including funerary rites – and other social or supernatural transactions were conducted; as dwellings of spirits or ancestors; as shrines or cult houses).

At this stage, we do not attempt to discriminate between these possibilities, although it is anticipated that the acquisition of a detailed radiocarbon chronology for the sites and for the Durrington complex as a whole will illuminate the issue.

References

Barrett, J.C. 1994 *Fragments From Antiquity: An Archaeology of Social Life in Britain, 2900-1200 BC.* Oxford: Blackwell.

Cleal, R.M.J., Walker, K.E. and Montague, R. 1995 *Stonehenge in its Landscape: twentieth-century excavations.* London: English Heritage.

Cunnington, M.E. 1931 The 'Sanctuary' on Overton Hill, Near Avebury. *Wiltshire Archaeological and Natural History Magazine* 45: 300-35.

David, A., Cole, M., Horsley, T., Linford, N., Linford, P. and Martin, L. 2004 A rival to Stonehenge? Geophysical survey at Stanton Drew, England. *Antiquity* 78: 341–358.

Gibson, A. 1998 *Stonehenge and Timber Circles.* Stroud: Tempus.

MacKie, E. 1977 *Science and Society in Prehistoric Britain.* London: Elek.

Mercer, R. 1981 The excavation of a Late Neolithic henge-type enclosure at Balfarg, Markinch, Fife, Scotland, 1977-8. *Proceedings of the Society of Antiquaries of Scotland* 111: 63-171.

Parker Pearson, M. and Ramilsonina 1998 Stonehenge for the ancestors: the stones pass on the message. *Antiquity* 72: 308-26.

Pitts, M. 2000 *Hengeworld.* London: Arrow Books.

Pitts, M. 2001 Excavating the Sanctuary: new investigations on Overton Hill, Avebury. *Wiltshire Archaeological and Natural History Magazine* 94: 1-23.

Pollard, J. 1995 Inscribing space: formal deposition at the later Neolithic monument of Woodhenge, Wiltshire. *Proceedings of the Prehistoric Society* 61: 137-56.

Pollard, J. 2001 The aesthetics of depositional practice. *World Archaeology* 33: 315-33.

Renfrew, A.C. 1973 Monuments, mobilisation and social organisation in Neolithic Wessex. In: C. Renfrew (ed.) *The Explanation of Culture Change.* London: Duckworth. 539-558.

Richards, C.C. and Thomas, J.S. 1984 Ritual activity and structured deposition in later Neolithic Wessex. In R. Bradley and J. Gardiner (eds) *Neolithic Studies: a review of some current research.* Oxford: BAR (British Series) 133. 189-218.

Speak, S. and Burgess, C. 1999 Meldon Bridge: a centre of the third millennium BC in Peeblesshire.

Proceedings of the Society of Antiquaries of Scotland129: 1-118.

Thomas, J.S. 1999 *Understanding the Neolithic*. London: Routledge.

Thomas, J.S. 2004 The later Neolithic architectural repertoire: the case of the Dunragit complex. In: R. Cleal and J. Pollard (eds.) *Monuments and Material Culture: Papers on Neolithic and Bronze Age Britain in Honour of Isobel Smith*. East Knoyle: Hobnob Press. 98-108.

Wainwright, G.J. 1989 *The Henge Monuments.* London: Thames and Hudson.

Wainwright, G.J. and Longworth, I.H. 1971 *Durrington Walls: excavations 1966-1968*. London: Society of Antiquaries.

Chapter 14

A return to Woodhenge:
the results and implications of the 2006 excavations

Joshua Pollard and David Robinson

Department of Archaeology & Anthropology, University of Bristol

Introduction

Woodhenge is an integral component of the Durrington Walls/Avon riverside late Neolithic complex. Although lying outside the circuit of the Durrington henge, the two monuments may originally have been linked via a southern entrance through the Durrington earthwork. The size and structural complexity of the Woodhenge timber circles find ready analogy with those making up the Southern Circle inside Durrington Walls, and both share plan similarities with the Phase 3 stone settings of Stonehenge, providing an architectural link across different media that substantiates the claims for these monuments being elements of a single, contemporary ritual complex (Parker Pearson and Ramilisonina 1998; Parker Pearson *et al.* 2006*)*.

Woodhenge also occupies an important position within the history of archaeological research, being the one of the first monuments to be identified from the air - or at least its timber component - during a flight by Squadron Leader Insall in December 1925. It then became the first later Neolithic multiple timber circle to be excavated; the work being led over two seasons in 1926 and 1927 by Maud Cunnington of the Wiltshire Archaeological and Natural History Society (with prompt publication in 1929; Cunnington 1929). Those excavations represent a pioneering engagement with prehistoric timber architecture, undertaken over a decade before Gerhard Bersu's work at Little Woodbury revealed the recoverability of post-built prehistoric domestic structures in lowland Britain (Evans 1989). The Cunnington work involved trenching across the whole of the interior in order to reveal the plan of the timber rings, and the cutting of sections through the bank and ditch on the north, east, south and west sides. The resulting plan was of a setting of six concentric oval rings (A-F: outer-inner) of post-holes within an oval earthwork enclosure c.85m in diameter, broken by a northeasterly entrance (Cunnington 1929). In the southern part of the monument two putative stone-holes were discovered between posts B8 and 9, and C5 and 6.

In 1970 further, small-scale, excavations took place. Directed by John Evans and Geoff Wainwright, the work involved the cutting of a single 27m-long trench through the ditch and bank on the south-eastern side (Evans and Wainwright 1979). A detailed environmental sequence was obtained from mollusca in the ditch fills and buried soil under the bank; dates on antler and animal bone from

the base of the ditch and primary fills respectively placed the construction of the earthwork in the third or fourth quarter of the 3rd millennium BC: 2470-2030 BC (BM-677) and 2340-2010 BC (BM-678), at 95.4% confidence (calibrated using OxCal v.3.10). Inevitably, this was not the end of the story, since many questions relating to the full chronology and character of activity at the monument remained unaddressed.

Subsequent re-assessments of the monument (Pollard 1995a; Pitts 2000; Gibson 2005) highlighted several aspects that required clarification. There is a suspicion that the henge ditch was dug after the timber structure had been erected, the axis of the earthwork being 'off-set' to the north of that of the timber rings. Alex Gibson argues, on the basis of Grooved Ware sealed under the bank and analogy with reinterpreted sequences at other henge-enclosed timber circles, that the earthwork is later than the timber circles (Gibson 2005: 46, 66). Stepped profiles to a number of the post-holes suggest that individual posts within rings A, B, D, E and F may have been subject to replacement on one or more occasions, as can now be demonstrated at the analogous site of the Sanctuary, near Avebury (Pitts 2001). This process of replacement may have been linked to practices of renewal, remembrance and commemoration, metaphorically symbolised by post erection, rotting and subsequent deposition.

Another issue relates to the unusual character of the pre-bank deposits, which included un-weathered Grooved Ware sherds, plentiful animal bone and ash-filled pits. Rather than representing the residue of pre-monument occupation, the possibility arises that these deposits relate to episodes of feasting and midden deposition contemporary with the timber circles. Similar deposits were encountered in 2005 from beneath the henge bank of Durrington Walls (Parker Pearson this volume).

Studies by one of the authors and Julian Thomas (Pollard 1995; Thomas 1999: 82-3) have drawn attention to complex patterns of artefact, animal bone and human bone deposition within the monument. The earthwork entrance was marked out by elaborate deposits that included human bone and Grooved Ware sherds with circular motifs; much of the deposition within the timber rings, including that of carved chalk objects, focused on the south-east sector; cattle bones were concentrated in the inner rings, pig in the outer; and so forth. Combined with the way that the architecture of the timber rings engendered a particular pattern of movement, experience and sequence of encounter, Bradley (2000: 124-31) has argued that the deposits were structured according to a narrative quality 'concerned with how the world came into being, and ... how the human population is related to the past and the supernatural' *(ibid.*: 127).

We now understand that the large quantities of artefactual and faunal material recovered during the 1967 excavations at the Southern Circle in Durrington Walls were not associated with the standing posts of that monument, but had been placed in re-cuts dug into the tops of the post-holes after the timbers had rotted or been removed. Therefore, much of the identified depositional patterning at that monument relates to a series of commemorative or re-animative acts undertaken several generations after the construction of the circles (Thomas, this volume). It is highly likely, although it can no longer be tested through excavation, that a similar process was in operation at Woodhenge. The published sections of the post-holes appear to show large pits filled with dark soil (previously considered to be 'weathering cones', but in fact too large) cut into the tops of these features (Cunnington 1929: pl. 12). It is from these contexts that the majority of the pottery, bone and lithics recovered during the 1920s excavations was retrieved. Considering the deposits in the timber rings as deliberate burials of selected assemblages of material in re-cuts would explain a number of anomalies, such as the survival of carved chalk objects (including the famous axes), which would have shattered and decayed if originally placed in an exposed surface context. So Woodhenge, like the Southern Circle, underwent a transformation from a complex setting of timber rings to, effectively, a multiple pit circle, in which deposits of material curated from middens or other contexts had been placed. There is an obvious analogy with the processes of re-cutting and deposition seen at the pit henge on Wyke Down, Dorset (Barrett *et al.* 1991). We argue that at Woodhenge the phase of re-cutting and deposition may have occurred when the monument underwent a wholesale transformation, marked by its enclosure through the creation of the henge earthwork and the erection of megalithic settings.

The rationale for the 2006 excavations

The work in 2006 was undertaken in order to address a series of questions relating to the chronology of the various components of the monument, constructional processes, and the character of the pre-henge activity (so addressing points raised in the recent Stonehenge landscape research framework: Darvill 2005: 112-3). Refining the date of the timber circles and establishing their sequential relationship both with the enclosure and with developments at Durrington Walls and Stonehenge were key concerns. This could only be achieved by recovering suitable samples for radiocarbon dating. Although the interior of the monument and all the post-holes were subject to 'total excavation' in 1926-7, recent

re-excavations at the Sanctuary (Pitts 2001) showed that Cunnington did, on one occasion, miss pockets of feature fill in which antler or freshly-deposited bone might occur. Published photographs of the 1920s excavation make it quite clear that an open-area technique was not employed, and that the work was messy by modem standards (Cunnington 1929: pl. 17).

Cunnington claimed to have discovered two stone-holes ('h' and 'i') and spreads of sarsen fragments in the southern part of the monument, between posts B8 and B9, and C5 and C6 (Cunnington 1929: 14). While the published details relating to these features are sufficiently scant to raise questions over the veracity of Cunnington's claim that they were stone-holes, support came from timber-to-stone sequences at other multiple timber circles such as the Sanctuary and Site IV, Mount Pleasant (Cunnington 1931; Wainwright 1979). In order to attempt to secure dateable material from the post settings, and to establish the character of the 'stone-hole' features, a 10m x 7m trench (Trench 17) was excavated in the southern part of the monument's interior around post-holes A15-17, B8-9 and C5, and 'stone-holes' 'h' and 'i' (Figure 14.1). This is also an area that produced high densities of finds, including antler, from the post-hole fills (Pollard 1995a). In re-excavating this area, backfill was removed from the features explored previously, and 'missed' finds recovered in the process, while the features themselves were recorded in plan and profile. Specific attention was paid to identifying and excavating *in situ* deposits and features that had been missed in the 1920s. This was not just an exercise in prehistory, but an investigation into the historical archaeology of the history of archaeology.

In order to investigate the practices that led to the generation and deposition of material prior to the creation of the earthwork, a 10m x 5m trench (Trench 16) was excavated through the bank and buried soil on the south-eastern side of the monument, adjacent and to the south of that dug in 1970 (Figure 14.1). This comprised the investigation of *c.* 5% of the likely remaining bank deposits and underlying buried soil (though difficulty exists in knowing the extent of the excavations through the bank undertaken by Cunnington in the 1920s and the general survival of truncated bank material).

Results

Trench 17: *the post- and stone-holes*
The excavation showed that the post-holes of rings A, B and C had been marked accurately by the concrete posts set up soon after the original excavation (Figures 14.2 and 14.3). The markers proved to be lengths of capped, pre-cast concrete pipe - from which the term 'post-pipe' was apparently derived (Mike Pitts pers. comm.) - filled with soil. As a first stage, work concentrated on removing the excavated fill from these post-holes, the two stone-holes ('h' and 'i') and 'extra hole d'. It soon became apparent that the 1926 excavators had performed a very respectable job, especially given contemporary

WOODHENGE

N

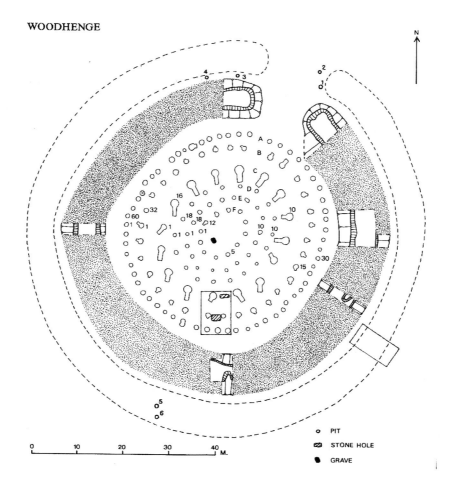

o	PIT	
⊘	STONE HOLE	
●	GRAVE	

0   10   20   30   40 M.

Figure 14.1 The locations of Trenches 16 and 17 at Woodhenge

Figure 14.2 Trench 17 within the Woodhenge timber structure, viewed from the south
(photographed by Adam Stanford of Aerial-Cam)

Figure 14.3 Trench 17 in close-up, viewed from the south (photographed by Adam Stanford of Aerial-Cam)

unfamiliarity with post-hole archaeology. With minor exceptions, the fill of these features had been identified correctly and fully removed, the excavations conforming to the original shapes of the features (i.e. there was little evidence of undercutting or over-cutting). Small quantities of worked flint (predominantly debitage) and a little bone and pottery came from the backfill deposits, but the impression gained was that the original level of finds recovery had been high (Figure 14.4). Sieves may even have been employed, since a deposit of very fine, sorted soil was encountered below the main backfill deposit in C5.

In three instances (A 15, A 17 and C5) small lenses of unexcavated *in situ* fill were encountered in the post-holes. That in the base of A15 included some charcoal flecking and a fresh piece of animal bone; charcoal was also present in C5. Whether any of the charcoal or animal bone can provide suitable samples for radiocarbon dating (in terms of their integrity with the erection of the posts) remains to be established.

The stone-holes and other features
Re-excavation of the two stone-holes investigated in 1926 confirmed that they had indeed once held large sarsens, and also revealed a more complex pattern and sequence of megalithic settings than initially envisaged. Stone-hole 'i', between posts B8 and B9, was a substantial and regularly cut oval pit, 2.65m x 1.90m, and 0.80m deep (Figure 14.5). The base was almost flat, though compressed and smoothed over an area of *c.* 1m x 0.5m on the northern side where a large stone had evidently been set. In this same area was a remnant patch of

original fill, comprising very compact and de-structured chalk with some light clay (patches of remnant soil). One curious feature of the stone-hole was a marked step on the southern side. Cunnington thought it was a ramp, and it is clear that the large stone held within the pit was brought in from this side. However, with its stepped profile it does not work well as a ramp, and in plan is slightly asymmetric in relation to the rest of the stone-hole cut. Its base also supported a patch of highly compacted chalk, an unusual deposit for a ramp fill. It is much more likely that the 0.3m-deep step is the remnant of a separate and probably earlier feature, and that this too once held a large stone.

Cunnington had felt confident that feature 'i' was a stone-hole and, we now know, had plans to mark its position, plans which for some reason were never realized. A temporary marker, in the form of a setting of three large concrete blocks enclosing several tightly-packed flint nodules, was found centrally against the northern edge of the stone-hole in the top of the backfill.

The re-excavation of stone-hole 'h' between C5 and C6 presented greater difficulties, not least because it had been backfilled with a chalk rubble matrix that was similar in character to *in situ* packing deposits. The stone-hole itself was oblong, 2.90m x 1.40m, and up to 0.48m deep, with an uneven base perhaps created by compression from the stone that it had held. The shape of the 1926 excavation cut followed the contours of the stone-hole closely, except on the northern side where an area of original compact chalk rubble packing had been missed. Some bone and worked flint was recovered from

Figure 14.4 Post-hole B8 after re-excavation, viewed from the south

Figure 14.5 Stone-hole 'i' with its additional lip visible on its south side

the latter, and a number of sarsen flakes from the backfill. As with stone-hole 'i', stepping on the east and north sides of the feature suggests it cut through an earlier pit (another stone-hole?).

The level of Cunnington's competence in feature recognition and interpretation was always going to be an issue, though the discovery in 2006 of several features that had been missed or poorly understood in the original excavation came as something of a surprise. In the northeast of the trench, stone-hole 'h' cut an earlier, oval pit that was almost clipped by post-hole C6. Having escaped notice in the 1926 excavation, the fill was intact, comprising chalk rubble in which were embedded several large flint nodules. Too broad and shallow to be a post-hole and, anyway, lacking a post-pipe, this feature is a candidate for another stone-hole. Two other features can also be identified as stone-holes: the first a pit previously recognized during the 1926 excavation (extra hole 'd'), and considered at the time to be a post-hole; the second adjacent to post B9. Both are similar in morphology with slight ramps on one side and near vertical faces on the other, and, critically, evidence of compression on their bases consistent with the former presence of medium-sized stones.

In the zone between rings B and C were four features - a large hollow, surrounded by two pits and a small post-hole - that had not been encountered by Cunnington. Cut through a seam of irregular chalk containing flint nodules and pockets of poorly structured parent rock, the hollow is best interpreted as a tree-throw pit that saw limited reworking in order to extract flint (Figure 14.6). In places (e.g. on the north and east) there were slight depressions in the sides where flint nodules had been removed. Two sherds of Early Neolithic pottery and several pieces of worked flint came from the upper soil fill; and other worked flint, including Late Mesolithic or Early Neolithic blades, came from close to the base. Of the small features surrounding the hollow, the pit on its eastern side contained a deposit of fresh worked flint and bone.

Trench 16: the bank and buried soil
It became clear after removal of the topsoil that Trench 16 inadvertently intersected, at a slightly oblique angle, the southern edge of the 1970 excavation. Furthermore, the 1970 trench had, in turn, cut into the edge of an earlier (1926) excavation along the same axis (this is not commented upon in the published report: Evans and Wainwright 1979)! As a result of these archaeological interventions and truncation of the rear of the bank by Roman to post-Medieval cultivation, an area of buried soil only 5.4m x 3.2m was left for investigation in the southern and western part of the trench.

Here, the buried soil comprised a grey-brown loam up to 0.17m deep (Figure 14.7). Upon exposure, quantities of bone, earlier Neolithic pottery and worked flint were immediately evident *within* this, especially on the southern side of the excavated area. The buried soil was sampled on a 0.5m grid: alternate squares being dug across a 1m-wide strip along the middle of the trench, while a second 1m-wide strip of buried soil was totally excavated against the southern section. Somewhat surprisingly, the full profile of the buried soil was not present. Comparison with the northern section of the 1970 excavation, only 2m to the north, shows that the top was here truncated by *c.*0.10m - it lacked the dark brown, stone-free turf-line and sorted line of flints visible in the Evans and Wainwright section (Evans and Wainwright 1979: fig. 41). The absence of later Neolithic artefacts within and on the buried soil is also telling. The obvious interpretation is that the turf and top of the buried soil were stripped in this area prior to the construction of the bank, and probably very soon before since a new turf-line did not have time to develop.

The buried soil and artefact spread ran into the top of a substantial hollow under the eastern tail of the bank (Figure 14.7). This proved to be a large oval tree-throw pit, 3.5m x 2.5m and 0.5m deep. The fills were asymmetric, beginning with a primary fill of chalk rubble, from which a small quantity of fresh animal bone was recovered. Sealing this was a brown loam and then an upper fill which looks to be a continuation of the buried soil, again lacking its full profile. Large quantities of bone (including mandible, rib and long-bone fragments from large mammals) were present in a loose concentration in the top of this soil; while below this was a concentration of pottery, most of the sherds lying horizontally in a 'carpet-like' spread. Bone and pottery, along with a reasonable amount of worked flint and unworked small nodules, had evidently been dumped, though not without structure, into the top of the partially filled tree-throw pit. All the sherds look to come from plain carinated bowls of early 4th millennium BC date. Representing an earliest Neolithic presence, the assemblage finds analogy with that from the Coneybury Anomaly, 2km to the southwest (Richards 1990).

Covering the area of the tree-throw - which had evidently survived as a discernable hollow into the later Neolithic - was a band of extremely compact chalk, made up of large angular blocks set two thick in places and rammed into place. The chalk was not simply a revetment to the rear of the bank, which is, anyway, not otherwise attested. Telling of the perceived significance of the earlier tree-throw during the late Neolithic, this capping looks very much like a deliberate act to 'seal' the tree-throw before or at the time that the bank was created.

Discussion

For such a limited excavation, and one that dealt in part with the re-evaluation of a site extensively trenched in 1926, the results of the 2006 work proved rather surprising. There are three themes that merit discussion: that of the marking place in the earlier Neolithic and memory of it; the position of the timber monument in the local sequence of monument development; and the

Figure 14.6 The large Early Neolithic hollow between post rings B and C, viewed from the east

Figure 14.7 Trench 16 with the half-sectioned tree-throw visible in the foreground and the buried soil beneath the henge bank visible between the two ranging rods, photographed from the east

165

transformation from timber to stone - the' lithicization' of Woodhenge.

Marking and memory

Although the cutting through the bank and buried soil failed to define the character of the immediate pre-henge activity, it did reveal important evidence relating to the long-term history of this location and the relationship between late Neolithic communities and their past. The large tree-throw is a significant feature, in that it provided the focus for occupation and deposition during the earliest part of the region's Neolithic, and it remained a visible landscape feature as a surface hollow into the later 3rd millennium BC. For some reason the turf was stripped from this area before the henge bank was created, resulting in an 'exposure' of earlier midden material. The result was an almost 'archaeological' encounter in which the late Neolithic monument builders came to face the residues of acts of occupation and deposition that had occurred a millennium and a half earlier. Perhaps some knowledge of these earlier events already existed, although how such historical landscape detail might be sustained over such a long period is debatable (see below). Alternatively, it may have been the hollow left by the tree-throw that attracted attention or anchored long-term memory. Certainly the capping of the tree-throw with a rammed chalk surface alludes to its significance, this act potentially serving to mark or control an ancestral presence.

It seems as though the siting of Woodhenge in relation to earlier episodes of activity may not have been coincidental. In fact, the relationship between later Neolithic monuments and the traces of earlier activity in general, both in this region and elsewhere, deserves more critical attention. Locally, one can note the position of the Coneybury henge adjacent to the massive earliest 4th millennium BC pit deposition of the Coneybury Anomaly (Richards 1990). Beaker pottery from the upper fills of the Anomaly *(ibid.:* 40) shows that this feature, like the Woodhenge tree-throw, retained a landscape signature as a visible hollow into the latest 3rd millennium BC. Was this why the Coneybury henge was built here? The same level of subtle later visibility and ascribed significance might have attached to the traces of the famous 8th millennium BC post-holes, *aligned on a tree-throw,* next to Stonehenge (Cleal *et al.* 1995: 43-7). There are many other curious instances of apparently long-term memory or re-engagement with traces of much earlier activity in the late Neolithic, from the siting of the North Mains henge in Perthshire over 4th millennium BC pits (Barclay 1983), to the deposition of later Neolithic ceramics in pits cutting features of the earlier Neolithic timber buildings at White Horse Stone, Kent (Oxford Archaeology 2000), and Fengate, Peterborough (Pryor 2001: 48-9). There are a sense that, in the 3rd millennium BC, many decisions about where to create monuments or engage in the formal deposition of material in pits were undertaken with reference to the histories of particular locations, and that subtle surface traces of earlier features could become

powerful mnemonics in sustaining long-term memory.

As for the question of why Woodhenge was created where it was, perhaps a convergence of factors and 'qualities' made this locale sufficiently special to monumentalize in a truly spectacular manner. The site lay on the axis of the earlier Stonehenge Cursus; it was a location with an important history that included a component of the first Neolithic presence in the area; and it overlooked two highly significant topographic features, the course of the Avon and Beacon Hill to the east (see Tilley *et al.* this volume).

Timber circles

The excavations were not successful in their goal of obtaining high-quality dateable material from the post-hole fills. For the present at least, their precise chronology remains uncertain; however, we now know that deposits of remnant fill remain in some of the post-holes and future work could continue to target these and potentially recover dateable material. None the less, we do have dates for the earthwork. If the timber phase pre-dates the earthwork by a margin of one or two hundred years, then it would still remain relatively late in the Durrington Walls/Stonehenge sequence.

Although Woodhenge may be seen as a structure equivalent to the Southern Circle at Durrington Walls, there are also important differences which may be indicative of distinct roles, or of the modification of an architectural tradition over time. The timber settings at Woodhenge are laid out in an oval rather than circular configuration - the structure has an axis that is defined by its overall shape rather than an elaborated entrance - and it possesses a more coherent ('planned') plan, with regularly-spaced and even-numbered posts. If the Woodhenge timber structure was built later in the 3rd millennium BC than the Southern Circle (whose process of 'messy' post replacement echoes similar re-workings in stone at Stonehenge), it perhaps commemorates earlier timber constructions. The argued alignment on the midsummer sunrise/midwinter sunset also sets it apart from the midwinter sunrise axis of the Southern Circle. Perhaps here is a timber version of Stonehenge's Phase 3iv settings, themselves copying wooden structures like the Southern Circle?

As work continues on the Stonehenge Riverside Project a sense of the diverse range of later Neolithic timber monuments in the region is beginning to emerge. Many of these are located in the riverside zone around Durrington Walls and Woodhenge. In addition to the multiple timber circles of Woodhenge and the Southern Circle, and the smaller though still monumental settings of the Northern Circle (Wainwright with Longworth 1971), work in the western interior of Durrington during 2006 revealed small circular timber structures within earthwork enclosures, one at least with a central arrangement of four posts set on each corner of a slightly sunken square floor (Thomas, this volume). Those structures are near-identical in plan to the dwellings found outside the south-eastern entrance, although there exists a critical distinction in that they are not associated with occupation debris. Their cleanliness is perhaps indicative of a special status as shrines or houses of venerated individuals.

To the immediate south of Woodhenge is the later Neolithic timber structure under Durrington 68 (Pollard 1995b), and slightly further afield a series of post settings inside the Coneybury henge (Richards 1990). With sizeable central settings of four posts, the first phase of the Southern Circle was not dissimilar to the Northern Circle and Durrington 68 (Wainwright with Longworth 1971), and all three find analogy with other rings containing four-post settings at Wyke Down, Knowth, Ballynahatty and perhaps Stanton Drew Northeast (Gibson 2005). These in turn appear to be monumentalized versions of the structures excavated in the western interior of Durrington and the contemporary dwellings outside the south-eastern entrance there. 'Squares within circles' provide a common late Neolithic architectural theme, seen in other media with Orcadian houses, the arrangement of monoliths inside the Maeshowe passage-grave (Richards 2005) and Mayburgh henge (Topping 1992). Does the importance of these four post/stone arrangements perhaps lie in their reference to schemes of cosmological quartering - the four points of the world?

As Bradley has noted (2003, 13), smaller late Neolithic dwellings such as those at Trelystan in Powys show the same organization of space as larger 'monumental' timber structures like the Northern Circle. This he sees as a 'ritualization of the domestic sphere', in which the format of everyday structures (in both the literal and cultural sense) was drawn upon and took on special qualities in certain contexts. Taking the diversity of late Neolithic timber structures as a whole, ranging in scale from those at Trelystan to the Wessex multiple circles (and here Stonehenge as a lithic version of such), it is possible to see an architectural continuum. Just as Richards argues in the case of Orcadian dwellings, henges and passage-graves (Richards 2005), the notion of the 'house' may have lain at the core of this. In one way or another, Woodhenge, the Southern Circle and Stonehenge cited the dwellings of the living.

From timber to stone and the enclosure of Woodhenge
Not only has confirmation been provided of the existence of megalithic settings at Woodhenge, but these can now be seen to be of more than one phase. The first was an arc of at least four small stones open on the west and, coincidentally or not, surrounding an earlier hollow. The latter, like that under the bank, was probably still visible in the later Neolithic and a significant feature in its own right. Whether the stones of this first megalithic phase were of sarsen, bluestone or a mixture of the two, it is impossible to tell. Those four stones were then removed and replaced by two much larger sarsen settings

represented by stone-holes 'h' and 'i'. The scale of stone-hole 'i' in particular suggests that these megaliths stood two or three metres high.

The fate of the stones is clearly an issue. To judge by the quantity of sarsen debris recovered in the 1926 and 2006 excavations, the substantial megaliths within stone-holes 'h' and 'i' were probably broken *in situ* and carted away at some point in time prior to the antiquarian investigations of this landscape beginning in the 16th century (Chippindale 2004). The earlier, smaller stones (taking the size of the stone-holes as an index of their dimensions) were removed in prehistory. They could have been taken to one of several locations: to Stonehenge, Durrington Walls (stone-holes were found in the Neolithic roadway excavated in 2005-2006), or to the site of the nearby Cuckoo Stone, for example. Given the propensity of stones to move around this landscape during the later Neolithic, assisted of course by human agency, one wonders how many other erstwhile megalithic settings might remain undetected.

Unfortunately, the 1926 work removed the relationship between stone-hole 'i' and post B9, depriving us of a clear understanding of the sequence, if such there was, of timber and stone. This said, analogy with other multiple timber circles would suggest that the stones were introduced after the posts had rotted. It was perhaps at this time that the earthwork was created - demarcating, even controlling, a potent and sacred space. Pits were cut into the tops of the post-holes, and material such as the famous chalk axes, pottery, lithics, animal bone and even token collections of human bone deposited within them. By this stage, Woodhenge had become a very different monument to that represented by the timber circles: one of stone, separated from the landscape of routine life by its deep ditch and chalk bank, and now more intimately associated with commemorative acts and ancestral veneration.

References

Barclay, G. 1983. Sites of the third millennium BC to the first millennium AD at North Mains, Strathallan, Perthshire. *Proceedings of the Society of Antiquaries of Scotland* 113: 122-81.

Barrett, J.C., Bradley, R. and Green, M. 1991. *Landscape, Monuments and Society: The Prehistory of Cranborne Chase.* Cambridge: Cambridge University Press.

Bradley, R. 2000. *An Archaeology of Natural Places.* London: Routledge.

Bradley, R. 2003. A life less ordinary: the ritualization of the domestic sphere in later prehistoric Europe. *Cambridge Archaeological Journal* 13(1): 5-23.

Chippindale, C. 2004. *Stonehenge Complete.* 2nd edition. London: Thames & Hudson.

Cleal, R.M.J., Walker, K.E. and Montague, R. 1995. *Stonehenge in its Landscape: twentieth-century excavations.* London: English Heritage.

Cunnington, M.E. 1929. *Woodhenge*. Devizes: Simpson.

Cunnington, M.E. 1931. The 'Sanctuary' on Overton Hill, near Avebury. *Wiltshire Archaeological and Natural History Magazine* 4: 300-35.

Darvill, T. 2005. *Stonehenge World Heritage Site: an archaeological research framework*. London and Bournemouth: English Heritage and Bournemouth University.

Evans, C. 1989. Archaeology and modern times: Bersu's Woodbury 1938 and 1939. *Antiquity* 63, 436-50.

Evans, J.G.E. and Wainwright, G.J. 1979. The Woodhenge excavations. In G.J. Wainwright, *Mount Pleasant, Dorset: excavations 1970-1971*. London: Society of Antiquaries. 71-4.

Gibson, A. 2005. *Stonehenge and Timber Circles*. 2nd edition. Stroud: Tempus.

Oxford Archaeology 2000. White Horse Stone: a Neolithic longhouse. *Current Archaeology* 168: 450-53.

Parker Pearson, M., Pollard, J., Richards, C., Thomas, J., Tilley, C., Welham, K. and Albarella, U. 2006. Materializing Stonehenge: the Stonehenge Riverside Project and new discoveries. *Journal of Material Culture* 11: 227-61.

Parker Pearson, M. and Ramilisonina 1998. Stonehenge for the ancestors: the stones pass on the message. *Antiquity* 72: 308-26.

Pitts, M. 2000. *Hengeworld*. London: Century.

Pitts, M. 2001. Excavating the Sanctuary: new investigations on Overton Hill, Avebury. *Wiltshire Archaeological and Natural History Magazine* 94: 1-23.

Pollard, J. 1995a. Inscribing Space: Formal deposition at the Later Neolithic monument of Woodhenge, Wiltshire. *Proceedings of the Prehistoric Society* 61: 137-56.

Pollard, J. 1995b. The Durrington 68 Timber Circle: a forgotten Late Neolithic monument. *Wiltshire Archaeological and Natural History Magazine* 88: 122-5.

Pryor, F. 2001. *The Flag Fen Basin: archaeology and environment of a Fenland landscape*. London: English Heritage.

Richards, C. (ed.) 2005. *Dwelling among the Monuments: the Neolithic village of Barnhouse, Maeshowe passage grave and surrounding monuments at Stenness, Orkney*. Cambridge: McDonald Institute.

Richards, J. 1990. *The Stonehenge Environs Project*. London: English Heritage.

Thomas, J. 1999. *Understanding the Neolithic*. London: Routledge.

Topping, P. 1992. The Penrith henges: a survey by the Royal Commission on the Historical Monuments of England. *Proceedings of the Prehistoric Society* 58: 249-64.

Wainwright, G.J. 1979. *Mount Pleasant, Dorset: excavations 1970-1971*. London: Society of Antiquaries of London.

Wainwright, G.J. with Longworth, I.H. 1971. *Durrington Walls: excavations 1966-1968*. London: Society of Antiquaries of London.

Chapter 15

Units of measurement in Late Neolithic southern Britain

Andrew Chamberlain and Mike Parker Pearson

Department of Archaeology, University of Sheffield

Introduction

The abilities of the prehistoric peoples of Britain to construct large-scale yet intricate monumental architecture incorporating standardised constructional designs, accurate astronomical alignments and detailed patterns of symmetry are now widely recognised, but this raises questions concerning the techniques of measurement that were in use in the British Late Neolithic (third millennium BC). The regularities in the plans of circular earthworks and timber and stone settings suggests that, at least at the level of individual monuments, a system of measurement was used to set out the positions of banks, ditches and orthostats. However, the spatial arrangements of the principal elements of these monuments could have been determined by regular pacing and the monumental architecture does not, of itself, necessitate the existence of a fixed unit of measurement in the Late Neolithic, let alone a *standard* unit that was widespread amongst the prehistoric peoples of Britain. The symmetry and astronomical alignments of prehistoric monuments are, to a certain extent, scale-independent and therefore do not require the existence of a fixed standard of measurement; nonetheless, if such a standard or standards did exist there would be important implications for our understanding of prehistoric technology and society.

Direct evidence for the existence of standard measurement units could be gained from rulers or measuring rods, but examples of these do not survive from the British Neolithic or indeed any other period of British prehistory (although later prehistoric examples have been found in Denmark, Germany and Ireland: Glob 1974: 38; Sievers 2002: 205; Raftery 1986: 51). An indirect procedure for discerning units of measurement is to look for regularities in the dimensions of prehistoric monuments, in the expectation that peaks in the distributions of lengths, breadths and diameters, and perhaps perimeters, will cluster at multiples of a fundamental unit or 'quantum'. This method of inference was applied by Alexander Thom to selected measurements from surveys of British prehistoric stone circles and stone rows (Thom 1955; 1967), but the resulting quantum of the Megalithic Yard failed to gain widespread acceptance amongst prehistorians and statisticians. Rigorous quantitative treatment of Thom's measurements found that the evidence for the use of a Megalithic Yard reached a satisfactory level of statistical significance only amongst a restricted sample of Scottish stone circles (Kendall 1974; Freeman 1976; Baxter 2003).

There are many difficulties that can frustrate the search for quanta in the dimensions of prehistoric monuments. Firstly, the level of precision of the survey data has to be high so that errors in estimated dimensions are small relative to the size of the quantum under investigation, otherwise any regularities that exist may be lost in the noise arising from measurement error. Many publications only provide small-scale plans of monuments, or report dimensions to the nearest metre, and these are insufficiently accurate for the purposes of metrological analyis. Secondly, ancient measurement systems often made use of multiple values for their base units (Michell 1981; Neal 2000) and thus different built structures may incorporate dimensions that are not commensurable as integer values within a single measurement system. The implication is that when measurements from different sites are combined in a single analysis the resulting pattern may be confused by the presence of multiple quanta. Thirdly, most previous exercises in detecting quanta in the dimensions of prehistoric monuments have been based on measurements of distances between the megalithic elements of the monument, yet these stone settings often represent later phases of activity that do not necessarily correspond to the dimensions of the original plan of the monument (and, as seen with the sequence of modifications at Stonehenge, megaliths are notoriously moveable markers).

The aim of the present study is to investigate a new source of measurement data for Late Neolithic monuments with a view to overcoming some of the above-mentioned difficulties. The data examined are the diameters of the circuits of earthworks and stone- and post-holes that by their very nature are more likely to retain their original positions and hence reveal the metric principles upon which the monuments were constructed. Also our analysis focuses primarily on the regularities observable *within* complex multicircuit monuments, rather than *between* separate monuments, to isolate and circumvent the problem that may arise when the unit of measurement varies between different structures.

Stonehenge

Stonehenge, near Amesbury in Wiltshire, is the most complex example of Late Neolithic ceremonial architecture in Britain. It consists of a doubled-banked circular earthwork enclosing a series of circular arrangements of pits, postholes and stone circles nearly all of which are arranged concentrically and symmetrically about a common central point and linear axis. The orientation of the monument and its constituent parts, at least in its later phases of use, were clearly related to the observance of celestial phenomena: the axis of the monument and its associated avenue were directed towards midsummer sunrise, and other stone settings within the monument may have been aligned on both solar and lunar horizon positions (Ruggles 1999).

In contrast to our progress in recognising and understanding these astronomical alignments, there is complete disagreement over the question of whether Stonehenge was constructed to a measured plan incorporating a standardised linear measure of distance. There is a long and chequered history of metrical analysis of the dimensions of Stonehenge which can only be touched upon very briefly here. The first topographical surveys and measurements of the site were carried out in the 17th, 18th and 19th centuries, most notably by Inigo Jones in about 1640, by William Stukeley in about 1723 and by William Flinders Petrie between 1874 and 1880 (Chippindale 1983; Piggott 1985; Pitts 2000), and ever more refined efforts to capture the monument in numerical form have continued up to the present day (Bryan and Clowes 1997; Bewley et al. 2005). Inigo Jones' early, stylised portrayal of the stone settings of Stonehenge as a symmetrical monument of Vitruvian proportions has been ridiculed for its inaccuracy (Chippindale 1983: 57) yet the internal diameters of the trilithon, bluestone and sarsen settings on Jones' plan are within 5% of modern values. Whatever the motivations behind Jones' attempt to capture the dimensions of the rude stone monument within an integrated classical architectural design, he was more successful in depicting the groundplan of Stonehenge than has subsequently been credited.

Stukeley had deduced the precise length of the Roman foot of 0.96 statute feet (0.293m) used in masonry construction in Roman Britain, but his best estimate for a unit of measurement at Stonehenge was 20.8 inches (or 1.73 statute feet, equal to 0.528m), a length Stukeley recognised as being incommensurate with the British Roman unit (Chippindale 1983: 75; Piggott 1985: 90). Petrie, however, found that the inner diameter of the Stonehenge sarsen circle amounted to 100 Roman feet, though Petrie's version of the Roman foot (0.973 statute feet, or 0.297m) was a few millimeters longer than the Roman foot employed by Stukeley. Petrie also deduced that the earthworks and station stones at Stonehenge were laid out on a different unit, which he estimated as 1.873 feet, or 0.571m (Chippindale 1983: 137; Burl 1987: 183). Thom and Thom (1988) found that the average centre-line diameter of the sarsen circle at Stonehenge was 37 Megalithic Yards of 2.722 statute feet (0.830m), a unit of measure which Thom (1967) claimed was in widespread use for the construction of stone monuments in Britain.

These attempts to determine a unit of measure at Stonehenge have little in common other than that they have mainly focused on the dimensions and distances amongst the stone settings and especially the sarsen circle, the arrangement of large standing stones and lintels that was designed to form a complete 30m diameter arcade near the centre of the monument. The sarsen circle, however, represents an intermediate phase in the development of Stonehenge when the site was transformed by the incorporation of dressed stones brought from distances as far away as 250km.

The initial stages of construction at Stonehenge, which are assigned to Phase 1 (Cleal et al. 1995), consisted of the careful laying out of a circular earthwork enclosure comprising the counterscarp bank, the ditch, and the main bank. Also probably assignable to Phase 1 are the Aubrey Holes, a regularly spaced circuit of 56 pits located just inside the aforementioned earthworks. Some of the Aubrey Holes held timber posts and some were reopened in Phase 2 when they received deposits of wood ash or cremated bone. Later stages in the development of Stonehenge included the erection of the sarsen circle and trilithons (Phase 3ii), the positioning of the bluestones in various arrangements (Phases 3i to 3iv) and culminated in the construction of the bluestone circle (Phase 3v) and the creation of the Y and Z hole circles (Phase 3vi).

The diameters of the various circular structures at Stonehenge, taken from data and plans in Cleal et al. 1995, are given in Table 15.1. We have not included the short arcs of Phase 2 postholes which may have been parts of more complete circles but for which "no plausible circular structures have been identified" (Cleal et al. 1995: 151). Trial calculations suggested that the measured diameters of the Phase 1 components can be approximated most closely by a series of concentric circles with modular diameters computed in multiples of 30 from a base unit that is termed here a 'long' foot, equal to 1.056 modern or statute feet (0.32187m.). The errors between these modular diameters and the measured diameters of these components of Stonehenge are small (less than half of one foot) and are within the precision of the original survey measurements, given the uncertainty of estimating the centre lines of large structures within prehistoric monuments.

The subsequent components of construction at Stonehenge are assigned to subdivisions of Phase 3, and these elements of the monument include concentric arrangements of postholes and stone settings (the Y and Z holes) and the sarsen and bluestone circles. While maintaining the radial symmetry of the pre-existing monument these additional components do not obviously lie on circles with diameters that are multiples of 30 'long' feet, with the exception of the Z holes at a diameter very close to 120 'long' feet. However, the Y holes and the bluestone circle appear to respect the overall pattern by exhibiting intermediate diameters of approximately 165 and 75 'long' feet.

Phase	Structural Component	Diameter (metres)	Diameter (stat. ft)	Diameter ('long' ft)	Modular Diameter	Absolute Error
1	*Counterscarp bank*	116.00	380.58	360.40	360	0.40
1	*Ditch (lowest point)*	106.28	348.69	330.20	330	0.20
1	*Bank*	96.60	316.93	300.12	300	0.12
1	*Aubrey Holes*	87.05	285.60	270.45	270	0.45
3vi	*Y holes*	53.57	175.76	166.44	?	-
3vi	*Z holes*	38.57	126.55	119.84	120	0.16
3ii	*Sarsen circle*	30.69	100.68	95.34	?	-
3v	*Bluestone circle*	24.25	79.56	75.34	?	-

Table 15.1: Diameters between centre lines of the major concentric structural components of Stonehenge in units of metres, statute feet and a 'long foot' of 1.056 statute feet (0.32187m). The diameters of the Ditch, Bank and Aubrey Hole circuits are based on computer-generated circles fitted to the present-day centre lines of these structures Cleal *et al.* (1995:24-26). The diameters of the other features were computed directly from plans in Cleal *et al.* (1995) using the same method, whereby the diameter of a circle is calculated geometrically from the distances between three points spaced around the perimeter. The diameter of the centre line of the Ditch, given by Cleal *et al.* (1995:24) as 107.0m, has been reduced by 0.72m because excavations have demonstrated that the centre line of the ditch at surface is displaced away from the centre of the base of the ditch by an average of 0.36m radially towards the exterior of the monument, probably as a result of differential sedimentation from the large internal bank and the lower external counterscarp bank. The actual diameters of some of the circular components of Stonehenge match the modular diameters of circles whose radii are incremented in multiples of 15 'long' feet (i.e. diameter increments of 30 'long' feet). The final column of the table expresses the error in the model as the absolute difference between the measured and the modular diameters: these errors are within the range of precision of the survey measurements given the difficulty of estimating the positions of centre lines of large stone settings and pits.

Phase	Structural Component	Diameter (metres)	Diameter (stat. ft)	Diameter ('long' ft)	Modular Diameter	Absolute Error
2	2F	10.73	35.20	33.33	?	-
2	2E	15.09	49.52	46.90	?	-
2	2D	22.55	73.99	70.06	70	0.06
2	2C	29.01	95.17	90.12	90	0.12
2	2B	35.46	116.35	110.18	110	0.18
2	2A	38.46	126.19	119.50	120	0.50

Table 15.2: Diameters of the Phase 2 concentric structural components of the Durrington Walls Southern Circle, taken from Wainwright with Longworth (1971: fig. 14). The measured diameters of the outer circuits of postholes (components 2D to 2A) are very close to a set of modular diameters that expand in increments of 20 'long' feet.

Other Late Neolithic sites in the Stonehenge area

An appropriate independent test of the concept of a base unit measurement at Stonehenge is provided by the layout of timber post settings at Durrington Walls, a Neolithic henge monument which is located 3km to the northeast of Stonehenge. Excavations at Durrington Walls in 1966-1968 (Wainwright with Longworth 1971) revealed just over two thirds of the ground plan of a concentric arrangement of postholes, designated the Durrington Walls Southern Circle (Table 15.2). Two phases of construction were recognised from the pattern of postholes, with the smaller Phase 1 postholes being laid out on the same diameters as the larger Phase 2 post settings. Recent radiocarbon dating has shown that pits cut into the decayed fill of the Phase 2 timber settings at the Durrington Walls Southern Circle were contemporaneous with the Phase 3ii sarsen circle at Stonehenge (Parker Pearson *et al.* in press), thus the initial laying out of the Durrington Walls Southern Circle most likely took place during or shortly before Phase 3ii at Stonehenge.

The diameters of the outer four of the six Phase 2 post settings at the Durrington Walls Southern Circle demonstrate the use of the same measurement system that was employed at Stonehenge, i.e. based on multiples of 10 of the 'long' foot of 1.056 modern statute feet. However, the increment between diameters at Durrington is 20 'long' feet, compared to the 30 feet increment at Stonehenge, implying radial increments of 10 and 15 'long' feet respectively. The errors between the model (i.e. the modular diameters in multiples of 10 'long' feet) and the actual diameters of the outer circuits of postholes at the Durrington Walls Southern Circle are comparable with those at Stonehenge and are less than half of one foot. These errors may be attributable either to the precision of the construction of the monument or to the precision of modern estimates of the centre lines of the post settings.

Monument and Component	Diameter (metres)	Diameter (stat. ft)	Diameter ('short' ft)	Diameter ('long' ft)
Woodhenge F (axial)	11.80	38.71	40.33	36.66
Woodhenge E (axial)	17.30	56.76	59.12	53.75
Woodhenge D (axial)	22.50	73.82	76.89	69.90
Woodhenge C (axial)	29.40	96.46	100.48	91.34
Woodhenge B (axial)	38.10	125.00	130.21	118.37
Woodhenge A (axial)	44.10	144.69	150.71	137.01
Durrington North Circle (outer)	14.55	47.72	49.71	45.19
Durrington 68 (axial)	14.60	47.90	49.89	45.36
Coneybury	23.68	77.70	80.94	73.58
Sanctuary G	4.11	13.50	14.05	12.77
Sanctuary F	4.32	14.17	14.76	13.42
Sanctuary E	6.05	19.83	20.68	18.80
Sanctuary D	9.75	32.00	33.32	30.29
Sanctuary C	14.17	46.50	48.43	44.02
Sanctuary B	19.66	64.50	67.19	61.08
Sanctuary A	39.32	129.00	134.38	122.16

Table 15.3: Woodhenge, Durrington North Circle and the Sanctuary: measurements taken from Wainwright with Longworth (1971); Durrington 68: measurements taken from Pollard (1995); Coneybury: measurements taken from Richards (1990: 130).

Despite the remarkable parallels between Stonehenge and the Durrington Southern Circle, it appears that the 'long' foot was not the sole unit of measurement used in this region of prehistoric Britain. The dimensions of five other timber monuments in the vicinity of Stonehenge that date to the third millennium BC indicate that the Durrington North Circle, Durrington 68, Woodhenge and (less convincingly) Coneybury may all have utilised a unit based on the 'short' foot measure of 0.96 statute feet (Table 15.3). This 'short' foot unit, which is identical to one version of the Roman foot, was recognised by Cunnington (1929) to have been used at Woodhenge. However, the diameters of the rings of pits and postholes at the Sanctuary do not appear to utilise either the 'short' or the 'long' foot, although regularities in the spacing between the circuits at the Sanctuary suggest that a third unit, perhaps based on a multiple of approximately 1.3 statute feet, may have been used at this site.

A possible relationship between the 'short' and the 'long' foot

At face value the data presented above appear to support the following statements: (a) regularities in the spacing of concentric circuits of Late Neolithic monuments are indicative of the purposeful use of some form of measurement in constructing the monuments; (b) the monuments were constructed using a variety of units of measurement, with perhaps three different units being represented in the small sample studied here; (c) the different measurement units were sometimes shared between geographically proximate and chronologically contemporary structures (Stonehenge and Durrington Southern Circle; Woodhenge and the other Durrington Circles); and (d) the units of measurement were expedient and were not part of a universal measurement system.

The latter statement, however, ignores the interesting numerical relationship between the empirically derived values of the 'short' and 'long' foot, whereby 11 units of the 'short' foot make a length that is identical to 10 units of the 'long' foot.

The 11:10 ratio is found in some historically documented systems of linear measurement, including the British statute system in which the modular lengths of chain, furlong and mile are based on multiples of 11 statute feet (Connor 1987). One reason for using a system with separate units of measurement that are related in the ratio 11:10 stems from the observation that a wheel with a diameter of seven units in the 'short' measure has a perimeter extremely close to 20 units in the 'long' measure. This property arises because the ratio $22 \div 7$ approximates to the mathematical constant Pi (the ratio of a circle's perimeter to its diameter) very closely, in fact to an accuracy close to one part in 2500. The effect of the 11:10 conversion ratio between the measurement systems reduces the perimeter length of 22 units of the 'short' measure to 20 units of the 'long' measure. Thus the 'long' measure would have served as an appropriate base unit for laying out the dimensions of monuments using an odometer or wheel whose diameter was calibrated in multiples of the 'short' unit. As is the case with measuring rods, no evidence for a measurement wheel has been found at a British prehistoric site, although the construction of such a device could have been accomplished by skilled wood-workers such as the builders of Stonehenge. More generally, the existence of a precise 11:10 ratio between two of the measurement units used to lay out the Late Neolithic monuments in the Stonehenge area is suggestive of a relatively sophisticated system of measurement that may warrant further investigation.

Discussion

We view these findings as interesting but note also that they are preliminary and in need of corroboration using a larger sample of accurate data for the dimensions of earthen, timber and stone monuments of the Late Neolithic. Such data are best obtained from original plans and publications, as the dimensions presented in secondary sources have often been rounded up or down to the nearest metre (e.g. Gibson 1998) or even to the nearest 5 or 10 feet (e.g. Burl 1969). Previous attempts to demonstrate the existence of quanta in the dimensions of prehistoric monuments have shown that substantial samples of accurate data are required to achieve statistical significance at a level that satisfies scientific criteria (Kendall 1974; Freeman 1976). The data from multicircuit Neolithic monuments currently available to us are as yet too limited to be subject to a formal statistical analysis, and we condition our conclusions accordingly.

The regularities in the spacing of the concentric circuits at Stonehenge, Woodhenge and the Durrington circles suggest the use of at least two units of measurement in the designs of the Late Neolithic monuments of the Stonehenge area. The base units of these measurement systems, which are designated here the 'long' and 'short' foot, are linked by a simple numerical ratio and they may therefore be alternatives within a single measurement system. It is also possible that the base units actually used in laying out the monuments were five times larger than these foot-sized units, as the radii of the concentric circuits at all of the monuments appear to be spaced in increments of 5, 10 or 15 feet.

The use of multiple base measurements in prehistory adds substantially to the complexity of the problem of detecting quanta in data sets comprising the dimensions of prehistoric monuments. This complication can be addressed by distinguishing between two patterns of regularity: those contained *within* single constructional phases at individual monuments (for example, Stonehenge Phase 1), and those observed *between* different phases of construction or between different monuments. We suspect that a single unit of measurment was used for any given phase of construction, a proposition that is testable at sites like Stonehenge where the chronology of construction is now reasonably well established (Cleal *et al.* 1995; Parker Pearson *et al.* in press).

Some variation in the base unit of measurement across Neolithic Britain might be expected, both on the broad grounds that strongly regional styles of monument design and construction characterise the British Neolithic (Harding, 1995), and on the more specific grounds that the analyses by Kendall (1974) and Freeman (1976) of Alexander Thom's stone circle data found only regional (i.e. Scottish) evidence for Thom's postulated prehistoric measurement unit. The findings reported here tend to confirm these conjectures by indicating heterogeneity of measurement units within a geographically and temporally constrained sample, although we have also shown that some of the different base units in use in the Stonehenge area may be co-ordinated elements of a common measurement system.

We believe that the dimensions recorded from archaeologically excavated monuments are superior to those obtained from field survey measurements of megalithic structures, primarily because the dimensions of stone circles may be affected by later rebuilding phases (both in prehistoric times and in the modern era – cf. Barnatt and Moir, 1984). We also note that the use of a unit of measurement may be reflected more faithfully in the spacing between circuits within a single monument than in a composite data set compiled from measurements of different monuments that may have been constructed by unrelated groups at various times.

References

Barnatt, J. and Moir, G. 1984. Stone circles and megalithic mathematics. *Proceedings of the Prehistoric Society* 50: 197-216.

Baxter, M. 2003. *Statistics in Archaeology*. London: Arnold.

Bewley, R.H., Crutchley, S.P. and Shell, C.A. 2005. New light on an ancient landscape: lidar survey in the Stonehenge World Heritage Site. *Antiquity* 79: 636-647.

Bryan, P.G. and Clowes, M. 1997. Surveying Stonehenge by photogrammetry. *Photogrammetric Record* 15: 739-51.

Burl, H.A.W. 1969. Henges: internal features and regional groups. *Archaeological Journal* 126: 1-28.

Chippindale, C. 1983. *Stonehenge Complete*. London: Thames and Hudson.

Cleal, R.M.J., Walker, K.E. & Montague, R. 1995 *Stonehenge in its Landscape: Twentieth-Century Excavations*. London: English Heritage.

Connor, R.D. 1987. *The Weights and Measures of England*. London: HMSO.

Cunnington, M.E. 1929. *Woodhenge*. Devizes: Simpson.

Freeman, P.R. 1976. A Bayesian analysis of the Megalithic Yard. *Journal of the Royal Statistical Society A* 139: 20-55.

Gibson, A. 1998. *Stonehenge and Timber Circles*. Stroud: Sutton.

Glob, P.V. 1974. *The Mound People: Danish Bronze Age man preserved*. London: Faber.

Harding, J. 1995. Social histories and regional perspectives in the Neolithic of lowland England. *Proceedings of the Prehistoric Society* 61: 117-136.

Kendall, D.G. 1974. Hunting quanta. *Philosophical Transactions of the Royal Society of London A* 276: 231-266.

Michell, J. 1981. *Ancient Metrology*. Bristol: Pentacle Books.

Neal, J. 2000. *All Done with Mirrors*. London: The Secret Academy.

Parker Pearson, M., Cleal, R., Marshall, P., Needham, S., Pollard, J., Richards, C, Ruggles, C., Sheridan, A., Thomas, J. Tilley, C., Welham, K., Chamberlain, A., Chenery, C., Evans, J., Knüsel, C., Linfords N., Martin, L., Montgomery, J., Payne, A. and Richards. M. Forthcoming. The age of Stonehenge. *Antiquity*.

Petrie W.M.F. 1880. *Stonehenge: Plans, Descriptions and Theories*. London: Stanford.

Piggott, S. 1985. *William Stukeley. An Eighteenth Century Antiquary*. Revised and enlarged edition. London: Thames & Hudson.

Pitts, M. 2000. *Hengeworld*. London: Century.

Pollard, J. 1995. The Durrington 68 timber circle: a forgotton Late Neolithic Monument. *Wiltshire Archaeological and Natural History Magazine* 88: 122-125.

Raftery, B. 1986. A wooden trackway of Iron Age date in Ireland. *Antiquity* 60: 50-53.

Richards, J. 1990. *The Stonehenge Environs Project*. London: English Heritage.

Ruggles, C. 1999. *Astronomy in Prehistoric Britain and Ireland*. New Haven: Yale University Press.

Sievers, S. 2002. Auf dem Weg zur Stadt: die keltische Oppidazivilisation. In M. Nawroth, R. von Schnurbein, R.-M. Weiss and M. Will (eds) *Menschen – Zeiten – Raume: archäologie in Deutschland*. Berlin: Staatliche Museen zu Berlin. 203-09.

Stukeley, W. 1740. *Stonehenge: a Temple Restor'd to the British Druids*. London: Innys and Manby.

Thom, A. 1955. A statistical examination of the megalithic sites of Britain. *Journal of the Royal Statistical Society A* 118: 275-291.

Thom, A. 1967. *Megalithic Sites in Britain*. Oxford: Clarendon Press.

Thom, A. and Thom, A. 1988. The metrology and geometry of Megalithic man. In Ruggles, C.L.N. (ed.) *Records in Stone: papers in memory of Alexander Thom*. Cambridge: Cambridge University Press. 132-151.

Wainwright, G.J. with Longworth, I.H. 1971 *Durrington Walls: excavations 1966-1968*. London: Society of Antiquaries.

Chapter 16

Stonehenge – Olenok, Siberia: universals or different phenomena? Ethnoarchaeological observations of a midsummer rite

Ole Grøn and Maria Magdalena Kosko

Langelands Museum, Denmark, and Institute of Archaeology, University College London

Introduction: variability and similarity

The idea of cultural universals has played an important role in anthropology through time (*e.g.* Murdock 1957; Pinker 2002; Tylor 1889). Even though the notion of general cultural traits appears to play a peripheral role in the recent archaeological and ethnoarchaeological debate, behavioural repeatability at different scale-levels forms the backbone of the analysis of archaeological data, as already formulated by the Swede Sven Nilsson who, inspired by Cuvier's 'Comparative Anatomical Method', applied his own 'Comparative Ethnological Method' to Swedish archaeological material, and thus preceded and influenced later systematic ethnoarchaeological approaches. A central question is to what degree and how such phenomena can be utilised in cultural interpretation (Deetz 1968; Grøn 1991; Nilsson 1835, 1868).

One problem is that cross-cultural similarities that can be observed are often of a character so variable in their appearance that they are difficult to fit into a strict and well-defined terminology, in spite of the fact that their central elements appear to be general. The bear ritual is a good example. There appears to have been a shared attitude in circum-polar hunter-gatherer societies to the bear yet the ritual manifestations of this are expressed in a multitude of ways, related to different expressions of identities of social groups at different scales, with groupings at the clan level having a key role (Barth 1969; 1987; Frobenius 1904; Grøn *et al.* 2003; Myrstad 1996; Paproth 1976; Shirokogoroff 1935:11-39; Tanner 1979: 162-181).

A central terminological problem appears to be that general behavioural elements do not act in isolation but interact with other elements. For instance, the general idea of the bear ritual appears to interact with the universal tendency of neighbouring groupings to express their difference through variations in their ritual (Barth 1987).

Another problem is obviously that different features can have meanings so similar that they can substitute for each other. Amongst Evenk hunter-gatherers, for instance, the tree, the tripod and the hearth express the same basic idea: communication between the three worlds (the upper world of fire, winds and unborn souls; the middle world of earth where we live; and the underworld of water and dead souls). This is why the riding-reindeer of the deceased Evenk in some areas was/is hung on a tree, but

in other areas was/is hung on a tripod – in both cases connected to a hearth. The arrangement is supposed to facilitate the soul of the animal in following its master to serve him/her in the upper world.

In a number of cases it has been observed that the Evenk put the clothes of the deceased, and a pillow or a pair of shoes on the stump of a tree, felled on the spot where somebody died. In each case the body was buried in the local village cemetery in a typical Russian 'state burial'. In Evenk terms the significant feature, however, is that the remains of the soul of the deceased are preserved in the material deposited at the tree, consonant with a traditional 'air-burial' in which the coffin/dugout-boat/tree-trunk, supported by two felled trees, formerly contained the body.

In general, all cultural aspects that can be varied are used to mark the identity of different groups. 'Everybody wants to be a little bit different' as one Evenk expressed it. Language can vary so much that neighbouring clans have problems understanding each other (Donner 1915: 75). Ornamental aspects of material culture that do not interfere with its practical function are typically used to mark identity. Aspects of it that are, to a higher degree, dictated by its practical function are normally found to vary less. Variations in ritual and cosmology are used as well. It is my subjective feeling that the whole complex of possibilities for marking identity is used in a dynamic way to express the relations between different groups (Barth 1969; Donner 1915: 75; Shirokogoroff 1935: 11-39). In some cases, identity-marking seems to be able to over-ride the practical aspects of material culture such as the example of Sami hats being worn by males (Hætta 2002: 99-100).

It is important to understand that small-scale societies' logic and basic principles for perceiving are considerably more variable and pragmatic than those used by industrial societies. In the former, logically consistent systems do not play an important role as a standard for co-ordination and exchange of observations within large areas, but are based on what can be agreed on in smaller groups as being reasonable (Shirokogoroff 1935: 117-120).

Assemblies and circular sacred sites in ethnoarchaeological perspective

The discussion of a universal idea expressed in a number of different but related ways seems relevant for the

Fig. 16.1. Stonehenge with earthworks and stones (photo by Mike Parker Pearson).

understanding of the large range of British and even European circular timber and stone structures, typically dating to the Late Neolithic and Early Bronze Age, such as Stonehenge (Figure 16.1), Woodhenge and the 'seahenges' Holme I and II (Behrens 1981; Champion 2000; Clark 2005; Cunnington 1927; Fowler 1996; Parker Pearson and Ramilisonina 1998).

It is well known that stones in 'megalithic' barrows can be replaced by timber (Ashbee 1970: 33-54; Madsen 1997). Therefore it is no surprise to see that circular structures can be expressed in both stone and timber (Parker Pearson and Ramilisonina 1998).

In some cases circular structures with a central grave are regarded as features related to burial-mounds with central burials, such as a Danish example (Ramskou 1970). Even Woodhenge has a central burial (Cunnington 1927). The question is whether these two categories of features exclude each other or should be regarded as similar phenomena sometimes related to burials.

Circular or, at times, square features or arrangements can symbolise the 'Tent of the Universe' enclosing a central feature symbolising the World Tree or *axis mundi* (pole, hearth, altar *etc.*); their use for annual rituals including

contests and circular dances as well as in other important rituals is known in a large number of small-scale cultures all over the world. It is often the case that the basic layout, manifested in different ways materially, can be used for all types of celebrations from general group assemblies to local low-level celebrations. The time of the year when general assemblies are held depends, according to ethnographic and ethnoarchaeological information, to a large extent on the group's economic activities. They are, therefore, not necessarily held at the time of the solstice. For the Evenk hunter-gatherers who hunt migrating reindeer in the Olenok area in Siberia, ceremonies are held in the autumn in relation to the main migration of the reindeer (for this and other examples see Bauer 1996; Campbell 1988: 135-146, 159, 216-231; Grøn 2005; Gusinde 1931: 808-1083; Holmberg 1922; Thomas 1959: 251-257; Parker Pearson and Ramilisonina 1998; Radcliffe-Brown 1948: 128-132, 215-216; Schmidt 1935: 88-89; 1941; 1955: 442-456).

In a prehistoric context it would be natural to think that the more elaborate the structure the more central a role it played. Even though assemblies of recent small-scale cultures, in some cases, seem tied to a single site over longer periods, one should be open to the possibility that they can move or change, for instance, in relation to

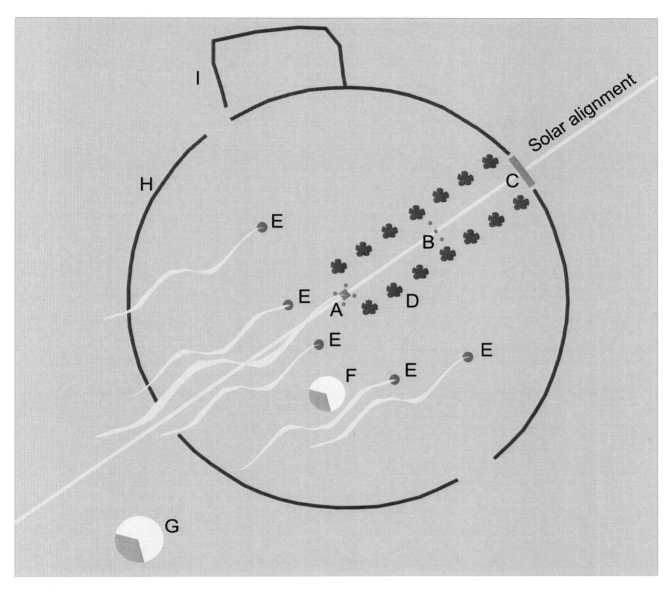

Fig. 16.2. The place of celebration of the midsummer ritual in Olenok, Siberia. A: The central altar and fireplace with four 'three-world-poles' with onion-shaped tops. Each pole symbolises the three worlds. This is where the shaman carried out the main part of his activities during the ritual, facing the position where the sun would rise. B: Three 'three-world-poles' on a line perpendicular to the solar alignment. C: Large wooden sun symbol. D: Alley of young larch trees from the forest 'planted' in the ground and decorated with garlands of coloured rags on strings meant to keep evil spirits away. E: Fires lit before the fire on the altar is lit. F: Tent without cover – apparently an area for placing requisites so that they should not be damaged by the dancers or the audience. G: The large tent where the shaman stayed when he was not performing. H: Pole-fence marking the border of the site ornamented with garlands of coloured rags meant to keep evil spirits away. I: enclosure for the dancers to change their costumes.

changes or 'reformations' of the local cult. This can be observed at other central Evenk sites which have been abandoned because they 'stink' and their vegetation needs regeneration (Barth 1987: 46-54; Grøn 2005; Grøn *et al.* in press a). This would fit the observation in places like Durrington Walls of several timber circles close to each other (Cunnington 1927; Parker Pearson and Ramilisonina 1998).

An Evenk midsummer festival

Early in the morning of 7th July 2001 we were invited to participate in the local midsummer celebration or 'yizik'

in a 'secret place' in Olenok after a festival with dancing, singing and wrestling on 6th July. This was the first legal celebration of this ritual after it had been prohibited for a long period during the Communist regime. As well as the normal excitement, this in itself caused the whole business to be ridden with conflict from the beginning.

The Sacha Republic (Yakutia) is dominated by Yakut pastoralists and farmers who penetrated into this area in the 17th century when it was dominated by an old population of Evenk and Eveni hunter-gatherers co-existing with some other groups (Долпих 1960; Гурвич 1966:268-269). In the 20th century the Yakuts have actively been suppressing the other ethnic groups in the republic in the most chauvinistic way and officially and actively support research promoting the idea that the Yakut culture is the traditionally dominant culture in the area.

In the northern Olenok area the advancing Yakuts had to give up their 'Neolithic' economy and turn to hunting and gathering like the local Evenk, a process that created an interesting mixture of the two cultures with Yakutian as the spoken language but with an economy, material culture, cosmology and ritual life that is mainly Evenk.

The government of the Sacha Republic in Yakutsk had sent a cultural consultant to help 'reconstruct' the 'yizik'. His presence caused problems not only with the local Evenk but also with the local Yakut who generally enjoy good relations with the large local population of Evenk. The cultural consultant had unsuccessfully demanded that somebody should provide him with two horses for the ritual of which one should be white. However, the horse is a central Yakut symbol and nobody was willing to help. The Evenk use a white reindeer. In the end he became so furious at the resistance he met that he left the area prematurely.

The celebrations must be seen as a fusion between Yakut and Evenk cultural elements including Yakut reconstruction of some of the details. However, the participation of the local Evenk in the event as well as their whole attitude to it (apart from the confrontations with the presence of a Yakut official) seemed to reflect that it was acceptable and well-known to them. It is most likely that the tradition has continued in this area through its period of prohibition. The Evenk are known to have hidden their ritual places and shamans in the forest through critical periods. With the pragmatism that was displayed by many local administrations on this point such a practice was in many cases unlikely to cause problems. The main features of the ritual must therefore be assumed to be in accordance with Evenk tradition.

During the celebrations, the shaman first lights fires at 'E' and then on the central altar at 'A' (Figure 16.2). The dancing is carried out in the ritual alley marked by the larch trees and is continued southwest of the central altar inside the surrounding fence by groups of dancers of different ages (Figure 16.3). Generally the male dancers occupy its southwest side and the female dancers its northeast side. When the sun rises they raise their hands and praise it. After that the young dancers begin a round-dance, southwest of the central altar, symbolising – among other things - the sun. After some time the shaman and the audience join the round-dance.

The celebration area is organised and thought of as a large tent 'of the universe' with its entrance against the rising sun. The alley matches the entrance zone where firewood is normally placed. The shaman's place is in the back of the tent, which is also the position he takes when visiting the tents of households other than his own (Odgaard et al. 2006).

The ritual lasted a couple of hours. After that, the participants went home and slept for a couple of hours. At 11:30am the festival continued with round-dances and more official speeches in the dancing area.

Discussion

It is tempting to see the 'yizik' in Olenok as a likely model for activities that were carried out within Stonehenge. It is not proposed as an exact model, but as an approximation or 'rough-out' because the detailed configuration of the rituals of different groups can be expected to have varied from clan to clan and through time, as is the case for most other cultural expressions in small-scale societies (Barth 1987: 46-54; Grøn et al. 2003). According to this approach, the differences that can be observed between various circular structures are to be expected rather than being a surprise.

The Olenok site demonstrates that such sites can be organised so that they focus on astronomical phenomena without being 'observatories' (e.g. Hoyle 1967; Trotter 1927). Its alley is oriented simply to match the position of the sun at the time that the ritual is to be carried out. In a way, this can be conceived as a 'clock'.

Because the central gatherings of the different groups, that can be or have been observed recently, can be held at different times of the year, the prehistoric structures should not all be expected to focus on this particular solar alignment. However, this may be an important feature for agricultural societies as opposed to hunter-gatherer communities.

A co-location of central ritual and assembly sites with the burials of the forefathers/ancestors of the different groups could logically lead to the combination of burial-mound like features and central circular structures. And, on the other hand, the burials of prominent members of society could be accompanied by rituals drawing on spatial patterns and frames of the same character as those of the central assembly sites. The main thing is to understand the important role of individual variations in ritual and ritual features, and the mechanisms behind it (Barth 1987: 46-54; Grøn et al. 2003; Grøn et al. in press b).

The perspective of viewing circular structures as material reflections of a cultural 'universal' is an exciting one. It might be worth carrying out detailed registration of existing information on recent ritual contexts that could further elucidate their use and meaning. It might just be that Sven Nilsson's 1866 interpretation of Stonehenge, except for certain details that appear unlikely, did in principle hit the right keys (Nilsson 1866).

Fig. 16.3. Upper photograph (A): view from the central altar ('A' in Figure 16.2) down the ritual alley flanked by young larch trees cut from the forest and 'planted', with garlands of coloured rags between them. The three 'three-world-poles' are in the middle and the sun symbol at its end. Lower photograph (B): The shaman facing the altar and the sun just at the moment when it rises, with the male dancers behind him to his right and the female dancers behind him to his left. They are praising it.

References

Ashbee, P. 1970: *The Earthen Long Barrow in Britain.* London: Dent.

Barth, F. 1969. Introduction. In F. Barth (ed.) *Ethnic groups and boundaries.* Boston: Little, Brown & Company. 9-38.

Barth, F. 1987. *Cosmologies in the Making. A Generative Approach to Cultural Variation in Inner New Guinea.* Cambridge: Cambridge University Press.

Bauer, B.S. 1996. Legitimation of the state in Inca myth and ritual. *American Anthropologist* (new series) 98: 327-337.

Behrens, H. 1981. The first 'Woodhenge' in middle Europa. *Antiquity* 55: 172-181.

Campbell, J. 1988. *Historical Atlas of World Mythology. Vol. I: The Way of the Animal Powers. Part 2: Mythologies of the Great Hunt.* New York: Harper & Row.

Champion, M. 2000. *Seahenge: A Contemporary Chronicle.* London: Barnwell's Print Ltd.

Clark, B. 2003-2005. Photos of Holme 2. Accessed 3.10.2006.
http://www.megalithic.co.uk/article.php?sid=10631

Cunnington, M.E. 1927. Prehistoric timber circles. *Antiquity* 1: 92-95.

Deetz, J. 1968. The inference of residence and descent rules from archaeological data. In S.R. Binford and L.R. Binford (eds) *New Perspectives in Archaeology.* New York : Aldine. 41-48.

Долгих, В.О. 1960. *Родовой и племенной состав народов сибири в XVII в.* Москва: Издателъство Академиа Наук СССР.

Donner, K. 1915. *Bland Samojeder i Sibirien åren 1911-1913, 1914.* Helsingfors.

Frobenius, L. 1904. *Geografische Kulturkunde. Eine Darstellung der Beziehungen zwischen der Erde und der Kultur nach älteren und neueren Reiseberichten zur Belebung des geographischen Unterrichts.* Leipzig: Brandstetter.

Fowler, M.J.F. 1996. High-resolution satellite imagery in archaeological application: a Russian satellite photograph of the Stonehenge region. *Antiquity* 70: 667-671.

Grøn, O. 1991. A method for reconstruction of social organization in prehistoric societies and examples of practical application. In O. Grøn, E. Engelstad and I. Lindblom (eds) *Social Space. Proceedings of an interdisciplinary conference on human spatial behaviour in dwellings and settlements.* Odense: Odense University Press. 100-117.

Grøn, O. 2005. A Siberian perspective on the north European Hamburgian Culture: a study in applied hunter-gatherer ethnoarchaeology. *Before Farming* [online version] 2005/1: article 3.

Grøn, O., Kuznetsov, O. and Turov, M.G. 2003. Cultural micro-mosaics – a problem for the archaeological culture concept? In J. Bergstøl (ed.) *Scandinavian Archaeological Practice - in Theory. Proceedings from the 6th Nordic TAG, Oslo 2001.* Oslo: Oslo Archaeological Series no. 1. 342-350.

Grøn, O., Turov, M. and Klokkernes, T. Forthcoming a. Spiritual and material aspects of everyday ritual negotiation. Ethnoarchaeological data from the Evenk, Siberia.

Grøn, O., Klokkernes, T. and Turov, M. Forthcoming b. Cultural small-scale variations in a hunter-gatherer society – or – 'everybody wants to be a little bit different!'. An ethnoarchaeological study from Siberia.

Гурвич, И.С. 1966. *Этническая историа северо-востока сибири.* Москва: Издателъство «Наука».

Gusinde, M. 1931. *Die Feuerland Indianer. 1 Band. Die Selk'nam.* Vienna: Verlag der Internationalen Zeitschrift "Anthropos".

Holmberg, U. 1922. *Der Baum des Lebens. Götinnen und Baumkult.* Helsinki: Edition Amalia.

Hoyle, F. 1966. Speculations on Stonehenge. *Antiquity* 40: 262-276.

Hætta, O.M. 2002. *Samene. Nordkalottens urfolk.* Kristianssand: Norwegian Academic Press.

Madsen, T. 1997. Earthen long barrows and timber structures: aspects of the Early Neolithic mortuary practice in Denmark. *Proceedings of the Prehistoric Society* 45: 301-320.

Thomas, E.M. 1959. *The Harmless People.* New York: Alfred A. Knopf.

Murdock, G.P.1957. World ethnographic sample. *American Anthropologist* 59: 664-687.

Myrstad, R. 1996. *Bjørnegraver i Nord-Norge. Spor etter den samiske bjørnekulten.* Masters theses in archaeology, University of Tromsø, Norway.

Nilsson, S. 1835. *Skandinaviens Fauna, Foglarna, första & andra bandet. Andra och reviderade upplagan av Svensk Ornithologi eller Beskrifning öfver Sveriges Foglar.* Lund: Berlinska Boktryckeriet. XII-LII.

Nilsson, S. 1866. Stonehenge: an attempt to explain the above monument. *Transactions of the Ethnological Society of London* 4: 244-263.

Nilsson, S. 1868. *The Primitive Inhabitants of Scandinavia. A description of the implements, dwellings, tombs, and mode of living of the savages in the north of Europe during the Stone Age.* Longmans, Green & Co.

Odgaard, U., Fog Jensen, J., Grøn, O, and Anderson, D.G. 2006: Comments on David G. Andersons: Dwellings, Storage and Summer Site Structure Among Siberian Orochen Evenkis: Hunter-Gatherer Vernacular Architecture under Post-Socialist Conditions. *Norwegian Archaeological Review 39: 162-171.*

Paproth, H.-J. 1976. *Studien über das Bärenzeremoniell. I. Bärenjagdriten und Bärenfeste bei den tungusischen Völkern.* Uppsala: Skrifter utgivna av Religionshistoriska Institutionen i Uppsala.

Parker Pearson, M. and Ramilisonina 1998. Stonehenge for the ancestors: the stones pass on the message. *Antiquity* 72: 308-326.

Pinker, S. 2002: *The Blank Slate. The Modern Denial of Human Nature*. Penguin Books (Viking): London.

Radcliffe-Brown, A.R. 1948. *The Andaman Islanders*. Glencoe IL: The Free Press.

Ramskou, T. 1970. Et Dansk Stonehenge? *Nationalmuseets Arbejdsmark* 1970: 59-66.

Schmidt, P.W. 1935. *Der Ursprung der Gottesidee. Eine Historish-Kritische und Positive Studie. Band VI. 9. Abteilung: Die Religion der Urvölker V*. Münster in Westfalen: Aschedorffsche Verlagsbuchandlung.

Schmidt, P.W. 1941. Die heilige Mittelpfal des Hauses. *Anthropos* 35-36: 966-969.

Schmidt, P.W. 1955. *Der Ursprung der Gottesidee. Eine Historish-Kritische und Positive Studie. III. Teil. Der Religionen der Hirtenvolker VI. XII. Band. Synthesis der Religionen Der Asiatischen und der Afrikanischen Hirtenvölker*. Münster in Westfalen: Aschedorffsche Verlagsbuchandlung.

Shirokogoroff, S. 1935. *Psychomental Complex of the Tungus*. London: Kegan Paul, Trench, Trubner & Co.

Tanner, A. 1979. *Bringing Home Animals. Religious Ideology and Mode of Production of the Mistassini Cree Hunters*. London: C. Hurst & Co.

Trotter, A.P.1927. Stonehenge as an astronomical instrument. *Antiquity* 1: 42-53.

Tylor, E.B. 1889. On a method of investigating the development of institutions; applied to laws of marriage and descent. *The Journal of the Anthropological Institute of Great Britain and Ireland* 18: 245-272.

Chapter 17

Stonehenge - its landscape and its architecture: a reanalysis

Christopher Tilley, Colin Richards, Wayne Bennett and David Field

Department of Social Anthropology, UCL, School of Arts, Histories and Cultures, University of Manchester, Dillington House, Somerset, and English Heritage, Swindon

Introduction

Almost all twentieth century considerations of Stonehenge have, perhaps understandably, ignored the fact that Stonehenge exists in, is related to, and is embedded in a landscape. The focus of attention has always been the stones themselves and the chronology and structural development of the monument. Thus Gowland (1902), Hawley (1921-28) and Atkinson (1956) make no reference to the landscape setting of Stonehenge at all and only Atkinson mentions and provides a map of monuments in its vicinity (*ibid.*: 146). The Royal Commission of Historical Monuments usefully puts Stonehenge into a wider spatial context in terms of an inventory of other sites in the Stonehenge 'environs' (RCHME 1979) while *The Stonehenge Environs Project* (Richards 1990) reports on the results of fieldwalking and excavations within a 33km square box centered on Stonehenge. However, in both of these studies the landscape contexts and interrelationships of monuments are not considered either from the perspective of Stonehenge or from anywhere else. The landscape, in both cases, is simply a more or less blank spatial field for analysis. Previous generations of archaeologists have diligently worked in the Stonehenge landscape while simultaneously ignoring it!

The first publication to actually start to seriously consider the landscape around Stonehenge was published little more than a decade ago (Cleal *et al.*1995). In an excellent discussion Mike Allen considers, in some detail, the geographical and topographical setting of the monument in relation to Bronze Age barrow cemeteries, and Julie Gardiner the view to it from the Avenue (Allen in Cleal *et al.* 1995: 34-40 and Gardiner in Cleal *et al.* 40), research that will be discussed in some detail below. Elsewhere in the book other monuments in more or less the same spatial box used by the RCHME (1979) and Julian Richards (1990) are briefly considered in relation to various proposed phases of Stonehenge. The title of this book *Stonehenge in its Landscape* promises a great deal but the subtitle 'Twentieth Century Excavations' indicates what is, in fact, its main concern. Exon, Gaffney, Woodward and Yorston (2000), in contrast, devote a short book to a discussion of the landscape around Stonehenge. However, their study is almost exclusively concerned with monument inter-visibility, combining primarily the use of GIS data with some phenomenological fieldwork. Although they discuss the approach to Stonehenge along the Avenue and from

elsewhere in some detail (see below) they do not consider Stonehenge itself, presumably because of Allen's pre-existing work on the visual field from the monument itself. Both of these studies very usefully concern themselves with issues of monument visibility, providing important insights which inform the discussion in this paper. But other aspects of the landscape around Stonehenge, principally the form and topographic character of the hills and ridges, the river valleys and coombes, or dry valleys, are scarcely considered at all. Discussion of such landscape features around Stonehenge is confined by Allen to mentioning which nearer or more distant ridges or hills can be seen. Exon *et al.* throughout their book rarely consider any other aspect of the landscape beyond monument visibility and intervisibility. In both these studies, the Stonehenge landscape and its topography tend to be considered only in terms of a series of monuments that at various times are visible or not. In other words, 'culture' is writ large in these studies but 'nature' has been virtually excluded. A much more holistic approach is adopted in this paper paying as much attention to the 'natural environment' of Stonehenge as to the positioning and visibility of monuments within it.

The aim of the first part of this paper is to address, and to attempt to answer, one simple question: why is Stonehenge located where it is in the landscape? Why here? Why *this* place? In all the voluminous literature on Stonehenge this question never actually appears to have been directly addressed. In attempting to provide an answer to this question we attempt to show the manner in which a consideration of the monument in its landscape context provides the basis for a novel interpretation of the architecture of Stonehenge itself and the locations of the Bronze Age barrow cemeteries around it, which forms the second part of the discussion.

In relation to the question raised above the paper presents a few of the preliminary results of a phenomenological landscape survey forming part of the Stonehenge Riverside Project (see Parker Pearson *et al.* 2006). This survey involves the description and analysis of a 180sq km area of land with the henge monument of Durrington Walls at its centre (Figure 17.1). The area covered in this survey includes the entire landscape area covered in the 'Stonehenge environs' project (Richards 1990; Figure 17.2), that in Cleal *et al.* (1995), the far wider area considered by Exon *et al.* (2000), except to the south of their 'enlarged study area'. It extends considerably further to the east of the Avon and to the north in the

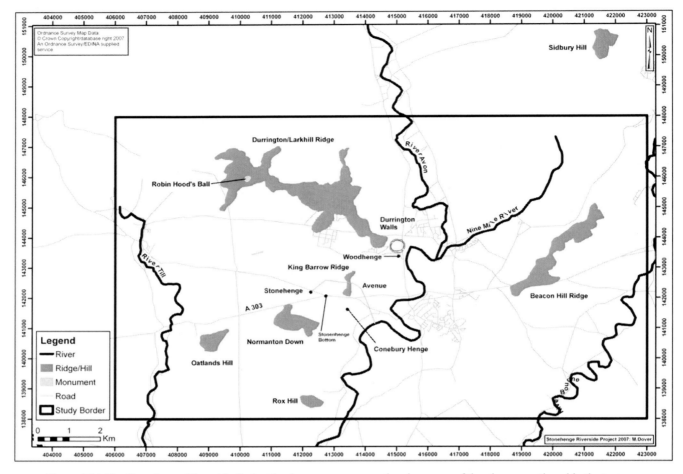

Figure 17.1 The Stonehenge Riverside Project landscape survey area showing some of the places mentioned in the text

Salisbury Plain army training ranges than the Exon *et al.* landscape study. Research has involved walking this entire landscape and studying in the field all known barrows and the locations of ring ditch sites recorded from aerial photographs.

Stonehenge in its landscape

What is remarkable about the location of Stonehenge in its immediate landscape is that it appears to be absolutely unremarkable. Allen rightly notes that when looking towards Stonehenge from any direction the location is undistinguished: 'without the monument in place it would not easily be distinguished from the gently undulating surrounding countryside, and it cannot be said to form an obviously important landscape feature from any direction' (Allen in Cleal *et al.* 1995: 37). The monument is located on virtually flat ground on a very gentle west-east slope which steepens markedly as it approaches the dry valley system of Stonehenge Bottom some 400 m distant to the east. Immediately to the north and south of the enclosing bank and ditch the land dips away towards shallow coombes running down to Stonehenge Bottom. The drop in height to the bottoms of these coombes is about 10 m in about 300m to the north and 500m to the south. To the west the land rises by a similar amount. The area in the immediate vicinity of Stonehenge is

ambiguously delimited. It is not located on a well-defined ridge or spur, of which there are many in the surrounding landscape. The land on which it is built is only 100m high. There is absolutely no drama with regard to its location. The drama and theatrical power of the monument seems to derive entirely from the sheer size and height of the stones, and without these the place would long since have been forgotten.

In essence Stonehenge confounds the, perhaps all too contemporary expectation, that such an impressive monument might be located elsewhere in the landscape, for example on the top of the Beacon Hill Ridge 7km to the east or perhaps on the Sidbury Hill summit 12km to the northeast or, nearer, on the Durrington/Larkhill ridge 2km to the north (see Figure 17.1). However, monuments and barrows of any kind seldom occupy the very highest hill and ridge summits in the 180sq km considered in the landscape survey, and even some more localised high points and ridges are often entirely avoided. Similarly, very few barrows are located in the 'depths' of this landscape, at or near the bottom of coombes or river valleys. The vast majority occur in intermediate locations often on the mid points of gently sloping ridges and spurs. The location of Stonehenge is thus quite typical for that occupied by the many and somewhat later Bronze Age barrow cemeteries in the area. It is absolutely

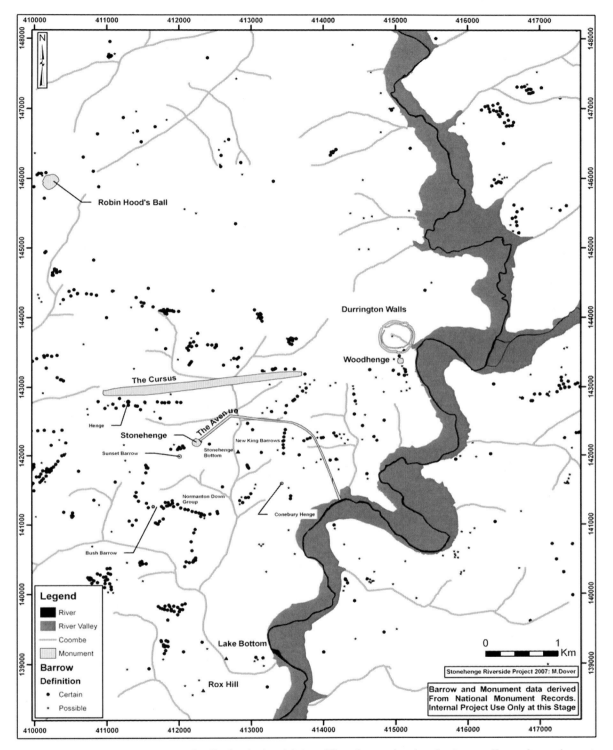

Figure 17.2 The landscape and barrow distribution in the vicinity of Stonehenge showing the Avon valley and coombe systems

ordinary in this respect. Perhaps this is not so surprising in the light of its use as a major cremation cemetery in Phase 2 before the erection of the stones (Cleal *et al.* 1995: 115). In many respects its location might be regarded as conforming to an expected norm. But while it conforms to the position of many later Bronze Age barrows it is actually built 500-1000 years earlier.

Allen (in Cleal *et al.* 1995) discusses Stonehenge in relation to a 'visual envelope' around it and considers both views out from Stonehenge and views into the monument in relation to a 'foreground', the nearest ground to the ditched enclosure, a 'near horizon' created by slight ridges, and a 'far' and a 'distant' horizon. Such horizons at different distances from the monument frequently merge and, in practice, it is very difficult to

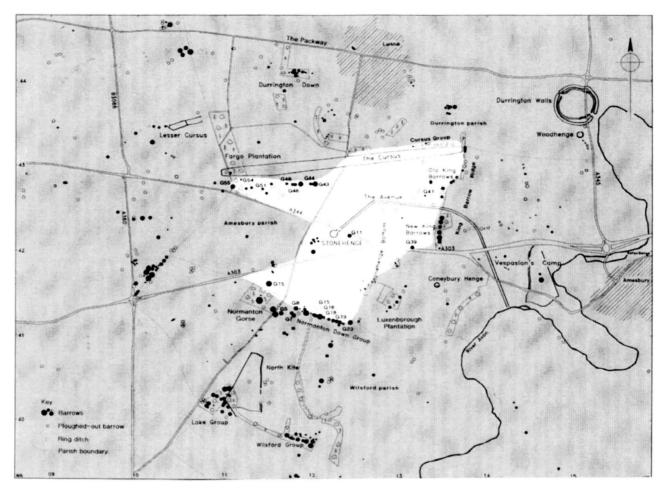

Figure 17.3 The visual envelope in the immediate vicinity of Stonehenge. The area bounded by the near horizon is unshaded (from Allen in Cleal *et al.* 1995)

distinguish between them. Furthermore even within parts of the immediate 'visual envelope' around Stonehenge there are lower lying areas along Stonehenge Bottom, to the north and east, which cannot be seen from the monument, nor is it visible from them. The interior of the visible field is thus more complex than that represented and gives a misleading impression that everything within it is visible (see Figure 17.3). Allen shows how important Bronze Age barrow cemeteries, principally those to the south on Normanton Down, to the east, those running along King Barrow ridge (the New and Old King Barrows), and the Cursus group of barrows to the northwest run along the edges of his 'near' or 'far' horizons indicating that they were deliberately located so as to be visible, running along the skyline, from Stonehenge itself.

Some, but by no means all, of these barrows are indeed monumental and dominant landmarks when seen from the perspective of the Stonehenge enclosure. Beyond this horizon barrows cannot be seen but other topographic features are visible in the far distance, notably the Beacon Hill Ridge to the east and Rox Hill to the south.

This is a rolling chalk downland landscape in which topographic distinctions are subtle. It has been, and still is, primarily shaped by the agency of water. Throughout the study area the following seven main topographic elements may be distinguished:

1. the Avon river valley, the only perennial water source
2. the winterbourne river valleys of the Till, the Bourne and Nine Mile Rivers to the west and east
3. the coombes or dry valley systems which run into these perennial or seasonal watercourses
4. well-defined and smoothly sloping ridges and spurs of various forms running between these valleys and coombes
5. more rounded localised high points such as Rox Hill and Oatlands Hill and Robin Hood's Ball
6. more amorphous and ambiguously defined sloping areas of slightly higher ground dissected by coombes
7. the Beacon Hill Ridge with a pronounced northern scarp slope and a much gentler and more irregular and dissected southern dip slope

Stonehenge is located in a position in the landscape which may be classified as category 6 above. It is directly linked to the Avon by the ceremonial pathway of the Avenue. The Avon itself is directly or indirectly linked to all the other winterbournes and coombes in the study area or beyond it to the south. The Till is linked to it via the Wylye to the west, the Bourne joins it to the east as does the Nine Mile River. All the coombe systems link in to the same overall dendritic system. Thus the Avon effectively articulates and joins together the entire immediate and larger landscape around Stonehenge. The link created between Stonehenge and the Avon thus positions (see below) the monument at the centre of a localised world defined by water, the source of all life.

Stonehenge is also directly linked to the Avon by a 'natural' route: the course of the Stonehenge Bottom/Spring Bottom coombe system, across which the Avenue itself passes to the northeast. Looking out from the Stonehenge enclosure the line of Stonehenge Bottom can be seen quite clearly, in particular the eastern side. This coombe system is by far the longest and most reticulated in the study area. It runs from Lake, on the Avon, for over 5km, twisting and turning and branching to the west and the east (Figures 17.1 and 17.2). Not only is it the longest coombe it is also the most complex and is also unusual in taking a northsouth course for much of its length (most other coombes run from the NW to the SE or the NE to the SW). Its shorter western branches run to the south and north of Stonehenge whose immediate landscape is thus contained or enclosed on three sides, to the east, north and south, by this coombe. By the River Avon the 'entrance' to this coombe system is marked by a large and prominent barrow to the south situated high up on the edge of the coombe and by three further barrows (now ring ditch sites) to the north, a point also cogently noted by Exon et al. (2000: 91) who suggest that this represents a portal into the Stonehenge landscape from the south. This barrow is one of a very few in the entire landscape visible from the River Avon on a canoe journey down the river from the north to the south. It appears to mark a turning point towards Stonehenge and away from the river. The place name 'Lake', deriving from 'lacu' meaning a stream or, in particular, a side-channel oro tributary of a river, is very interesting as it suggests the presence of a watercourse in Stonehenge/Lake bottom that might have been running for much of the year (Gelling and Cole 2000: 20).

Geomorphological research has demonstrated that Stonehenge Bottom has virtually no colluvium within it ,whereas thick colluvial deposits do occur in the coombe around which Durrington Walls was constructed (Richards 1990: 210-11). The reasons for this remain uncertain but one of the possibilities is the removal of colluvium by running water. It is interesting to note that water has been observed flowing in Stonehenge Bottom south of the A303 road by the present landowners and flooding has occurred at Lake near to the Avon. At times of heavy rainfall there is often standing water. Stonehenge Bottom differs from other coombes and river valleys in the area in that it is neither truly a dry valley

nor a seasonal Winterbourne. Stonehenge is thus directly linked with both the only perennial source of water in the area, the Avon, and an exceptional coombe system of unpredictable character. In general, our knowledge of the Neolithic water table is inadequate and water extraction has drastically reduced it affecting river and stream levels throughout the area. The Nine Mile River, which the military started tapping in the early twentieth century, is now completely dry in the summer for most of its course, as is the Bourne.

The river valleys and coombe systems both define and divide this landscape. Their courses delimit areas of higher ground and provide well defined routes of movement through it. They can be conceptualized in terms of boundaries, transition points from the lowest to the highest ground, and as providing pathways to follow through the landscape. They are also the places where sarsen stones are typically exposed and 'congregate' as we know from the few dramatic sarsen filled coombes that still exist (having survived quarrying) in the Marlborough Downs to the north of the Stonehenge landscape. The coombes, mythologically understood, give birth to sarsen stones. They may also give birth to water either seasonally or unpredictably. The association of coombes with water in various ways would have been noticed by prehistoric populations as would their resemblance to river valleys with water such as the Avon. A problem that might have required a mythological explanation could have been: why did these rivers of the past run dry?

Another important factor in the location of Stonehenge was its visual relationship to the Beacon Hill Ridge to the east and Sidbury Hill to the northeast. Both the Beacon Hill Ridge and Sidbury Hill punctuate the skyline in a distinctive manner in this landscape. They are, relatively speaking, 'jagged' compared with the rest of the Stonehenge Landscape where the localised topography of the rises and ridges and coombe systems winding their way through the chalk downland is either slight and indistinct, or if higher, rounded and smoothly rolling. These are by far the highest hills in the area, and indeed some of the highest in Wiltshire, with the Beacon Hill Ridge reaching a maximum height of 204m at its western end and Sidbury Hill rising to 223m.

The Beacon Hill Ridge (Figure 17.4) is by far the most dramatic in the study area. At the end of their landscape study Exon et al. state that 'we became overpowered by the influence of Beacon Hill. Lying towards the eastern margin of our study area its high and jagged profile forms a visual focus for many monuments' (Exon et al. 2000: 108). This is indeed the case. The ridge extends for about 4km on an approximate southwest to northeast alignment. Stonehenge is located in the landscape so that most of the northern scarp slope of this ridge with its distinctive summit areas is visible. Had it been sited further to the south only the far western edge of the ridge would be visible and the effect of seeing different summit areas

Figure 17.4 The Beacon Hill Ridge seen from the west

Figure 17.5 Pebbles on the Beacon Hill Ridge

Figure 17.6 Sidbury Hill seen looking out from the entrance to Woodhenge

would be lost. This ridge is comprised of five distinctive summit areas with lower ground in between and, because of its orientation, most of this ridge can be seen from Stonehenge. Three of these summit areas (Jukes Brown 1905 only notes two) and Sidbury Hill have a thin but nevertheless distinctive capping of smooth and rounded flint and quartz pebbles in a clayey soil overlying the chalk, known geologically as the Reading Beds (Jukes Brown 1905: 40). These pebbles are round or oval in form, the largest being 5-6cm in diameter, the smallest 2cm. They are water-worn and perfectly smooth and rounded. They vary considerably in colour from white to black, to red, yellow and brown (Figure 17.5) Their presence explain the unusual stepped form of the Beacon Hill Ridge contrasting with all other chalk ridges in the Stonehenge area which have much more rounded and even contours, lacking distinctive and discrete summit areas.

Now, the final section of the Avenue, after it dramatically bends to turn and run up directly to Stonehenge, is orientated on a direct NE line towards Sidbury Hill (the very highest point in this landscape). The rising midsummer sun striking the Heel Stone before shining into the interior of Stonehenge emerges from behind Sidbury Hill in the distance thus emphasizing the symbolic significance of this pebble-capped summit (Figure 17.6). Today Sidbury Hill cannot be seen from Stonehenge because trees and buildings on the Larkhill/Durrington ridge to the northeast block the view. GIS generated viewsheds produced by Mark Dover of the Stonehenge Riverside Project team show that the summit

area of Sidbury Hill would probably have just been visible in the Neolithic standing on the western or northern sectors of the bank of the Stonehenge Phase 1 monument (assuming a relatively open and treeless landscape as demonstrated by Allen 1997).

In view of the visual and symbolic significance of the Beacon Hill Ridge and Sidbury Hill a number of the architectural features of Stonehenge itself in its final phase, seen today, can be understood in a new manner. First of all, the internal space framed by the trilithons and taller bluestones is orientated on the same NE-SW axis as the Beacon Hill Ridge. This axis is also the same as the perfectly straight final stretch of the Avenue leading up to Stonehenge. This emphasis on a NE-SW axis is shared with a number of other approximately contemporary later Neolithic monuments. The oval timber rings at Woodhenge (Cunningham 1929) are arranged on a NE-SW axis and the single entrance faces to the northeast as did the single entrance to the Coneybury henge (J. Richards 1990: 123). From both these monuments Sidbury Hill is visible today (see Figure 17.6) looking out through the entrances and the midsummer sun can be seen rising up from behind it.

The significance of the Beacon Hill Ridge may have been important both much earlier and prior to the construction of Stonehenge, and after the final phase of its construction. It is intriguing to note that the line of earlier Mesolithic pine timber posts discovered in the Stonehenge car park (Cleal *et al.* 1995: 43-7) is orientated toward it. The ridge is visible from almost all the *c.* 25

Figure 17.7 Stonehenge seen from the northeast as one approaches the monument along the final stretch of the Avenue

Neolithic long barrows and *c.* 450 round barrows in the study region. By far the greatest concentration of Bronze Age barrows in the study region flank the Nine Mile River, a winterbourne stream running roughly NE-SW. This river arises to the east in the same part of the landscape as Sidbury Hill and flows along the foot of the north facing scarp of the Beacon Hill Ridge. Its confluence with the Avon is just to the east of the Durrington Walls henge. By comparison the Avon, Till and Bourne rivers that flow approximately north-south have far fewer barrows and barrow cemeteries associated with them. Thus a general NE – SW axis appears to have become the auspicious directional axis in the entire landscape after the final phase of the construction of Stonehenge and throughout the early Bronze Age (see also Darvill 1997: 180-1). At Stonehenge this orientation is present during the initial erection of the bluestones around 2600 BC.

The approach from the Avenue

Stonehenge as a locale in the landscape cannot be understood simply in terms of constituting a fixed place i.e. in terms of its specific location. Part of its meaning and significance was created through the process of the experience of moving towards it in the right way, and from the most propitious direction following the path of the rising sun. In the final phase of the construction of the monument at least we know this to have been by walking along the Avenue. This is by no means the shortest or easiest or 'least cost' route to Stonehenge whether dragging bluestones along it or not as Exon *et al.* (2000: 72) have shown. In brief, the approach involves

ascending from the Avon to the top of the King Barrow ridge from which Stonehenge can be seen for the first time from the east, descending into and across Stonehenge Bottom where it disappears from sight and then a dramatic change of direction to approach the monument again when it is very near indeed. Here we analyze in detail the final part of this journey to the stones and into the interior of the monument.

Approaching Stonehenge walking along the final part of the Avenue from the northeast the arrival at the monument takes the form of an ascending pathway which flattens off as you approach and enter the sarsen ring. The internal arrangement of trilithons gradually disappears becoming concealed by the lintel stones of the outer sarsen stone ring. They only become visible again as trilithons after one has finally entered the outer ring. The tallest and most impressive part of the monument thus goes out of sight while the outer ring of stones dominates the visual perspective. In effect this external ring of stones becoming more and more dominant and higher and higher in relation to a person approaching the monument continues the ascending path of the Avenue in a most dramatic and outrageous way. Passing the Heel stone and the Slaughter stone, to the left, glimpses into the interior of the monument are very limited. The details of its internal structures are almost entirely concealed from view. From the outside there is no obvious entrance into the sarsen ring, but rather a series of slots to pass through, which one might choose. The two stones through which one should pass remain unmarked. One is confronted with a massive structure of strong verticals and bold horizontals (Figure 17.7). The landscape beyond the

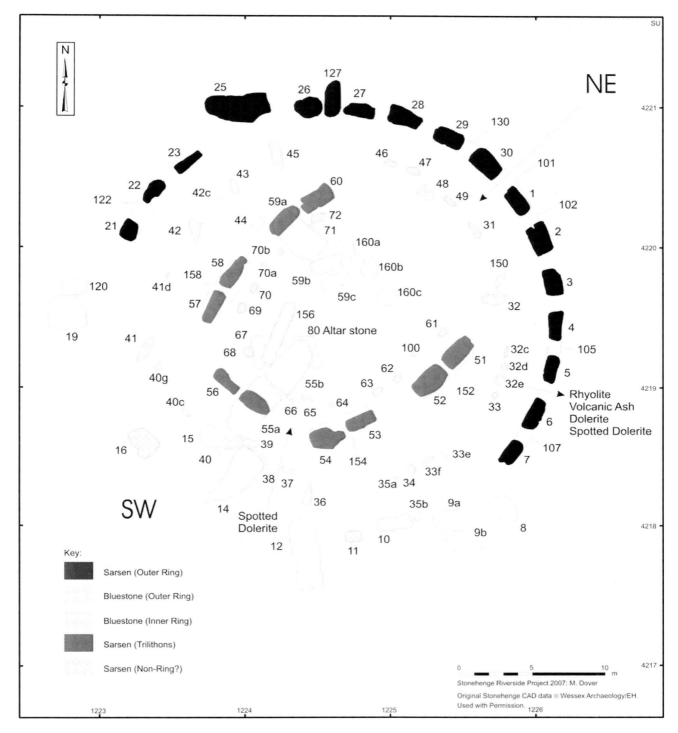

Figure 17.8 Plan of Stonehenge showing the arrangements of sarsens and bluestones

monument to the southwest is entirely blocked out. The only other monuments visible in the landscape are a few of the most monumental and massive barrows at the eastern end of the Normanton Down group to the south. These also disappear from sight as one walks up to the stones. It is clear that anyone entering the monument for the first time in the correct way would need to be led, or provided with guidance, from someone with an insider's knowledge of the internal structure.

Inside the stones

Passing through the outer circle of sarsen stones one encounters a ring of bluestones, the two highest of which (stones 49 and 31: see Figure 17.8), concealed from the outside, flank the entrance way through this circle. It is only having passed through the outer sarsen ring that the horseshoe-shaped internal arrangement of trilithons and bluestones become apparent and the outer circle of

191

17.9 View across the central area of Stonehenge showing the grading of height
of the bluestones in the inner 'horseshoe'

bluestones surrounding it. The concealment of this inner structural arrangement from the outside world and a view of almost all the bluestones from whatever direction you approach the monument, creates a crucial distinction between the internal and external spaces of the monument, creating a fundamental distinction between Stonehenge as viewed from the outside and as seen from the inside.

The inner space of the monument is effectively graded, both by the increasing height of the sarsen trilithons and bluestones from front to back (or to the southwest) and the enclosing architecture of the horseshoe (Figure 17.9). The permeability of the outer sarsen ring thus contrasts with the terminal space of the horseshoe arrangements of stones beyond which one should not pass. There was only one correct way into the inner part of the monument and only one way out. Such an architectural arrangement of stones, it might be noted, is typical, of Neolithic passage graves where similarly, there is only one entrance and exit from the internal space of the structure and in which the internal arrangements of stones and corbelling rises to the back. All this suggests that the central interior space of Stonehenge was an unroofed temple constructed using the same general design principles as earlier megalithic tombs. Such an observation strengthens an interpretation that this monument was associated with the ancestral dead (see Whittle 1997: 163; Parker Pearson and Ramilisonina 1998; Parker Pearson *et al.* 2006).

While acknowledging the graded nature of the central bluestone horseshoe, and the overpowering grandeur of

the similarly graded encasing sarsen trilithons, it was to the pale sandstone Altar Stone that this entire architectural edifice referred. Today, the Altar Stone lies little noticed embedded in the turf and partially covered by the lintel (156) and fallen eastern upright (55) of the tallest sarsen trilithon. Indeed, its upper face is worn and polished through generations of visitors walking over its surface to gaze at the collapsed great sarsen trilithon. At one time, however, this stone stood proud in a central position enclosed by the inner bluestone horseshoe (Atkinson 1956: 45), and providing a striking focal point (Stone 1924: 1). When erect, it stood to *c.* 4m in height and, although dwarfed by the great trilithon, it towered above the surrounding bluestones.

The hidden presence of the bluestones within the monument situated both inside the outer sarsen ring and inside the trilithon setting strongly suggests that the whole building project was designed to guard, shield, and conceal the exotic bluestones from the outside world. The bluestones were also of great antiquity having formed the first stone architecture at Stonehenge (*cf.* Bradley 2000: 94). Consequently, they may have needed to be surrounded by the sarsen stones to protect their magical powers and symbolic connotations.

Furthermore, there are important distinctions between the outer ring of bluestones, the internal horseshoe shaped arrangement and the central Altar Stone. All but two now fallen stones (nos. 36 and 42) which once formed lintels for trilithons, in the outer ring of bluestones are unshaped and retain their natural forms and individual character.

192

Figure 17.10 Axe blade shaped bluestones forming the inner 'horseshoe'

The size and shapes of these stones are very variable resembling those that may be observed on the Preseli mountains today (Darvill and Wainwright 2003). These stones are of mixed local origin but may all come from nearby sources at the eastern end of the Preseli mountains (Thorpe *et al.* 1991). Rhyolite, spotted and unspotted dolerite and volcanic ash are all used. The inner bluestones are much taller, all are skilfully dressed and of spotted dolerite except for one (Atkinson 1956: 42). The uniformity of the material used for the stones in the inner horseshoe thus contrasts with the diversity of types of stone employed to construct the outer bluestone ring. Atkinson notes that 'in every case where the upper part of the pillar survives intact, its top surface has been dressed flat and level…two pillars at least once terminated in a tenon' (*ibid.*: 43). At least six, possibly seven of these stones formed part of a previous structure which included at least two trilithons (*ibid.*: 44).

Of great consequence is that this megalithic architecture was of a form unlike that of any other stone monument in late Neolithic Britain. Its complexity is demonstrated not only by shaped components of trilithons, but also the presence of more complex forms of stone 'joinery'. Bluestone 68 has the beautiful groove running down its western side. Atkinson identifies the presence of the broken bluestone stump 66 with the remains of a tongue in a corresponding position: "it may be accepted that at one time these stones stood side by side, the tongue of one fitting into the groove on the other" (1956: 44). But the previous bluestone structure was of even greater complexity than envisaged by Atkinson in employing at least two pairs of 'tongue and groove' jointed stones. This is revealed in J. F. S. Stone's observation that of the remaining tongue-and-groove stones (bluestones 66 and 68) neither actually fitted one another (1953: 13). Hence, not only were the bluestones forming the inner horseshoe exotic in being derived from South Wales but also in being components of a unique and incredible megalithic monumental architecture.

Again, apart from its enhanced stature, the central Altar Stone stands out in its difference. While the inner bluestone horseshoe is the remnants of an earlier monument presumably mainly formed of spotted and unspotted dolerite, the Altar Stone is a pale, fine-grained calcareous sandstone. Previously identified as originating from the Cosheston Beds which outcrop around Milford Haven (Thomas 1923: 244-5; Atkinson 1956: 46), the 6 tonne stone has now been recently suggested to derive from the Senni Beds, possibly from a more eastern location near the Brecon Beacons (Kellaway 2002: 59). A more cautious approach to provenance is adopted by Ixer and Turner (2006: 7), who suggest that the important issue is not the exact source location within the Senni Beds but rather that they outcrop in locations far removed from either the Preseli Hills or Milford Haven. In this respect the nearly 5m-long Altar Stone assumes even greater significance in being 'exotic' in comparison to the commonality of the Preseli dolerites of the inner horseshoe (and earlier bluestone monument).

Many of the bluestones forming the inner horseshoe were re-shaped so as to resemble ground stone axe blades thrust into the ground with their blades facing down (Figure 17.10). None of the bluestones in the outer circle look like axes at all. These differences between dressed and undressed bluestones, taller and thinner stones, stones that resemble axes and those that do not, are further accentuated by the contrast between the outer

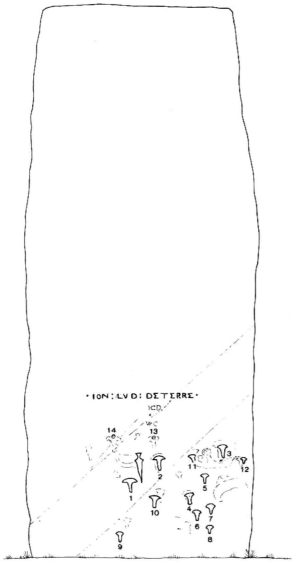

Figure 17.11 Axe carvings on the inner face of stone 53 (from Cleal *et al.*1995: fig. 20)

signficance of axe symbolism from the Neolithic into the Bronze Age. However, there is a significant difference insofar as the bluestones are shaped in the form of Neolithic axe blades which are located at the inner core of the monument. The axe carvings on the sarsens thus indicate both symbolic continuity with the past and difference and only some, unlike the bluestone axes, are hidden within the inner sanctum of the monument. Those on the external faces of stones 3 and 4 would be dramatically illuminated and highlighted by the equinoxal sunrise and do not relate at all to movement towards the monument along the Avenue.

The shaped bluestones forming the inner arrangement are hidden within the horseshoe trilithon arrangement also consisting of dressed stones with both the outer sarsen ring and the inner trilithons being furnished with lintels. The bluestones that never supported lintels form a permeable ring alluding perhaps to a yet earlier bluestone circle never elaborated with trilithons. Its presence and that of the bluestones in the inner oval arrangement thus served to objectify the presence of earlier structures at Stonehenge and the past in its present and final form in which the exotic bluestones once visible from the landscape and the outside became hidden inside. At the same time it was only the more local sarsen stones that had lintels or were used for trilithons. They were clearly chosen for their brute monumentality dwarfing a person and their presence would clearly make any attempt to retain a bluestone trilithon structure appear like the work of lesser beings in comparison.

The trilithons forming the inner part of the structure were carefully chosen pairs of stones with capping lintels. The fact that these and all the other extant sarsen stones in the monument were dressed does not mean that their surfaces are smooth and uniform. Whittle has made the important observation that the surfaces and dressing of the trilithon uprights is very different and differs between the external and internal faces from stone to stone (Whittle 1997: 155). Examining the internal broad faces of these stones seen from within the innermost oval space of the structure there are a striking series of repetitive contrasts between each pair of stones. Many are riddled with hollows and holes and have a very uneven surface. In each of the surviving three pairs of stones, in which both stones are still standing, one of the stones has a comparatively rough surface with many surface depressions, holes and irregularities. The other, by contrast, is almost perfectly smooth and regular in form all over its surface. So in each stone pair one of the stones retains a surface, or parts of a surface, which uniquely individuates it while the other is artificially shaped in such a manner as to remove all traces of its individual and original identity as a 'natural' or unworked stone (Figures 17.12 and 17.13). In each case it is the monolith on the left hand side of the pair that is smooth and regular in form and that to the right that is much more irregular. This pattern of pairing stones with smooth and rough internal surfaces is likely to have been repeated in the cases of the two trilithons where today

circular space formed by the bluestones and the inner oval space, open to the northeast.

The axe-shaped form of the bluestones is particularly interesting to note in relation to the occurrence of copper axe engravings on some of the sarsens and the presence of functionally useless but symbolically powerful chalk axes deposited at Woodhenge (Pollard 1995: 149). No carvings are known on any of the bluestones themselves. These carvings occur on the outer faces of stones 3 and 4 and on the inner face of stone 53, one of the trilithons. Another may occur on stone 5 but its position is unknown (Lawson and Walker in Cleal *et al.* 1995: 30-32). These carvings all occur on the lower parts of the stones with the lowest immediately above ground level. The majority resemble flanged axes of early Bronze Age date (Figure 17.11). All are unhafted axe blades with the blades pointing vertically up the stones. These, and the axe-blade shaped bluestones, clearly indicate the continuing

Figure 17.12 The inner faces of stones 51 and 52 (left) and 53 and 54 (right)

Figure 17.13 The inner faces of stones 53 and 54

one of the stones (55 and 59) has collapsed with only the outer faces visible and both irregular. This consistent contrast between comparatively smooth and comparatively rough broad faces of the stones seen from the inside is, however, not repeated when the same stones are seen from the outside. The external faces of stones 51 and 52 are both quite uniform and smooth. Stones 53 and 54 and 55 and 56 have external faces that are both smooth and rough. Stones 57 and 58 possess smooth external faces while stones 59 and 60 both have rough external faces. So while all combinations of smooth and rough or smooth and smooth faces occur on the outside of the trilithon oval, a deliberate choice was made to choose stones with a rough and a smooth surface to erect on the inside, a deliberate pairing of stones with very different and contrasting surface characteristics creating an internal architectural space that was very different when seen from the inside. Here it is worthwhile noting that, from a human-sized perspective, all the broad surfaces of the stones of the inner trilithon can only be seen when standing and looking around in the inner space. As one walks around and outside the same stones as the broad face of one comes into view the previous stone disappears out of view. Thus a consistent pairing of stones with rough and smooth surfaces would not be likely to be appreciated or be so visually striking when seen from the outside.

Stone 54 and the fallen stone 55 (see Figure 17.8) in the arrangement of trilithons contrast significantly with all the others. The other stones are all grey in colour. These two stones are unusually brown. This strongly suggests that at least two different sources of sarsens were utilized to construct the inner arrangement of trilithons and that, in two out of the five trilithons - including the highest of all - stones from these different sources were deliberately paired together. This replicates the use of different kinds of bluestones from different sources in the outer ring.

The inner arrangement of sarsen trilithons differs substantially from the outer ring of sarsens, not only in terms of their height and dimensions, but also in terms of the gaps between the pairs of uprights through which nothing of the outside landscape can be seen. Standing in the central space of the monument the outside world is completely screened off. This outside world is only partially visible when one moves and looks through the

gaps between the trilithons. Stonehenge, from the inside, is very much a monument that focuses attention on its internal architecture. Unlike every other stone circle in Britain the intention seems to have been to exclude the outside world. Although many of the locations of the numerous Bronze Age barrows in the surrounding landscape appear to have been deliberately chosen in relation to Stonehenge, they were not visible from the central part of the interior (Figure 17.14).

Only two massive bell barrows are visible, when one moves around in the central space and looks out through the gaps between the trilithons, the bell barrow to the southwest of Stonehenge behind which the sun sets on the shortest day of the year (the so-called Sunset Barrow, Amesbury 15), and the Bush Barrow with its fabulously rich grave goods (Ashbee 1960: 76-8; see Figure 17.2). This strongly suggests that these two barrows were located in a very specific relationship to the central space of the monument following its construction in the form that we see today. The locations of many of the other Bronze Age barrows indicate that while a view to Stonehenge from them was important they were not located so as to be seen from the centre of the monument. In other words views to Stonehenge from outside it and the surrounding landscape, were far more significant than views of that landscape from the central space of the monument defined by the internal trilithons and bluestones. Thus part of the significance of Stonehenge in its final phase of construction was that it was deliberately designed so as to be seen from a distance rather than being a place from which to view the world beyond. There is often a substantial difference between the

Figure 17.14 The view out from the centre of Stonehenge looking east

Figure 17.15 The New King Barrows seen from the Stonehenge enclosure looking east

distance from which one can see from Stonehenge looking out from the monument and see to it from the surrounding landscape. This is, of course, because the outer sarsen ring, and particularly the trilithons, are substantially taller than the height of an observer standing in the circle, in fact more than three or four times the height of a person (6m to over 7m high). Thus it is possible to see the tops of the trilithons from some parts of Stonehenge Bottom to the east but not the bottom of this coombe from Stonehenge itself. Similarly the tips of the trilithons of Stonehenge can be seen from the eastern end of the Winterbourne Stoke barrow cemetery to the east but none of these barrows are visible from the monument. Stonehenge can be seen from Oatlands Hill, 3km to the southwest, but Oatlands Hill cannot be seen from Stonehenge. From the barrow cemetery at Durrington Down to the north, Stonehenge can be seen but not *vice versa* (see further discussion of these landscape views into the monument below).

A more substantial view of the landscape beyond the monument is possible when walking a circuit between the outer bluestone and sarsen rings. The sarsens, with their lintels, continually frame and break-up this perception of the landscape. It has to be experienced in terms of a series of windows breaking up the continuity of the topographic forms of the ridges, groups of barrows, and the line of Stonehenge Bottom. By far the most dramatic view is to the east to the King Barrow ridge forming the near horizon and the Beacon Hill Ridge beyond, forming the distant horizon (Figure 17.15). Walking out from Stonehenge through the tallest bluestones in the outer

ring and sarsens 30 and 1 it is interesting to note that this is the last gap between the five pairs of sarsens on the northeast side (stones 5-29) through which the Beacon Hill Ridge can be seen directly in front of you looking out.

On the western side the view is curtailed by gently rising land to only about 250m. To the southwest the horizon is considerably longer while to the south, Rox Hill 3.5km away, is on the distant horizon but this is only very prominent today because of the distinctive clump of trees on its summit. By far the most prominent Bronze Age barrows seen from the monument, apart from the Bush Barrow and the Sunset Barrow and the nearby bell barrow immediately to the east of it, are the six massive New King Barrows running along a ridge 1km distant to the east.

Architectural order and the ordering of the landscape

Whittle notes that the stepped character of the sarsen settings is an important aspect of the architecture of Stonehenge (Whittle 1997: 150). He suggests that in some way this might be linked symbolically with a hierarchy of spirits or beings, the most powerful being high up and associated with the air. Going beyond this some more precise observations with regard to the stepped character of the stone settings can be made in relation to its landscape. There are five trilithons at Stonehenge precisely matching the number of summits on the Beacon Hill Ridge. The Beacon Hill summits are graduated in height with the highest at the southwest end.

197

Figure 17.16 Gravels in the bed of the Nine Mile River

The tallest trilithon at Stonehenge is similarly located at the southwest end of the central space thus suggesting a mimetic relationship between the orientation and graded height of the trilithons and the sequence of ridge summits. The inner horseshoe shaped arrangement of bluestones is similarly graduated in height to the southwest. So the cultural form of the interior of the monument is the landscape in microcosm. Furthermore the materials of the summit areas of the pebble-capped Beacon Hill Ridge and the Sidbury summit are alien to the area. Water-worn pebbles are found nowhere else in this landscape. In contrast to the pebbles on these hill tops the stones encountered in the beds of the Avon, Nine Mile River, Bourne and Till rivers in the vicinity of Stonehenge and along Stonehenge Bottom itself, are all jagged, angular and irregular (Figure 17.16). So pebbles do not occur in the river valleys directly associated with water, where we might perhaps most expect to find them, but on the very highest points in the landscape, where they might be least expected. This appears to be an inverted world!

The six New King Barrows on the nearby ridge to the east of Stonehenge stand out from all the others in the Stonehenge landscape in a number of important respects. They are all huge and monumental bowl barrows more or less equally spaced along the ridge top with significant gaps between each barrow. Nowhere else in the study area is such a large number of huge and regularly spaced barrows found in such close proximity.

In other places, and in other barrow cemeteries in the study region, there are barrows of similar or even greater dimensions but they only occur singly or in pairs and

their spacing is often irregular, or they may be conjoined as on Normanton Down and in the Cursus group. Clearly these barrows, which we know to have been built of stripped turves with a chalk cap obtained from digging the surrounding ditch (Cleal and Allen 1994), were constructed so as to be as prominent as possible from Stonehenge. Seen from Stonehenge these six massive mounds punctuate the skyline breaking up the otherwise smooth and rounded contours of the ridge in a manner that simply does not occur in relation to the barrows elsewhere running along the edge of its 'visibility envelope' (Figures 17.15 and 17.17). Our interpretation is that their relationship to the five summits of the Beacon Hill Ridge and to the summit of Sidbury Hill is again mimetic (six mounds and six summits).

The monumental New King Barrows thus reiterate the symbolic significance of these pebble-capped hills to their east in relation to Stonehenge itself. These barrows have an inverted stratigraphy, chalk covering the soil, just as the presence of pebbles on the hill summits to the east is an inversion of a norm. Rather than beach pebbles being found low down by the sea, they are instead encountered far inland and next to the sky. The upside-down King Barrows mimic the inversion of the wider world found on the ridge top.

Pebbles may have signified the sea and the connectedness of communities travelling by water and its buoyant potency. Pebbles from the summit areas of either the Beacon Hill Ridge and/or Sidbury Hill have been recorded from the recent excavations at Woodhenge in 2006 directed by Joshua Pollard. A substantial hollow was found directly underneath the bank of the late

Figure 17.17 One of the New King Barrows seen from the west

Neolithic henge on the southeast quadrant of the monument. This hollow was created by a fallen tree. In it early Neolithic pottery (the remains of a carinated bowl) was found, together with bones and flint in the upper fill. Both were directly associated with a deposit of pebbles brought from the Beacon Hill Ridge. At Stonehenge Hawley records the presence of pebbles in two of the Y holes (Hawley 1925: 37-8) although as these, unlike the sarsen and bluestone chippings were unlikely to have been of any interest to him, how many were left unrecorded remains uncertain. In this respect Green remarks, in the context of a general review of stones found in the 'Stonehenge layer' that well-rounded flint pebbles occur at Stonehenge 'over the whole period of its construction' (Green 1997: 5).

While the bluestones were an alien material from an exotic and distant source, the pebbles on the hill summits were an exotic local material. Excavations at Stonehenge have revealed that the entire interior of the monument was covered with sarsen and bluestone chippings. The bluestone chippings outnumber those of sarsen in a ratio of 1:3 (*ibid.*:). This is surprising in view of the fact that the dressing of the huge sarsen blocks would create much more waste material. It seems likely that during the construction of the final phase of the monument at least the bluestones were being dressed *in situ* while the sarsen blocks were largely dressed away from the monument and were then brought to the site and erected. Alternatively, many bluestone chippings were collected to be deliberately deposited within the circle. Whilst it is very easy to appreciate the significance of the imported

bluestones themselves, what is perhaps more surprising is the fact that bluestone mauls were brought from Southwest Wales too, further emphasizing the magical significance and power of these stones.

An unfinished structure?

The existing arrangement of sarsens, with or without lintels, in the outer circle of Stonehenge covers only about three-quarters of the circumference of the circle. There are many stones absent on the southwest side where the visual field from the monument is shortest and directly opposite the most significant axis of approach to Stonehenge along the Avenue. The outer sarsen ring of Stonehenge was, we think, never completed (*cf.* Ashbee 1998) and the reason may well be either that there simply were no stones of sufficient size to finish the building project or that a complete ring of sarsens with lintels was never intended or required on the southwest side of the monument where the horizon line is restricted and from which Stonehenge was never meant to be approached.

The internal trilithons, somewhat reduced in height, would have been sufficient in number to complete the perfect outer ring in the absence of any other stones of suitable size. Precisely where, in the landscape, surrounding Stonehenge, the sarsens were obtained still remains a mystery since today there are none of a similar size either in the immediate vicinity of Stonehenge or anywhere on the Marlborough Downs (see Stone 1924: 44-57; 1926; Bowen and Smith 1977; Green 1997a: 5-7; 1997b: 260-3).

Figure 17.18 View towards Stonehenge from the south

The idea of an external perfect sarsen ring was only fully realised on the northeast side of the monument facing towards the important approach from the Avenue. Approaching from this direction Stonehenge appears as relatively 'open'. Seen from the southern side through the entrance through the outer bank and ditch the visual perspective is totally different with the interior oval space defined by the trilithons and the tall bluestones being completely concealed (Figure 17.18). A smaller monolith (stone 11) and an adjacent sarsen stone (no. 10) completely block any view into the inner space. This side of the circle acts effectively as a screen effectively blocking off movement into the circle itself from this direction. Stone 11 is both much shorter in height and significantly different in shape from the other sarsens in the outer ring (Figure 17.19). Although in the correct position to continue the outer ring on the southern side it could never have supported a lintel. Atkinson suggests that the upper part may have been broken off and removed (Atkinson 1956: 24), but there is absolutely no evidence for this. Not only is this stone much shorter than the others, it is also significantly smaller in breadth and thickness. Hence, while there exists the collapsed upright (stone 12) and socket for missing stone 13 in the southwest, even if these once comprised a standing trilithon arrangement it was never connected to the outer circuit of sarsens. This lack of conjoining stones reveals Stonehenge was built in a piecemeal and probably different manner at the 'rear' of the monument.

Similarly stone 16, again, in the correct position to continue the outer sarsen ring on the southwest circuit of

Figure 17.19 Stone 11 (left)

Stonehenge is completely anomalous in shape (Figure 17.20). Its sinuous form, thick base and sides, and tapering form bear far more resemblance to a menhir and

200

Figure 17.20 Stone 16

its thin top is unlikely to have supported a lintel. Indeed, this stone is famous for its clear tool-marked surface (*e.g.* Atkinson 1956: fig. 8; Cleal *et al.*1995: plate 7.1), however, careful examination allows these marks to be re-interpreted as the results of extensive episodes of axe polishing subsequently pecked over. Overall, there is no evidence for a continuation of the outer sarsen circle beyond the socket for stone 13 in the southwest and the socket for stone 20 in the northwest.

In suggesting that the rear (southwest) area of the final Stonehenge monument was open and incorporated special and anomalous stones, it is worth recalling the initial bluestone architecture of Stonehenge. Here too a semi-circular arrangement was present with an entrance having a NE-SW axis (Cleal *et al.*1995: fig. 80). Significantly, Cleal suggests that at this early time the focus of the semi-circular bluestone arrangement may have been the Altar Stone then standing in socket WA3639, C17 (*ibid.*: 188).

The huge stones used for the five internal trilithons were used to mark out the auspicious NE-SW axis of the internal space of the monument to which the Avenue leads. It seems to have been far more important to mark out this axis rather than complete the external sarsen ring whose integrity was either sacrificed or never intended. In this respect we can note that of all the surviving upstanding stones in the outer sarsen ring stones 29, 30 and 1 are the most uniform and perfectly shaped on both their inner and outer faces. The inner faces of stones 27,

28 and 2 seen when exiting the circle towards the Avenue, are also very uniform in character whereas their outer faces are much more irregular with bulbous areas and/or hollows. Elsewhere in the ring stone faces which are irregular in form may be facing either towards the inside or outside of the ring and there appears to be no coherent pattern with regard to whether the 'best' (i.e. most uniform and regular face of the stone) faces outside or inside. This situation contrasts with the consistent pairing of stones with smooth or rough surfaces, seen from the inside, within the central arrangement of trilithons discussed above.

Stonehenge, in its final megalithic form, as in its earliest, was never a circular stage set for ceremonies and performances. It was an oval stage open to the northeast. From the very beginning discussion, analysis and representations of Stonehenge have always assumed that Stonehenge originally was constructed in terms of a Platonic and perfect circular geometry (see illustrations in Chippendale 2004), despite the presence of stones 11 and 16 which contradict such a view entirely. Throughout his book Atkinson (1956) works with the idea of completed bluestone and sarsen circles for successive stages of the monument while also admitting that 'there is no compelling reason for insisting that all the sarsen stones are components of a single and united plan, conceived and executed as a whole' (*ibid.*: 69). Perhaps we have all been misled by the plan of the monument and assumed the imperfections in it are the result of the ruinous state of Stonehenge and the removal of some stones, for which, it should be noted, there are no documentary accounts whatsoever, contrasting with those we have in relation to the burning and the breaking-up of the stones at Avebury. Stones could have been cleared for agricultural purposes but there is no evidence for cultivation at the monument itself and in any case the monument provides a ready-made site for a clearance cairn. One might expect other stones to be cleared to it rather than taken away. Furthermore there is little evidence for the use of sarsen as a building stone in the nearest settlement, Amesbury. It seems somewhat peculiar that this destruction should have taken place solely on one sector of the circle perimeter that in terms of the landscape setting of the monument is the most insignificant. What we have attempted to demonstrate here is that a phenomenological interpretation of the monument in its landscape setting provides an altogether different view. Our suggestion is that the final appearance of the monument in its latest phase was in fact rather similar to that encountered today.

Conclusions: Stonehenge through time

In relation to the seemingly continual process of the construction and reconstruction of Stonehenge some dramatic changes can be outlined in terms of the relationship of the monument to the landscape. In the earliest phase (phases after Cleal *et al.* 1995) – Phase 1 of the monument when it consisted of a bank and ditch with the 56 internal Aubrey Holes with its single entrance

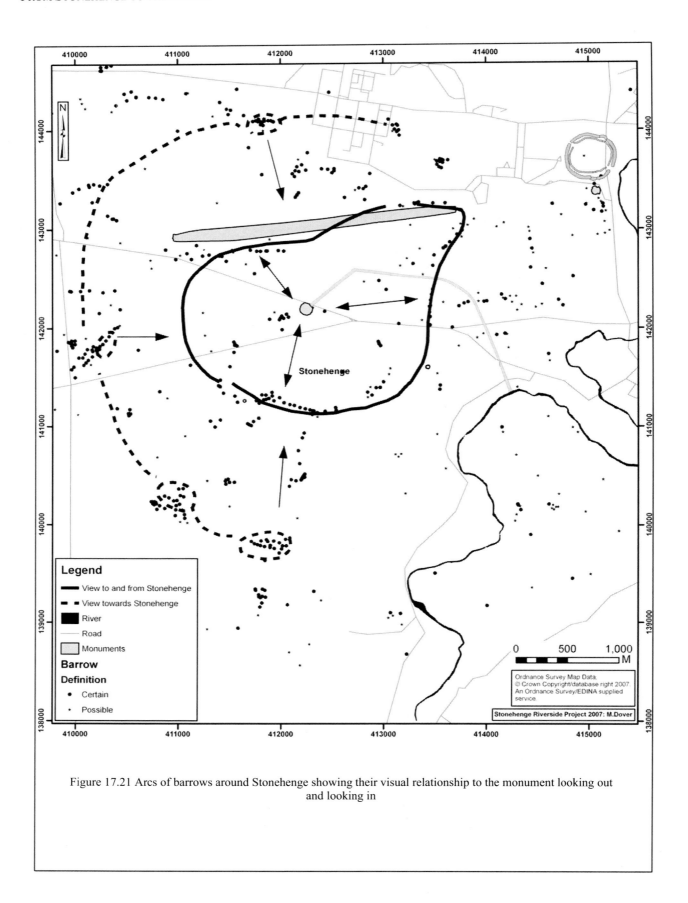

Figure 17.21 Arcs of barrows around Stonehenge showing their visual relationship to the monument looking out and looking in

facing northeast - Stonehenge would not have been highly visible in the landscape irrespective of how much tree cover there remained and by this time most of the landscape appears to have been open grassland (Allen in Cleal *et al.* 1995: 65; Allen 1997; Cleal *et al.* 2004). The possible presence of timber posts in the Aubrey Holes, estimated to have been as much as 4m high (Cleal *et al.* 1995: 112), would have increased its visibility but it might only appear to be a significant place from Normanton Down to the south or, from further away, the top of the King Barrow ridge to the east. It was a place from which, perhaps, one looked out to the landscape, but it would never have been a very prominent landscape marker within it.

In Phase 2 when internal timber structures were built - perhaps mortuary houses associated with its use as a cremation cemetery - the entrance was blocked by a palisade. The visual focus of the monument remained externally directed. In Phase 3i, the erection of the bluestones significantly altered the place irrevocably. Now these arrangements of bluestones, of whatever form, would not have effectively blocked out the landscape beyond. They would have formed a permeable membrane to the world that, while defining and screening the central activities, still permitted the inside to be connected to the outside. With the exception of the Altar Stone, the tallest of these stones would not have been all that much higher than a person. One could see out from Stonehenge and see to Stonehenge from the surrounding landscape from pretty much the same distance corresponding to Allen's 'visual envelope'. The bluestones, particularly the pale gleaming Altar Stone, so obviously exotic, would have constituted an incredible spectacle. In Phase 3ii, the sarsens and trilithons were erected and the bluestones were now hidden within them and were no longer visible from the landscape beyond. Stonehenge would thus appear to be a local monument made of local stone. The erection of the sarsens, as discussed above, not only hid the bluestones but also had the intended or unintended effect of blocking out most views of the landscape from within the centre of the monument except on the uncompleted side. The erection of the huge sarsens now further monumentalized the place.

For the first time one could now see the monument from a far greater distance away in the landscape than one could look out to that landscape from anywhere in the Stonehenge enclosure itself, a very significant change in visual perspective. The significance of this in relation to the location of Early Bronze Age barrow cemeteries around Stonehenge has been entirely overlooked previously (*cf.* Allen in Cleal *et al.*1995; Woodward and Woodward 1996; Exon *et al.* 2000). In relation to the monument itself, the visual focus changed again to being a monument that was more to be looked at from the outside than to look out from. After this final stone construction phase, Bronze Age barrow cemeteries were located both in relation to the margins of the 'visibility envelope' and intervisible with Stonehenge, but also

much further afield from Stonehenge but still within visual 'reach' of it, while themselves not being visible from the monument. This explains why there is an inner and outer arc of barrow cemeteries around Stonehenge to the west, north and south. No such arc of large and important barrow cemeteries exists to the east because the King Barrow ridge blocks all views beyond it looking from either side of it apart from the view to the Beacon Hill summit from Stonehenge and *vice versa*. Thus from the Durrington Down barrow cemetery to the north, from the eastern end of the Winterbourne Stoke barrow cemetery to the west, from the Lake and Wilsford groups to the southwest and south respectively, one can see to Stonehenge while from Stonehenge itself these barrow cemeteries remain invisible (see Figure 17.21).

If, in the final phases of the construction of the monument (that which we see today), the landscape was effectively shut out from the interior this does not imply that it was forgotten. The approach to Stonehenge down the Avenue was highly structured producing specific experiential effects of the monument in the landscape while moving towards it. We have also argued that the internal space of the monument bore a mimetic relationship to the landscape and the Beacon Hill Ridge in particular. The midsummer sun rising over the sacred and pebble capped Sidbury summit would have been highly symbolically charged. Both it and the western end of Beacon Hill were far too significant for any monuments or barrows to be built on them. The interior of Stonehenge would have provided the perfect symbolic and ritual space for telling mythological stories about the origins of the lived world, the landscape and everything in it. We will never know the content of these stories but we can surmise some of the problems they tried to address and answer: why were most of the rivers in the Stonehenge landscape dead? Why was it that only the Avon flowed throughout the year? Why were beach pebbles on the hilltops next to the sky? Why did huge sarsen blocks litter the coombes? If such matters were understood in terms of the mythical exploits and activities of ancestral beings then such exploits might be emulated to confer power and prestige on the monument building group. Hence the extraordinary feats of transporting the bluestones from south Wales and the sarsen stones from elsewhere in the landscape.

Acknowledgements

This paper was written by Christopher Tilley, with contributions by Colin Richards, Wayne Bennett and David Field, for the Stonehenge Riverside Project. It is based on fieldwork undertaken within Stonehenge during 2006 by Chris Tilley, Colin Richards and Wayne Bennett and fieldwork within the Stonehenge Riverside Project landscape survey area during fieldwork seasons 2004-2006 undertaken by Tilley, Bennett, Richards and Field. Mark Dover kindly prepared the figures and carried out GIS analysis.

References

Allen, M. 1997. Environment and land-use: the economic development of the communities who built Stonehenge (an economy to support the stones)' in C. Renfrew and B. Cunliffe (eds.) *Science and Stonehenge*. Oxford: Oxford University Press for the British Academy. 115-44.

Ashbee, P. 1960. *The Bronze Age Round Barrow in Britain*. London: Phoenix House.

Ashbee, P. 1998. Stonehenge: its possible non-completion, slighting and dilapidation. *Wiltshire Archaeological and Natural History Magazine* 91: 139-42.

Atkinson, R. 1956. *Stonehenge*. London: Hamish Hamilton.

Bowen, H. C. and Smith, I. F. 1977. Sarsen stones in Wessex: the Society's first investigations in the evolution of the landscape project. *Antiquaries Journal* 57: 185-97.

Bradley, R. 2000. *An archaeology of natural places*. London: Routledge.

Chippendale, C. 2004. *Stonehenge Complete*. London: Thames and Hudson.

Cleal, R. and Allen, M. 1994. Investigation of tree damaged barrows on King Barrow ridge and Luxenborough plantation, Amesbury. *Wiltshire Archaeological and Natural History Magazine* 97: 218-48.

Cleal, R.M.J., Allen, M. and Newman, C. 2004. An archaeological and environmental study of the Neolithic and later prehistoric landscape of the Avon valley and Durrington Walls environs. *Wiltshire Archaeological and Natural History Magazine* 97: 218-48.

Cleal, R., Walker, K. and Montague, R. 1995. *Stonehenge in its Landscape*. London: English Heritage.

Cunningham, M. 1929. *Woodhenge*. Devizes: Simpson.

Darvill, T. 1997. Sacred Geographies. In B. Cunliffe and C. Renfrew (eds) *Science and Stonehenge*. Oxford: Oxford University Press for the British Academy. 167-202.

Darvill, T.C. and Wainwright, G.J. 2003. Stone circles, oval settings and henges in south-west Wales and beyond. *Antiquaries Journal* 83: 9-45.

Exon, S., Gaffney, V., Woodward, A. and Yorston, R. 2000. *Stonehenge Landscapes*. Oxford: Archaeopress.

Gelling, M. and Cole, A. 2000. *The Landscape of Place-names*. Stanford: Shaun Tyas.

Gowland, W. 1902. Recent excavations at Stonehenge. *Archaeologia* 58: 38-119.

Green, C. P. 1997a. Stonehenge: geology and prehistory. *Proceedings of the Geologists Association* 108: 1-10.

Green, C. P. 1997b. The provenance of the rocks used at Stonehenge. In B. Cunliffe and C. Renfrew (eds) *Science and Stonehenge*. Oxford: Oxford University Press for the British Academy. 257-70.

Hawley, W. 1920-8. Excavations at Stonehenge. *Antiquaries Journal* 1: 19-41; 2:36-52; 3: 13-20; 4:30-9; 5:21-50; 6:1-16; 7: 149-76.

Ixer, R. A. and Turner, P. 2006. A detailed re-examination of the petrography of the Altar Stone and other non-sarsen sandstones from Stonehenge as a guide to their provenance. *Wiltshire Archaeological and Natural History Magazine* 99: 1-9.

Jukes Brown, A. 1905. *The Geology of the Country South and East of Devizes*. London: HMSO.

Kellaway, G. A. 2002. Glacial and tectonic factors in the emplacement of the Bluestones of Salisbury Plain. *Survey of Bath and District* 17: 57-71.

Parker Pearson, M. and Ramilisonina 1998. Stonehenge for the ancestors: the stones pass the message. *Antiquity* 72: 308-26.

Parker Pearson, M., Pollard, J., Richards, C., Thomas, J., Tilley, C., Welham, K. and Albarella, U. 2006. Materializing Stonehenge: the Stonehenge Riverside Project and new discoveries. *Journal of Material Culture* 11: 227-61.

Pollard, J. 1995. Inscribing space: formal deposition at the later Neolithic monument of Woodhenge, Wiltshire. *Proceedings of the Prehistoric Society* 61: 137-56.

RCHME 1979. *Stonehenge and its Environs: Monuments and Land Use*. Edinburgh: Edinburgh University Press.

Richards, J. 1990. *The Stonehenge Environs Project*. London: English Heritage.

Stone, E. H. 1924. *The Stones of Stonehenge*. London: Robert Scott.

Stone, E. H. 1926. Stonehenge – concerning the sarsens. *Man* 26: 202-4.

Stone, J. F. S. 1953. *Stonehenge: in light of modern research*. Salisbury: P. Jay & Son.

Thomas, H. H. 1923. The source of the stones of Stonehenge. *Antiquaries Journal* 3: 239-60.

Thorpe, R., Williams-Thorpe, O., Jenkins, D. and Watson, J. 1991. The geological sources and transport of the bluestones of Stonehenge, Wiltshire, UK. *Proceedings of the Prehistoric Society* 57: 103-57.

Whittle, A. 1997. Remembered and imagined belongings: Stonehenge in its traditions and structures of meaning. In B. Cunliffe and C. Renfrew (eds) *Science and Stonehenge*. Oxford: Oxford University Press for the British Academy. 145-62.

Woodward, A. and Woodward, P. 1996. The topography of some barrow cemeteries in Bronze Age Wessex. *Proceedings of the Prehistoric Society* 62: 275-91.

Chapter 18

Neolithic phallacies: a discussion of some southern British artefacts

Anne Teather

Department of Archaeology, University of Sheffield

Introduction

It is paradoxical that despite a comment by Richard Bradley in his analysis of Maumbury Rings over thirty years ago that the discovery of phalli on Neolithic sites is 'almost ubiquitous' (1975: 25), they have only been mentioned by academic authors in general discussions of the Neolithic (*e.g.* Thomas 1996; 1999; Piggott 1954: 86-8; Childe 1940: 39-40). Indeed, along with other objects such as chalk plaques, balls, cups or beads, there appears to be a distinct lack of attention to them (but see Varndell 1991; 1999). When one considers the nature of archaeological discourse of the last twenty years this is most surprising. Following the post-processual archaeology of the 1980s and the rise of both ethnographic and structured-depositional approaches, more attention has been levelled at traditional data sets in order to interpret complex, ritualised behaviours. These have encompassed the ritualization of what were previously seen as 'domestic' archaeology – pottery and flint products - perhaps most easily exemplified through Richards and Thomas's paper of 1984 (Richards and Thomas 1984; also see Pollard 1995). Furthermore, the architecture of Neolithic monuments has been given attention, with interpretations offered in terms of restriction and access (Barrett 1994; Thomas 1996; Whittle *et al.* 1999), with further arguments concerning whole prehistoric landscapes (Tilley 1994; Cummings and Whittle 2004).

The fact that this ritualization appears to have had a broader focus of meaning across Neolithic communities should be taken into account: in many senses, schemes of meaning and of relationality between main artefact groups such as flint or pottery have taken priority in order to encompass larger dialogues. The exclusion of these phallic artefacts from such discussions is most likely linked to the relatively small numbers so far recorded in Neolithic and Bronze Age archaeology (though one must acknowledge the circular argument - that they are not published so they are not studied; and they are not studied because comprehensive and encompassing publications do not exist). It is also the case that whilst secure contexts within half a metre are available for many phalli, some are unstratified. Despite this, I believe that the very objects most likely to be fruitful in investigating ritual interpretations, or in adding to existing ones, have been sidelined.

Integration

There are multiple reasons for this omission. One stems from a meshing of embarrassment and identification. It seems we have been previously unable to specify categorically what these objects are and represent, and therefore individual authors in attempting to include single artefacts into wider dialogues through short articles find the task daunting and best avoided. My first case study illustrates this through the discovery of a phallic flint flake on Magham Down, East Sussex. Mr Syd Jeffries is an active archaeological enthusiast in Sussex who supplied the results of his 2000-2001 fieldwalking on Magham Down, East Sussex to Dr. Chris Butler for a report produced in the *Sussex Archaeological Collections* of 2002 (Butler 2002: 139-144). I met Mr Jeffries during the *Time Team* excavation on Blackpatch in June 2005 when he told me of the flint flake he had discovered as part of the above fieldwalking and brought it for me to photograph (Figure 18.1; its line drawing is supplied by Chris Butler as Figure 18.2). In the article the flake was not described separately and is only referred to as part of

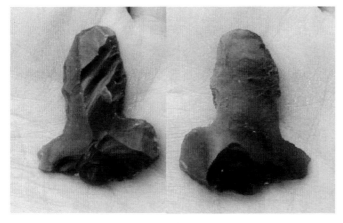

Figure 18.1: Photograph of both sides of Neolithic flint flake

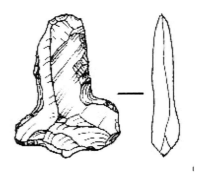

Figure 18.2: Flint flake drawing (from Butler 2002: 140)

a group of Late Neolithic/Early Bronze Age flintwork, with no comment as to its phallic appearance (Butler 2002: 141).

This both saddened and surprised me. Yet, as we do not have an academic discourse on prehistoric phalli in the Neolithic and Early Bronze Age, there is no place for objects such as this to be acknowledged. This is the first reported artefact where a phallus is represented by a flint flake in this period of prehistory and, as academics and researchers with responsibilities to our discipline, we must open a dialogue for these artefacts to be included. If we do not, we are by default excluding them and they will not form part of our archaeological record of the Neolithic. If I were to suggest that we ignore any other class of accepted artefact there would be an outcry. Had it not been for a chance encounter with Mr Jeffries, I would not be able to highlight this for our wider academic audience.

However, even with already excavated artefacts acknowledged as phallic, we have evidence of a problem caused by their omission from wider publications. During study visits for my PhD research I wished to examine three phalli from Neolithic sites: the Cissbury flint phallus from Worthing Museum, the Itford Hill chalk phallus and The Trundle bone phallus both in Lewes Museum. Unfortunately at the time, and to the present date, these cannot be located. It appears that they were all available in the 1980s, and the photo of the Cissbury phallus (Figure 18.3) was taken during the 1990s.

Figure 18.3: Cissbury flint phallus (photo courtesy of David Field, English Heritage)

Effective location management controls are now fully in place at both institutions, and today objects such as these would not be able to slip through the curatorial net. It seems in all three cases that the objects were made available for study and stolen. Both museums have highlighted to me their regret and have consented to the publication of this case study. I would like to propose that, while we can accept and regret the museums' failings, we must also consider our responsibilities as academics and researchers for their loss.

While we have been studiously examining pottery sherds, thin sections, inclusions and distributions, and refitting flints, sourcing locations, routeways and fieldwalking landscapes, our inattention and lack of publication has led to a widespread misunderstanding of the archaeological importance of phalli. Had we as academics and researchers supported the importance of these objects, potential thieves may have felt they were harming our archaeological record by their removal. They may have felt that the objects were of such importance that it was not appropriate to remove them from general access and further study. What we have achieved instead, through our lack of attention, is the implication that whoever removed them almost certainly felt they were not important and would not be missed. Additionally, we should acknowledge that odd flint flakes and pottery sherds are almost certainly not as interesting to non-specialists as archaeological phallic representations and their attraction to potential thieves is undoubtedly heightened through their form.

Frequency and form of phallic objects

It is not widely acknowledged that we can be certain that these objects represent the human male phallus, yet no arguments have been suggested to counter this. I firmly believe we should accept that these objects represent the male human penis. They are of the anatomically correct shape and size within a few centimetres. As can be seen from Figure 18.4, variation in the size and shape of the human penis is, in contemporary social publications, the norm. When compared to the Neolithic and Bronze Age phalli found (Figure 18.5), it seems sensible that this premise should be adopted. Having conceded that they are representations of the male human penis, in all its natural variability, we can begin to include them in our interpretations.

While phalli have been found on many Neolithic sites, their numbers are relatively few. As part of my Masters research in 2003 I studied the depositional context of 13 chalk or flint phalli of English Neolithic/Bronze Age provenance (Pangbourne 2003). Table 18.1 gives brief details of these and others subsequently excavated (or to which my attention has been drawn); more are almost certainly known. It seems clear that during the Neolithic and Bronze Age, phalli were accepted, although rare artefacts which were occasionally selected for deliberate deposition.

New discoveries

One must acknowledge that the biases of different excavators may affect the recovery of such finds and may result in the odd example being discarded. As discussed earlier, it is hoped that, with the publication of this and any future articles, excavators will take care to record and note phallic, or other unusual artefacts during excavation. The interest of the Durrington Walls excavators has

Figure 18.4: Variations in penis size (courtesy of FHM 2005)

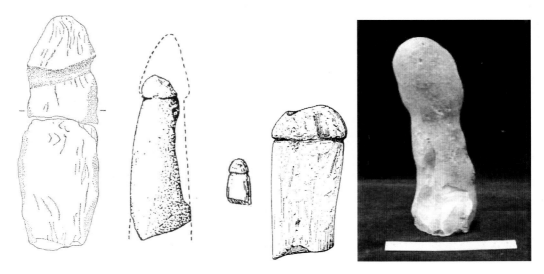

Figure 18.5: Different Neolithic phalli
(from left: Maumbury Rings, Thickthorn Down, the Trundle, Mount Pleasant, and Easton Down)

Site	Number	Substance	Primary Context	Secondary Context	Unstratified
Windmill Hill	4	Chalk	1	1	2
The Trundle	1	Bone	1		
Thickthorn Down	2	Chalk	2		
Maumbury Rings	1	Chalk	1		
Mount Pleasant	2	Chalk	2		
Magham Down	1	Flint flake			1
Cissbury	1	Flint	1		
Winterbourne Stoke Crossroads long barrow	1	Flint	1		
Itford Hill	1	Chalk	1		
Easton Down	1	Flint	1		
Grimes Graves	2*	Chalk	2		
	1	Flint	1		
Durrington Walls	3	Flint	1	2	
	1	Iron Pyrites	1		
TOTAL	21		15	3	3

*NB: I have not included the Pit 15 chalk phallus as I am doubtful of its authenticity

Table 18.1: Phalli at different Neolithic sites

ensured that many artefacts have been discovered and their details follow.

Figure 18.6: Flint phallus from the 'sex pit' (photo courtesy of Mike Parker Pearson)

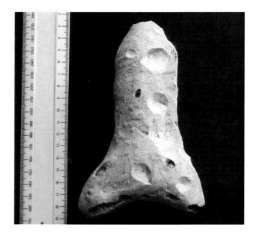

Figure 18.7: Flint nodule in phallic shape from the Southern Circle, Durrington Walls

During excavations conducted at Durrington Walls in 2004, a pit was discovered now referred to as the 'sex pit' (Parker Pearson *et al.* 2006). In this pit a flint nodule, in the shape of a phallus, was discovered alongside two flint balls (Figure 18.6) in the pit fill, close to a pelvis-shaped flint which was set into the wall of the pit and covered with a large block of flint. Excavations in 2005 uncovered another two flint nodules also in the shape of phalli (one of them, pictured in Figure 18.7, came from the western part of the Southern Circle; see Thomas this volume). These two have some similarity with the phallic nodules excavated at Easton Down, at Cissbury (Worthing Museum AC 1961/1584) and at Grimes Graves by Armstrong in 1939 (Varndell 1991: 148). At Cissbury and Grimes Graves these depositions of geologically formed flint in phallic shapes were extracted

from the chalk and placed back in the ground in an archaeological context.

The flint phallus from the 'sex pit' has been modified; and while most of its surface modifications are of geological origin (Andy Farrant, Mark Wood and Peter Hopson pers. comm.) the double groove at its tip is the result of human action. In this case, the flint nodule uncovered in its natural state could be said to be more representative of a male penis than any other discovered to date. It is possible that this double groove has been made to represent the female vulvae and clitoris. It was then deposited with two flint balls, seemingly to represent testes, within a pit whose lining included the flint nodule shaped as a pelvis. In 2006 a lump of iron pyrites in the shape of a phallus with attached testes was excavated from a house floor at Durrington Walls, within its abandonment layer and associated with Grooved Ware. It is small at approximately 6cm in length and is unlike many phalli both in its size and also in that the prepuce is present; it looks very much like the relaxed genitalia of a young or baby boy.

Discussion

It is hoped that I have established that the phallic objects retrieved during excavation can be seen as representations of the male penis and that our reluctance to do so in the past has created problems. I would like to suggest that we now need to examine how the inclusion of these artefacts into our discourses of the Neolithic can enhance our interpretations. Gender, form and substance have individual interpretative histories affecting these within the Neolithic.

Once we acknowledge that these were artefacts with significance, our challenges could be said to commence with understanding their form. Traditionally, this interpretation directs us towards discussions which collide with our own cultural preconceptions of sex and/or gender relations. When we imagine that the object (phallus) which, in a modern sense, biologically represents men (or a man), so many culturally instinctive reactions of suppression and dominance come immediately to mind that interpretation beyond our experience becomes extremely difficult. In theoretical terms, our immediate preconceptions towards artefacts have been challenged through the later understandings of phenomenology and critical theory. As contemporary archaeologists, we are expected to challenge our own intuitive understandings in favour of reflexive approaches (Hodder 1999); hence it is possible for us to acknowledge that we instinctively recognise certain shapes as being representative of a male penis without forcing our intuitive understandings onto it. This can also be applied to chalk plaques, flint balls, fossils or other artefacts. While we recognise the form, material, or substance that they constitute, their archaeological context aids their interpretation. Form can provide indications as to use, but information from form alone does not provide meaning.

Paradoxically, there has been a strong desire to see representations of female figures, or goddesses, in British prehistory. Hutton (1997) has provided a very useful summary of the rise of interest in 'the Goddess' during the 19th and 20th centuries based on literary, cultural and archaeological evidence that is unnecessary to repeat here. British archaeologists have been at the forefront of these views, from Sir Arthur Evans (1901), to the work of Jane Ellen Harrison (1903), H.J. Massingham (1932), Jacquetta Hawkes (1951), with both V. Gordon Childe and Stuart Piggott (albeit briefly) advocating the single Goddess in the 1950s (Hutton 1997: 96). While the desire to find goddesses in British prehistory was present, the archaeological evidence was not.

Hence, the discovery of prehistoric phalli challenges not only our present cultural understanding but also our history of research in this discipline. Theoretically, ethnographic approaches to archaeology have emphasised themes of practice with regard to objects. The inalienability of artefacts, the possession of biographies by artefact, and how objects can be representative of persons, or be regarded as persons in their own right have been advocated by many authors (Jones 2002; Tilley 1996; 1999; Thomas 1996; also see Fowler 2004 for a comprehensive discussion of personhood). However, while we can easily say that deposited artefacts have importance, and that this importance is socially created, reinforced and manipulated, it matters little what type of artefact it is. As all of the objects discussed in this manner are, to our preconceptions, 'ungendered' (such as a pottery sherd), it highlights our lack of experience when examining phalli. We do not have an open, academic, gendered approach to objects in the British Neolithic. Ethnographic accounts provide us with contextual evidence which cannot be gleaned from archaeology alone.

Despite this lack of open dialogue in the British Neolithic, there is a general trend to see flint objects as male (or owned and manufactured by men or boys), with pottery associated with femaleness. As Edmonds stated with regard to the larger and well-worked flint and stone tools: 'many accounts talk of a symbolic and practical link with men and, while axes were probably used by women too, there may have been times when these more categoric links were brought into focus', (1999: 41). The inference in this is that men and boys have a more categoric link with flint tools. Similar inferences to females and potting can be found (Thomas 1999: 97; Whittle 2003: 11).

We are trying, it seems, to move forward with dual constraints: a historical focus towards female deities without any archaeological foundation and a lack of open, gendered discussion on artefacts, with a tacit acceptance of gendered division based on technology and substance. An analysis of phalli cannot be based on substance, for if we were to examine flint phalli as separate from chalk phalli, or bone phalli, would it be productive? How can we separate form and material effectively in interpretation? Instead, phallic objects need to be examined as a category in themselves, exploring the contexts and deposition of these artefacts. This is both difficult and challenging; phallic objects are likely to be embedded in the spiritual life of Neolithic persons, yet this should not exclude them from analysis (Insoll 2004).

While the full discussion of meanings and implications of phalli and other objects is beyond the scope of this paper, brief conclusions may be offered. Comparisons with other types of phallic imagery can be useful. Bevan argues that, as male sexuality creates our cultural 'norms', an absence of the phallus in ithyphallic representations means female (subservient) whilst its presence is male (dominant) (2001: 65-6). Thus, the attachment of phalli to human representations creates our view as 'male'. Furthermore, she suggests that if biological sex were not important it would not be referenced; hence a lack of sexual attributes in art may express egalitarianism in society. Ethnographically, the phallus itself can appear ritually, (e.g Eliade 1964). In this example the wooden phalli among the Kumandin of Tomsk are used by three young men during the horse sacrifice (*ibid.*: 79). They wear masks and gallop around the spectators, touching them with the wooden phallus between their legs as part of the ritual to strengthen the men of the group sexually. In this role the phalli enhance the existing male characteristics of the men.

Thus the phallus, as a separate entity, can be said to create gender by influencing the natural gendered characteristics of the person or object it is linked to. This could be argued as being seen in the deposition of the 'sex pit' at Durrington Walls, where the addition of the phallus and flint balls to the pelvic-shaped flint in its slit-shaped pit was to somehow balance male and female biological characteristics within a single depositional event. Other Neolithic artefacts have been excavated where female characteristics are combined with male. The "god-dolly" excavated at the Somerset Levels, carved from wood, has both breasts and a peg-like phallus (Coles and Hibbert 1968: 256). A similar peg-like chalk object was uncovered at Grimes Graves (Varndell 1991: 149, C321) which appears to have broken away from a larger piece of chalk. Two figurines discovered at Windmill Hill (C11 and C12) were suggested by Smith to represent thighs and lower parts of a torso (1965: 130); however, they may also reference a male glans and female vulva. These hermaphroditic objects support an argument for the recognition of balance, conjoining, or equanimity of biological sexual difference. Therefore, following Bevan (2001), we could argue that the representation of sexual characteristics was socially relevant but the combination of these in a variety of contexts implies a multiplicity of meanings. Furthermore, portable objects such as these can allow for meanings to be created and also subverted (*e.g.* Thomas 1996: 141-82).

Conclusion

In monument building, extraction of flint, creation of mounds and digging of ditched enclosures, the engagement of Neolithic people with the chalk bedrock of parts of southern Britain resulted in the discovery of different natural objects. Flint nodules, iron pyrites and fossils all occur naturally in the chalk, the rock itself having different textures and hardness depending on the depth from which it was excavated. Fossil casts can also be left in the chalk; regular impressions of shell surfaces sometimes appear not unlike the linear designs on some plaques, or Grooved Ware, and some chalk objects especially from Sussex appear to represent fossils themselves (Curwen 1931).

Fossils, chalk objects and other artefacts were subject to specific depositional practices in different contexts (Thomas 1996: 168). Bradley has suggested that the re-deposition of chalk objects into chalk was culturally appropriate, being returned to where it was formed (2000: 121). If we combine these experiences of engagement with the earth and the different, natural shapes encountered – particularly those which appear to have represented the phallus, or other human forms - I believe that Neolithic peoples would have viewed uncovering the soil as an evocative and intense experience. Rather than examining these naturally occurring objects as oddities, they may well have seen themselves as humans, part of a wider integration with the earth at depth. Our contemporary notions of separation from the natural world would not have been present; instead, such objects provided a reinforcement and confirmation of people's rights and presence in the chalklands. People may have seen themselves as literally coming from the earth: the earth *as* ancestor. Following Bradley (*ibid.*), prehistoric interest in manufactured chalk objects (many representing phalli) and fossils may be seen as an elaboration of this connection: the symbolic representation of acting in a way that the earth had done on its own, re-deposition being the feeding back to the earth of an active engagement with a living entity.

Within this paper through case studies I have attempted to draw attention to the apparent importance of the representation of human male and, at times, female genitalia, or their combination into hermaphroditic forms in the British Neolithic. I have suggested that the lack of current discourse and publications on these may have directly influenced the opportunity to steal certain artefacts. Furthermore, this omission has encouraged silence towards new discoveries which may assist our interpretations. These interpretations allow us to broaden and enrich our views of Neolithic people and their active engagement with the earth. It is likely that these portable objects may have signified human biological sex, and that their application in social situations may, at times, have been contradictory. While we tend to see Middle and Late Neolithic artefact types as being more elaborate and complex than before, many of the unusual objects and

phalli were already present on Early Neolithic sites such as the Trundle or Thickthorn Down. In this way we should perhaps instead view these later artefacts as continuations of a complex practice which became more visible over time.

I hope that, through the publication of this paper, more unusual objects will be recognised through excavation and published. I would advocate the use of photography in addition to artefact drawings, as the objects in many cases provide a greater visual impact as photographs and aid better recognition of their form. Finally, I would hope to encourage wider discussion and dialogue in this fascinating area.

Acknowledgements

I would like to thank Diana Peek of Worthing Museum; Emma O'Connor of Lewes Museum; the staff at Salisbury Museum; Syd Jeffries; Dr Andy Farrant, Dr Mark Woods and Dr Peter Hopson of the British Geological Survey for their help. Chris Fowler, Tim Insoll, Colin Richards and Julian Thomas, together with other staff at the University of Manchester initially provided me with an open environment to raise these issues, a process continued through Bob Johnston and Mike Parker Pearson at the University of Sheffield. My thanks to all. Comments made by Ian Heath and Mike Parker Pearson on this contribution were gratefully received, any errors and omissions remain my own.

References

Barrett, J. 1994 *Fragments from Antiquity: an archaeology of social life in Britain, 2900-1200 BC.* Oxford: Blackwell.

Bevan, L. 2001. Gender bias or biased agenda? Identifying phallic imagery, sexual scenes and initiation in rock art. In L. Bevan (ed.) *Indecent Exposure*. Glasgow: Cruithne Press. 64-88.

Bradley, R.J. 1975. Maumbury Rings, Dorchester: the excavations of 1908-13. *Archaeologica* 105: 1-97.

Bradley, R.J. 2000. *An Archaeology of Natural Places.* London: Routledge.

Butler, C. 2002. A Mesolithic site and later finds at Magham Down, near Hailsham, East Sussex. In *Sussex Archaeological Collections* 140: 139-52.

Childe, V.G. 1940. *Prehistoric Communities of the British Isles*. London: Chambers.

Coles, J.M. and Hibbert, F.A. 1968. Prehistoric road and tracks in Somerset, England: 1 Neolithic. *Proceedings of the Prehistoric Society* 34: 238-258.

Cummings, V. and Whittle, A. 2004. *Places of Special Virtue: megaliths in the Neolithic landscapes of Wales*. Oxford: Oxbow.

Curwen, E.C. 1931. Excavations in The Trundle, second season 1930. *Sussex Archaeological Collections* 72: 100-50.

Edmonds, M. R. 1999. *Ancestral Geographies of the Neolithic*. London: Routledge.

Eliade, M. 1964. *Shamanism: archaic techniques of ecstasy*. London: Penguin.

Evans, Sir A. 1901. The Neolithic Settlement at Knossos and its place in the history of the early Agean culture. *Man* 1: 184-6

Fowler, C. 2004. *The Archaeology of Personhood*. London: Routledge.

Harrison, J.E. 1903. *Prolegomena to the study of Greek religion*. Cambridge: Cambridge University Press.

Hawkes, J. 1951. *A land*. London: Cresset

Hodder, I. 1999. *The Archaeological Process: an introduction*. Oxford: Blackwell.

Hutton, R. 1997. The Neolithic great goddess: a study in modern tradition. *Antiquity* 71: 91-9.

Insoll, T. 2004. *Archaeology, Ritual, Religion*. London: Routledge.

Jones, A. 2002. *Archaeological Theory and Scientific Practice*. Cambridge: Cambridge University Press.

Massingham, H.J. 1932. *World without end*. London:Cobden-Sanderson.

Pangbourne, A.M. 2003. Male Sexual Symbolism in the English Neolithic. Unpublished MA Paper, University of Manchester.

Parker Pearson, M., Richards, C., Allen, M. and Welham, K. 2006 A new avenue at Durrington Walls. *Past* 52.

Piggott, S. 1954. *The Neolithic Cultures of the British Isles*. Cambridge: Cambridge University Press.

Pollard, J. 1995. Inscribing space: formal deposition at the later Neolithic monument of Woodhenge, Wiltshire. *Proceedings of the Prehistoric Society* 61:137-56.

Richards, C.C. & Thomas, J.S. 1984. Ritual activity and structured deposition in later Neolithic Wessex. In R.J. Bradley and J. Gardiner (eds.) *Neolithic Studies*, 189-218. Oxford: British Archaeological Reports.

Smith, I.F. 1965. *Windmill Hill and Avebury, Excavations by Alexander Keiller 1925-1939*. Oxford: Clarendon Press.

Thomas, J.S. 1996. *Time, Culture and Identity: an interpretive archaeology*. London:Routledge.

Thomas, J.S. 1999. *Understanding the Neolithic*. London: Routledge

Tilley, C. 1994 *A Phenomenology of Landscape: places, paths and monuments*. London: Berg.

Tilley, C. 1996. *An Ethnography of the Neolithic*. Cambridge: Cambridge University Press.

Tilley, C. 1999. *Metaphor and Material Culture*. Oxford: Blackwell.

Varndell, G. 1991. The worked chalk. In I.H. Longworth, A. Herne, G. Varndell and S. Needham, *Excavations at Grimes Graves, Norfolk 1972-76*. London: British Museum Press. 94-153.

Varndell, G. 1999. An Engraved Chalk Plaque from Hanging Cliff, Kilham. *Oxford Journal of Archaeology* 18: 351- 355.

Whittle, A., Pollard, J. and Grigson, C. 1999. *The harmony of symbols: the Windmill Hill causewayed enclosure, Wiltshire*. Oxford: Oxbow.

Whittle, A. 2003. *The Archaeology of People*. London: Routledge.

Chapter 19

The lithic landscape of the Newgrange environs: an introduction

Conor Brady

Dundalk Institute of Technology

Introduction

Brú na Bóinne, in Co. Meath on the east coast of Ireland has long been recognised as an prehistoric landscape of international significance and is well known as home to one of the most important Neolithic passage-tomb cemeteries in Western Europe (Stout 2002; Bradley 1998a; 1998b: 101-6; Whittle 1996: 244; Eogan 1986). In recognition of its importance, the area was awarded UNESCO World Heritage Site status in 1993 and a management plan for the area has been published (Stout 2002: 181; Anon. 2002). There is limited evidence for activity here during the Later Mesolithic and Earlier Neolithic periods, but the area is best known for the Middle Neolithic passage tomb cemetery, the largest being the sites of Newgrange and Knowth, both of which have been extensively excavated in recent decades, and Dowth (Eogan 1963; 1968; 1974; 1984; 1986; Eogan and Roche 1997; O'Kelly 1982; O'Kelly *et al.* 1978; O'Kelly *et al.* 1983; Lynch 1989; 1990a and b). There are also up to forty smaller passage tombs in the area. Many other monuments also survive from the Later Neolithic period including earthen hengiform enclosures, of which the one at Dowth is still relatively intact. The example at Monknewtown was excavated during the 1970s before development of the site (Sweetman 1976), Sites A and P, which are much flattened by ploughing, remain visible in certain conditions in the fields below the Newgrange monument. A cursus monument beside the main tomb at Newgrange and a number of possible ritual ponds (Stout 1991; Meenan 1997; Condit 1997a and b). Also uncovered by excavation is a series of Late Neolithic timber enclosures and other structures – two adjacent to the monument at Newgrange (Sweetman 1985; 1987) and another is located outside the front of the entrance to the eastern tomb at Knowth (Eogan and Roche 1994).

The research carried out within the area to date has been essentially site-based, concentrating only on the areas in and around the monuments. While excavation has revealed much about these monuments and the activities carried out immediately adjacent to them, the same may not be said about the picture of settlement activity for the area. What data are available regarding settlement have emerged more by accident than by design as by-products of the investigations of the monuments. Evidence has been uncovered at Newgrange and Knowth that, in both cases, has been interpreted as domestic settlement (Eogan 1984; 1997; O'Kelly *et al.* 1983). However, this evidence has come from close to or beneath very important ritual

and ceremonial monuments, which raises the question of whether these can be regarded as representing everyday settlement and habitation activities of the general population of the area at the time (Sheridan 2004: 28).

Attempts to devise a chronology of settlement for Brú na Bóinne have relied heavily on the excavations at Knowth, Newgrange and, to a lesser extent, Monknewtown henge (e.g. Eogan 1991; Roche and Eogan 2001). When looking at the settlement history of the area, the excavations at Knowth are particularly useful because, in addition to the passage tomb activity, there is clear evidence of occupation and habitation activity from the Early Neolithic to the Beaker Period. The problem with this is that these excavations and the resulting interpretations of activity for the area have been site-based rather than taking the landscape as the starting point. These models of settlement for the region have, of necessity, been based on evidence that has been discovered incidentally during these investigations (e.g., van Wijngaarden-Bakker 1974; 1986; O'Kelly *et al.* 1983: 52-3; Woodman 1985; Mitchell 1986: 114-5; Mitchell and Ryan 1997: 177; Cooney 1991; 2000; Mount 1994; Cooney and Grogan 1994; 1998; Whittle 1996: 245; Bradley 1998a and b). Critical questions that this data does not adequately cover relate to the nature, distribution and extent of settlement evidence across the wider Brú na Bóinne landscape over the course of the Neolithic. The current work was designed to address these questions directly and was prompted by an earlier pilot surface collection survey in the area, the Red Mountain Transect, a small-scale pilot survey designed to draw attention to the potential of surface collection survey to answer such questions in the Brú na Bóinne area (Brady 2006; Cooney and Brady 1998). Preliminary results from this work indicated that there were highly significant densities of lithic material concentrated in certain parts of the landscape and that the distributions were also highly patterned.

The main aim of the present research was to identify evidence for settlement in the wider Brú na Bóinne landscape and to examine the character of that evidence. One question arising from this was whether there was a focus solely within the bend of the river in the core area of Brú na Bóinne or whether there was also settlement evidence on the southern side of the river Boyne which is an area almost devoid of upstanding archaeology yet within easy walking distance and visual contact of the area of the bend on the north side. Central to this work was the examination and interpretation of landscape use

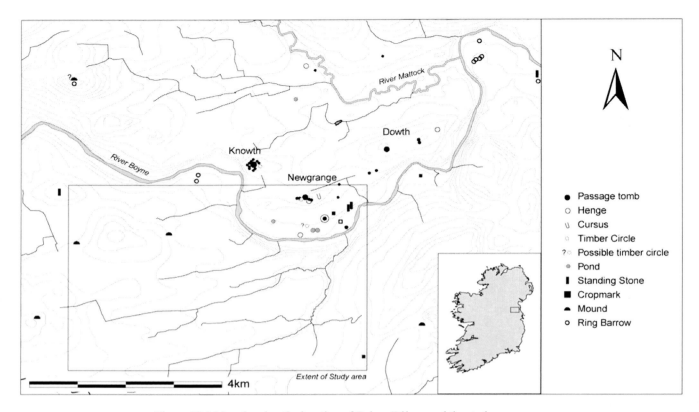

Figure 19.1 Map showing the location of Brú na Bóinne and the study area

from the Mesolithic to the Early Bronze Age based on surface-collected lithics distributions. The nature of lithic resource use over time was also examined.

The study area

Brú na Bóinne is a 16sq km area defined by the course of the River Boyne as it flows eastwards. The bend begins just below and to the west of the site at Knowth, marking the western edge of the area. It then flows in an easterly direction for a couple of kilometres below and south of Newgrange and gradually veers northwards in a series of bends around and east of Dowth, eventually resuming its easterly direction several kilometres downstream (Figure 19.1). The River Mattock defines the northern boundary of this monument zone. Because of the goals and the resources of the study, the area chosen was limited in size to a simple 6km by 4km quadrat. This was designed to straddle the River Boyne in order to be able to compare what was happening inside and outside the core area. The slope of the valley on the southern side of the river within the study area is quite steep while the lands on the northern side of the river terrace gently upwards to the knoll on which the monument of Newgrange stands. This creates a natural amphitheatre and gives striking views from much of the land south of the river, forming the crest of the valley slope into the core area. There would have been a series of fords across the river in prehistoric times and it has been demonstrated that the tidal reach of the river would have also been at the eastern edge of the study area (Phillips *et al.* 2002). The landscape of the southern side is relatively undulating, dominated by

Cullen hill on the western side which reaches 92m OD. There is a series of small streams flowing eastwards and northwards through the study area into the River Boyne.

Methodology

The primary data collection method used during this study was systematic surface collection and all available tilled land in the study area was walked – amounting to 623ha out of a total area of 24sq km. With field size in the study area averaging 0.9ha it would not have been practical to use a methodology like that used in Wessex because of the amount of time that would have been involved in setting up each field grid, so the sampling unit used was the individual field (*e.g.* Woodward 1978; Richards 1990). Transects were set out across each field at 10m intervals giving 20% coverage of surveyed ground. Each transect was subdivided into stints 25m long and all lithic finds were recorded and bagged by stint to which Irish National Grid Coordinates were attached, facilitating the creation of a GIS model of the study area which was used to store and analyse data gathered. Subsequent to the surface collection phase, targeted geophysics, geochemical survey and test excavation was carried out (Brady 2006).

For comparative purposes, the approach to lithic analysis was based on a modification of the model used for the excavated assemblages from Knowth (Dillon 1997) which itself was based on Peterson's (1990) model for the analysis of the assemblages from the Bally Lough survey (Zvelebil *et al.* 1987; Green and Zvelebil 1990; Zvelebil

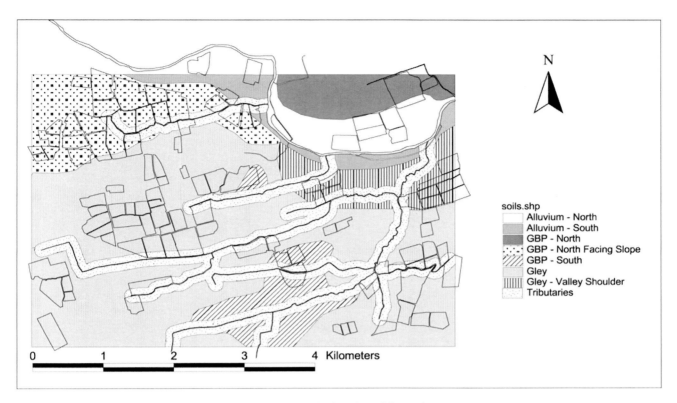

Figure 19.2 Ecological zoning of the study area

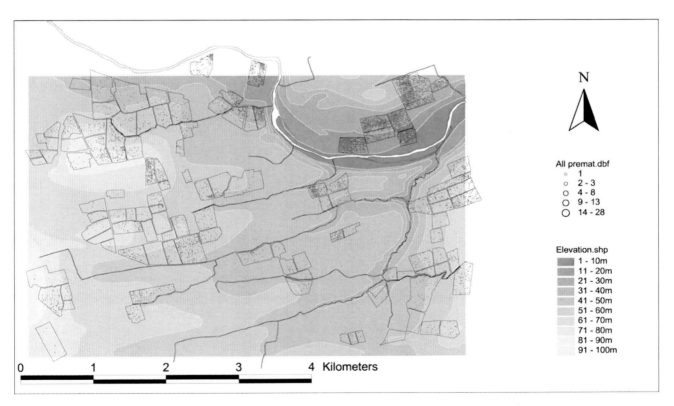

Figure 19.3 The distribution of lithics finds

et al. 1992) which examined the Mesolithic-Neolithic transition in southeast Ireland.

The study area was split into ecological zones in order to try to explore the relationships between the lithics distributions as an indicator of human activity and the landscape. Eight ecological zones or ecozones were identified and were based on a range of factors including soils, elevation, aspect and proximity to tributary streams and views (Figure 19.2). Whole fields were assigned to ecological zones for the purposes of analysis (Brady 2006).

Results

In all, 111 fields were walked and over 8,600 worked lithics were recovered (Figure 19.3). There was significant variation both in lithic densities and in individual field assemblage composition across the study area. As might have been expected, the highest densities were recorded in Newgrange townland on the northern side of the river close to the monuments with the highest field density reaching 92 artefacts per hectare. The highest density recorded for an individual stint was 28 artefacts in Field 45 on the ridge *c.*300m east of the Newgrange passage tomb. A remarkable 'doughnut' effect was apparent in the lithic plots for the fields centred on the monument at Newgrange whereby a curvilinear zone of high lithic density 100m wide and with a radius of 300m, with a low-density core closer to the monument, was recorded (see Figure 19.4). As well as confirming the high levels of activity on the north side of the river Boyne, survey results revealed that there were

also many areas of significant density on the southern side of the river. The most notable of these extend along the crest of the valley south of the river in locations with excellent views northwards towards the main area of monuments and also with good access to what would have been fording points across the river in the Neolithic. There were also significant densities of material extending up the shoulder of Cullen Hill towards the highest point in the study area (Brady 2006).

Using the excavation data from Knowth as a starting point, raw material procurement strategies for the area were examined. Here it was found that, for certain periods, significant quantities of chalk flint were being imported directly from Antrim, the only source of this type of flint in Ireland (Dillon 1997: 199, fig. 39). Chalk flint was found throughout the survey area but its density varied by ecozone. Over 11.5% of the flint collected on the north side of the river was chalk flint while this proportion was 7.2% on the south side. Pebble flint, the most significant raw material type, was not available in any great quantities within the study area and, where it did occur, it corresponded with areas of high lithic density, suggesting that this raw material was in all likelihood being gathered and transported from coastal areas where flint often forms a significant component of shingle beaches. Surface collection work in adjacent coastal areas of counties Louth, Meath and Dublin have repeatedly revealed very high densities of lithic material, with assemblages often containing an important industrial component (Collins 1997; Guinan 1992; Hodgers 1973; 1975; 1979; 1992; 1994). Medium-distance and, to a lesser extent, long-distance movement into and out of

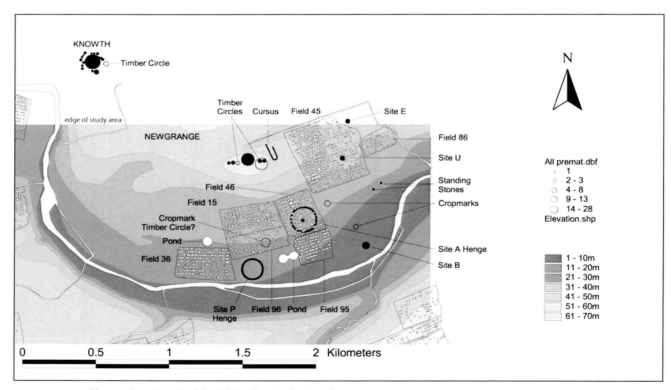

Figure 19.4: Detail of the lithics distribution in relation to the monuments north of the River Boyne

Brú na Bóinne appears to have been quite a routine activity, if varying over time. This pattern of movement has recently been underscored by a positive identification of the quarry locations of the structural stones used to construct many of the passage tombs at Clogher Head, on the coast about 20km to the northeast (Phillips *et al.* 2001; 2002). Chert and other materials were also present in small quantities in the assemblages and varied across the ecozones.

The assemblage composition was found to vary considerably both at field level and at ecozone level. It seems that procurement and much initial processing of material was taking place outside the study area. However, the assemblages suggest slightly more industrial activity in certain areas of the landscape especially on the northern side of the river. Even greater variation is apparent in the figures relating to production. Retouched tools accounted for high proportions of field assemblages in some zones and, in the 'tributaries' zone, they represented 20.2% of those assemblages strongly indicating the use of this zone for residential settlement (Brady 2006).

The analysis of the chronology of any lithics assemblage is problematic and even more so in an Irish context. Due to a lack of large well-contexted assemblages, the understanding of lithic technology in Ireland is not sufficiently clear to make extensive use of technological attributes resulting in a reliance on diagnostic artefacts to indicate lithic chronology. As is the case in Britain, it is only possible to discern broad stylistic differences between an 'earlier' and a 'later' Neolithic, despite the more usual division of the period into Early, Middle and Late Neolithic. The excavated assemblages from the various levels at Knowth were carefully examined to create a chronology as specific to Brú na Bóinne as possible. Unfortunately, the number of diagnostic pieces recovered during the survey was low, especially for the Mesolithic and Earlier Neolithic, and it seems highly likely that activity during these time periods is grossly underrepresented by the diagnostics relative to later periods when diagnostics are more abundant.

No Early Mesolithic artefacts were recovered during the survey but one Late Mesolithic piece was found, the upper portion of a broad flake. This was disappointing given that over thirty Late Mesolithic artefacts were recovered during the excavation at Newgrange (Lehane 1983: 142-5). Six artefacts could be assigned an Earlier Neolithic date and included leaf-shaped arrowheads, an unpolished javelin head and an elongated plano-convex knife. Many other artefacts were found which are traditionally viewed as earlier Neolithic in date (e.g. end-scrapers), but their presence in levels subsequent to Early Neolithic levels at Knowth cautioned against viewing them as representing activity during just one period. In addition to this, a single sherd of an Early Neolithic

carinated bowl was also recovered, the only piece of prehistoric pottery recovered during the survey. Although small in number, this group of finds comes from the southern side of the river and is located primarily between the 50m and 60m contours.

Ninety-eight artefacts were assigned a Later Neolithic date and these were distributed throughout the study area. A further thirty-seven artefacts were assigned a Beaker/Early Bronze Age date and, again, were found well distributed on the southern side of the river. However, diagnostics of this period were almost totally absent from the northern side, in spite of the significant numbers of these artefacts to come from the various excavations at Newgrange and Knowth. There also appears to be an avoidance of land below the 50m contour.

Because of the relatively fine resolution of the survey data, an attempt was made to examine the distributions at a deeper level than just field density. Thus, it was decided to make use of the idea of concentrations whereby areas of higher density than their surroundings were identified. Using the GIS database, the finds from these areas were then isolated and analysed. One hundred and nineteen concentrations were identified and 12 of these contained 95 or more artefacts but most contained less than 80 artefacts. Identification of the edges of concentrations was particularly difficult north of the river where finds densities are highest and most likely to be palimpsests. The distribution of concentrations, not surprisingly, follows the areas of highest overall density. However, one surprise to emerge from this analysis was the Tributaries zone which produced the highest overall number of concentrations despite being relatively low in density terms. These concentrations all tended to be small, averaging around 25 artefacts which, taking into account estimates of the proportion of a total lithics assemblage represented by the component visible on the surface of a ploughed field, could represent a total assemblage of 1250 and 4000 subsurface artefacts (see discussion and calculations in Clark and Schofield 1991). Looking at the occurrence of diagnostics in concentrations, 44 of the 119 concentrations contained diagnostics indicating activity from the Earlier Neolithic to the Early Bronze Age. Thirty-eight had diagnostics from one single period while six concentrations had diagnostics from more than one period indicating either the longevity of some tool forms or, alternatively, that these sites are likely to be palimpsests (Brady 2006). While conventional wisdom cautions against the automatic equation of lithic scatters with settlement sites, it is argued here that, given the likely high population levels in the Brú na Bóinne landscape over much of the Neolithic and Early Bronze Age and the high proportion of retouched artefacts in the concentrations identified, many of these locations are likely to represent settlement foci.

217

Additional fieldwork

Further geophysical, geochemical and test-pit investigations were carried out at a number of selected locations. The most successful of the geophysical investigations was the magnetic susceptibility survey which covered, at least partially, the locations of a number of concentrations. There was a close degree of correspondence between the lithic distributions and the magnetic susceptibility data (Brady 2006). This correspondence of data in my view reinforces the interpretation of the strong settlement character of the individual field assemblages and concentrations of lithics. This hypothesis is testable in locations where archaeological deposits remain undisturbed beneath the ploughsoil.

Conclusion

The densities of material recovered during this survey are among the highest recorded so far in Ireland and point to intensive and prolonged use of this landscape over the Neolithic period. The composition of the assemblages in terms of artefacts and raw materials point to routine contact with areas outside Brú na Bóinne, some considerable distances away, and highlight its position as a core area from at least the Middle Neolithic to the Early Bronze Age. The impression from the diagnostics, although imperfect indicators, is that there was considerable development and expansion of the population over time with a certain amount of continuity as well as the opening up of new areas of the landscape. The recognition of concentrations in the lithics distribution was analytically useful and, although many are probably palimpsests which accumulated over long periods of time and may result from a variety of different activities, a proportion of these may be viewed as settlement locations. Much of the material does give the impression of settlement residues because of the consistently high proportion of retouch in many of the assemblages. This is supported to a degree by the magnetic susceptibility data which show a close but not identical spatial correspondence in the two datasets. However, detailed geophysical survey and excavation hold considerable potential for exploring the nature of the data (*e.g.* Richards 2005).

While providing only a broad outline of the project and a summary of some of the results of the survey, it is hoped that what has been said here offers a new perspective on the character of activity during the Neolithic in the Brú na Bóinne landscape. It represents a fresh approach to the region at an appropriate scale which, while complementing the data from the excavations of the monuments, allows new themes and avenues to be explored.

Acknowledgements

This project was part-funded by a Government of Ireland Postgraduate Scholarship from the Irish Research Council for the Humanities and Social Sciences. I wish also to thank Professor Gabriel Cooney for comments on an earlier draft of this paper.

References

Anon. 2002. *Brú na Bóinne World Heritage Site Management Plan.* Dúchas (the Heritage Service), Department of the Environment and Local Government. Dublin: The Stationery Office.

Bradley, R. 1998a. *The Significance of Monuments.* London: Routledge.

Bradley, R. 1998b. Stone circles and passage graves – a contested relationship. In A. Gibson and D. Simpson (eds) *Prehistoric Ritual and Religion.* Stroud: Sutton Publishing. 2-13.

Brady, C. 2006. A Landscape Survey of the Newgrange Environs: Earlier Prehistoric Settlement At Brú Na Bóinne, Co. Meath. PhD thesis, School of Archaeology, University College Dublin.

Clark, R.H. and Schofield, A.J. 1991. By experiment and calibration: an integrated approach to archaeology of the ploughsoil. In A.J. Schofield (ed.) *Interpreting Artefact Scatters: Contributions to Ploughzone Archaeology.* Oxford: Oxbow. 93-105.

Collins, K. 1997. Prehistoric landuse at Bremore, north County Dublin: the evidence from fieldwalking and lithic analysis. M.A. dissertation, Department of Archaeology, University College Dublin.

Condit, T. 1997a. Late Neolithic ritual – earthen ceremonial enclosures. *Archaeology Ireland (supplement)* 41: 22-3.

Condit, T. 1997a. The Newgrange cursus and the theatre of ritual. *Archaeology Ireland (supplement)* 41: 26-7.

Cooney, G. 1991. Irish Neolithic Landscapes and Land Use Systems: The Implications of Field Systems. *Rural History* 2: 123-39.

Cooney, G. 2000. *Landscapes of Neolithic Ireland.* London: Routledge.

Cooney, G. and Brady, C. 1998. The Red Mountain transect: the results of a pilot fieldwalking study in the Boyne Valley area. Unpublished report for Dúchas (the Heritage Service). Department of Archaeology, University College, Dublin.

Cooney, G. and Grogan, E. 1994. *Irish Prehistory: a social perspective.* Dublin: Wordwell.

Cooney, G. and Grogan, E. 1998. People and place during the Irish Neolithic: exploring social change in time and space. In M. Edmonds and C. Richards (eds) *Understanding the Neolithic of North-Western Europe.* Glasgow: Cruithne Press. 456-80.

Dillon, F. 1997. The lithics. In G. Eogan, and H. Roche, *Excavations at Knowth (Volume 2).* Dublin: Royal Irish Academy.

Eogan, G. 1968. Excavations at Knowth, Co. Meath. *Proceedings of the Royal Irish Academy* 66C: 299-382.

Eogan, G. 1974. Report on the excavations of some passage graves, unprotected inhumation burials and a settlement site at Knowth, Co. Meath. *Proceedings of the Royal Irish Academy* 74C: 11-112.

Eogan, G. 1984. *Excavations at Knowth, voume. 1: smaller passage tombs, Neolithic occupation and Beaker activity.* Dublin: Royal Irish Academy.

Eogan, G. 1986. *Knowth and the Passage-Tombs of Ireland.* London: Thames & Hudson.

Eogan, G. 1991. Prehistoric and early historic culture change at Brugh na Bóinne. *Proceedings of the Royal Irish Academy* 91C: 105-132.

Eogan, G. and Roche, H. 1994. A Grooved Ware wooden structure at Knowth, Boyne Valley, Ireland. *Antiquity* 68: 322-30.

Eogan, G. and Roche, H. 1997. *Excavations at Knowth (Volume 2).* Dublin: Royal Irish Academy.

Green, S. and Zvelebil, M. 1990. The Mesolithic colonisation and agricultural transition of south-east Ireland. *Proceedings of the Prehistoric Society* 56: 57-88

Guinan, B. 1992. Ploughzone archaeology in north Dublin: the evidence from a lithic collection and fieldwalking survey. M.A. dissertation, Department of Archaeology, University College, Dublin.

Hodgers, D. 1973. A report on surface finds from County Louth. *County Louth Archaeological and Historical Journal* 18(1): 46-59.

Hodgers, D. 1975. A report on further surface finds from County Louth. *County Louth Archaeological and Historical Journal* 18(3): 198-210.

Hodgers, D. 1979. A third collection of surface finds from County Louth. *County Louth Archaeological and Historical Journal* 19(3): 227-237.

Hodgers, D. 1992. An investigation of a surface collection of prehistoric artefacts from Co. Louth. PhD thesis, Department of Geography, University of Dublin, Trinity College.

Hodgers, D. 1994. The Salterstown surface collection project. *County Louth Archaeological and Historical Journal* 23(2): 240-268.

Lehane, D. 1983. The flint work. In M.J. O'Kelly, R. Cleary, and D. Lehane, *Newgrange, Co. Meath, Ireland: the Late Neolithic/Beaker period settlement.* Oxford: BAR (International) Series 190. 118-167.

Lynch, A. 1989. Newgrange. In I. Bennett (ed.) *Excavations 1988: Summary accounts of archaeological excavations in Ireland.* Dublin: Organisation of Irish Archaeologists. 33.

Lynch, A. 1990a. Newgrange. In I. Bennett (ed.) *Excavations 1988: Summary accounts of archaeological excavations in Ireland.* Dublin: Organisation of Irish Archaeologists. 42-3.

Lynch, A. 1990b. Dowth. In I. Bennett (ed.) *Excavations 1988: Summary accounts of archaeological excavations in Ireland.* Dublin: Organisation of Irish Archaeologists. 42.

Meenan, R. 1997. Monknewtown ritual pond. *Archaeology Ireland (supplement)* 41: 23.

Mitchell, G.F. 1986. *Shell Guide to Reading the Irish Landscape.* Dublin: Country House.

Mitchell, G.F. and Ryan M. 1997. *Reading the Irish Landscape.* Dublin: Town and Country House.

Mount, C. 1994. Aspects of ritual deposition in the Late Neolithic and Beaker periods at Newgrange, Co. Meath. *Proceedings of the Prehistoric Society* 60: 433-443.

O'Kelly, M.J. 1982. *Newgrange: Archaeology, Art and Legend.* London: Thames and Hudson.

O'Kelly, M.J., Lynch, F. and O'Kelly, C. 1978. Three passage-graves at Newgrange, Co. Meath. *Proceedings of the Royal Irish Academy* 78C: 249-359.

O'Kelly, M.J. and O'Kelly, C. 1983. The tumulus of Dowth, Co. Meath. *Proceedings of the Royal Irish Academy* 83C: 135-90.

Peterson, J.D. 1990. From foraging to food production in south-east Ireland: some lithic evidence. *Proceedings of the Prehistoric Society* 56: 89-99.

Phillips, A., Corcoran, M. and Eogan G. 2001. Derivation of the source localities for the kerb, orthostat and standing stones of the Neolithic passage graves of the Boyne Valley, Co. Meath. Unpublished report for the Heritage Council. Department of Geology, Trinity College Dublin.

Phillips, A., Corcoran, M. and Eogan G. 2002. Identification of the source area for megaliths used in the construction of the Neolithic passage graves of the Boyne Valley, Co. Meath. Unpublished report for the Heritage Council. Department of Geology, Trinity College Dublin.

Richards, C. (ed.) 2005. *Dwelling Among the Monuments: The Neolithic Village of Barnhouse, Maeshowe Passage Grave and Surrounding Monuments at Stenness, Orkney.* Cambridge: McDonald Institute Monographs.

Richards, J. 1990. *The Stonehenge Environs Project.* London: English Heritage.

Roche, H. and Eogan, G. 2001. Late Neolithic activity in the Boyne Valley, County Meath, Ireland. *Revue archéologique de l'Ouest (supplement)* 9: 125-40.

Sheridan, A. 2004. Going round in circles? Understanding the Irish Grooved Ware 'complex' and its wider complex. In H. Roche, E. Grogan, J. Bradley, J. Coles and B. Raftery (eds) *From Megaliths to Metals: essays in honour of George Eogan.* Oxford: Oxbow. 26-37.

Stout, G. 2002. *Newgrange and the Bend of the Boyne.* Cork: Cork University Press.

Stout, G. 1991. Embanked enclosures of the Boyne region. *Proceedings of the Royal Irish Academy* 91C: 245-84.

Sweetman, P.D. 1976. An earthen enclosure at Monknewtown, Slane, Co. Meath. *Proceedings of the Royal Irish Academy* 76C: 25-72.

Sweetman, P.D. 1985. A Late Neolithic/Early Bronze Age pit circle at Newgrange, Co. Meath. *Proceedings of the Royal Irish Academy* 85C: 195-221.

Sweetman, P.D. 1987. Excavation of a Late Neolithic/Early Bronze Age site at Newgrange, Co. Meath. *Proceedings of the Royal Irish Academy* 87C: 283-298.

Whittle, A. 1996. *Europe in the Neolithic.* Cambridge: Cambridge University Press.

van Wijngaarden-Bakker, L.H.1974. The animal remains from the Beaker settlement at Newgrange, Co. Meath: first report. *Proceedings of the Royal Irish Academy* 74C: 313-83.

van Wijngaarden-Bakker, L.H. 1986. The animal remains from the Beaker settlement at Newgrange, Co. Meath: final report. *Proceedings of the Royal Irish Academy* 86C: 17-112.

Woodman P.C. 1985. Prehistoric settlement and environment. In K.J. Edwards and W.P. Warren (eds) *The Quaternary History of Ireland.* London: Academic Press. 251-78.

Woodward, P. 1978. A problem-oriented approach to the recovery of knapped flint debris: a field walking strategy for answering questions posed by site distributions and excavations. In J.F. Cherry, C. Gamble and S. Shennan (eds) *Sampling in Contemporary British Archaeology.* Oxford: BAR (British) Series 50. 121-28.

Zvelebil, M., Moore, J., Green, S. and Henson, D. 1987. Regional survey and the analysis of lithic scatters: a case study from south-east Ireland. In P. Rowley-Conwy, M. Zvelebil and H.P. Blankholm (eds) *Mesolithic Northwest Europe: Recent Trends.* Sheffield: Department of Archaeology and Prehistory, University of Sheffield. 9-32.

Zvelebil M., Green S.W. and Macklin M.G. 1992. Archaeological landscapes, lithic scatters and human behaviour. In J. Rossignol and L.A. Wandsnider (eds) *Space, Time, and Archaeological Landscapes.* London: Plenum Press. 193-226.

Chapter 20

'The Heart of Neolithic Orkney' World Heritage Site: building a landscape

Nick Card,[1] Jonathan Cluett,[2] Jane Downes,[3] John Gater[4] and Susan Ovenden[5]

[1] Projects Unit, Archaeology Centre, Orkney College UHI
[2] School of Biological and Environmental Sciences, University of Stirling
[3] Archaeology Dept., Orkney College UHI
[4] GSB Prospection Ltd, Cowburn Farm, Market Street, Thornton, Bradford
[5] Geophysics Unit, Archaeology Centre, Orkney College UHI

Introduction

In 1999 'The Heart of Neolithic Orkney' was inscribed as a World Heritage Site (WHS), a designation which applies to six discrete sites in west Mainland – Maes Howe chambered tomb; the henge monuments of Stones of Stenness and the Ring of Brodgar; the Watchstone and the Barnhouse Stone (Figure 20.1); and Skara Brae settlement. Although the designation of the WHS is monument specific, the work that has gone into both the subsequent management and research of the Orkney WHS has pushed these boundaries out both spatially and temporally (Downes *et al.* 2005). The focus of this paper is on the archaeological fieldwork that has been undertaken since designation within the Inner Buffer Zone (IBZ) surrounding Maes Howe and the henge monuments (Figure 20.1), and the results as they pertain to the late Neolithic.

A programme of geophysical investigations within the Inner Buffer Zone (IBZ) of the World Heritage Site started in 2002 and, to date, some 215ha (Figure 20.1) have been investigated by fluxgate gradiometry (GSB 2002; 2003a and b; 2004; OCGU 2004; 2005a and b; 2006a and b). It is normal to define the nature and extent of sites, sometimes over large areas (Gaffney and Gaffney 2000), and vast areas have been investigated by gradiometer scanning to determine possible sites within proposed development areas (Gaffney and Gater 2003). However, the use of large-scale detailed gradiometry within a broader research agenda is unusual. The main focus of archaeological research in what is now the WHS IBZ had been on the extant monuments and, before the current programme of geophysical investigations, the use of geophysics within the wider area had been somewhat piecemeal. The current geophysical investigation has provided a clearer image of past landscapes.

Geophysical surveys

Survey to date has revealed a wide variety of responses within the WHS IBZ (Figure 20.1). Vast magnetically quiet areas, significant in themselves, have been identified around the Ring of Brodgar, with well-defined zones of strong magnetic anomalies indicative of settlement being located to the northwest at Wasbister and to the southeast on the Ness of Brodgar (Figure 20.1).

Gradiometer survey at Wasbister over a suspected Bronze Age 'double house', surviving as earth and stonework, produced magnetically strong and clear anomalies within a complex of responses indicative of a major settlement site of around six hectares (Figure 20.1). The strong anomalies are thought to represent an accumulation of midden, burnt structures, building remains and debris. In addition, a number of lesser buildings may have been identified with the suggestion of a complex arrangement of 'cells' forming larger structures.

Survey of the southern tip of the Ness of Brodgar isthmus (south of Brodgar Farm), revealed a previously unknown and unexpectedly high density of anomalies (Figures 20.1 and 20.2). The data suggest midden deposits, burnt features and remains of stone structures. Some of the responses correspond with antiquarian and more recent excavations (see below). The extent of the activity (*c.* 240m long northwest-southeast) as revealed by the geophysics is substantial and is reflected in the topography of the area (Figures 20.2 and 20.3 insets). The land rises gradually from Brodgar Farm to the northwest to a maximum elevation of *c.* 7.8m OD close to the dwelling of Lochview. The land then slopes more abruptly down towards the Bridge of Brodgar and the shores of the Lochs of Stenness and Harray on either side to form an extensive elongated 'whaleback' mound.

To the south and east of the Stones of Stenness the nature of the gradiometer responses changes showing much variation and greater complexities (Figure 20.1). Results are dominated by strong linear anomalies crossing the landscape and show the location of buried igneous dykes and sills. Survey has also detected numerous parallel linear responses indicative of past ridge and furrow cultivation. Numerous alignments suggesting a palimpsest of land use are apparent. These show some correlation with the pattern of the presumed medieval cultivation visible on Thomas' plan of 1852. Superimposed alignments also hint at reorganisation of the landscape at some point during the medieval period.

Overlying the geological responses, and sometimes distorted by subsequent land use, are further anomalies indicative of buried archaeological deposits. Survey to the east of the Stones of Stenness over a suspected broch, Big Howe (Figure 20.1), recorded responses indicating a

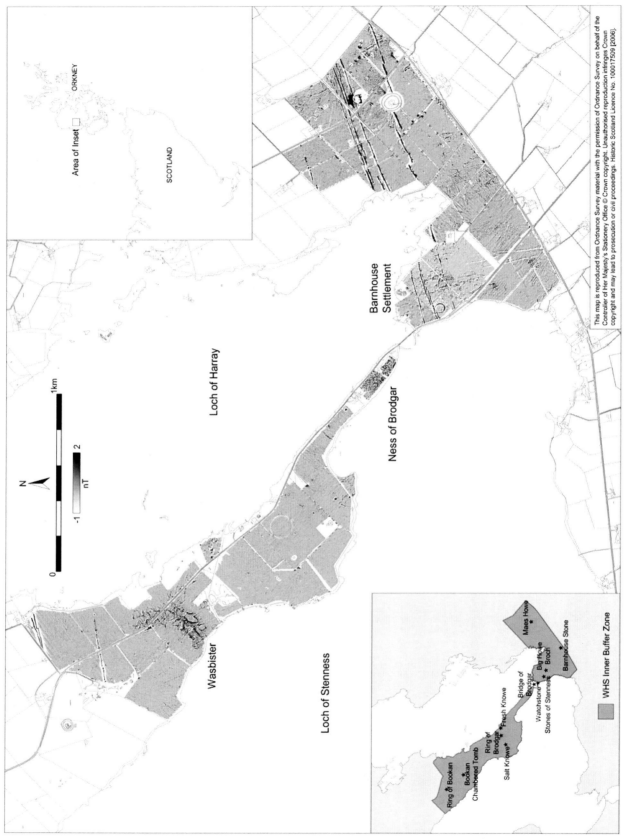

Figure 20.1Location plans and summary greyscale image of gradiometer survey within the Orkney World Heritage Sites Inner Buffer Zone

Figure 20.2 Ness of Brodgar: gradiometer data interpretation, trench location and contour survey (inset)

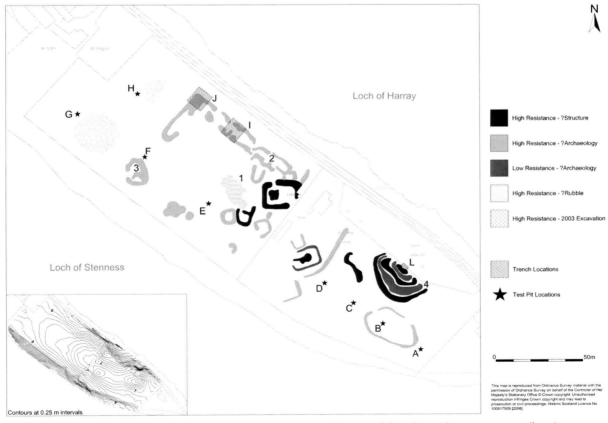

Figure 20.3 Ness of Brodgar: resistance data interpretation, trench location and contour survey (inset)

probable 40m-diameter interior bank/ditch enclosed within a larger 'light bulb-shaped' bank/ditch. The elongated and squared off northern end suggests a defended entrance as recorded at other broch sites. The interior produced a very strong level of magnetic response that is consistent with midden heaps and hearths. The gradiometer survey has provided a wealth of information about this broch site thereby confirming the most notable evidence for Iron Age activity very close to the Neolithic monuments of the WHS. Gradiometer data collected in the fields to the west of Maes Howe are dominated by responses associated with World War II structures and activity. However, even with these high levels of modern magnetic disturbance new sites have still been identified including a previously unknown barrow *c.* 340m north of Maes Howe.

The gradiometer survey of the landscape within the IBZ is providing interesting and significant information. It is however, a reconnaissance technique and just the first phase in the geophysical investigations of the WHS IBZ. The gradiometer surveys provide a wealth of information regarding previously unknown settlement areas, known sites and past land use, but it does not reveal a complete image of the buried landscape. The technique cannot provide detailed plans of stone structures and for this objective targeted area resistance survey was subsequently utilised. Gradiometry and resistance used together can provide a detailed plan of the buried past, within the top one metre or so of the ground surface, for example on the Ness of Brodgar. On some sites it is not a two-dimensional plan that is required but a three dimensional understanding of the site. This is especially true of the many artificial mounds within the area, for example Salt Knowe and Fresh Knowe (Figure 20.1), on which conventional gradiometry and area resistance survey are not suitable due to the topography and depth of potential targets. Here the use of ground penetrating radar and electrical imaging are vital to assist in the interpretation of these sites.

The Ness of Brodgar Neolithic complex

Geophysical techniques are, however, but one tool available to the archaeologist and should not be viewed in isolation (Gater 2005: 98). Nineteenth century cartographic and literary sources have aided the interpretation of several geophysical anomalies and others have been tentatively interpreted by analogy, but the need to ground truth the results of the geophysics is clear. Although some of the geophysical results provide compelling evidence for intensive activity or settlement, in particular on the Ness of Brodgar (Figures 20.1, 20.2 and 20.3) and at Wasbister (Figure 20.1), the nature of these sets of anomalies could only be identified by excavation. The opportunity to start this process came with the chance discovery during ploughing of a large notched slab at the Ness of Brodgar. The association of cremated bone with this stone and the previous discovery of a series of conjoined 'cists' in the same field (Marwick

Figure 20.4: Structure uncovered by GUARD in 2003 at the Ness of Brodgar (Photo: Orkney Archaeological Trust)

1925) prompted the slab to be considered part of a cist. Under the 'Human Remains Call-off Contract', Historic Scotland commissioned Glasgow University Archaeological Research Division (GUARD) to investigate the find spot. No evidence for a cist was found, but part of a large structure was uncovered (Figure 20.4), very reminiscent of Structure 2 at Barnhouse; that later Neolithic settlement (Richards 2005) is located barely 300m to the southeast (Figure 20.1). This structure was defined on the exterior by an arc of upright slabs. Within the arc were the remains of a double-faced coursed stone wall forming two rectangular recesses, suggestive of an overall cruciform internal space (Ballin Smith 2003). Although not excavated, probing suggested that these walls survived to at least 0.3m in height. This structure corresponds to a large oval anomaly, *c.* 20m by 15m, on the gradiometry survey (Figure 20.2, anomaly 1). This structure lay immediately below the ploughsoil and was surrounded and infilled by what the excavator termed 'midden deposits' (Ballin Smith 2003).

The discovery of this late Neolithic building near the apex of this 'whaleback' mound had implications both in terms of the date and nature of the other geophysical anomalies (Figure 20.1) that form this extensive complex of features. In order to define the built archaeology more clearly and complement the gradiometry survey, a resistivity survey of the area was undertaken (Mackintosh and Damianoff 2003). The resistance survey confirmed the presence of several of the structures revealed by the gradiometry but also several new structures. Most prominent was a large double linear anomaly over 70m in length (Figure 20.3, anomaly 2).

A preliminary, limited excavation on the Ness of Brodgar was undertaken in June 2004 (Card 2004). Eight test trenches (Figures 20.2 and 20.3, A-H) were opened across the area to examine the depth, nature and extent of archaeological deposits. The trenches were deliberately located away from significant geophysical anomalies in order to avoid disturbing potential structures that could not be fully understood in such small trenches. However stone structures were revealed at varying depths in all but one trench and the character of the deposits and stonework implied the presence of substantial buildings. In Trench F, near the northwest extremity of the 'whaleback' mound, substantial stonework similar to that found in chambered tombs was revealed in close association with a large, oval, resistance anomaly (Figure 20.3, anomaly 3).

At the same time as the trial trenching, samples were taken as part of systematic geoarchaeological research within the WHS IBZ (Cluett forthcoming). This research aimed to ascertain the influence of anthropic activities upon soils and sediments within the WHS IBZ and has characterised soil properties using a combination of field observations and analyses including thin section micromorphology, total phosphorus, magnetic susceptibility and particle size distribution. Results at the Ness of Brodgar have identified an anthropic sediment which was a silty clay containing abundant, fine to very fine inclusions of charcoal, burnt stone, cremated bone and occasional non-cremated bone and pieces of pottery. This sediment has formed entirely as a result of anthropic sedimentation processes involving the stripping of turf, the burning of this turf within domestic activity (presumably for light and heat) and the subsequent mixing of this burnt turf with other domestic waste immediately prior to, or during deposition.

The inclusions within this sediment are consistent with those from other Late Neolithic settlements (Guttmann 2005). However this sediment has only been deposited upon a discrete area of the Ness of Brodgar and to a considerable depth (0.65m). It is also worth noting that it differs significantly from the anthropic soils at Wasbister (Figure 20.1) that contain only occasional and fine charcoal but no other domestic waste. These very different soil histories between the two areas may also reflect marked contrasts in settlement and cultivation. This sediment at the Ness of Brodgar overlies some structural archaeology within Trench E (Figures 20.2 and 20.3), but may also correspond to the 'midden deposits' noted by GUARD as surrounding and infilling the structure revealed in 2003 (Ballin Smith 2003). The absence of micro-horizons and textural pedofeatures in thin section samples from this sediment suggests that

accumulation was an ongoing process with no standstill phases allowing exposure to surface weathering.

Recent research within the Orcadian Neolithic highlights the importance of the resource selection and utilisation of anthropic soils and sediments to settlement function and sustenance (Simpson *et al.* 2006*)*. A post-depositional function of the anthropic sediment upon the Ness of Brodgar is difficult to ascertain although the homogenised nature of the deposit may suggest its use subsequent to deposition within arable agriculture. Despite the yet unascertained function of this anthropic sediment, field observations clearly identify a significant volume of anthropic sediment at the Ness of Brodgar requiring a re-evaluation of the 'whaleback' landform that has previously been attributed to formation through geomorphological processes.

Radiocarbon analyses were undertaken upon inclusions of cremated bone and charcoal from the anthropogenic sediment within two of the test trenches E and C (Figures 20.2 and 20.3) in order to ascertain the most likely period of the sediment formation. The results (Trench E charcoal 3020-2860 cal BC; bone 2910-2830 cal BC; Trench C charcoal 3080-3060 cal BC; bone 2900-2620 cal BC) indicate a similar time period within the Late Neolithic. Despite the potential problems and limitations inherent within the attempt to provide radiocarbon dates for periods of cultural activity involved in anthropogenic sediment formation, the use of multiple samples of different origins from the same archaeological context does allow confidence in this interpretation and suggests that anthropogenic sediment formation upon the Ness of Brodgar is solely a product of relatively intense Late Neolithic cultural activity between *c.* 3000 and *c.* 2800BC.

Further excavation on the Ness of Brodgar in 2005 (Card and Cluett 2005) concentrated on the large double linear anomaly revealed by resistivity survey (Figure 20.3, Trench I), and tentatively interpreted it as a causeway or processional way. A stratigraphic sequence of badly plough-truncated structures was uncovered 'eroding' out of the northeast slope of the 'whaleback' mound (Figure 20.5). Most of these exhibit elements found in the repertoire of known Neolithic structures in Orkney – stalls, drains, large square stone hearths and stone 'furniture' (including part of another notched slab which formed an upright division within one structure). Trench J (Figure 20.3), opened over the northern external 'corner' of this linear anomaly, revealed a section of a monumental stone wall of natural boulders covered by cairn-like material and faced internally.

The apparent unity of the 'causeway' feature was shown to be a product of the interpretation of the resistance results, and the amalgamation of responses from several separate features and structures. A refinement of the resistivity survey at 0.5m intervals has since been undertaken which confirms this lack of unity.

Figure 20.5: Aerial view of Trench I (11m x 10m) in 2005 (Photo: 59° north, Frank Bradford)

Figure 20.6: Trench J in 2006 showing the monumental stone wall enclosing the oval structure (Photo: Orkney Archaeological Trust)

In 2006 a larger area expanding Trench J was excavated around the boulder-constructed walled structure, revealing that the substantial wall was an outer element of a far larger structure over 15m in diameter (Figure 20.6). Within this outer element was an oval structure *c.* 8m by 6m with radial divisions and a short entrance passage to the southeast. Although the complexity and depth of archaeological remains encountered prevented the excavation of the full depth of deposits within the oval structure, the remains were clearly multi-phased. Several phases of collapse and use were identified within the oval structure including a later phase associated with a hearth and the insertion of a large drain (Figure 20.6). Ephemeral wall lines, a rectangular stone setting, hearths, peat-ashy spreads, a flint cache and a triangular cist indicated later activity after the abandonment of these structures. Two conjoining thin stone slabs from the top of the cist exhibited lightly incised Neolithic motifs similar to some from Skara Brae. Although the monumental stone wall encloses the oval structure and they appear concentric to each other in the area excavated, the resistivity results suggest that the wall may extend to the southwest across the peninsula, separating the Ness of Brodgar complex from the Brodgar area to the northwest (Figure 20.3).

Another element of the Ness of Brodgar Neolithic complex is the remains of a large mutilated mound on the southeast side of the 'whaleback' mound close to the Bridge of Brodgar (Figures 20.2 and 20.3, anomaly 4). Finds recovered from the site in the 19th century of a Neolithic carved stone ball (Anon. 1885) and a decorated 'stone sinker', possibly Iron Age in date (Noble 1888), suggested a multi-phase site. This appeared to be borne out by the geophysical results that revealed a series of concentric anomalies centred on the mound (Figures 20.2 and 20.3). The nature and strength of these responses were initially presumed to be "indicative of habitation… more likely a broch type structure… rather than a burial cairn" (GSB 2002: 1.1). However, exploratory excavations (Figures 20.2 and 20.3, Trench L) in the spring of 2006 (Card 2006a) to assess a potential collapse of the top of this mound recovered only Neolithic finds, in particular Late or final Neolithic Grooved Ware with applied decoration and a flake of Arran pitchstone. These finds and the mound's apparent relationship with the other elements of the Ness of Brodgar complex imply that it is also Late Neolithic in date, rather than a broch. The concentric anomalies corresponding to either revetments, similar to those seen in the primary construction or later modifications at chambered cairns (such as those at Bookan; Card 2006b), or a building incorporating concentric walls similar to Structure 8 at Barnhouse (Richards 2005) or Structure 8 at Pool, Sanday (Hunter 2000). At *c.* 40m in diameter, however, its overall size is only comparable to Maes Howe itself.

The excavation and geophysics results to date would indicate that much of the mounded effect of the Ness of Brodgar is artificial, comprising structures, middens and deep midden-enhanced soils. Although the full depth of stratigraphy has yet to be revealed across most of the mound, it seems likely that at least 2m of stratigraphy is present near the apex of the 'whaleback' mound. This is supported by evidence from the 1925 discovery of the cists in this field (Marwick 1925: 36). Marwick noted a further 'cist' at a depth of '5 feet' (*c.* 1.5m) below those initially encountered. The diagnostic Late Neolithic finds, the building styles encountered and the radiocarbon dates from the Ness of Brodgar suggest that all the evidence discovered so far dates to the later fourth and early third millennia BC.

Conclusion

Fifteen years before the designation of the Orkney WHS, Colin Richards successfully employed systematic fieldwalking in this part of west Mainland and discovered several lithic scatters indicative of Neolithic settlement (Richards 2005). One of these scatters, located less than 150m to the north of the Stones of Stenness, was the first indication of the Barnhouse Neolithic settlement that was excavated subsequently (ibid). The extraordinary nature of some of the buildings at Barnhouse appears to mark it out as an unusual settlement when compared with Skara Brae and other Orcadian Late Neolithic settlements. Moreover, as Richards comments, 'at last the label 'ritual landscape or monument' could be deconstructed' (Richards 2005: 205) and the dichotomy which had been drawn between domestic and ritual in terms of landscape use could finally disappear.

Although there is not space here to evaluate fully the implications of the recent findings we have been describing, they are obviously very significant in both landscape and site-specific terms. The extensive nature of the geophysical survey, and the limited but intensive soil sampling and excavation, has placed Barnhouse and the henge monuments in a yet more clearly defined landscape context. The extremely dense clustering of Neolithic buildings on the Ness of Brodgar is striking especially when one considers that the areas which seem relatively blank in comparison on the geophysical survey (Figure 20.1) have a fair density of later Neolithic/earlier Bronze Age remains (such as standing stone sockets, pits and hearths that were located and excavated in the Odin field between the Stones of Stenness and the Bridge of Brodgar [Challands *et al.* 2005]). The buildings excavated so far at the Ness of Brodgar appear to combine traits both of domestic and funerary structures (tombs and cists), and aggrandized elements of the Barnhouse 'monumental' Structures 2 and 8 (Richards 2005). The character of these buildings finds some resonance with the congruence of houses and tombs in Ireland, for example at Knowth and Newgrange (*cf.* Grogan 2004; Brady this volume). The situation of the buildings on the Ness of Brodgar emphasizes the axial role this spit of land may have played both as a causeway between the two henges and other monuments, and as a barrier between two different environments or habitats –

that is the salt water of Stenness Loch and the fresh water of Harray Loch, and the most striking parallel in all respects is, of course, with the new discoveries by the Stonehenge Riverside Project at Durrington Walls (Parker Pearson this volume).

Acknowledgements

The authors acknowledge with thanks the support and funding from Historic Scotland in the Orkney WHS research. Thanks also to James Moore for preparing the illustrations and for his helpful comments.

References

Anonymous 1885. Articles exhibited. *Proceedings of the Society of Antiquaries of Scotland* 19: 134-139.

Ballin Smith, B. 2003. *A New Late Neolithic House at Brodgar Farm, Stenness, Orkney.* GUARD Project 1506. Unpublished report for Historic Scotland.

Card, N. 2004. *Ness of Brodgar Excavations 2004, Data Structure Report.* Unpublished report for Orkney Archaeological Trust.

Card, N. 2006a. *Ness of Brodgar Excavations 2006, Data Structure Report.* Unpublished report for Historic Scotland.

Card, N. 2006b. Excavations at Bookan Chambered Cairn. *Proceedings of the Society of Antiquaries of Scotland* 135 (2005): 163-190.

Card, N. and Cluett, J. 2005. *Ness of Brodgar Excavations 2005, Data Structure Report.* Unpublished report for Historic Scotland.

Challands, A., Edmonds, M. and Richards, C. 2005. Beyond the village: Barnhouse Odin and the Stones of Stenness. In C. Richards (ed.) *Dwelling among the Monuments: excavations at Barnhouse and Maeshowe, Orkney.* Cambridge: MacDonald Institute. 205-227.

Cluett, J. Forthcoming. Soils-based Cultural Records and the Heart Of Neolithic Orkney World Heritage Site. PhD thesis, University of Stirling.

Downes, J., Foster, S.M. and Wickham-Jones, C.R. with Callister, J. 2005. *The Heart of Neolithic Orkney World Heritage Site Research Agenda.* Edinburgh: Historic Scotland.

Gater, J. 2005. Geophysics. In J. Downes, S.M. Foster and C.R. Wickham-Jones with J. Callister (eds) *The Heart of Neolithic Orkney World Heritage Site Research Agenda.* Edinburgh: Historic Scotland. 98-100.

Gaffney C. and Gaffney V. (eds) 2000. Non-invasive investigations at Wroxeter at the end of the twentieth century. *Archaeological Prospection* 7:2.

Gaffney, G. and Gater, J. 2003. *Revealing the Buried Past: geophysics for archaeologists.* Stroud: Tempus.

Grogan, E. 2004. The implications of Irish Neolithic houses. In I.A.G. Shepherd and G.J. Barclay (eds) *Scotland in Ancient Europe.* Edinburgh: Society of Antiquaries of Scotland. 103-114.

GSB Prospection 1999. *Report on the Geophysical Survey at Stones of Stenness.* GSB Prospection, Report 99/55. Unpublished report for Historic Scotland.

GSB Prospection. 2002. *Orkney World Heritage Site, Geophysical Report, Phase I.* GSB Report 2002/61. Unpublished report for Historic Scotland.

GSB Prospection 2003A. *Report on the Geophysical Survey at Orkney WHS, Phase II.* GSB Prospection Report 03/12. Unpublished report for Historic Scotland.

GSB Prospection 2003B. *Report on the Geophysical Survey at Orkney WHS, Phase III.* GSB Prospection Report 03/84. Unpublished report for Historic Scotland.

GSB Prospection 2004. *Report on the Geophysical Survey at Orkney WHS Phase IV.* GSB Prospection, Report 04/17. Unpublished report for Historic Scotland.

Guttmann E.B.A. 2005. Midden cultivation in prehistoric Britain: arable crops in gardens. *World Archaeology* 37: 224-239.

Historic Scotland 1998. *Nomination of the Heart of Neolithic Orkney for inclusion in the World Heritage List.* Edinburgh: Historic Scotland. Unpublished document submitted to UNESCO.

Hunter, J.R. 2000. Pool, Sanday, and a sequence for the Orcadian Neolithic. In A. Ritchie (ed.) *Neolithic Orkney in its European Context.* Cambridge: McDonald Institute. 117-26.

Mackintosh, A. and Damianoff, D. 2003. *Ness of Brodgar: a geophysical survey report.* Unpublished report for Orkney Archaeological Trust.

Marwick, J.G. 1926. Discovery of Stone Cists at Stenness, Orkney. *Proceedings of the Society of Antiquaries of Scotland* 60: 34-6.

Noble, J. 1888. Notice of a stone, apparently a sinker, with incised figures of animals, from a tumulus at Bridge of Brodgar, Stennis. *Proceedings of the Society of Antiquaries of Scotland* 22: 266-7.

Orkney Archaeological Trust 2002. *Project Design for a Geophysical Survey in the Inner Buffer Zone of World Heritage Site.* Kirkwall: Orkney Archaeological Trust.

OCGU 2004. *Report on the Geophysical Survey at Orkney WHS Phase V.* Orkney College Geophysics Unit (Report Number 0 4/08). Unpublished report for Historic Scotland.

OCGU 2005a. *Report on the Geophysical Survey at Orkney WHS Phase VI.* Orkney College Geophysics Unit (Report Number 05/01). Unpublished report for Historic Scotland.

OCGU 2005b. *Report on the Geophysical Survey at Orkney WHS Phase VII.* Orkney College Geophysics Unit (Report Number 05/06). Unpublished report for Historic Scotland.

OCGU 2006a. *Report on the Geophysical Survey at Orkney WHS Phase VIII.* Orkney College Geophysics Unit (Report Number 06/03). Unpublished report for Historic Scotland.

OCGU 2006b. *Report on the Geophysical Survey at Orkney WHS Phase IX.* Orkney College Geophysics Unit (Report Number 06/13). Unpublished report for Historic Scotland.

Richards, C. (*ed.*) 2005. *Dwelling among the Monuments: excavations at Barnhouse and Maeshowe, Orkney.* Cambridge: MacDonald Institute.

Ritchie, A. (*ed*) 2000. *Neolithic Orkney in its European Context.* Cambridge: McDonald Institute.

Simpson, I. A. Guttmann, E. B. Cluett, J and Shepherd, A. 2006. Characterising midden in Neolithic Settlement: an assessment from Skara Brae, Orkney. *Geoarchaeology* 21: 221-235.

Thomas, F. W. L. 1852. An account of some of the Celtic antiquities of Orkney, including the Stones of Stenness, tumuli, Picts houses *etc*. with plans. *Archaeologia* 34: 88-136.